CONTENTS

5 WHERE TO EAT 71

6 EXPLORING SEATTLE 118

7 CITY STROLLS 169

8 SEATTLE SHOPPING 189

9 SEATTLE AFTER DARK 208

10 SIDE TRIPS FROM SEATTLE 230

11 PLANNING YOUR TRIP TO SEATTLE 300

LIST OF MAPS

ABOUT THE AUTHOR

Karl Samson lives in Oregon, where he spends his time juggling his obsessions with traveling, gardening, outdoor sports, and wine. Each winter, to dry out his webbed feet, he flees the soggy Northwest to update the *Frommer's Arizona* guide. Karl is also the author of *Frommer's Portland*, *Frommer's Oregon,* and *Frommer's Washington State*.

HOW TO CONTACT US

In researching this book, we discovered many wonderful places—hotels, restaurants, shops, and more. We're sure you'll find others. Please tell us about them, so we can share the information with your fellow travelers in upcoming editions. If you were disappointed with a recommendation, we'd love to know that, too. Please write to:

Frommer's Seattle, 10th Edition
John Wiley & Sons, Inc. • 111 River St. • Hoboken, NJ 07030-5774
frommersfeedback@wiley.com

ADVISORY & DISCLAIMER

Travel information can change quickly and unexpectedly, and we strongly advise you to confirm important details locally before traveling, including information on visas, health and safety, traffic and transport, accommodation, shopping, and eating out. We also encourage you to stay alert while traveling and to remain aware of your surroundings. Avoid civil disturbances, and keep a close eye on cameras, purses, wallets, and other valuables.

While we have endeavored to ensure that the information contained within this guide is accurate and up-to-date at the time of publication, we make no representations or warranties with respect to the accuracy or completeness of the contents of this work and specifically disclaim all warranties, including without limitation warranties of fitness for a particular purpose. We accept no responsibility or liability for any inaccuracy or errors or omissions, or for any inconvenience, loss, damage, costs, or expenses of any nature whatsoever incurred or suffered by anyone as a result of any advice or information contained in this guide.

The inclusion of a company, organization, or Website in this guide as a service provider and/or potential source of further information does not mean that we endorse them or the information they provide. Be aware that information provided through some Websites may be unreliable and can change without notice. Neither the publisher or author shall be liable for any damages arising herefrom.

FROMMER'S STAR RATINGS, ICONS & ABBREVIATIONS

Every hotel, restaurant, and attraction listing in this guide has been ranked for quality, value, service, amenities, and special features using a **star-rating** system. In country, state, and regional guides, we also rate towns and regions to help you narrow down your choices and budget your time accordingly. Hotels and restaurants are rated on a scale of zero (recommended) to three stars (exceptional). Attractions, shopping, nightlife, towns, and regions are rated according to the following scale: zero stars (recommended), one star (highly recommended), two stars (very highly recommended), and three stars (must-see).

In addition to the star-rating system, we also use seven feature icons that point you to the great deals, in-the-know advice, and unique experiences that separate travelers from tourists. Throughout the book, look for:

Special finds—those places only insiders know about

Fun facts—details that make travelers more informed and their trips more fun

Kids—best bets for kids and advice for the whole family

Special moments—those experiences that memories are made of

Overrated—places or experiences not worth your time or money

Insider tips—great ways to save time and money

Great values—where to get the best deals

The following abbreviations are used for credit cards:

AE American Express

DISC Discover

V Visa

DC Diners Club

MC MasterCard

TRAVEL RESOURCES AT FROMMERS.COM

Frommer's travel resources don't end with this guide. Frommer's website, www.frommers.com, has travel information on more than 4,000 destinations. We update features regularly, giving you access to the most current trip-planning information and the best airfare, lodging, and car-rental bargains. You can also listen to podcasts, connect with other Frommers.com members through our active-reader forums, share your travel photos, read blogs from guidebook editors and fellow travelers, and much more.

1

THE BEST OF SEATTLE

Imagine yourself sitting in a park on the Seattle waterfront, a latte and a marionberry scone close at hand. The snowy peaks of the Olympic Mountains shimmer on the far side of Puget Sound, while ferryboats come and go across Elliott Bay. It's a sunny summer day, not a cloud in the sky. It just doesn't get much better than this, unless maybe you take in a 9:30pm summer sunset from the Space Needle or the Olympic Sculpture Park and then head to a brewpub. No wonder people love this town.

Things to Do For a bottom-to-top tour of Seattle, join the **Underground Tour** and hide out beneath the streets of historic Pioneer Square, then later take an elevator to the clouds at the **Space Needle.** Between these extremes, you can walk the **waterfront,** watch salmon climb the fish ladder at Ballard Locks, see fish fly at **Pike Place Market,** and sail off into the sunset. If the Space Needle isn't spacey enough, visit **EMP/SFM,** a museum dedicated to rock music and science fiction.

Active Pursuits If you visit Seattle and don't get out on the **water** while you're in town, you're missing out on what makes this city so distinctive. With lakes Union and Washington, Elliott Bay, and Puget Sound surrounding the city, you'll have ample opportunities to go **boating.** However, the quintessential Seattle outing is a paddle around Lake Union in a **sea kayak.** You'll paddle past houseboats, see floatplanes, and even have the chance to tie up at a waterfront restaurant.

Eating & Drinking In a city where people discuss the merits of oysters from different local bays and anxiously await the annual return of Copper River salmon, it

PREVIOUS PAGE: Day or night, Pike Place Market is one of the places that define where to go, what to do, and how to eat in Seattle. ABOVE: Ferries gliding across Elliott Bay are a quintessential Seattle scenic view.

should come as no surprise that **Pike Place Market,** with its fishmongers and food stalls, is one of Seattle's top attractions. A day spent noshing in the market can be a foodie's dream come true. Visit such popular dining districts as **Capitol Hill** and **Ballard,** and you'll quickly learn that this is a city obsessed with eating locally.

Nightlife & Entertainment If you think Seattle nightlife still means grunge music, dude, wake up! The grunge scene died with Kurt Cobain, but that doesn't mean there's nothing to do here at night. Whether you're into Wagner or weird, Seattle's got you covered. **Seattle Center** and **Benaroya Hall** keep the cultured crowd happy, while **Pike Place Market** has clubs staging wild cabaret acts. You can even do dinner and the circus at **Teatro ZinZanni.** Then again, you just might want to raise a pint of local ale to Kurt's memory.

THE most UNFORGETTABLE SEATTLE EXPERIENCES

- **Eating Your Way Through Pike Place Market:** Breakfast at Le Pichet, espresso at what was once the only Starbucks in the world, lunch at Cafe Campagne, a martini at The Pink Door, dinner at Matt's in the Market, Celtic music at Kells, and a nightcap at Il Bistro—that's how you could spend a day at Pike Place. Between stops on this rigorous itinerary, you can people-watch, listen to street musicians, and shop for everything from fresh salmon to tropical fruits, to magic tricks, to art glass. See chapters 5 and 9.
- **Strolling the Olympic Sculpture Park:** With views of Puget Sound and the Olympic Mountains, and sculptures by Alexander Calder, Claes Oldenburg, and Richard Serra, this terraced park at the north end of the Seattle waterfront is great for a stroll any time of day, but is absolutely sublime at sunset. See p. 122.

A piece of art in Olympic Sculpture Park frames the Space Needle.

Get under the surface of Seattle with the Underground Tour.

- **Joining the Underground:** Rome has its catacombs, Paris has its sewers, and Seattle has its underground. Now, some people, including my own brother, think I'm nuts for enjoying the Seattle Underground Tour, but corny sewer jokes aside, this tour is fascinating and a great introduction to the seamier side of Seattle's early history. See p. 140.
- **Spending an Afternoon in the Ballard Neighborhood:** Watch the salmon climb the fish ladders and swim past viewing windows at the Hiram M. Chittenden (Ballard) Locks. Check out the exhibits at the Nordic Heritage Museum, and then stroll the shady streets of old Ballard. Have a meal at Ray's Boathouse, keeping an eye out for bald eagles, and then finish the day on the beach at Golden Gardens Park. See chapter 6.
- **Taking a Cruise:** Seattle is best seen from a boat, and there are plenty of vessels that will take you out on the water. Personally, I prefer sailboat outings from the waterfront, but for a more informative and diverse excursion, take the Argosy Cruises tour from Lake Union to the waterfront. If you don't mind flaunting the fact that you're a tourist, there's the daffy Seattle Duck Tour. See p. 153.
- **Visiting Volunteer Park:** Whether the day is sunny or gray, this park on Capitol Hill is a great spot to spend an afternoon. You can relax in the grass, study Chinese snuff bottles in the Seattle Asian Art Museum, marvel at the orchids in the conservatory, or simply enjoy the great view of the city from the top of the park's water tower. See p. 146.
- **Riding the Water Taxi to Alki Beach:** The water taxi that operates between the Seattle waterfront and Alki Beach, on the far side of Elliott Bay, is practically the cheapest boat ride you can take in Seattle. Once you get to Alki Beach, you can dine with a killer view of the Seattle skyline, and then go for a walk or bike ride on the beachfront path. See p. 306.

THE best THINGS TO DO FOR FREE (OR ALMOST)

- **Taking in the Sunset from the Waterfront:** On clear summer days, the setting sun silhouettes the Olympic Mountains on the far side of Puget Sound and makes sunset on the Seattle waterfront a not-to-be-missed experience. Try the rooftop park at the Bell Street Pier, Myrtle Edwards Park at the north end of the waterfront, the lounge at The Edgewater hotel, or, my personal favorite sunset spot, the Olympic Sculpture Park, which is adjacent to Myrtle Edwards Park. See "The Waterfront," in chapter 6.
- **Riding a Ferry Across Puget Sound:** Sure, you could spend $20 or $30 for a narrated tour of the Seattle waterfront, but for a fraction of that, you can take a ferry to Bremerton or Bainbridge Island and see not just Elliott Bay, but also plenty more of Puget Sound. Keep an eye out for porpoises and bald eagles. See p. 306.
- **Relaxing over a Latte:** If the rain and gray skies start to get to you, there is no better pick-me-up (short of a ticket to the tropics) than a frothy latte in a cozy cafe. Grab a magazine and just hang out until the rain stops (maybe sometime in July). See "Coffee, Tea, Bakeries & Pastry Shops," in chapter 5.
- **Riding the Monorail:** Though the ride is short, covering a distance that could easily be walked in a half-hour, the monorail provides a different perspective on the city. The retro-futurist transport, built for the Seattle World's Fair in 1962, ends at the foot of the Space Needle and even passes right through the Experience Music Project building. See p. 305.
- **Exploring a Waterfront Park:** Seattle abounds with waterfront parks, where you can gaze at distant shores, wiggle your toes in the sand, or walk through a remnant of old-growth forest. Some of my favorites include Discovery Park, Seward Park, Lincoln Park, and Golden Gardens Park. See "Parks & Public Gardens" and "Outdoor Pursuits," in chapter 6.

You can get around town on Seattle's famous monorail.

- **Museum-Hopping on First Thursday:** On the first Thursday of each month, almost all of Seattle's museums are open late, and most offer free admission for all or part of the day. Get an early start, and be sure to check the opening and closing times of the museums. Talk about a great way to save bucks on your vacation! See chapter 6.
- **Taking a Free Boat Ride on Lake Union:** Every Sunday afternoon, the Center for Wooden Boats on Lake Union offers free boat rides in classic wooden boats. You can watch noisy floatplanes landing and taking off as you sail serenely across the waves. See p. 128.
- **Strolling Through the Arboretum in Spring:** Winters in Seattle may not be long, but they do lack color. So when spring hits, the sudden bursts of brightness it brings are reverently appreciated. There's no better place in the city to enjoy the spring floral displays than the Washington Park Arboretum. See p. 150.
- **Stopping to Smell the Flowers:** Whether it's a cold rainy day or a sunny summer afternoon, a visit to the Volunteer Park Conservatory is a free ticket to the tropics. There are always plenty of beautiful orchids in bloom, as well as lots of other unusual tropical plants. See p. 136.

THE best OUTDOOR ACTIVITIES

- **Sea Kayaking on Lake Union:** Lake Union is a very urban body of water, but it has a great view of the Seattle skyline, and you can paddle right up to several waterfront restaurants. For more natural surroundings, kayak over to the marshes at the north end of the Washington Park Arboretum. See p. 162
- **Cycling the Burke-Gilman Trail:** Seattle-area cyclists are blessed with a plethora of great cycling paths, and the granddaddy of them all is the Burke-

The Northwest Folklife Festival is one of Seattle's many outdoor concerts.

Gilman Trail, which stretches for more than 14 miles from the Ballard neighborhood to the north end of Lake Washington. The Sammamish River Trail extends the trail for another dozen miles or so. There's even a gravel extension of the trail along the east shore of Lake Sammamish. See p. 161.

- **Going to an Outdoor Summer Movie or Concert:** When the summer sun shines, Seattleites spend as much time outdoors as they can, and among the city's favorite outdoor activities is attending outdoor concerts and movies. Whether in parks or parking lots, these outdoor performances bring out the lawn chairs and blankets. See "The Performing Arts" and "Movies," in chapter 9.
- **Hiking up Mount Si:** There's no getting around the fact that this hike is a real killer, but ooh, the view from the top! Mount Si is less than 45 minutes east of Seattle and rises straight up from the valley of the Snoqualmie River. The trail also goes straight up, so if you aren't in good shape, don't even think of trying this hike. See p. 160.
- **Day-Tripping to Mount Rainier National Park:** With growling glaciers, meadows full of colorful wildflowers, and thousand-year-old trees, Mount Rainier National Park always gets my vote for best day trip from Seattle. In summer, the opportunities for hiking are abundant and the views are absolutely breathtaking; and, in winter, cross-country skiing and snowshoeing provide opportunities for exploring a snowy landscape. See "Mount Rainier," in chapter 10.

THE best OFFBEAT EXPERIENCES

- **Adding Your Contribution to the Gum Wall:** Hey, when your gum has lost its flavor, don't spit it out on the sidewalk; instead, turn it into alfresco art by adding it to the "Gum Wall," Pike Place Market's self-adhesive display of ABC (already been chewed) art. See p. 172.
- **Making Music Even If You Can't Carry a Tune in a Bucket:** Even the musically challenged can make beautiful music (well, sort of) at a couple of unusual Seattle attractions. At the Experience Music Project, you can let your inner rock 'n' roller go wild on simulated musical instruments, while at the Soundbridge Seattle Symphony Music Discovery Center, fans of classical music can play a cello or conduct an orchestra. See p. 130 and 128.
- **Counting Salmon at Ballard's Chittenden Locks:** If you find yourself sleepless in Seattle, forget about counting sheep. Try counting salmon. In fact, even if you aren't suffering from insomnia, during the summer, the fish ladder and underwater viewing windows at the Hiram M. Chittenden (Ballard) Locks are great places to count salmon. See p. 138.
- **Believing It or Not at Ye Olde Curiosity Shop:** Two-headed calves, the Lord's Prayer on a grain of rice, a human mummy. These are just some of the unbelievable items on display at Ye Olde Curiosity Shop, Seattle's waterfront temple of the bizarre. See p. 140.
- **Buying a Flying Fish at Pike Place Market:** At Pike Place Market, the pigs may not fly, but the fish do. If you purchase a fresh salmon from the Pike

The salmon get help climbing upstream at Chittenden Locks.

Place Fish stall, you'll get to watch it go sailing over the counter as the overalls-clad fishmongers put on one of the best floor shows in the market. See p. 206.

THE best THINGS TO DO ON A RAINY DAY

- **Hang Out at Elliott Bay Book Company:** Nothing beats hanging out in a big bookstore on a rainy day, especially when the bookstore feels as if it has been around for a century and has its own cafe. See p. 196.
- **Go Wine Tasting in Woodinville:** Who needs sunshine if you're going to be indoors sampling the fruits of the vine? This rainy-day outing is best on Saturdays, when dozens of wineries open their doors in the nearby Woodinville wine country. See "The Woodinville Wine Country," in chapter 10.
- **Get Jazzed Up at an Espresso Bar:** When it's cold and dark and wet out in Seattle, you need powerful medicine to keep the blues at bay. You need espresso. Along with the ubiquitous (Seattle-originated) Starbucks, you can get your caffeine on at local chains like Tully's Coffee, Caffe Ladro, and Caffé Vita, as well as Monorail Espresso, Ancient Grounds, Local Color, and Zeitgeist Art/Coffee, among many others. Bring a book or your laptop and sit and sip all day, just like a Seattle native. See "Coffee, Tea, Bakeries & Pastry Shops," in chapter 5.
- **Spend the Day at Volunteer Park:** A park might not at first seem like the place to spend a rainy afternoon, but Volunteer Park, on Capitol Hill, is home to the Seattle Asian Art Museum, the Volunteer Park Conservatory, and a water tower with views over the city. See "Neighborhoods in Brief" in chapter 3 and "Parks & Public Gardens" in chapter 6.

You can sample the fruit of the vine in Woodinville.

THE best ACTIVITIES FOR FAMILIES

- **Wandering the Seattle Waterfront:** Yes, it's touristy, but with an aquarium, a carousel, boat-tour docks, and, best of all (at least as far as I'm concerned), Ye Olde Curiosity Shop, this is the sort of waterfront that keeps kids entertained for hours. See "The Waterfront," in chapter 6.
- **Doing a Daffy Duck Tour:** It's an open-air bus tour. No, it's a boat tour. No, it's both, and it's exceedingly silly, especially if you opt for your own duck-billed "quacker" noisemaker. Kids love these daffy duck tours aboard army surplus amphibious vehicles. Just remind them that the family minivan does not belong in the lake. See p. 155.
- **Seeing Seattle Center:** With a science museum, an IMAX theater, a children's museum, a children's theater, and a choreographed multimedia fountain to play in, this is Seattle's ultimate kid zone. See "Seattle Center & Lake Union" and "Especially for Kids," in chapter 6.
- **An Outing to the Snoqualmie Valley:** Little ones enamored of Thomas the Tank Engine will adore the Northwest Railway Museum and affiliated Snoqualmie Valley Railroad. In summer, you can pick berries on local "U-pick" farms; and, in the fall, you can see salmon spawning at a fish hatchery. Then there's Camlann Medieval Village, where there are all sorts of fun activities all year. See "Snoqualmie Falls & the Snoqualmie Valley," in chapter 10.
- **EMP/SFM (Experience Music Project/Science Fiction Museum):** If you've got teenagers in tow, drop them at this pair of affiliated museums and they'll stay happy for hours. EMP focuses on rock music with lots of cool interactive exhibits, while the SFM has loads of props from Hollywood's most famous sci-fi movies. See p. 130.

2

SEATTLE IN DEPTH

Ever since 1851, when a boatload of settlers landed on a windswept beach on Puget Sound, Seattle has had grand aspirations. The pioneers who rowed ashore that day named their settlement New York Alki, appending the local Native American word for "by and by" to that of the East Coast's largest city, in hopes that this new community would one day be a bustling metropolis to rival New York. It took more than 150 years, but their dreams have come true—just not quite the way they had first imagined.

First, those early settlers discovered that the spot where they had set up camp was more than just windswept; it was downright blustery in winter. So they moved across Elliott Bay and changed the name of their community to Seattle, in honor of a local Native American chief who had befriended them. For nearly 50 years, Seattle remained a rough-and-tumble place surrounded by wilderness, but when gold was discovered in the Yukon and miners began emptying their pockets before and after they'd gone north to Alaska, Seattle turned from town to city.

However, even as Seattle has turned into a sprawling metropolis, it has remained tightly connected to its natural surroundings. With the waters of Puget Sound and lakes Union and Washington shaping the city's topography, Seattle is a city of splendid vistas, and many of those views are tinted a deep green, which has given the city its nickname—the Emerald City. Take a little time to read through this chapter, and you'll get a feel for this jewel of the Pacific Northwest.

SEATTLE TODAY

Let's say you're sitting in your local Starbucks using your laptop to order something from Amazon.com. Your wife calls you on your T-Mobile cellphone to ask if you made the plane reservations on Expedia.com. You reach into your R.E.I day pack and pull out the printout of the tickets. "Yup, got 'em right here, honey," you tell her. "They're on Alaska Airlines." As you hang up the phone, you bump your latte and spill it all over your new Eddie Bauer shorts and the Tommy Bahama Hawaiian shirt you got on sale at Nordstrom. It's becoming one of those days, and you realize you really, *really* need this Seattle vacation.

Whether you know it or not, you have just immersed yourself (pardon the pun) in a big chunk of the Seattle aesthetic without ever setting foot in the city. Of course, you probably already knew that Starbucks got its start in Seattle and that the plane you're going to take to Seattle was probably built in the area by Boeing. However, you might not be aware that such familiar companies as Amazon.com, T-Mobile, Expedia.com, R.E.I, Nordstrom, and Eddie Bauer are all headquartered in or near Seattle. Despite the fact that their names imply otherwise, even Alaska Airlines and Tommy Bahama are Seattle-area companies. Go figure. Oh yes, and if the laptop you're using is a PC, chances are good that you're running software by another Seattle-area company—Microsoft.

OPPOSITE PAGE: **Pearl Jam, led by frontman Eddie Vedder, is one of the many important musical acts that came from Seattle.**

Seattle is a major urban center nestled in a gorgeous natural setting.

Many of these companies are directly or indirectly responsible for making Seattle what it is today. Starbucks, of course, gave birth to the city's lively cafe culture, and today there seems to be an espresso bar on every block. The plethora of high-tech companies filled the city with young, well-educated computer nerds. The forests, mountains, lakes, and bays hemming in Seattle's edges gave rise to both the city's outdoor-clothing companies and the many manufacturers of outdoor-recreational equipment.

Few cities in the United States are as immersed in the outdoor aesthetic as Seattle. The Cascade Range lies less than 50 miles to the east of downtown Seattle, and across Puget Sound stand the Olympic Mountains. In the spring, summer, and fall, the forests and mountains attract hikers, mountain bikers, anglers, and campers, while in winter the ski areas of Snoqualmie Pass, Stevens Pass, and Crystal Mountain draw snowboarders and skiers. Impressive mountains line the city's eastern and western horizons, but it takes but a glance to the southeast on a sunny day to reveal Seattle's most treasured sight—Mount Rainier, a 14,410-foot-tall dormant volcano that looms so large and unexpected that it demands your attention. When "the Mountain is out," as they say here in Seattle, the natives head for the hills.

As important as "the Mountain" is to Seattle, it is water that truly defines the city's character (and I don't mean the city's infamous rain). To the west lies Elliott Bay, an arm of Puget Sound; to the east is Lake Washington; and right in the middle of the city is Lake Union. With so much water, Seattle is a city of boaters, who take to the water in everything from regally appointed yachts to slender sea kayaks. Want to paddle a kayak up to a restaurant and order a dozen raw oysters? You can do it here. Putter around in a steam-powered wooden boat? Easy. Sail off into the sunset? No problem. Consequently, the opening day of boating season has become one of Seattle's most popular annual festivals.

Each spring, however, even boating takes a back seat to gardening. The mild climate, tempered by the waters of Puget Sound, has made Seattle one of the

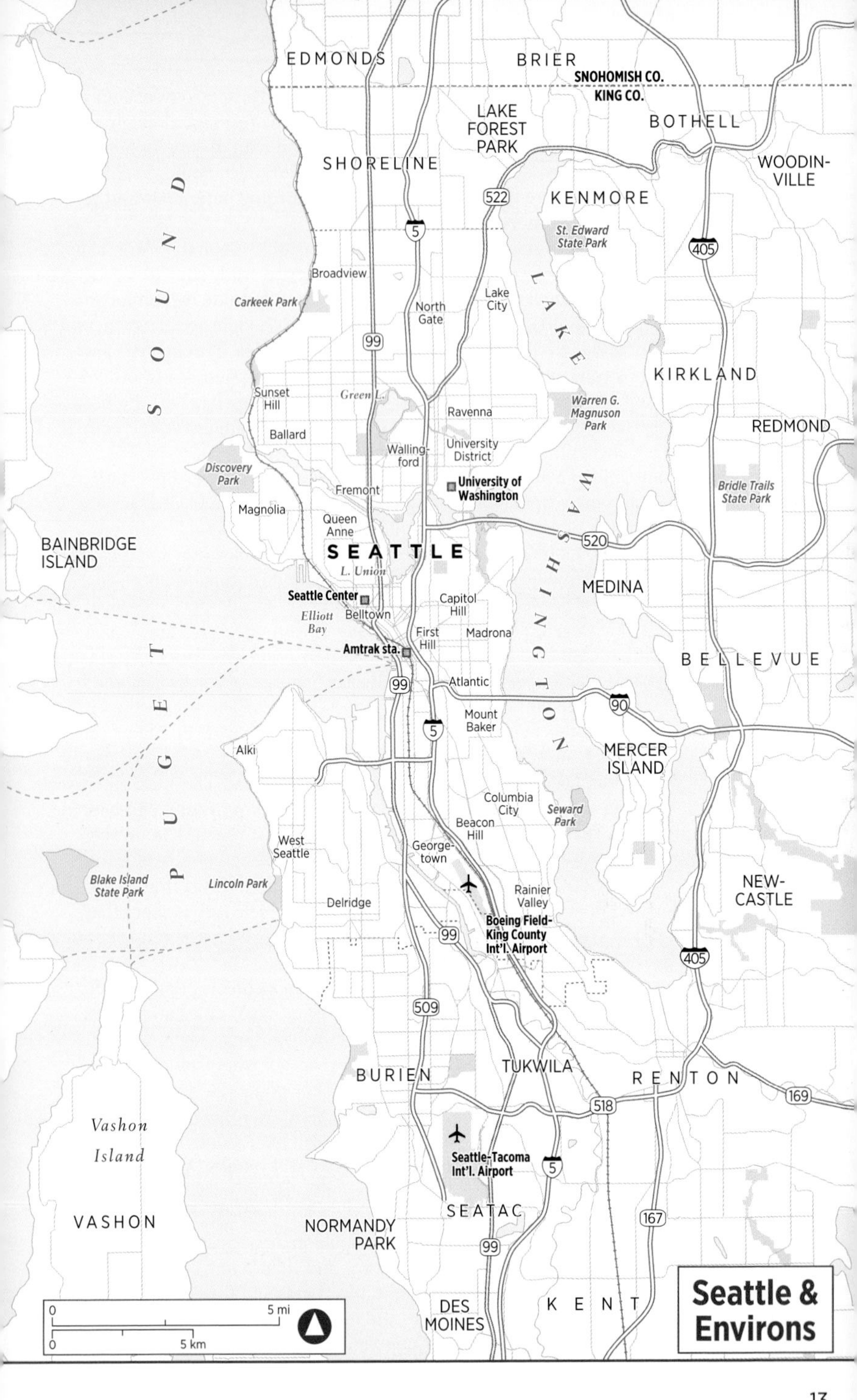

Seattle & Environs
EDMONDS
BRIER
SNOHOMISH CO.
KING CO.
LAKE FOREST PARK
BOTHELL
SHORELINE
WOODINVILLE
KENMORE
St. Edward State Park
PUGET SOUND
Broadview
Carkeek Park
North Gate
Lake City
LAKE WASHINGTON
KIRKLAND
Sunset Hill
Green L.
Ravenna
Warren G. Magnuson Park
REDMOND
Ballard
Walling-ford
University District
Discovery Park
Fremont
University of Washington
Bridle Trails State Park
Magnolia
Queen Anne
BAINBRIDGE ISLAND
SEATTLE
L. Union
MEDINA
Seattle Center
Capitol Hill
Elliott Bay
Belltown
First Hill
Madrona
Amtrak sta.
BELLEVUE
Atlantic
Mount Baker
Alki
MERCER ISLAND
Columbia City
Seward Park
Beacon Hill
West Seattle
George-town
Blake Island State Park
Lincoln Park
Rainier Valley
NEW-CASTLE
Delridge
Boeing Field-King County Int'l. Airport
BURIEN
TUKWILA
RENTON
Vashon Island
Seattle-Tacoma Int'l. Airport
VASHON
SEATAC
NORMANDY PARK
DES MOINES
KENT
0
5 mi
0
5 km
5
99
405
522
520
90
509
518
169
167

most garden-obsessed cities in the nation. Spring in Seattle sees city residents flocking to public gardens, and a drive or walk around any residential neighborhood in April can serve as a de facto garden tour. I spend a lot of time in Seattle each spring and early summer, and just one visit to the Queen Anne neighborhood makes me wish I were back in my own garden dividing perennials and reconstructing my mixed borders.

Boats and gardens aside, Seattle is known as the coffee capital of America. To understand Seattle's coffee addiction, it is necessary to study the city's geography and climate. Seattle lies at almost 50 degrees north latitude, which means that winter days are short. The sun comes up around 7:30am, goes down as early as 4:30pm, and is frequently hidden behind leaden skies. Through the gray days of winter, a strong stimulant is almost a necessity to get people out of bed. Seattleites love to argue over which espresso bar or cafe in town serves the best coffee (and the answer isn't always Starbucks, despite the famous coffee company's global expansion from its humble beginnings in Seattle).

Spend any time in a Seattle cafe, and you're likely to catch the conversation veering from espresso to express lanes. Seattle has become infamous on the West Coast for its traffic congestion, and Seattleites love to gripe about their city's transportation issues. Yet, despite a reputation for foot-dragging when it comes to public transit, Seattle finally got a light-rail system up and running in 2009; and, in 2010, service began between Seattle-Tacoma International Airport and downtown Seattle. There's even a streetcar line linking downtown with Lake Union, and a monorail that connects downtown with Seattle Center, the former World's Fair campus that is now home to numerous theaters, museums, and attractions, including the Space Needle.

Not surprisingly, the city still can't seem to decide what to do about the Alaskan Way Viaduct, an elevated highway that runs along the Seattle waterfront, which was damaged by the 2001 Nisqually earthquake. The most likely solution is a tunnel similar to Boston's Big Dig. However, a proposed city-wide monorail project in years past never got off the ground, so it remains to be seen whether ground will ever be broken for a viable viaduct replacement. As if traffic congestion on land weren't bad enough, the Seattle area also suffers from an aging and undersized floating bridge and a passenger-and-vehicle ferry system that, while the largest in the nation, has had to cut back on sailings due to budget cuts brought on by the ongoing economic recession.

The sluggish economy has also put many Seattle-area construction projects on hold, but the city is still doing better than many other major cities around the country. Growth and construction continue to transform both downtown and many outlying neighborhoods around the city. In the case of Microsoft cofounder Paul Allen's ambitious South Lake Union development project, a neighborhood just north of downtown is being transformed from low-rise warehouses and apartments into high-rise condominiums and hotels and will be, among other things, home to the world headquarters of online bookseller and retailer Amazon.com. With its glass-and-steel towers, this new development is completely changing the look and feel of urban Seattle.

With nearly 3.5 million people in the metropolitan area, Seattle is the largest west-coast U.S. city north of San Francisco, and, like San Francisco, it is famously liberal and has a large LGBT community. Consequently, Seattle today embraces diversity as much as it embraces the outdoors and the latest technology. The area's many tech jobs keep the population surprisingly young for such

a large metropolitan area, and Seattle's youthful character is most readily apparent on the streets of Belltown, Ballard, and Capitol Hill, three of Seattle's hippest neighborhoods and main nightlife districts. With upscale restaurants, stylish bars, and hip nightclubs, these neighborhoods are where many of the beautiful people of Seattle spend their evenings. Capitol Hill, long Seattle's main gay neighborhood, and Ballard, once a stodgy Scandinavian neighborhood, are also now the city's main epicenters of culinary expansionism. New restaurants have been opening in these two neighborhoods at a surprising pace considering the state of the economy; high-end restaurants have also been opening on the ground floors of the many new condominium towers in the South Lake Union neighborhood.

Gaze across the rooftops of Seattle from the observation deck of the cloud-impaling Space Needle, and you'll see a modern metropolis, a Pacific Rim powerhouse, but the modern high-rises of South Lake Union and the bustle of a workday amid the downtown office buildings belie the true nature of this city on the shores of Puget Sound. Seattle today is far more than just a place to do business. It is a city of forward-thinking young computer nerds who, after a week of staring out their office windows at the sparkling waters of Elliott Bay, the snowy bulk of Mount Rainier, or the jagged peaks of the Olympic Mountains, grab their hiking boots, kayak, or bike and head outdoors. Smartphone-wielding Seattleites, seduced by the city's many scenic vistas, fueled by espresso, and favoring Keens over Jimmy Choos have turned the concept of casual Fridays into a lifestyle choice.

LOOKING BACK: SEATTLE HISTORY

By East Coast standards, Seattle got a late start in U.S. history. Although explorers visited the region as far back as the late 1700s, the first settlers didn't arrive until 1851. Capt. George Vancouver of the British Royal Navy—who lent his name to both Vancouver, British Columbia, and Vancouver, Washington—had explored Puget Sound as early as 1792. However, there wasn't much to attract anyone permanently to this remote region. Unlike Oregon to the south, Washington had little rich farmland, only acres and acres of forest. It was this seemingly endless supply of wood that finally enticed the first settlers.

Pioneer Years

The region's first settlement was on Alki Point, in the area now known as West Seattle. Bad choice. Because this location was exposed to storms sweeping in off the Pacific Ocean, the settlers soon decided to move across Elliott Bay to a more protected spot that has since grown into the city of Seattle. The new location for the village was a tiny island surrounded by mud flats. Some early settlers wanted to name the town New York

> **Wisdom from Seattle's Namesake**
>
> ***Every part of this country is sacred to my people. Every hillside, every valley, every plain and grove has been hallowed by some fond memory or some sad experience of my tribe.***
>
> **—Chief Sealth, for whom Seattle is named**

The Seattle area's rich stores of lumber helped the settlement grow into a city.

Alki—even then, Seattle had grand aspirations—but chose "Seattle" as a tribute to Chief Sealth, a local Native American who had befriended the newcomers.

In the middle of town, on the waterfront, Henry Yesler built the first steam-powered lumber mill on Puget Sound. It stood at the foot of what is now Yesler Way, which for many years was referred to as Skid Road, a reference to the way logs were skidded down to the sawmill from the slopes behind town. Over the years, Skid Road developed a reputation for its bars and brothels. Some say that after an East Coast journalist incorrectly referred to it as Skid Row in his newspaper, the name stuck and was subsequently applied to derelict neighborhoods all over the country. To this day, despite attempts to revamp the neighborhood, Yesler Way continues to attract the sort of visitors you would expect (due in part to the presence in the neighborhood of missions and homeless shelters), but it is also in the center of the Pioneer Square Historic District, one of Seattle's main tourist destinations.

Up from the Ashes

By 1889, Seattle had more than 25,000 inhabitants and was well on its way to becoming the most important city in the Northwest. On June 6 of that year, however, 25 blocks in the center of town burned to the ground. By that time, the city, which had spread out onto low-lying land reclaimed from the mud flats, had begun experiencing problems with mud and sewage disposal. The fire gave citizens the opportunity to rebuild their town. The solution to the drainage and sewage problems was to regrade the steep slopes to the east of the town and raise the streets above their previous levels.

That #@&•#! Hill

The section of First Hill that rises above the Pioneer Square area was once referred to as Profanity Hill because it was so #@&*#! hard to climb.

> ### All Fired Up
>
> **The fire remembered as the Great Fire *transformed* Seattle from a town to a city.**
>
> **—Greg W. Lange**

Because the regrading lagged behind the rebuilding, the ground floors of many new buildings eventually wound up below street level. When the new roads and sidewalks were constructed at the level that had previously been the second floor of most buildings, the former ground-floor stores and businesses moved up into the light of day and the spaces below the sidewalk were left to businesses of shady characters. Today you can tour sections of this Seattle underground (see "Good Times in Bad Taste," in chapter 6).

Among the most amazing post-fire engineering feats was the leveling of two hills. Although Seattle once had eight hills, there are now only six—nothing is left of either Denny Hill or Jackson Street Hill. Hydraulic mining techniques, using high-powered water jets to dig into the hillsides, leveled both mounds. Today the Jackson Street Hill has become the flat area to the west of the International District, while Denny Hill is the flat neighborhood south of Seattle Center. This latter area was historically known as the Denny Regrade but today is known as Belltown.

Eight years after the fire, another event changed the city almost as much as the fire. On July 17, 1897, the steamship *Portland* arrived in Seattle from Alaska, carrying a ton of gold from the recently discovered Klondike goldfields. Within the year, Seattle's population swelled with prospectors heading north. Few of them ever struck it rich, but they all stopped in Seattle to purchase supplies and equipment, thus lining the pockets of local merchants and spreading far and wide the name of this obscure Northwest city. When the prospectors came south again with their hard-earned gold, much of it never left Seattle, sidetracked by beer halls and brothels.

The Boeing Years

In 1916, not many years after the Wright brothers made their first flight, Seattle residents William Boeing and Clyde Esterveld launched their first airplane, a

Boeing, founded in 1916, still sends planes skyward from Seattle.

floatplane, from the waters of Lake Union. Their intention was to operate an airmail service to Canada. Their enterprise eventually became the Boeing Company, which grew to be the largest single employer in the area. Until recently, Seattle's fortunes were so inextricably bound to those of Boeing that hard times for the aircraft manufacturer meant hard times for the whole city. While Boeing still employs thousands of people in the Seattle metropolitan area, it no longer controls the city's economic fate. With the founding of a little computer-software company called Microsoft, Seattle's economy began to diversify, and with that has come a new, broad-based prosperity that has profoundly changed Seattle's landscape and character.

Seattle's Really Not That Bad

I grew up in Seattle, but I always knew I wanted to leave.

—David Guterson, author of *Snow Falling on Cedars* and *The Other*

SEATTLE IN POPULAR CULTURE

Books

If, after a few hikes through the wild areas in and around Seattle, you decide you want to keep a bit of this wildness close at hand, pick up a copy of Terry Donnelly and Mary Liz Austin's *Wild Seattle: A Celebration of the Natural Areas In and Around the City* (Sierra Club Books, 2004), a coffee-table book filled with beautiful photos.

David Guterson's immensely popular *Snow Falling on Cedars* (Vintage, 1995), though not set in Seattle, does take place on a fictionalized Puget Sound island that sounds a lot like the Seattle bedroom community of Bainbridge Island. More recently, the Asian-American experience in Seattle is also the focus of Jamie Ford's novel *Hotel on the Corner of Bitter and Sweet* (Ballantine, 2009).

Fans of murder mysteries should be sure to check out J.A. Jance's series of J.P. Beaumont mysteries, which feature a Seattle homicide detective. Although Seattle author Mary Daheim's Emma Lord mysteries aren't set right in Seattle, they take place in a fictitious town not far away.

If you've already been on the Seattle Underground tour, you know all about William Speidel's *Sons of the Profits (Or, There's No Business Like Grow Business: The Seattle Story 1851–1901* [Nettle Creek Publishing Company, 2003]). This entertaining account of the first 50 years of Seattle history tells it like it was, much to the chagrin of straight-laced historians who didn't like the way Speidel dredged up the exploits of profiteers and prostitutes in writing this fun book. Despite the title, *Skid Road: An Informal Portrait of Seattle* (University of Washington Press, 2003), by Murray Morgan, is a more straightforward history of Seattle, and equally readable.

Films & TV

While the gray skies of Seattle aren't exactly the favorite backdrops of filmmakers, there have been some memorable films shot in Seattle over the years. Of course, *Sleepless in Seattle* (1993), starring Tom Hanks and Meg Ryan, is perhaps the best known of these, and boat tours of Seattle's Lake Union always point out the houseboat that was used in the movie. *Singles* (1992), directed by Cameron Crowe and starring Matt Dillon, Kyra Sedgwick, and Bridget Fonda, features

20-somethings and the famous Seattle grunge music club scene. Long before the days of grunge, Elvis Presley made his way to Seattle in *It Happened at the World's Fair;* the 1963 film is set at the 1962 Seattle World's Fair, which gave Seattle the Space Needle. The Seattle jazz club scene is the backdrop for 1989's *The Fabulous Baker Boys,* which stars brothers Jeff and Beau Bridges and Michelle Pfeiffer.

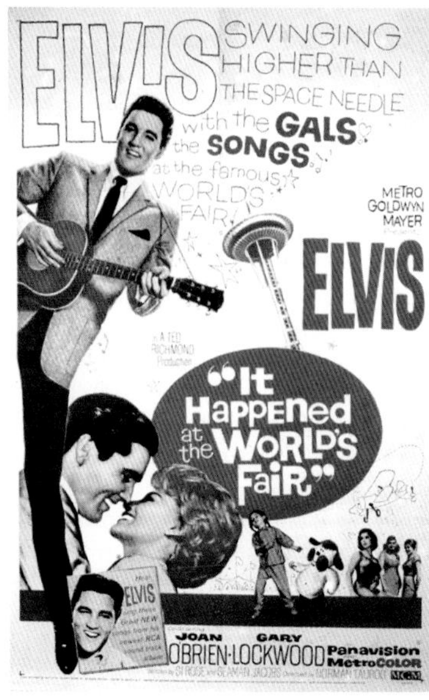

The 1962 World's Fair gave Elvis Presley a chance to rock Seattle on film.

Early Seattle history was the focus of *Here Come the Brides* (1968–70, ABC), about an 1870s logging company that brings 100 women to Seattle as wives for the lumberjacks, and its title song, "Seattle," was a hit single for both Perry Como and "Brides" star Bobby Sherman. In 1960, John Wayne and Stewart Granger starred in *North to Alaska,* a story of romance and the lust for gold.

The Last Mimzy (2007), a family film about two kids who develop paranormal powers after they find a box of special toys, is set partly in Seattle and partly on nearby Whidbey Island. In *Life or Something Like It* (2002), Angelina Jolie stars as a Seattle TV reporter who is told by a psychic homeless man that she has only a few days to live. Nearby Tacoma serves as the backdrop for *10 Things I Hate About You* (1999), starring Heath Ledger and Julia Stiles, a retelling of Shakespeare's *The Taming of the Shrew.* In Bernardo Bertolucci's *Little Buddha* (1993), with Keanu Reeves, Bridget Fonda, and Chris Isaak, a reincarnated Tibetan lama turns up in Seattle. The red-hot dot com days are the backdrop for *Disclosure* (1994), with Michael Douglas and Demi Moore.

ABC's *Grey's Anatomy* (2005–present) is set in Seattle; and, if you were a fan of the TV show *Frasier,* you've seen plenty of Seattle scenery and heard lots about this city.

Music

Although many rock-music fans might think that Seattle music started and ended with grunge, that's just not true. Seattle has been producing noteworthy music and musicians for more than 60 years.

Long before grunge—in 1948, to be precise—a young, blind musician named Ray Charles moved to the Emerald City and made his first record. A decade later, legendary guitarist Jimi Hendrix, who was born in Seattle in 1942, began playing in his first local band. Although Hendrix's career would not take off until long after he had left Seattle, the musician is much celebrated here in his hometown. EMP (Experience Music Project), Microsoft cofounder Paul Allen's music museum, started out as a place for Allen to show off his extensive collection of Hendrix memorabilia and eventually grew into a major shrine to popular music. Up on Capitol Hill, at the corner of Broadway Avenue and East

Pine Street, there's a statue of Hendrix. The guitarist's grave is at Greenwood Memorial Park, in the nearby suburb of Renton.

In the mid-1980s, a new sound emerged in Seattle. It merged heavy metal with punk music and came to be known as "grunge." The Sub Pop recording label was the premier grunge-music record company, and Seattle bands such as Nirvana, Pearl Jam, Alice in Chains, Mudhoney, and Soundgarden quickly came to dominate the airwaves with their new sound. However, the grunge scene effectively came to a screeching halt when Nirvana bandleader Kurt Cobain committed suicide in 1994.

Legendary guitarist (and Seattle native) Jimi Hendrix was the inspiration for the Experience Music Project.

EATING & DRINKING

Although it is mere coincidence that the words Seattle and **seafood** both start with the same three letters of the alphabet, it takes only a stroll through Pike Place Market to see for yourself that Seattle is a seafood-lover's nirvana. Silvery salmon, hefty Dungeness crabs, clams, mussels, and dozens of varieties of oysters are the seafood stars in this city on the shores of Puget Sound. Salmon, although not always local, is a Northwest icon that shows up both fresh and smoked on Seattle menus. Wish you could take some salmon home? Not a problem. Pike Place Market fishmongers will pack fresh salmon for you to take home on the plane, and some vacuum-packed smoked salmon doesn't even need to be refrigerated. Oysters are such an obsession here that one of my favorite restaurants, Elliott's Oyster House, even has an oyster "New Year" celebration every year in early November.

Washington's bounty doesn't end where the surf meets the turf. The state's temperate climate is ideal for growing everything from apples to zucchinis. Small farms grow such a wide variety of fresh produce throughout the year that the locavore movement (eating locally as much as possible) has rapidly gained ground among chefs at the city's top restaurants. *Fresh, organic, local,* and *sustainable* are the watchwords at an ever-increasing number of restaurants in town, such as Tilth, Agua Verde Cafe, and Portage Bay Café. Even espresso stands around town have jumped on the wagon, serving organic, fair-trade, and shade-grown coffees. Perhaps best of all, Seattle's Theo Chocolate, a company that gives tours of its chocolate factory, roasts its own organic and fair-trade cocoa beans. Finally, guilt-free chocolate!

Of course, as nearly everyone on the planet knows, **coffee** leviathan Starbucks got its start in Seattle, and espresso here has been raised to an art form. However, from dawn to dark, Seattle cups and glasses stay filled with more than just double-tall skinny lattes.

Washington State is one of the nation's top **wine** producers, and while there are few vineyards in the vicinity of Seattle, many of the state's best and biggest wineries are in the town of Woodinville, just a 30-minute drive north of the city. Washington wineries are best known for their cabernet sauvignon and merlot, but you should also keep an eye out for excellent syrahs and semillons. Many of the city's top restaurants emphasize Washington wines on their wine lists, and wine bars around the city provide opportunities to sip and sample regional fruits of the vine. Seattle is also home to quite a few craft breweries; some are tiny brewpubs, but others are major brewers that craft distinctive **beers.** While Pyramid Breweries and the Red Hook Ale Brewery are the two major players in the area, smaller brewpubs worth searching out include Big Time Brewery & Alehouse and the Elysian Brewing Company, two of my personal favorites.

Enjoy the bounty of fresh produce that packs the markets and restaurants in Seattle.

WHEN TO GO

Weather

Let's face it: Seattle's weather has a bad reputation. As they say out here, "The rain in Spain stays mainly in Seattle." I wish I could tell you it isn't so, but I can't. It rains in Seattle—and rains and rains and rains. However, when December 31 rolls around each year, a funny thing happens: They total up the year's precipitation, and Seattle almost always comes out behind such cities as Washington, Boston, New York, and Atlanta. So it isn't the *amount* of rain here that's the problem—it's the number of rainy or cloudy days, which far outnumber those of any of the rainy East Coast cities.

Most of Seattle's rain falls between October and April, so if you visit in the summer, you might not see a drop the entire time. But just in case, you should bring a rain jacket or at least an umbrella. Also, no matter what time of year you plan to visit Seattle, be sure to pack at least a sweater or light jacket. Summer nights can be quite cool, and daytime temperatures rarely climb above the low 80s Fahrenheit (upper 20s Celsius). Winters are not as cold as they are in the East, but snow does fall in Seattle.

Because of the pronounced seasonality of the weather here, people spend as much time outdoors during the summer as they can, and accordingly summer is when the city stages all its big festivals. Because it stays light until 10pm in the middle of summer, it's difficult to get Seattleites indoors to theater or music performances. But when the weather turns wet, Seattleites head for the theaters and performance halls in droves.

To make things perfectly clear, here's an annual weather chart:

Seattle's Average Temperature & Days of Rain

	JAN	FEB	MAR	APR	MAY	JUNE	JULY	AUG	SEPT	OCT	NOV	DEC
TEMP. (°F)	41	44	46	51	57	61	65	65	61	54	47	43
TEMP. (°C)	5	6	8	11	14	16	18	18	16	12	8	6
RAIN (DAYS)	18	16	17	14	11	9	5	6	8	11	18	18

HOLIDAYS

Banks, government offices, post offices, and many stores, restaurants, and museums are closed on the following legal national holidays: January 1 (New Year's Day), the third Monday in January (Martin Luther King, Jr., Day), the third Monday in February (Presidents' Day), the last Monday in May (Memorial Day), July 4 (Independence Day), the first Monday in September (Labor Day), the second Monday in October (Columbus Day), November 11 (Veterans' Day/Armistice Day), the fourth Thursday in November (Thanksgiving Day), and December 25 (Christmas). The Tuesday after the first Monday in November is Election Day, a federal government holiday in 2012 and in all presidential-election years (held every 4 years).

Seattle Calendar of Events

Seattleites will hold a festival at the drop of a rain hat, and summers here seem to revolve around the city's myriad celebrations. To find out what special events will be taking place while you're in town, check the "NW Ticket" arts-and-entertainment section of the Friday *Seattle Times,* or pick up a copy of *Seattle Weekly.* Remember, festivals here take place rain or shine. For more specific dates than those listed here, take a look at the calendar of events on Seattle's Convention and Visitors Bureau website **(www.visitseattle.org),** which is updated as dates become available.

In addition to the festivals listed here, a series of more than a dozen cultural community festivals is held every year at Seattle Center. Called **Festál,** this series celebrates Seattle's cultural diversity. In the past, they've held Vietnamese, African, Japanese, Filipino, Brazilian, and Tibetan festivals. For information, contact **Seattle Center** (✆ **206/684-7200;** www.seattlecenter.com).

For an exhaustive list of events beyond those listed here, check **http://events.frommers.com**, where you'll find a searchable, up-to-the-minute roster of what's happening in cities all over the world.

JANUARY

Chinatown/International District Lunar New Year Celebration (✆**206/382-1197;** www.cidbia.org). Each year's date depends on the lunar calendar. In 2012, the Chinese New Year celebration starts January 23.

FEBRUARY

Northwest Flower & Garden Show (✆ **253/756-2121;** www.gardenshow.com), Seattle. This massive 5-day show for avid gardeners has astonishing floral displays. Late February.

MARCH

Moisture Festival (✆ **206/297-1405;** www.moisturefestival.com), various venues. This month-long festival is a sort of modern vaudeville celebration of classic comedy/varietè performances and burlesque. Mid-March to early April.

APRIL

Seattle Cherry Blossom and Japanese Cultural Festival (✆ **206/684-7200** or 206/723-2003; www.seattlecenter.com), Seattle Center. Traditional Japanese spring festival. Early to mid-April.

Skagit Valley Tulip Festival (✆ **360/428-5959;** www.tulipfestival.org), La Conner. An hour north of Seattle, acres and acres of tulips and daffodils cover the Skagit Valley with broad swaths of color every spring, creating an enchanting landscape. Lots of festivities. All month.

MAY

Opening Day of Boating Season (✆ **206/325-1000;** www.seattleyachtclub.org), Lake Union and Lake Washington. A parade of boats and much fanfare take place as Seattle boaters bring out everything from kayaks to yachts. First Saturday in May.

Seattle Maritime Festival (✆ **206/787-3163;** www.portseattle.org). Tugboat races are the highlight of this annual Port of Seattle event. Festivities are centered on the Bell Street Pier (Pier 66) on the Seattle waterfront. Early May.

University District StreetFair (✆ **206/547-4417;** www.udistrictstreetfair.org), University District. This is the first big street fair of the season in Seattle and includes lots of crafts booths, food vendors, and live music. Mid-May.

International Children's Festival (✆ **206/684-7338;** www.giantmagnet.org), Seattle Center. Maori musicians, Chinese puppets, Japanese storytellers, West African drummers and dancers—these are just some of the acts you might see at this children's festival that celebrates world cultures through the performing arts. Mid-May.

Seattle International Film Festival (✆ **206/324-9996;** www.siff.net), at theaters around town. New foreign and independent films are screened over several weeks during this highly regarded film festival. Late May to mid-June.

Northwest Folklife Festival (✆ **206/684-7300;** www.nwfolklife.org), Seattle Center. This is one of the largest folklife festivals in the country, with dozens of national and regional folk musicians performing on numerous stages. In addition, you'll find crafts vendors from all over the Northwest, lots of good food, and dancing. Memorial Day weekend.

JUNE

Edmonds Art Festival (✆ **425/771-6412;** www.edmondsartsfestival.com), Edmonds. This is the first big art festival of the year in the Puget Sound area, and many of the region's top artists and craftspeople attend. Third weekend in June.

Fremont Fair (✆ **206/632-1500;** www.fremontfair.org). A celebration of the summer solstice with a wacky parade, naked bicyclists, food, arts and crafts, and entertainment in one of Seattle's favorite neighborhoods. Third weekend in June.

Seattle Pride (✆ 206/322-9561; www.seattlepride.org), Capitol Hill. With several days of revelry leading up to and including the last weekend in June, this is the largest gay, lesbian, bisexual, and transgender parade and festival in the Northwest. Last week in June.

JULY

Family 4th at Lake Union (✆ **206/281-7788;** www.familyfourth.org), Gas Works Park. Seattle's main Fourth of July fireworks display. July 4th.

Lake Union Wooden Boat Festival (✆ **206/382-2628;** www.cwb.org), Center for Wooden Boats. Wooden boats, both old and new, from all over the Northwest are displayed. Demonstrations, food, and entertainment. July 4th weekend.

Out to Lunch (✆ **206/623-0340;** http://downtownseattleevents.com). Free Friday and Wednesday lunchtime music concerts in plazas and parks throughout downtown. Mid-June through August.

Seafair (✆ **206/728-0123;** www.seafair.com). This is the biggest Seattle event of the year, with an abundance of festivities—parades, hydroplane boat races, an air show with the Navy's Blue Angels, the Torchlight Parade, ethnic festivals, sporting events, and tours of naval ships. Events take place all over Seattle. Early July to early August.

Chinatown International District Summer Fest (✆ **206/382-1197;** www.cidbia.org). Music, dancing, arts, and food of Seattle's Asian district. Second weekend in July.

Viking Days (✆ **206/789-5707;** www.nordicmuseum.org), Ballard. Seattle's Ballard neighborhood was founded by Scandinavians, and that heritage is still celebrated every summer at the Nordic Heritage Museum. Lots of Scandinavian crafts and foods. Mid-July.

Pilchuck Glass School Open House (✆ **206/621-8422;** www.pilchuck.com), Stanwood. If you're a fan of glass artist Dale Chihuly, you won't want to miss an opportunity to visit the school that helped him make a name for himself. The open house is immensely popular, so buy tickets early. Mid-July.

Bite of Seattle (✆ **425/295-3262;** www.comcastbiteofseattle.com), Seattle Center. Sample bites from local restaurants or taste some wines. Third weekend in July.

Sequim Lavender Festival (✆ **360/681-3035;** www.lavenderfestival.com). The town of Sequim, on the north side of the Olympic Peninsula, is a 30-minute ferry ride and an hour's drive from Seattle. Every summer the purple haze of lavender farms adds splashes of color to the landscape. This festival features farm visits and vendors selling lavender-themed art, crafts, cosmetics, and foods. Third weekend in July.

Bellevue Arts Museum ArtsFair (✆ **425/519-0770;** www.bellevuearts.org), Bellevue Square, Bellevue. This is the largest arts-and-fine-crafts fair in the Northwest. Last weekend in July.

Camlann Medieval Village Summer Village Festivals (✆ **425/788-8624;** www.camlann.org), Carnation. Come all ye lords and ladies and enjoy knightly combat, demonstrations of long bows, wandering minstrels, and medieval banquets. Weekends late July to late August.

AUGUST

Chief Seattle Days (✆ **360/598-3311;** www.suquamish.nsn.us), Suquamish tribal headquarters. A celebration of Northwest Native American culture across Puget Sound from Seattle. Third weekend in August.

SEPTEMBER

Bumbershoot (✆ **206/281-7788;** www.bumbershoot.org). Seattle's second-most-popular festival derives its peculiar name from a British term for an umbrella —an obvious reference to the rainy weather. Rock music and other events pack Seattle's youthful set into Seattle Center and other venues. You'll find plenty of arts and crafts on display, too. Labor Day weekend.

Fremont Oktoberfest (✆ **206/633-0422;** www.fremontoktoberfest.com). With beer gardens, a "Miss Buxom" contest, a chainsaw pumpkin-carving competition, and a 5K "Brew Ha-Ha" walk/run, this fun festival puts Fremont's funky spin on the German tradition. Late September.

OCTOBER

Issaquah Salmon Days Festival (✆ **425/392-0661;** www.salmondays.org). This festival in Issaquah, 15 miles east of Seattle, celebrates the annual return of salmon that spawn within the city limits. First full weekend in October.

Earshot Jazz Festival (✆ **206/547-6763;** www.earshot.org). With three weeks of jazz concerts at venues around the city, this is Seattle's premier jazz festival. Mid-October to early November.

NOVEMBER

Seattle Marathon (✆ **206/729-3660;** www.seattlemarathon.org), around the city. With all the hills, you have to be crazy to run a marathon in Seattle, but plenty of people do it every year. Sunday after Thanksgiving.

DECEMBER

Argosy Cruises Christmas Ships Festival (✆ **888/623-1445** or 206/622-8687; www.argosycruises.com), various locations. Boats decked out with imaginative Christmas lights parade past various waterfront locations. Argosy Cruises offers tours; see p. 155 for details. Throughout December.

New Year's at the Needle (✆ **800/937-9582** or 206/905-2100; www.spaceneedle.com), Seattle. The Space Needle ushers in the new year with a big fireworks show when midnight strikes. December 31.

RESPONSIBLE TOURISM

Before you even reach your hotel in Seattle, you can do your part for the environment by taking the **Link light rail** (p. 302) from the airport to downtown Seattle. If you must rent a car, you can get a hybrid car from Enterprise or Avis.

If you don't want to be sleepless in Seattle worrying about the environmental impact of your vacation, book a room at the **Hyatt at Olive 8** (p. 51). When it opened in 2009, it became the first Seattle hotel certified by Leadership in Energy and Environmental Design (LEED), an organization that certifies environmentally sustainable construction practices. Although this is primarily a business and convention hotel, it is conveniently located and offers some great amenities, including a spa and a pool. The **Kimpton Hotels chain** (www.kimptonhotels.com), which operates the **Alexis Hotel, Hotel Vintage Park,** and **Hotel Monaco,** also goes out of its way to be environmentally friendly and socially responsible. See chapter 4 for information on all of these hotels.

When it comes to eating out in Seattle, you've got loads of eco-friendly options. At many of the restaurants listed in this book, you'll find that the chefs rely on local and organic produce as much as possible. The locavore movement (eating foods grown or raised nearby) has been wholeheartedly embraced here in Seattle. Restaurants emphasizing organic and sustainably produced ingredients include **Tilth** (p. 101), **Spur Gastropub** (p. 84), **Portage Bay Café** (p. 95), and **Agua Verde Cafe** (p. 100).

Caffe Ladro (p. 107) espresso bars serve organic, fair-trade coffee, and **Theo Chocolate** (p. 201), a local maker of chocolate bars and other chocolate confections, uses fair-trade cocoa beans. You can even tour its factory in the Fremont neighborhood.

If you plan on heading out of town on an adventurous outing, consider booking your tour with **EverGreen Escapes** (p. 153), which uses biodiesel tour vehicles. In addition to the resources for Seattle listed above, see **frommers.com/planning** for more tips on responsible travel.

SPECIAL-INTEREST TRIPS

Adventure & Wellness Trips

If you want to turn a trip to Seattle into an adventure, book a multiday kayak tour with **Northwest Outdoor Center,** 2100 Westlake Ave. N, Ste. 1 (✆ **800/683-0637** or 206/281-9694; www.nwoc.com), which offers a variety of sea-kayak tours. Also see "The San Juan Islands," in chapter 10, for kayak-tour companies offering trips through the San Juan Islands.

For a very different sort of hiking tour, contact **Deli Llama** (**✆ 360/757-4212;** www.delillama.com), which offers llama trekking tours in Olympic National Park.

With its biodiesel vans and Jeeps, **EverGreen Escapes** (**✆ 866/203-7603** or 206/650-5795; www.evergreenescapes.com) is an environmentally conscious tour company specializing in adventurous getaways. Hiking, rafting, kayaking, and bicycling are all options on this company's tours.

Food & Wine Trips/Cooking Classes

Seattle is the sort of city that foodies and wine lovers dream about—great restaurants with access to superb local ingredients and dozens of wineries within 30 minutes of the city. If you'd like to focus on food or wine on your vacation, check out some of the offerings from these cooking schools and wine-tour companies.

One of my favorite Seattle chefs, Tom Douglas, offers 5-day summer culinary camps ($2,500). To learn more, visit **www.tomdouglas.com**. Another local chef, Christine Keff, offers cooking classes through her restaurant, **Flying Fish,** 300 Westlake Ave. N. (**✆ 206/728-8595;** www.flyingfishseattle.com). The lunchtime classes cost $55.

If you want to add a cooking class to a day spent ogling all the great produce at Pike Place Market, check the calendar at **Diane's Market Kitchen,** 1101 Post Alley (**✆ 877/624-6114** or 206/624-6114; www.dianesmarketkitchen.com), a cooking school just a few blocks away from the market. Local cooking store **Dish it up!** (http://dish-it-up.com) with two locations—in the Magnolia neighborhood at 2425 33rd Ave. W, Ste. B (**✆ 888/322-2665** or 206/281-7800), and in the Ballard neighborhood at 5320 Ballard Ave. NW (**✆ 206/971-0400**)—offers a wide range of classes, many of which feature local chefs. At **Auberge Edge of Seattle Cooking School,** 16400 216th Ave. NE, Woodinville, WA 98077 (**✆ 425/844-4102;** www.edgeof-seattle-cooking.com), you can stay in wine country and spend a couple of days learning new cooking techniques.

For a tour of the nearby Woodinville wine country, get in touch with **Bon Vivant Wine Tours** (**✆ 206/524-8687;** www.bonvivanttours.com), which offers day tours of the area and also does full-day tours to eastern Washington's wine country.

3 SUGGESTED SEATTLE ITINERARIES

When you're not familiar with a city, it can be daunting trying to figure out how to organize your time on a brief visit. To help you plan your trip to Seattle, I've put together three suggested itineraries. The first, a 1-day itinerary, hits all the must-see attractions and, I have to admit, packs a lot into a single day. Still, if you've got only a day to do Seattle, you probably want to get the most out of your time, and that's exactly what the first itinerary provides. The other two itineraries pick up some of Seattle's more interesting neighborhoods and outlying attractions.

Neighborhoods in Brief

THE WATERFRONT The Seattle waterfront, which stretches along Alaskan Way from roughly Washington Street in the south to Broad Street and Myrtle Edwards Park in the north, is the most touristy neighborhood in Seattle. In addition to the tacky gift shops, greasy fish and chips windows, and tour-boat docks, you'll also find the city's only waterfront hotel (The Edgewater), the Seattle Aquarium, and a few excellent seafood restaurants. The waterfront is also a residential neighborhood; at the north end of Alaskan Way are water-view condominiums.

DOWNTOWN This is Seattle's main business district and can roughly be defined as the area from Pioneer Square in the south to around Pike Place Market in the north, and from First Avenue to Eighth Avenue. It's characterized by steep streets, high-rise office buildings, luxury hotels, and a high density of retail shops (primarily national chains). This is also where you'll find the Seattle Art Museum and Benaroya Hall, which is home to the Seattle Symphony. Because hotels in this area are convenient to both Pioneer Square and Pike Place Market, this is a good neighborhood in which to stay. Unfortunately, the hotels here are the most expensive in the city.

SOUTH LAKE UNION Stretching from the north side of downtown to the southern shore of Lake Union, this is Seattle's newest and trendiest neighborhood. Developed in recent years by Microsoft cofounder Paul Allen. The SLU, as it's known by locals, is home to Amazon's headquarters and some of the city's best restaurants. A streetcar line runs through the middle of the neighborhood linking it to downtown.

FIRST HILL Because it is home to several large hospitals, this hilly neighborhood just east of downtown and across I-5 is called "Pill Hill" by Seattleites. First Hill is home to the Frye Art Museum and a couple of good hotels.

CAPITOL HILL To the northeast of downtown, centered on Broadway near Volunteer Park, Capitol Hill is Seattle's main gay neighborhood and has

PREVIOUS PAGE: **You can experience music (at the EMP) and lots of other Seattle sights and sounds with our suggested itineraries.**

long been a popular youth-culture shopping district. Broadway sidewalks are always crowded, and it is nearly impossible to find a parking space here. However, the area has undergone a renaissance in recent years, with new condominiums being built on Broadway. Also, along 12th Avenue, near the intersection with Pike Street, there are more than a half-dozen good restaurants. Capitol Hill is also where you'll find many bed-and-breakfasts, in some of the neighborhood's impressive old homes and mansions. Unfortunately, this area is also Seattle's main hangout for runaways and street kids.

PIONEER SQUARE The Pioneer Square Historic District, known for its restored 1890s buildings, is centered on the corner of First Avenue and Yesler Way. The tree-lined streets and cobblestone plazas make this one of the prettiest downtown neighborhoods. Pioneer Square (which refers to the neighborhood, not a specific square) is full of antiques shops, art galleries, restaurants, bars, and nightclubs. Because of the number of bars, late nights are not a good time to wander this neighborhood. Also, during the day, the number of street people in this area is off-putting to many visitors.

THE CHINATOWN/INTERNATIONAL DISTRICT Known to locals as the I.D., this is one of Seattle's most distinctive neighborhoods and is home to a large Asian population. Here you'll find the Wing Luke Asian Museum, Hing Hay Park (a small park with an ornate pagoda), Uwajimaya (an Asian supermarket), and many small shops and restaurants. The Chinatown/International District begins around Fifth Avenue South and South Jackson Street. This neighborhood is interesting for a stroll, but there aren't many attractions.

BELLTOWN In the blocks north of Pike Place Market, between Western and Fourth avenues, Belltown is ground zero for hip bars and nightclubs. There are also quite a few decent restaurants in this neighborhood of high-rise

Chinatown is one of Seattle's most distinctive neighborhoods.

The Japanese Garden in Madison Park provides a tranquil setting.

condos. Because Belltown's establishments attract crowds of the young, the hip, and the stylish, the neighborhood also draws a lot of nighttime panhandlers.

QUEEN ANNE HILL Queen Anne is just northwest of Seattle Center and offers great views of the city. This affluent neighborhood, one of the most prestigious in Seattle proper, is where you'll find some of Seattle's oldest homes. Today it's divided into the Upper Queen Anne and Lower Queen Anne neighborhoods. Upper Queen Anne is very peaceful and abounds in moderately priced restaurants; Lower Queen Anne, adjacent to theaters and Marion Oliver McCaw Hall at Seattle Center, is something of a theater district and has a more urban character.

MADISON PARK One of Seattle's more affluent neighborhoods, Madison Park fronts the western shore of Lake Washington, northeast of downtown. The University of Washington Arboretum, which includes the Japanese Gardens, is the centerpiece of the neighborhood. Several excellent restaurants cluster here at the end of East Madison Street.

THE UNIVERSITY DISTRICT As the name implies, this neighborhood in the northeast section of the city surrounds the University of Washington. The U District, as it's known to locals, provides all the amenities of a college neighborhood: cheap ethnic restaurants, pubs, clubs, espresso bars, and music stores. Several good hotels here offer substantial savings over comparable downtown accommodations.

WALLINGFORD This is another of Seattle's quiet, primarily residential neighborhoods with an interesting commercial/retail district. Located just west of the University District and adjacent to Lake Union, it's filled with small restaurants, some of which are quite good. You'll also find interesting little shops and an old school that has been renovated and is now home to boutiques and restaurants.

FREMONT North of the Lake Washington Ship Canal, between Wallingford and Ballard, Fremont is home to Seattle's best-loved piece of public art—*Waiting for the Interurban*—as well as the famous *Fremont Troll* sculpture. This is Seattle's wackiest neighborhood, filled with eclectic shops and ethnic restaurants. During the summer, there are outdoor movies on Saturday nights, a Sunday flea market, and a solstice festival.

MAGNOLIA This affluent residential neighborhood lies to the west of Queen Anne Hill. Magnolia's few cafes, restaurants, and bars are frequented primarily by area residents, but it's also home to Palisade, one of Seattle's best waterfront restaurants. The west side of Magnolia borders sprawling Discovery Park, Seattle's largest green space.

BALLARD If you have time to visit only one neighborhood outside of downtown, make it Ballard. In northwest Seattle, bordering the Lake Washington Ship Canal and Puget Sound, Ballard is a former Scandinavian community that retains visible remnants of its past. Known for its busy restaurant and nightlife scene, Ballard is also a great place to discover off-the-beaten-path gems. Art galleries and interesting boutiques and shops are set along the tree-shaded streets of the neighborhood's old commercial center. Here in Ballard, you'll also find the Nordic Heritage Museum, which often has excellent art exhibits.

SODO This neighborhood lies to the SOuth of DOwntown, hence its name. It is home to Qwest Field and Safeco Field, and while primarily an industrial and warehouse district, it does have a smattering of interesting shops and restaurants.

COLUMBIA CITY Connected to downtown Seattle via the Central Link light-rail line, this is one of south Seattle's neo-bohemian neighborhoods. With numerous decent restaurants and bars, and a weekly farmers market, it's a good place to rub shoulders with young, hip Seattleites.

GEORGETOWN In this up-and-coming neighborhood south of SoDo and just north of Boeing Field, youthful urban pioneers are turning old industrial buildings into art galleries, nightclubs, cafes, and restaurants.

THE EASTSIDE Home to Bill Gates, Microsoft, countless high-tech spinoff companies, and seemingly endless suburbs, the Eastside lies across Lake Washington from Seattle proper and comprises the cities of Kirkland, Bellevue, Redmond, and a few other smaller communities. As the presence of Bill Gates's mansion attests, there are some pretty wealthy neighborhoods here; but wealth doesn't necessarily equal respect, and the Eastside is still much derided by Seattle citizens, who perceive it as an uncultured bedroom community.

WEST SEATTLE West Seattle, across the wasteland of the port facility from downtown, is not just the site of the terminal for ferries to Vashon Island and the Kitsap Peninsula. It's also the site of Seattle's favorite beach, Alki, which is as close to a Southern California beach experience as you'll find in the Northwest. Here, too, is Salty's on Alki Beach, the waterfront restaurant with the best view of Seattle.

BAINBRIDGE ISLAND Seattle's most exurban bedroom community is only a 35-minute ferry ride away, though Bainbridge feels quite far from the inner-city asphalt to the east. Green, green, green is the best way to characterize this rural residential island. Downtown Bainbridge Island (formerly known as Winslow), the island's main commercial area, has the feel of an upscale San Francisco Bay–area community. When you hear about Seattle's quality of life, this is what people are talking about.

THE BEST OF SEATTLE IN 1 DAY

Lace up your walking shoes, grab an umbrella if it looks like rain, and hit the streets early if you want to experience the best of Seattle in a single day. Luckily, two of the city's top attractions—Pike Place Market and the Olympic Sculpture Park—open early, so you should get started as early as possible. For visitors, the fact that the market is only 2 blocks from the waterfront makes connecting the dots in this town fairly easy. Late in the afternoon, after delving into the city's history, you'll visit Seattle Center, which is home to Seattle's most familiar icon, the Space Needle. ***Start:*** *Walk or take a taxi to the Olympic Sculpture Park.*

---

1 Olympic Sculpture Park ★★★

Set at the north end of the waterfront and home to monumental sculptures by Alexander Calder, Claes Oldenburg, and Richard Serra, this multilevel park is the most beautiful open space in Seattle. There are stunning views across Puget Sound to the Olympic Mountains, native-plant gardens, and a tiny man-made beach that looks as wild as any beach on the Olympic Peninsula. See p. 122.

Walk south along the waterfront (or catch the free Waterfront Streetcar bus) to Pier 59 and the Pike Street Hill Climb.

2 Pike Place Market ★★★

At the top of the hill-climb stairs, you'll find Pike Place Market, Seattle's sprawling historic market complex. Grab a grande latte at the Starbucks that kicked the whole espresso scene into high gear, and then pick out a pastry at one of the market bakeries. With fortification in hand, peruse the many stalls selling fresh salmon and Dungeness crabs, local and exotic produce, and cut flowers. By midmorning, the market's arts-and-crafts vendors are usually set up and you can shop for distinctive gifts and souvenirs. Wander through the dark depths of the market to search out unusual specialty shops. See p. 126.

Take the Pike Street Hill Climb back down to the waterfront.

3 The Waterfront ★★

Just as at San Francisco's Fisherman's Wharf, the Seattle waterfront is ground zero for tacky tourist shops, fish and chips counters, and mediocre, overpriced restaurants. However, the waterfront does have its redeeming features: On a clear day, the view across Elliott Bay to the Olympic Mountains is unforgettable. And a wide sidewalk along the waterfront is perfect for strolling. The real stars of the waterfront, though, are the Seattle Aquarium and, of course, the Olympic Sculpture Park. See p. 120.

Directly across the street from the stairs of the Pike Street Hill Climb is Pier 59.

Taste test some of the delicacies at Pike Place Market, like these jams and jellies.

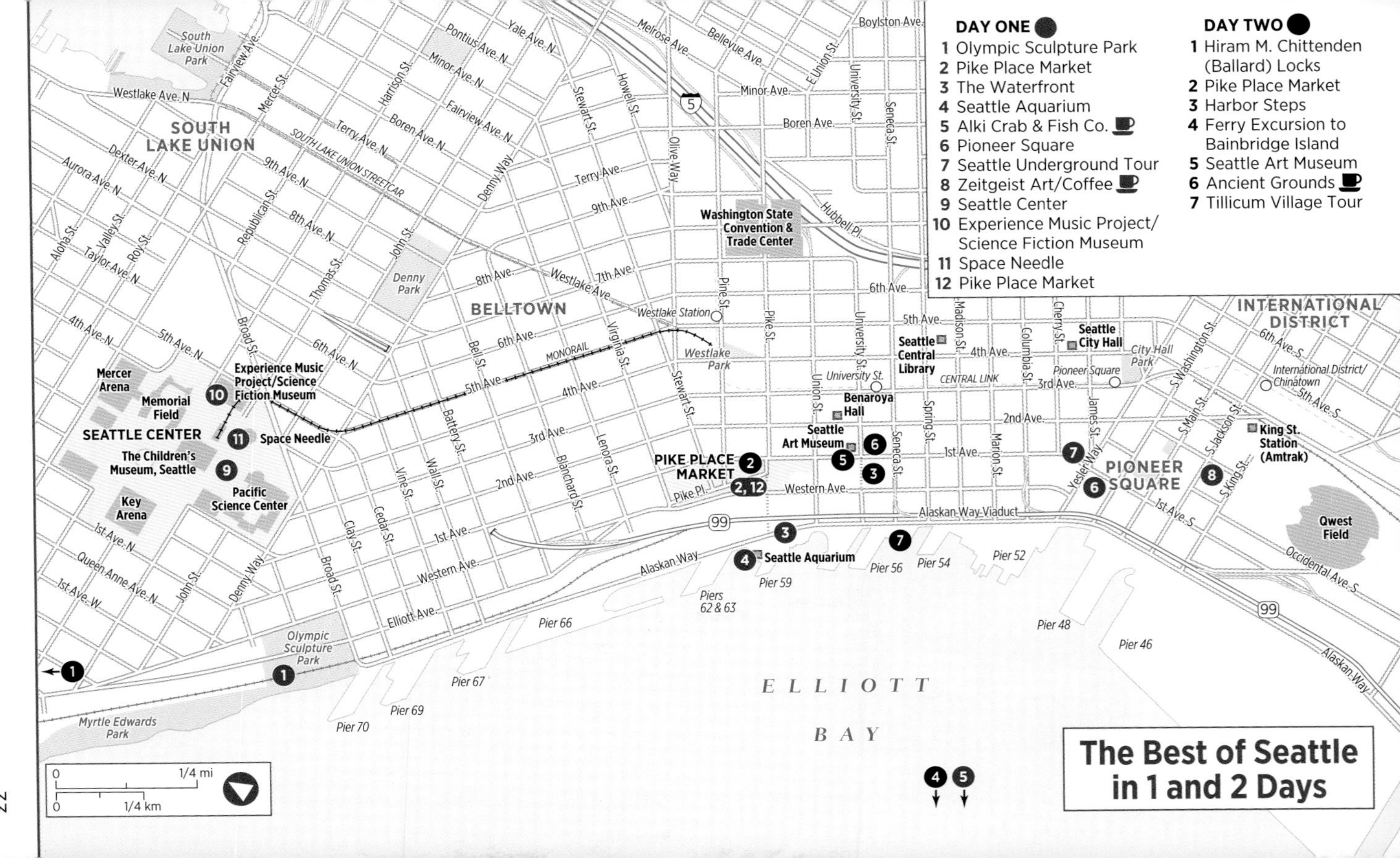

The Best of Seattle in 1 and 2 Days
DAY ONE
1 Olympic Sculpture Park
2 Pike Place Market
3 The Waterfront
4 Seattle Aquarium
5 Alki Crab & Fish Co.
6 Pioneer Square
7 Seattle Underground Tour
8 Zeitgeist Art/Coffee
9 Seattle Center
10 Experience Music Project/Science Fiction Museum
11 Space Needle
12 Pike Place Market
DAY TWO
1 Hiram M. Chittenden (Ballard) Locks
2 Pike Place Market
3 Harbor Steps
4 Ferry Excursion to Bainbridge Island
5 Seattle Art Museum
6 Ancient Grounds
7 Tillicum Village Tour
SOUTH LAKE UNION
South Lake Union Park
BELLTOWN
SEATTLE CENTER
Mercer Arena
Memorial Field
Experience Music Project/Science Fiction Museum
Space Needle
The Children's Museum, Seattle
Pacific Science Center
Key Arena
Denny Park
Washington State Convention & Trade Center
Westlake Station
Westlake Park
MONORAIL
SOUTH LAKE UNION STREETCAR
PIKE PLACE MARKET
Seattle Art Museum
Benaroya Hall
Seattle Central Library
University St.
CENTRAL LINK
Seattle City Hall
City Hall Park
Pioneer Square
PIONEER SQUARE
INTERNATIONAL DISTRICT
International District/Chinatown
King St. Station (Amtrak)
Qwest Field
Seattle Aquarium
Alaskan Way Viaduct
Alaskan Way
Olympic Sculpture Park
Myrtle Edwards Park
ELLIOTT BAY
Pier 46
Pier 48
Pier 52
Pier 54
Pier 56
Pier 59
Piers 62 & 63
Pier 66
Pier 67
Pier 69
Pier 70
Westlake Ave. N
Fairview Ave.
Mercer St.
Harrison St.
Pontius Ave. N
Yale Ave. N
Minor Ave. N
Terry Ave. N
Boren Ave. N
Fairview Ave. N
Dexter Ave. N
Aurora Ave. N
9th Ave. N
8th Ave. N
Republican St.
Denny Way
John St.
Thomas St.
Roy St.
Valley St.
Aloha St.
Taylor Ave. N
4th Ave. N
5th Ave. N
6th Ave. N
Broad St.
Stewart St.
Howell St.
Olive Way
Terry Ave.
9th Ave.
8th Ave.
7th Ave.
Westlake Ave.
6th Ave.
5th Ave.
4th Ave.
3rd Ave.
2nd Ave.
1st Ave.
Western Ave.
Elliott Ave.
Melrose Ave.
Bellevue Ave.
E Union St.
Minor Ave.
Boren Ave.
Boylston Ave.
University St.
Seneca St.
Hubbell Pl.
Pine St.
Pike St.
Union St.
Spring St.
Madison St.
Marion St.
Columbia St.
Cherry St.
James St.
Yesler Way
S Washington St.
S Main St.
S Jackson St.
S King St.
6th Ave. S
5th Ave. S
1st Ave. S
Occidental Ave. S
Virginia St.
Lenora St.
Blanchard St.
Bell St.
Battery St.
Wall St.
Vine St.
Cedar St.
Clay St.
Pike Pl.
1st Ave. N
Queen Anne Ave. N
1st Ave. W
0 1/4 mi
0 1/4 km

Get a window on the (underwater) world at Seattle Aquarium.

4 Seattle Aquarium ★★

Pier 59 is home to the Seattle Aquarium, where you can learn about the sea life of the region. Jellyfish, sea horses, salmon, and otters are just some of the popular attractions at this aquarium. See p. 123.

5 Alki Crab & Fish

Head to Pier 50, where you can catch the water taxi across Elliott Bay to **Alki** in West Seattle. The view back across the water to the Seattle skyline is beautiful, and right at the water-taxi dock on Alki, there's this inexpensive little fish and chips place with a million-dollar view. If service is fast and you remembered to ask for a transfer when you got on the boat, you can ride back across the bay without having to buy another ticket. 1660 Harbor Ave. SW. ✆ **206/938-0975.** See p. 106.

Take the water taxi back across Elliott Bay and then head away from the water on Yesler Way.

6 Pioneer Square ★

Historic Pioneer Square area is where Seattle got its start back in the 1850s. Today it is one of the city's only historic districts, and its tree-shaded streets are lined with brick buildings constructed after the Seattle fire of 1889. See "Walking Tour 2: The Pioneer Square Area," in chapter 7, for a recommended route to explore this area.

7 Seattle Underground Tour ★

To learn more about Seattle's early history, with an emphasis on the seamier side of life and the city's reconstruction after the fire of 1889, take the

Underground Tour, which begins at the corner of First Avenue and Yesler Way. This tour provides a little fun and paints an interesting picture of the characters who founded Seattle. Be forewarned that participants need an appreciation for bad jokes and should not have a fear of dark, musty basements. See p. 140.

8 Zeitgeist Art/Coffee ☕

With its big windows and local artwork, **Zeitgeist Art/Coffee** is popular with the Pioneer Square art crowd. A hip, low-key character makes this a pleasant place to kick back and get off your feet for a few minutes. 171 S. Jackson St. ✆ **206/583-0497.** See p. 108.

Head to the corner of James Street and Third Avenue, and catch a free bus through the Transit Tunnel to Westlake Station, which is beneath the Westlake Center shopping mall. From here you can take the monorail to Seattle Center.

9 Seattle Center ★★

Built for the 1962 World's Fair, this 74-acre campus is the cultural heart of Seattle and the city's premier family attraction. Seattle Center is home to the Seattle Opera, the Pacific Northwest Ballet, numerous theater companies, a children's museum, and a science museum. For most people, however, Seattle Center is primarily known as the home of the Space Needle and the bizarre Frank Gehry–designed building that houses EMP/SFM (the Experience Music Project/Science Fiction Museum). See p. 151.

10 Experience Music Project/Science Fiction Museum ★★

If you're a rock-music or science-fiction fan, explore this unusual museum. It's inside a huge blob of color that looks a bit like a melted-down electric guitar. If you're not interested in going inside, at least stroll around outside and marvel at the building's sweeping lines and colorful exterior. See p. 130.

11 Space Needle ★★

Of course, a visit to Seattle isn't complete without riding the elevator to the top of the Space Needle. From the observation deck, 520 feet above the ground, you have a superb panorama of Seattle and its surrounding mountains and many bodies of water. If it's summer and the sun is still

Hail, hail rock and roll at the Experience Music Project.

shining, see if you can pick out the route you followed during your earlier tour of the city. Keep in mind that during the summer, sunset isn't until after 9pm. If you're here at a time of year when the sun sets early, you'll get to enjoy the city's twinkling lights. See p. 132.

From Seattle Center, take the monorail back to Westlake Center and then walk 5 blocks west on Pine Street to Pike Place Market.

12 Pike Place Market ★★★

Finish your day back at Pike Place Market. By nightfall the fishmongers and flower vendors are long gone and the shops are closed. However, some of the city's best restaurants and most enjoyable bars are here. Catch an eclectic musical act at The Pink Door, listen to Irish music at Kells, or enjoy a romantic late dinner at Il Bistro.

THE BEST OF SEATTLE IN 2 DAYS

On your second day, start and end your day with salmon. Up in north Seattle's Ballard neighborhood, you can take in salmon and locks (not lox) at the Hiram M. Chittenden Locks (known as the Ballard Locks). Afterward, head back to Pike Place Market to shop for picnic supplies, and then hop aboard a ferry bound for Bainbridge Island. Once back in Seattle, take in world-class art at the Seattle Art Museum, and then head out for your second Puget Sound excursion of the day, this time to an island state park, where you'll be served a grilled salmon dinner (not lox this time either).

Head to the corner of Third Avenue and Pike Street downtown and catch the no. 17 bus north to the Ballard neighborhood; get off at the Hiram M. Chittenden Locks stop.

1 Hiram M. Chittenden (Ballard) Locks ★★

These locks separate the waters of Elliott Bay from those of Lake Union and allow everything from sea kayaks to commercial fishing boats to make their way between the two bodies of water. It's a slow, though fascinating, process that always draws crowds. However, for many summer visitors, the big attraction here is the fish ladder and its associated fish-viewing windows that allow visitors to watch salmon and steelhead migrating up-river. See p. 138.

Take the no. 17 bus back to downtown Seattle and walk down Pike Street to Pike Place Market.

2 Pike Place Market ★★

There's just so much to see at this market, you should visit again on your second day. Put together the ingredients for a picnic so you can have lunch on a ferry crossing Puget Sound. See p. 126.

Walk 2 blocks south from Pike Place Market on First Avenue.

3 Harbor Steps ★

The Harbor Steps, 2 blocks south of Pike Place Market, may not be as beautiful as Rome's Spanish Steps, but they are by far the prettiest route from downtown to the waterfront and are a popular hangout both for footsore tourists and downtown office workers hoping to soak up a little sunshine on

Watch the boats pass through the Ballard Locks.

their lunch hour. Waterfalls, fountains, and sculptures grace the terraces of the Harbor Steps, and several restaurants and shops flank the stairs.

Walk 3 blocks south along the waterfront to Pier 52.

4 A Ferry Excursion to Bainbridge Island

No visit to Seattle is complete without a ride on a ferry, and because the Bainbridge Island ferry takes only 35 minutes for the crossing, it's a good choice for an excursion if your time is limited. The big car ferries that shuttle back and forth across Puget Sound to both Bainbridge Island and Bremerton leave from Colman Dock at Pier 52. Once on Bainbridge Island, you can wander around the downtown area, where you'll find coffeehouses, restaurants, boutiques, galleries, and restaurants. You can even rent a sea kayak and paddle around Eagle Harbor while you're here. See "Ferry Excursions from Seattle," in chapter 10.

Once back in Seattle, head up the Harbor Steps for an afternoon of art.

5 Seattle Art Museum ★★★

Looming over First Avenue at the corner of University Street is Jonathon Borofsky's *Hammering Man,* a three-story animated silhouettelike sculpture that stands outside the front door of the Seattle Art Museum. This huge museum has impressive permanent collections and hosts numerous traveling exhibits throughout the year. Any time of year, the Northwest Coast Indian and contemporary Northwest art exhibits are well worth a visit. See p. 127.

6 Ancient Grounds ☕ ★

If you're interested in Native American artifacts, be sure to stop in at this eclectic establishment a half-block south of the Harbor Steps. Order a latte and then peruse the masks and wood carvings that fill the cases of this cabinet of curiosities. 1220 First Ave. ✆ **206/749-0747.** See p. 107.

Head back down the Harbor Steps to the waterfront's Pier 55.

Attend a traditional Northwest dance and have dinner in the "long house" at Tillicum Village.

7 Tillicum Village Tour ★★

Although it is a bit touristy, the Tillicum Village Tour, which departs from Pier 55 on the waterfront, includes not only a boat excursion to Blake Island State Park, but also a salmon dinner and a performance of traditional Northwest Coast Native American masked dances. The "long house," where the dinner and dances are held, was built as part of the same World's Fair that gave Seattle the Space Needle. The island setting is beautiful, and the masked dances are fascinating. I especially recommend this for families. Be sure to check the schedule for these tours. See p. 154.

A DAY AT MT. RAINIER NATIONAL PARK

On your third day, head out of the city to see some of the wild country for which the Northwest is famous. The only problem is that there are so many great choices that it can be difficult to decide where to go on a day trip from Seattle. Personally, I prefer the mountains, so I would steer you southeast to Mount Rainier, that great big bulk of a dormant volcano that looms over Seattle like a sleeping giant. The mountain and all its glaciers, wildflower meadows, and old-growth forests are preserved as Mount Rainier National Park. For this excursion, you'll need to rent a car; it's roughly 90 miles to the national park, and you should expect to take at least 2 hours to cover this distance. I recommend circling the mountain in a clockwise direction beginning at the park's northeast entrance, which is along Wash. 410 southeast of Enumclaw. Be aware, however, that this route is only possible during the summer months.

1 Sunrise ★★★

This is the highest point in the park accessible by car, and the in-your-face view of Mount Rainier is unforgettable. Also in view is the Emmons Glacier, which is the largest glacier in the 48 contiguous states. Hiking trails of

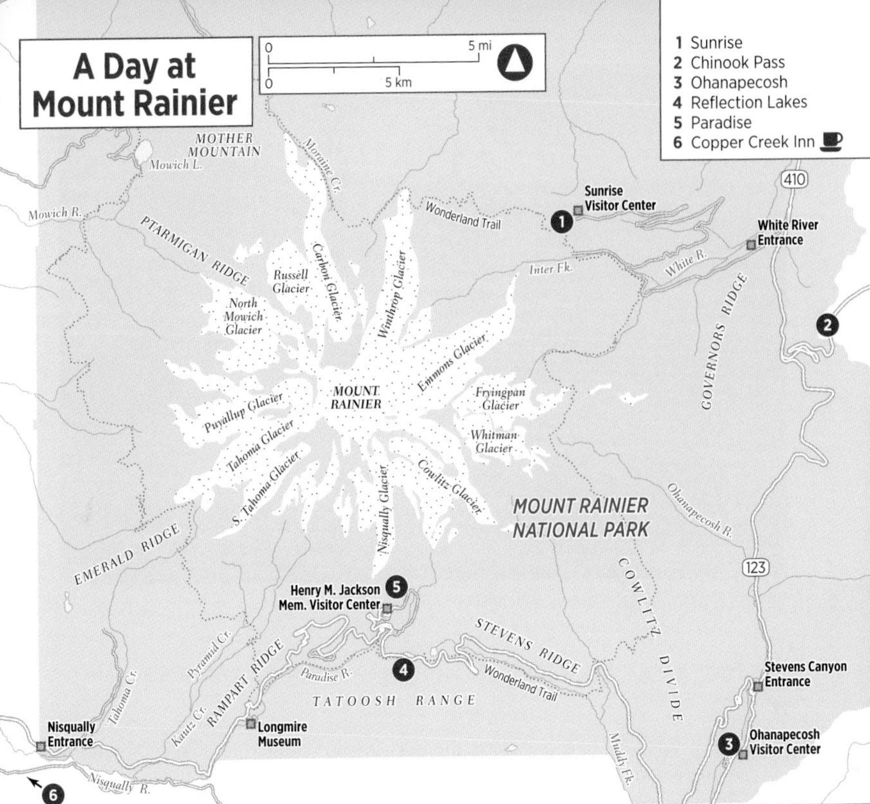

varying levels of difficulty radiate out from Sunrise, and every one of these trails has great views. Keep an eye out for mountain goats and elk. ***Bonus:*** Sunrise usually isn't as crowded as Paradise, on the other side of the mountain. See p. 277.

2 Chinook Pass ★

At Cayuse Pass, on the east side of the park, take a short side trip off the main 'round-the-mountain road by staying on Wash. 410, which will bring you to the lovely Chinook Pass. Here the tiny Tipsoo Lakes flank the highway and Naches Peak rises above the road. A 4.5-mile loop trail leads alongside the lake and around Naches Peak through forests and meadows. This is a good place to lose the crowds. See p. 278.

Head back the way you just came and turn south on Wash. 123 to Ohanapecosh.

3 Ohanapecosh ★★

You won't find any views of the mountain here, but you will find a .75-mile trail to some of the oldest trees in the state. The Grove of the Patriarchs trail, which begins just west of Wash. 123 near the park's Stevens Canyon entrance, leads to a streamside grove of Western red cedars that are estimated to be more than 1,000 years old. One of these trees is the largest red cedar in the park. See p. 278.

Observe a mirror image of beauty at Reflection Lakes.

From Ohanapecosh, drive west through the park on Stevens Canyon Road.

4 Reflection Lakes ★★

Make sure you have plenty of memory in your camera; the view of Mount Rainier from these pretty little alpine lakes, hands-down, is the most photogenic view in the park. If there's no wind, the reflection of the mountain in the waters of these lakes provides the answer to how these bodies of water were named. See p. 278.

Continue west on Stevens Canyon Road.

5 Paradise ★★★

This place isn't called Paradise for nothing. Mountainside meadows burst into vibrant color every summer, usually starting in mid- to late July. Trails of different lengths meander through these wildflower meadows and lead to the edges of snowfields and viewpoints overlooking rumbling glaciers. Because you've probably already done quite a bit of hiking, you may want to head straight to the Nisqually Vista overlook, where you can gaze down on the Nisqually Glacier.

6 Copper Creek Restaurant

Just after you leave the park via the Nisqually entrance and Wash. 706, keep an eye out for this rustic roadside diner. Sure, you can get a simple meal, but the real reason to stop here is for a slice of blackberry pie. It's the best in the area. 35707 Wash. 706 E., Ashford. ✆ **360/569-2326.**

WHERE TO STAY

4

Seattle, with its mountain and water views and its 10pm summer sunsets, is close on the heels of San Francisco as a West Coast summer-in-the-city destination. During those few short months when the city's notoriously gloomy skies turn blue, conventioneers, cruise-ship passengers, and summer vacationers all vie for rooms. For this reason, hotels stay pretty much booked solid for July and August. Plan far in advance for a summer visit, and, if you can afford a splurge, get a room with a view.

best SEATTLE HOTEL BETS

- **Best Splurges:** The modern **Four Seasons Hotel Seattle** has an enviable location adjacent to Pike Place Market and across the street from the Seattle Art Museum. See p. 48. If you love the romance of travel as much as I do, then you'll want to stay at the **Arctic Club Seattle.** Built in 1917 as an exclusive men's club, it has a sort of Art Deco travel theme in its decor. See p. 55. Big rooms have walls of glass that take in great views of the city and Elliott Bay at the **Hotel 1000,** and the bathrooms are works of art. A special golf room even lets you play virtual golf at more than 50 famous golf courses. See p. 49.
- **The Best Moderately Priced Hotels:** Although this luxurious lodge is located within a quarter mile of the Sea-Tac Airport, the **Cedarbrook Lodge** feels as though it is in a secluded setting miles from the bustle of the city. See p. 65. Only a block away from Seattle Center and close to the Space Needle, the **Maxwell Hotel,** plays up its connection to the nearby theaters; rooms are all colorfully decorated and have very theatrical decor. See p. 58. One of Seattle's most impressive historic hotels, the **Sorrento Hotel** is also

The Arctic Club was built in 1917 with Art Deco/explorer touches.

PREVIOUS PAGE: The Fairmont Olympic Hotel, styled after an Italian Renaissance palace, is the most impressive of Seattle's historic hotels.

one of the city's best values. You can immerse yourself in hundred-year-old luxuries. See p. 62.

Price Categories	
Very Expensive	**$275 and up**
Expensive	**$200–$274**
Moderate	**$125–$199**
Inexpensive	**Under $125**

- **Best for Families:** Just across the street from Lake Union, the **Silver Cloud Inn–Lake Union,** is far enough from downtown to be affordable—but not far from Seattle Center. Plus it has a great location overlooking the lake. There are indoor and outdoor pools and several restaurants right across the street. See p. 60.
- **Best Value:** You don't have to be a timber baron to be able to stay in one of the most impressive old mansions in Seattle. For less than $150 a night, you can spend the night at the **Shafer Baillie Mansion Bed & Breakfast,** a 100-year-old mansion on Capitol Hill's Millionaire's Row. See p. 61.
- **Most Romantic:** Though Seattle has quite a few hotels that do well for a romantic weekend, the **Inn at the Market,** with its Elliott Bay views,

WHAT YOU'LL really PAY

In the following listings, price categories are based on the high season, which generally runs from June through September (most hotels charge the same for single and double rooms). Keep in mind that the rates listed do not include **taxes,** which add up to **15.6%** in Seattle. Also be sure to factor in hotel parking fees—around $40 per day in downtown Seattle.

For comparison purposes, I list what hotels call "rack rates," or walk-in rates—but you should never have to pay these highly inflated prices. Various discounts and specials are often available, so make it a point to check, either online or over the phone, whether any discounts are being offered during your stay. At inexpensive chain motels, discounted rates are almost always available for AAA members and seniors. During slow times, you can usually obtain a room at an expensive property for the same rate as a more moderate one.

You can sometimes find discounted room rates when booking through websites such as **www.hotels.com** or **www.expedia.com** (see "Getting the Best Deal," on p. 69, for more tips). However, I've also found that hotel websites sometimes have lower rates than are available on any of the online reservation sites. It pays to check different sites, and the best way to do this is by going to **www.kayak.com**.

If you're the gambling type, you can bid for a room on Priceline (which also offers set rates that might tempt you). In May of 2011, travelers got rooms at the Grand Hyatt for $100 and the Sheraton for $79. These rates are as much as $100 less than published rates. To find out how much you'll need to bid to get a Seattle hotel room through Priceline, first go to **http://biddingfortravel.yuku.com**.

European atmosphere, and proximity to many excellent (and romantic) restaurants, is sure to set the stage for lasting memories. See p. 53.

- **Best Service:** With 24-hour room service, a 24-hour exercise room, free Wi-Fi, and a free town-car service to shuttle you around downtown, the **Pan Pacific Hotel Seattle** provides far more extras than other Seattle hotels. See p. 59.
- **Best Historic Hotel:** Built in 1924, the **Fairmont Olympic Hotel,** is styled after an Italian Renaissance palace and is by far the most impressive of Seattle's historic hotels. See p.48.
- **Best for Hipsters:** The **Hotel Ändra** is a boldly contemporary lodging. Best of all, it's on the edge of the Belltown neighborhood, which makes this an ideal base for club-crawling night owls. See p. 50.
- **Best B&B:** Set in the Capitol Hill neighborhood, the **Gaslight Inn** is a lovingly restored and maintained Craftsman bungalow filled with original Stickley furniture. Lots of public spaces, very tasteful decor, and a swimming pool in the backyard all add up to unexpected luxury. See p. 62.
- **Best Location:** On a pier right on the Seattle waterfront, the **Edgewater** is only 5 blocks from Pike Place Market and the Seattle Aquarium, and 3 blocks from the restaurants of Belltown. Ferries to Victoria, British Columbia, leave from the adjacent pier. See below.
- **Best Views:** If you're not back in your room by sunset at the **Westin Seattle,** you may not turn into a pumpkin, but you will miss a spectacular light show. Because this is the tallest hotel in the city, the Westin boasts fabulous views from its upper floors, especially those facing northwest. See p. 52.

THE WATERFRONT

Seattle's most touristy neighborhood, the waterfront has some of the city's finest views and is home to several worthwhile attractions and activities.

Best For: Views that cannot be beat. There's also easy access to a variety of boat tours; and many Alaska-bound cruise ships leave from the waterfront, making these hotels very convenient for a stay before or after a cruise.

Drawbacks: Lodging options limited to two hotels, only one of which is actually on the water. Shops along the waterfront are very touristy and restaurants, for the most part, are both touristy and overpriced.

Fish from Your Room at the Edgewater

When it first opened in the early 1960s, the Edgewater hotel (see below) advertised that you could fish from your room. Because the hotel is built on a pier jutting out into Elliott Bay, the claim was an easy one to make. In 1964, when the Beatles came to Seattle, they stayed at the Edgewater—and, of course, the Fab Four had to do a little fishing out the window of their room. The hotel has turned the room where John, Paul, George, and Ringo stayed into the Beatles Suite and filled it with Beatles memorabilia. Unfortunately, the hotel management now frowns on guests fishing from their room.

The Alexis Hotel is well located near Pike Place, Pioneer Square, and the waterfront.

Very Expensive

The Edgewater ★★ On a pier at the north end of the waterfront, the Edgewater is Seattle's only true waterfront hotel, and despite the urban setting, it manages to capture the feel of a classic Northwest wilderness retreat. The views out the windows are among the best in Seattle, and sunsets can be mesmerizing. On a clear day, you can see the Olympic Mountains across Puget Sound. The mountain-lodge theme continues in the rooms, which feature fireplaces and lodgepole-pine furniture. The least expensive units overlook the city (and the parking lot), so it's worth it to spring for a water view. The rooms with balconies are a bit smaller than others, although the premium waterview rooms, with claw-foot tubs and walls that open out to those great views, are hard to beat.
Pier 67, 2411 Alaskan Way, Seattle, WA 98121. www.edgewaterhotel.com. ✆ **800/624-0670** or 206/728-7000. Fax 206/441-4119. 223 units. Summer $350–$629 double, from $399 suite; other months $179–$469 double; from $379 suite. Children 17 and under stay free in parent's room. AE, DC, DISC, MC, V. Valet parking $34. Pets accepted (no fee). **Amenities:** Restaurant, lounge; concierge; exercise room and access to nearby health club; room service. *In room:* A/C, TV, hair dryer, minibar, Wi-Fi ($10/day).

Expensive

Seattle Marriott Waterfront ★★ Across Alaskan Way from Elliott Bay, this sleek hotel doesn't have superb views like the Edgewater, but it's the only other option if you want to stay on the waterfront. The hotel does a brisk business putting up people heading out on cruises (some cruise ships dock right in front of the hotel). If there isn't a cruise ship berthed across the street, the best views are from the large junior suites at the northwest corner of the property. Because of the way the hotel is designed, many standard rooms have only limited views, but they do have little balconies where you can stand and breathe in the salt air. In 2011, the guest rooms here got a major makeover.

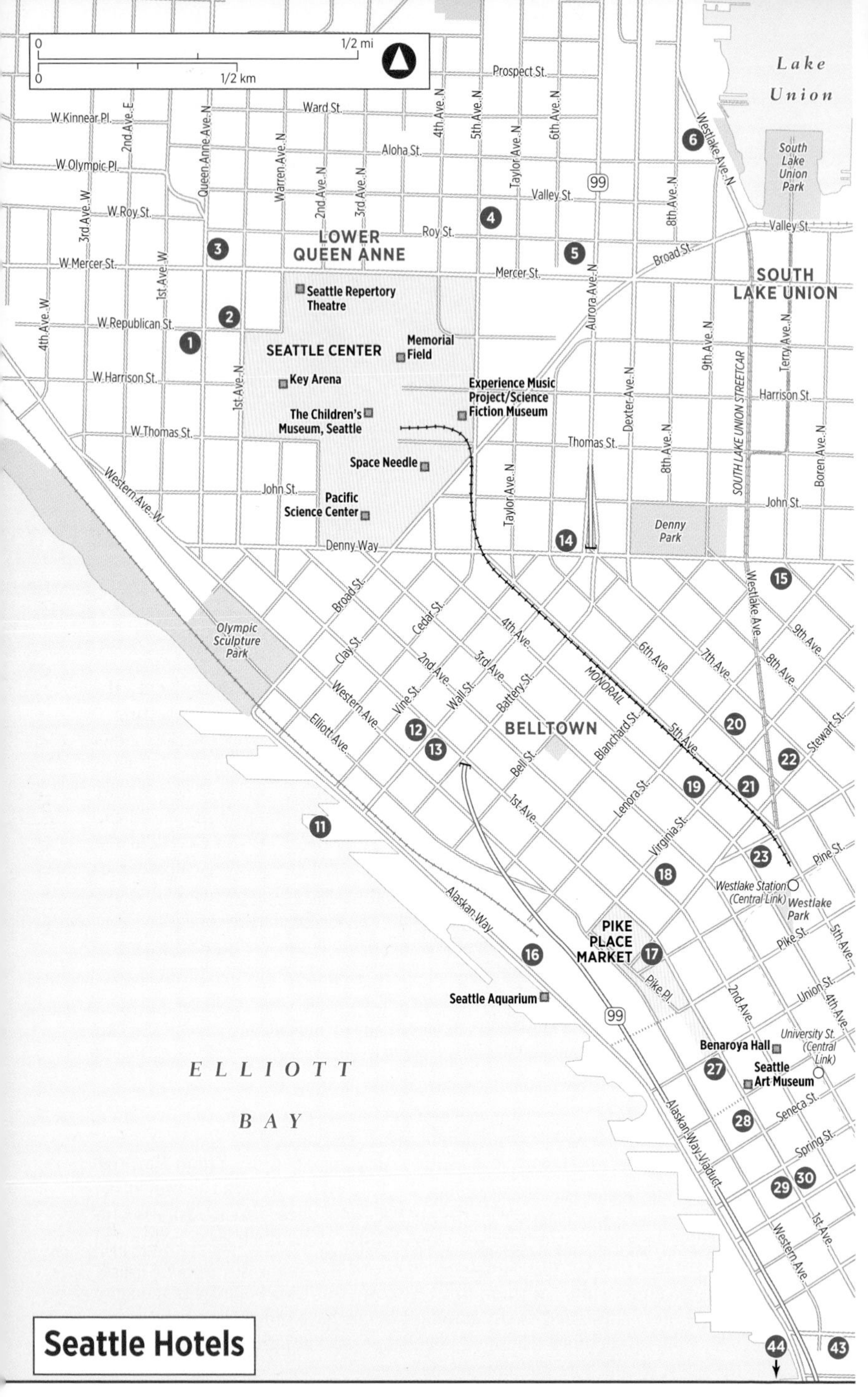

Seattle Hotels
Lake Union
South Lake Union Park
LOWER QUEEN ANNE
SEATTLE CENTER
SOUTH LAKE UNION
BELLTOWN
PIKE PLACE MARKET
ELLIOTT BAY
Seattle Repertory Theatre
Memorial Field
Key Arena
Experience Music Project/Science Fiction Museum
The Children's Museum, Seattle
Space Needle
Pacific Science Center
Denny Park
Olympic Sculpture Park
Seattle Aquarium
Westlake Station (Central Link)
Westlake Park
Benaroya Hall
Seattle Art Museum
University St. (Central Link)
MONORAIL
SOUTH LAKE UNION STREETCAR

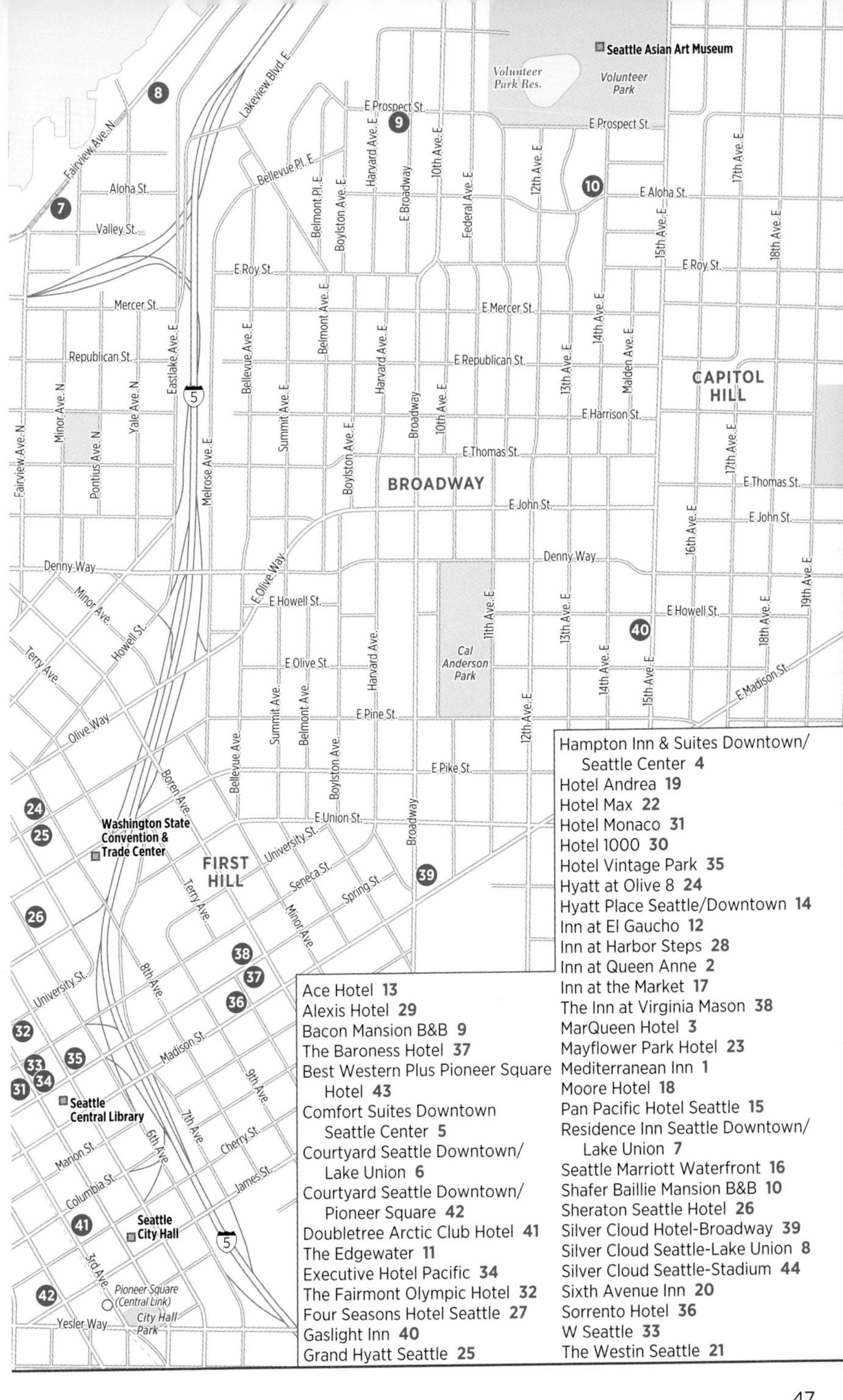
Seattle Asian Art Museum
Volunteer Park Res.
Volunteer Park
E Prospect St.
Lakeview Blvd. E
Fairview Ave. N
Aloha St.
Valley St.
Bellevue Pl. E
Belmont Pl. E
Boylston Ave. E
Harvard Ave. E
E Broadway
10th Ave. E
Federal Ave. E
12th Ave. E
E Aloha St.
15th Ave. E
17th Ave. E
18th Ave. E
E Roy St.
Mercer St.
E Mercer St.
Eastlake Ave. E
Bellevue Ave. E
Belmont Ave. E
14th Ave. E
Malden Ave. E
Republican St.
E Republican St.
13th Ave. E
CAPITOL HILL
Minor Ave. N
Yale Ave. N
Summit Ave. E
Harvard Ave. E
Broadway
E Harrison St.
Fairview Ave. N
Pontius Ave. N
Melrose Ave. E
Boylston Ave. E
E Thomas St.
BROADWAY
E John St.
16th Ave. E
Denny Way
Minor Ave.
E Olive Way
E Howell St.
Howell St.
Terry Ave.
11th Ave. E
13th Ave. E
19th Ave. E
E Olive St.
Harvard Ave.
Cal Anderson Park
14th Ave. E
15th Ave. E
E Madison St.
Olive Way
Summit Ave.
Belmont Ave.
E Pine St.
12th Ave. E
Boren Ave.
Bellevue Ave.
Boylston Ave.
E Pike St.
Washington State Convention & Trade Center
E Union St.
University St.
FIRST HILL
Seneca St.
Spring St.
Terry Ave.
Minor Ave.
University St.
8th Ave.
Madison St.
9th Ave.
Seattle Central Library
7th Ave.
6th Ave.
Cherry St.
Marion St.
Columbia St.
James St.
Seattle City Hall
3rd Ave.
Pioneer Square (Central Link)
City Hall Park
Yesler Way
5
Ace Hotel 13
Alexis Hotel 29
Bacon Mansion B&B 9
The Baroness Hotel 37
Best Western Plus Pioneer Square Hotel 43
Comfort Suites Downtown Seattle Center 5
Courtyard Seattle Downtown/Lake Union 6
Courtyard Seattle Downtown/Pioneer Square 42
Doubletree Arctic Club Hotel 41
The Edgewater 11
Executive Hotel Pacific 34
The Fairmont Olympic Hotel 32
Four Seasons Hotel Seattle 27
Gaslight Inn 40
Grand Hyatt Seattle 25
Hampton Inn & Suites Downtown/Seattle Center 4
Hotel Andrea 19
Hotel Max 22
Hotel Monaco 31
Hotel 1000 30
Hotel Vintage Park 35
Hyatt at Olive 8 24
Hyatt Place Seattle/Downtown 14
Inn at El Gaucho 12
Inn at Harbor Steps 28
Inn at Queen Anne 2
Inn at the Market 17
The Inn at Virginia Mason 38
MarQueen Hotel 3
Mayflower Park Hotel 23
Mediterranean Inn 1
Moore Hotel 18
Pan Pacific Hotel Seattle 15
Residence Inn Seattle Downtown/Lake Union 7
Seattle Marriott Waterfront 16
Shafer Baillie Mansion B&B 10
Sheraton Seattle Hotel 26
Silver Cloud Hotel-Broadway 39
Silver Cloud Seattle-Lake Union 8
Silver Cloud Seattle-Stadium 44
Sixth Avenue Inn 20
Sorrento Hotel 36
W Seattle 33
The Westin Seattle 21

2100 Alaskan Way, Seattle, WA 98121. www.seattlemarriottwaterfront.com. ✆ **800/455-8254** or 206/443-5000. Fax 206/256-1100. 358 units. Summer $229–$329 double, from $645 suite; other months $149–$239 double, from $645 suite. Children 18 and under stay free in parent's room. AE, DC, DISC, MC, V. Valet parking $38. **Amenities:** 2 restaurants, 2 lounges; concierge; executive-level rooms; exercise room and access to nearby health club; Jacuzzi; indoor/outdoor pool; room service; free Wi-Fi. *In room:* A/C, TV, fridge, hair dryer, MP3 docking station, Wi-Fi ($13/day).

DOWNTOWN

The heart of Seattle, downtown is filled with high-rise office towers, business hotels, major department stores, shopping centers, and national-chain clothing stores. This is the city's expense-account district, and if you're using frequent-travelers points at a major hotel chain, this is where you'll want to stay.

Best For: Business travelers and anyone here for a shop-'til-you-drop vacation. The transit tunnel, streetcar, and monorail provide easy access to other neighborhoods.

Drawbacks: Restaurants downtown are geared toward expense accounts; and with few views, this area could be in any city.

Very Expensive

The Fairmont Olympic Hotel ★★★ If you're looking for classically elegant surroundings, excellent service, and great amenities, then book a room at this gorgeous facsimile of an Italian Renaissance palace. This hotel has the grandest lobby in Seattle. Gilt-and-crystal chandeliers hang from the arched ceiling, while ornate moldings grace the hand-burnished oak walls and pillars. Although many of the guest rooms tend to be rather small, all are very tasteful. If you crave extra space, opt for one of the suites, of which there are more than 200 (however, be aware that the executive suites aren't much bigger than deluxe rooms). The **Georgian** (p. 75) is the most elegant restaurant in Seattle. Of all Seattle's luxury hotels, the Fairmont Olympic works the hardest at being eco-friendly by using compact fluorescent bulbs, providing in-room recycling bins, and sending food waste to be composted.

411 University St., Seattle, WA 98101. www.fairmont.com/seattle. ✆ **888/363-5022,** 800/821-8106 (in Washington), 800/257-7544 (in Canada), or 206/621-1700. Fax 206/682-9633. 450 units. Summer $329–$429 double, $379–$875 suite; other months $249–$329 double, $299–$875 suite. Children 18 and under stay free in parent's room. AE, DC, DISC, MC, V. Valet parking $39; self-parking $30. Pets accepted ($40 fee). **Amenities:** 2 restaurants, lounge; concierge; health club; Jacuzzi; indoor pool; room service. *In room:* A/C, TV, hair dryer, minibar, Wi-Fi ($14/day).

Four Seasons Hotel Seattle ★★★ This is one of the newest luxury hotels in Seattle, and it boasts a superb location adjacent to Pike Place Market and across the street from the Seattle Art Museum. The small lobby blends contemporary lines with natural stone and wood for a modern Northwest aesthetic. Guest rooms are wired to the max and have artworks by regional artists as well as walls of glass, and many of them look out to Elliott Bay. An infinity-edge pool with a water view may sound like it belongs in Hawaii or Mexico, but that's exactly what you'll find here on the terrace just outside the hotel's huge exercise room.

99 Union St., Seattle, WA 98101. www.fourseasons.com/seattle. ✆ **800/819-5053** or 206/749-7000. Fax 206/749-7099. 147 units. $375–$545 double; $795–$2,000 suite. Children 18 and

under stay free in parent's room. AE, DC, DISC, MC, V. Valet parking $39. Pets accepted (no fee). **Amenities:** Restaurant, lounge; babysitting; concierge; exercise room; Jacuzzi; year-round outdoor pool; room service; full-service spa. *In room:* A/C, TV/DVD, CD player, hair dryer, minibar, MP3 docking station, Wi-Fi ($11/day).

Hotel 1000 ★★ Geared toward techie business travelers, Hotel 1000 is the most luxurious and one of the most technologically advanced hotels in Seattle. However, what should really matter to you is that the rooms are bigger than at most downtown hotels, and all have floor-to-ceiling walls of glass to let in lots of light—and, if you're high enough up, views of Elliott Bay. Bathrooms in deluxe rooms are works of art, with freestanding bathtubs that fill dramatically from the ceiling. Golfers take note: This is the only downtown Seattle hotel with its own golf course. In fact, the hotel's virtual-reality "golf club" has more than 50 golf courses on offer, including St. Andrews, Pinehurst No. 2, and Pebble Beach.

1000 First Ave., Seattle, WA 98104. www.hotel1000seattle.com. ✆ **877/315-1088** or 206/957-1000. 120 units. Summer $279–$489 double, $429–$689 suite; other months $229–$359 double, $359–$509 suite. Children 18 and under stay free in parent's room. AE, DISC, MC, V. Valet parking $36. Pets accepted ($40 fee). **Amenities:** Restaurant, lounge; babysitting; concierge; exercise room and access to nearby health club; room service; full-service spa. *In room:* A/C, TV, hair dryer, minibar, MP3 docking station, free Wi-Fi.

W Seattle ★★ The W hotel chain has won plenty of national attention and devoted fans for its oh-so-hip accommodations, and here in the land of espresso and high-tech, the W is a natural. The lobby has the look and feel of a stage set, with dramatic lighting and sleek furniture; and, in the evening, the space transforms into a trendy lounge. Rooms are not only beautifully designed and filled with plush amenities, but they also tend to be larger than those at other W hotels. They're full of great perks, including goose-down comforters and HDTVs. Although the -09 and -02 "Cool Corner" rooms cost a bit more, they are worth requesting. The W also has an extensive array of amenities for your dog or cat, if yours happens to be traveling with you.

1112 Fourth Ave., Seattle, WA 98101. www.whotels.com/seattle. ✆ **877/946-8357** or 206/264-6000. Fax 206/264-6100. 424 units. Summer $289–$349 double, from $959 suite; other months $229–$299 double, from $959 suite. Children 18 and under stay free in parent's room. AE, MC, V. Valet parking $41. Pets accepted ($100 fee plus $25 per night). **Amenities:** Restaurant, lounge; babysitting; concierge; exercise room and access to nearby health club; room service. *In room:* A/C, TV/DVD, CD player, hair dryer, minibar, MP3 docking station, Wi-Fi ($15/day).

Expensive

Alexis Hotel Seattle ★★ This century-old building is a sparkling gem in an enviable location: halfway between Pike Place Market and Pioneer Square, and 3 blocks from the waterfront and the Seattle Art Museum. The Alexis is dedicated to the arts, and throughout the hotel, both in guest rooms and in public spaces, there are original works of art. The cheerful, personalized service and the pleasant mix of contemporary and antique furnishings give the Alexis a special atmosphere. About a quarter of the rooms are suites, and the spa suites are real winners, offering whirlpool tubs in luxurious bathrooms. The hotel also has complimentary evening wine tastings. As part of the Kimpton chain, the Alexis participates in the eco-friendly EarthCare program and does what it can to be green. See their website for details.

1007 First Ave. (at Madison St.), Seattle, WA 98104. www.alexishotel.com. ✆ **888/850-1155** or 206/624-4844. Fax 206/621-9009. 121 units. Summer $229–$319 double, $274–$579 suite; other months $175–$319 double; $210–$579 suite. Rates include evening wine reception. Children 17 and under stay free in parent's room. AE, DC, DISC, MC, V. Valet parking $36. Pets accepted (no fee). **Amenities:** Restaurant, lounge; concierge; executive-level rooms; exercise room and access to nearby health club; room service; Aveda day spa. *In room:* A/C, TV, hair dryer, minibar, free Wi-Fi.

Grand Hyatt Seattle ★★★ If you're accustomed to staying in only the finest hotels, book a room here. For luxury, contemporary styling, amenities, and service, this hotel is first-rate. A spacious lobby full of regionally-inspired art glass sets the tone the moment you arrive. There is, however, one catch: Unless you spring for something pricier than the basic "deluxe guest room," you're going to be a bit cramped; the least expensive units here are designed for solo business travelers. The health club is well outfitted but doesn't have a swimming pool; families searching for deluxe accommodations should probably opt for the Fairmont Olympic instead.

721 Pine St., Seattle, WA 98101. www.grandseattle.hyatt.com. ✆ **800/233-1234** or 206/774-1234. Fax 206/774-6120. 425 units. Summer $269–$339 double, $299–409 suite; other months $199–$339 double, $229–$389 suite. Children 17 and under stay free in parent's room. AE, DC, DISC, MC, V. Valet parking $39; self-parking $28. **Amenities:** 2 restaurants, 2 lounges; concierge; exercise room and access to nearby health club; room service; sauna; day spa. *In room:* A/C, TV, hair dryer, minibar, MP3 docking station, Wi-Fi ($10/day).

Hotel Ändra ★★ On the edge of the Belltown neighborhood and only a few blocks from both downtown shopping and Pike Place Market, this hotel melds a vintage building with bold, contemporary styling and manages to succeed even better than the local W hotel. Rooms feature contemporary furnishings and decor, with plush beds and ergonomic desk chairs. Just off the sophisticated little library-like lobby is **Lola** (p. 83), a Greek restaurant operated by Tom Douglas, one of my favorite Seattle chefs. Don't miss it. The hotel location, close to restaurants, bars, and nightclubs, makes this a great place to stay if you're in Seattle to check out the nightlife.

2000 Fourth Ave., Seattle, WA 98121. www.hotelandra.com. ✆ **877/448-8600** or 206/448-8600. Fax 206/441-7140. 119 units. Summer $209–$299 double, from $279 suite; other months $159–$279 double, from $229 suite. Children 18 and under stay free in parent's room. AE, DC, DISC, MC, V. Valet parking $39. Pets accepted (no fee). **Amenities:** 2 restaurants, lounge; babysitting; concierge; exercise room and access to nearby health club; room service. *In room:* A/C, TV, hair dryer, minibar, MP3 docking station, Wi-Fi ($10/day).

Hotel Monaco Seattle ★★ The Monaco is one of downtown's most stylish hotels, attracting a young, affluent clientele. If you appreciate cutting-edge style, you'll go for the eclectic, over-the-top, retro-contemporary design. The lobby has reproductions of ancient Greek murals, while in the guest rooms, you'll find wild color schemes, bold-striped wallpaper, and animal-print terry-cloth robes. Miss your pet back home? Call the front desk, and a staff member will send up a pet goldfish for the night. **Sazerac,** the hotel's Southern-inspired restaurant, is as boldly designed as the rest of the place. Be sure to order the restaurant's namesake cocktail at the adjacent bar.

1101 Fourth Ave., Seattle, WA 98101. www.monaco-seattle.com. ✆ **888/454-8397** or 206/621-1770. Fax 206/621-7779. 189 units. Summer $239–$329 double, $289–$329 suite; other months

$165–$329 double; $215–$329 suite. Rates include evening wine tasting. Children 17 and under stay free in parent's room. AE, DC, DISC, MC, V. Valet parking $36–$39. Pets accepted (no fee). **Amenities:** Restaurant, lounge; concierge; exercise room and access to nearby health club; room service. *In room:* A/C, TV, hair dryer, minibar, free Wi-Fi.

Hotel Vintage Park ★★ Small, classically elegant, and exceedingly romantic, the Vintage Park is a must for both lovers and wine lovers. The guest rooms, which are named for Washington wineries, are perfect for romantic getaways, and every evening, the hotel hosts a wine tasting in the lobby featuring Washington wines. Throughout the hotel are numerous references to grapes and wine. Deluxe rooms have the best views (including views of Mount Rainier). Standard rooms, though smaller and less lavishly appointed, are still very comfortable. Through its EarthCare program, this Kimpton hotel does its part to be eco-friendly. See website for more details.

1100 Fifth Ave., Seattle, WA 98101. www.hotelvintagepark.com. ✆ **800/853-3914** or 206/624-8000. Fax 206/623-0568. 124 units. Summer $239–$375 double, $475–$595 suite; other months $139–$315 double, $475–$595 suite. Children 17 and under stay free in parent's room. AE, DC, DISC, MC, V. Valet parking $34. Pets accepted (no fee). **Amenities:** Restaurant (Italian), lounge; concierge; exercise room; room service. *In room:* A/C, TV, hair dryer, minibar, free Wi-Fi.

Hyatt at Olive 8 ★★ This downtown hotel near the convention center is Seattle's first LEED-certified hotel. (LEED, or Leadership in Energy and Environmental Design, certifies environmentally sound buildings.) To that end, this hotel has such green features as a living roof, lights that turn off when you leave your room, dual-flush toilets, water-reducing shower heads, and lots of natural light. The hotel's restaurant uses primarily ingredients sourced in the Northwest, and even the spa features organic and environmentally aware products. On top of all that, the hotel is very stylish, boldly contemporary, and features relatively large guest rooms with all the electronic features you would expect in a modern business hotel.

1635 Eighth Ave., Seattle, WA 98101. www.olive8.hyatt.com. ✆ **800/234-1234** or 206/695-1234. Fax 206/676-4400. 346 units. Summer $264–$319 double, $449–$519 suite; other months $179–$239 double, $379–$519 suite. Children 17 and under stay free in parent's room. AE, DC, DISC, MC, V. Valet parking $39. **Amenities:** Restaurant, lounge; concierge; executive-level rooms; health club; room service; sauna; full-service spa w/lap pool and Jacuzzi. *In room:* A/C, TV/DVD, fridge, hair dryer, MP3 docking station, Wi-Fi ($10/day).

Inn at Harbor Steps ★ This inn's excellent location, on the lower floors of a modern apartment building across the street from the Seattle Art Museum, makes it convenient to all of downtown Seattle's major attractions. The guest rooms, which overlook a courtyard garden, feel spacious enough to be apartments. The surprisingly classical furnishings lend a comfortable, homey feel. Every unit has a gas fireplace, and the largest rooms have whirlpool tubs. The only real drawback is the lack of views.

1221 First Ave., Seattle, WA 98101. www.innatharborsteps.com. ✆ **888/728-8910** or 206/748-0973. Fax 206/748-0533. 28 units. $225–$300 double. (Call or check website for seasonal specials.) Rates include continental breakfast and afternoon tea and appetizers. Children 5 and under stay free in parent's room. AE, DC, DISC, MC, V. Parking $20. Pets accepted ($65 fee). **Amenities:** Concierge; health club; Jacuzzi; 2 indoor pools; sauna; Wi-Fi. *In room:* A/C, TV, CD player, fridge, hair dryer, free Wi-Fi.

The Westin Seattle ★ ☺ With its distinctive cylindrical towers, the 47-story Westin is the tallest hotel in Seattle and has the best views of any accommodation in the city. From rooms on the upper floors of the north tower's northwest side, you get breathtaking vistas of the Space Needle, Puget Sound, and the Olympic Mountains. Guest rooms here are also some of the nicest in town. Couple those great views (seen through unusual curved walls of glass) with the Westin's plush "Heavenly Beds," and you'll be sleeping—literally and figuratively—on clouds. Although the pool doesn't have the great views that the Sheraton's has, keep in mind that few downtown hotels have pools at all—which makes the Westin a good choice for families.

1900 Fifth Ave., Seattle, WA 98101. www.westinseattle.com. ✆ **800/937-8461** or 206/728-1000. Fax 206/728-2259. 891 units. Summer $209–$329 double, from $495 suite. (Call or check website for seasonal specials.) Children 12 and under stay free in parent's room. AE, DC, DISC, MC, V. Valet parking $39; self-parking $36. Pets accepted, (no fee). **Amenities:** Restaurant, 2 lounges; concierge; health club; Jacuzzi; large indoor pool; room service; sauna. *In room:* A/C, TV, hair dryer, minibar, Wi-Fi ($10/day).

Moderate

Hotel Max ★ 🎁 If you crave Philippe Starck–inspired furnishings but have an Ikea budget, this is the place for you. Every guest-room door is covered with a black-and-white photo mural. In fact, art is the main design theme here, and throughout the hotel there are works by dozens of regional artists. Stainless-steel sinks and bold color schemes make it clear that this place is designed to appeal to travelers with an artistic aesthetic. Rooms can be tiny to the point of claustrophobia, so the Max is best for solo travelers.

620 Stewart St., Seattle, WA 98101. www.hotelmaxseattle.com. ✆ **866/986-8087** or 206/728-6299. Fax 206/443-5754. 163 units. Summer $159–$259 double; other months $119–$179 double. Children 12 and under stay free in parent's room. AE, DC, DISC, MC, V. Valet parking $30. Pets accepted ($45 fee). **Amenities:** Restaurant; exercise room and access to nearby health club; room service. *In room:* A/C, TV, CD player, hair dryer, minibar, Wi-Fi ($12/day).

Mayflower Park Hotel ★ If your favorite recreational activities include shopping or sipping martinis, the Mayflower Park is for you. Built in 1927, this historic hotel is connected to the Westlake Center shopping plaza and is within a block of Nordstrom and Macy's. Most rooms are furnished with an eclectic blend of contemporary Italian and traditional European pieces. The smallest rooms are cramped, so if you crave space, ask for one of the larger corner rooms or a suite. Martini drinkers will want to spend time at **Oliver's** lounge (p. 222), which serves the best martinis in Seattle and has free hors d'oeuvres at happy hour. The hotel's **Andaluca** restaurant is a plush, contemporary spot serving a highly creative cuisine.

405 Olive Way, Seattle, WA 98101. www.mayflowerpark.com. ✆ **800/426-5100,** 206/382-6990, or 206/623-8700. Fax 206/382-6997. 160 units. Summer $189–$229 double, $249–$289 suite; other months $149–$199 double, $229–$289 suite. Children 18 and under stay free in parent's room. AE, DC, DISC, MC, V. Valet parking $20. **Amenities:** Restaurant (Mediterranean/Northwest), lounge; concierge; exercise room and access to nearby health club; Jacuzzi; room service. *In room:* A/C, TV, hair dryer, free Wi-Fi.

Sheraton Seattle Hotel ★ ☺ This hotel, with 1,258 rooms, is the largest in Seattle, and it is evident as soon as you arrive that big conventions are big business here. As an individual traveler, you're likely to feel a bit overlooked.

However, despite the impersonal nature of this hotel, I still recommend it, especially for families. Kids (and many adults) will love the 35th-floor swimming pool with great city views; there's an exercise room on the same floor. You also get good views from guest rooms on the higher floors. All units are fairly large, but if you are not traveling with the kids and want the maximum space, book one of the king rooms, which are designed for business travelers. Throughout the hotel, you'll find artworks that are part of a $6 million collection.

1400 Sixth Ave., Seattle, WA 98101. www.sheraton.com/seattle. ✆ **800/325-3535** or 206/621-9000. Fax 206/621-8441. 1,258 units. $165–$399 double; $300–$5,000 suite. Children 17 and under stay free in parent's room. AE, DC, DISC, MC, V. Valet parking $41. Pets accepted (no fee). **Amenities:** 2 restaurants, lounge; concierge; executive-level rooms; exercise room; Jacuzzi; indoor pool; room service; free Wi-Fi. *In room:* A/C, TV, hair dryer, Internet ($11/day), minibar.

Inexpensive

Executive Hotel Pacific ★ There aren't too many reasonably priced choices left in downtown Seattle, but this renovated and updated hotel, built in 1928, offers not only moderately priced rooms but also a prime location—halfway between Pike Place Market and Pioneer Square, and just about the same distance from the waterfront. Rooms and bathrooms have been updated, and the lobby has a very stylish and contemporary look. However, the rooms are small (verging on tiny) and sometimes quite cramped. Consequently, I recommend this place primarily for solo travelers.

400 Spring St., Seattle, WA 98104. www.executivehotels.net. ✆ **888/388-3932** or 206/623-3900. Fax 206/623-2059. 154 units. Summer $124–$179 double, $174–$279 suite; $89–$154 double, $154–$279 suite. Children 17 and under stay free in parent's room. AE, DC, DISC, MC, V. Valet parking $27; self-parking $23. Pets under 30 lbs. accepted (no fee). **Amenities:** Restaurant, lounge; concierge; exercise room. *In room:* A/C, TV, CD player, hair dryer, MP3 docking station, free Wi-Fi.

PIKE PLACE MARKET & BELLTOWN

Pike Place Market is Seattle's top attraction, a buzzing market packed with produce stalls, specialty food shops, restaurants, and unusual shops. Belltown, once Seattle's hippest neighborhood, has in recent years lost much of its cachet. However, there are still plenty of bars and nightclubs in the neighborhood, as well as a few good restaurants.

Best For: Foodies wanting to stay in the thick of things will want to stay in the market; young travelers on a budget and anyone in town to check out the Seattle club scene will find Belltown hotels convenient.

Drawbacks: The market is shoulder-to-shoulder with tourists during the day and can be overwhelming. In Belltown, a plethora of panhandlers hit the streets each night when the bars start filling up. When the bars close, light sleepers are often bothered by street noises.

Expensive

Inn at the Market ★★ For romance, convenience, and the chance to immerse yourself in the Seattle aesthetic, it's hard to beat this hotel in Pike Place Market.

A rooftop deck overlooking Elliott Bay provides a great spot to soak up the sun on summer afternoons. Don't look for a grand entrance or large sign; there's only a small plaque on the wall to indicate that the building houses a tasteful, understated luxury hotel. Be sure to ask for one of the waterview rooms, which have large windows overlooking the bay. Even if you don't get a water view, you'll find spacious accommodations, with mold-to-your-body beds, large bathrooms, and elegant decor that gives the feel of an upscale European beach resort. **Cafe Campagne** (p. 81) offers country-style French food amid casual surroundings.

86 Pine St., Seattle, WA 98101. www.innatthemarket.com. ✆ **800/446-4484** or 206/443-3600. Fax 206/448-0631. 70 units. Summer $255–$525 double, $399–$625 suite; other months $185–$395 double, $299–$399 suite. Children 17 and under stay free in parent's room. AE, DC, DISC, MC, V. Parking $29. **Amenities:** 2 restaurants, lounge; concierge; access to nearby health club; room service. *In room:* A/C, TV, hair dryer, minibar, MP3 docking station, free Wi-Fi.

Moderate

The Inn at El Gaucho ★ While low-budget hipsters have the Ace Hotel, those who are more flush can opt to stay at this plush little Belltown inn. It's located directly above, and affiliated with, the retro-swanky El Gaucho steakhouse. The nondescript street-level front door does nothing to prepare you for the luxurious little second-story lobby, which makes this place feel like a real find. After a night on the town, have breakfast in the plush feather bed. Leather chairs and sofas, help make rooms here well worth lingering in. Throw in fresh flowers, and you have a great place for a romantic weekend. One caveat: Be aware that the inn is up a flight of stairs.

2505 First Ave., Seattle, WA 98121. http://inn.elgaucho.com/inn.elgaucho. ✆ **866/354-2824** or 206/728-1133. 17 units. Summer $179–$289 suite; other months $149–$239 suite. No extra charge for 1 child in parents' room. AE, DISC, MC, V. Valet parking $25. **Amenities:** Restaurant, lounge; babysitting; concierge; access to nearby health club; room service. *In room:* A/C, TV, CD player, hair dryer, free Wi-Fi.

Inexpensive

Ace Hotel The Ace Hotel, in the heart of Belltown, is the city's hippest economy hotel. White-on-white and stainless steel are the hallmarks of the minimalist decor; even the brick walls and wood floors have been painted white. Wall decorations are minimal, except in those rooms with 1970s photo murals of the great outdoors. Platform beds and wool blankets salvaged from foreign hotels add to the chic feel, as do the tiny stainless-steel sinks and shelves in the rooms with shared bathrooms. Basically, aside from the eight large rooms with private bathrooms (ask about the room with the shower behind the bed), this place is a step above a hostel; it's aimed at the 20- and 30-something crowd. Be aware that some walls are paper-thin, and the clientele tends to keep late hours. Don't plan on going to sleep early.

2423 First Ave., Seattle, WA 98121. www.acehotel.com. ✆ **206/448-4721.** Fax 206/374-0745. 28 units, 14 with shared bathroom. $99–$109 double with shared bathroom; $175–$199 double with private bathroom. Rates include continental breakfast. Children 12 and under stay free in parent's room. AE, DC, DISC, MC, V. Parking $19. Pets accepted. *In room:* TV, free Wi-Fi.

The Moore Hotel In a historic building 2 blocks from both Pike Place Market and the Belltown restaurant and nightlife district, the Moore is a decent downtown choice for young and adventurous travelers on a tight budget. If you've ever traveled through Europe on the cheap, you'll know what to expect. It's not fancy, and if you aren't in a renovated room, the place can seem a bit dreary. But if you request one of the updated suites, you'll be surprised by the stylishly modern, large rooms with hardwood floors, full kitchens, and big windows. Ask for a room with a view of Puget Sound. The lobby, with its marble, tiles, and decorative moldings, hints at the Moore's historic character, but this is more budget accommodation than historic hotel. There's a hip **restaurant/lounge,** and an adjacent theater stages rock concerts.

1926 Second Ave., Seattle, WA 98101. www.moorehotel.com. ✆ **800/421-5508** or 206/448-4851. Fax 206/728-5668. 120 units, 30 with shared bathroom. $71 double with shared bathroom; $86–$97 double with private bathroom; $118–$190 suite. Call or check website for seasonal specials. Children 9 and under stay free in parent's room. MC, V. Parking $12. **Amenities:** Restaurant, lounge. *In room:* TV, free Wi-Fi.

PIONEER SQUARE, THE INTERNATIONAL DISTRICT & SODO

Pioneer Square is one of Seattle's only historic districts, and many of the brick-and-stone commercial buildings lining the shady streets date from the years just after the great Seattle fire of 1889. The International District lies a few blocks east of Pioneer Square. SoDo, which begins south of the Pioneer Square neighborhood, is home to the city's two main sports stadiums—Qwest Field and Safeco Field.

Best For: Soaking up Seattle's historic, gold-rush-era character.

Drawbacks: This is one of Seattle's main nightlife districts and can be a rowdy place at night. During the day, be prepared to encounter a lot of street people.

Expensive

The Arctic Club Seattle ★★ With distinctive ceramic walrus heads decorating the facade, this hotel was built in 1917 as an exclusive club for men who had struck it rich in the Alaska gold rush. Today the Arctic Club Seattle is one of the prettiest historic buildings in Seattle and should be your first choice if you enjoy staying in historic hotels. The lobby, with its bar, billiards table, and travel-themed Art Deco furnishings, feels like it could be in Singapore or Nairobi; you half-expect Humphrey Bogart to be sipping a gin and tonic in the corner. Guest rooms are decorated in keeping with the historic, adventure-travel theme. Be sure to sneak a peek inside the **Northern Lights Dome Room**, a grand hall with original frescoes, a stained-glass ceiling, and lots of ornate plasterwork and gilding.

700 Third Ave., Seattle, WA 98104. www.arcticclubhotel.com. ✆ **800/222-8733** or 206/340-0340. Fax 206/340-0349. 120 units. Summer $249–$349 double; other months $149–$269 double. Children 18 and under stay free in parent's room. AE, DC, DISC, MC, V. Valet parking $32. **Amenities:** Restaurant, 2 lounges; concierge; executive-level rooms; exercise room; room service. *In room:* A/C, TV/DVD, CD player, hair dryer, minibar, MP3 docking station, Wi-Fi ($10/day).

Best Western Plus Pioneer Square Seattle Hotel ★ This hotel, listed on the National Register of Historic Places, is in the heart of the Pioneer Square historic district, Seattle's historic art gallery and nightlife neighborhood. As such, things get raucous on weekend nights, and this hotel is only recommended for guests accustomed to dealing with street people and noise. However, if you're in town to party (or to attend a Mariners or Seahawks game), it is a good option. Guest rooms are fairly small (some are positively cramped) but are furnished in an attractive classic style. Be sure to stay aware of your surroundings on neighborhood streets late at night.

77 Yesler Way, Seattle, WA 98104. www.pioneersquare.com. ✆ **800/800-5514** or 206/340-1234. Fax 206/467-0707. 75 units. Summer $210–$280 double; other months $160–$220 double. Rates include continental breakfast. Children 16 and under stay free in parent's room. AE, DC, DISC, MC, V. Parking $20. **Amenities:** Concierge; access to nearby health club; room service. *In room:* A/C, TV, hair dryer, free Wi-Fi.

Silver Cloud Hotel–Stadium ★ ☺ If you're a sports fan, there is no better place to stay than here: This hotel is across the street from Safeco Field (where the Seattle Mariners play) and adjacent to Qwest Field (home of the Seattle Seahawks). Even if you're not a sports fan, this hotel is a great choice for its beautiful, modern rooms, which are almost as impressive as those at the Pan Pacific Hotel Seattle, on the other side of downtown. Families, take note: This is one of the few hotels in the area that has a swimming pool, and best of all, it's outside on a rooftop deck.

1046 First Ave. S., Seattle, WA 98134. www.silvercloud.com/stadium.php. ✆ **800/497-1261** or 206/204-9800. Fax 206/381-0751. 211 units. $249–$349 double, $319 suite. Call or check website for seasonal specials. Children 17 and under stay free in parent's room. AE, DC, DISC, MC, V. Valet parking $22. **Amenities:** Restaurant, lounge; exercise room; Jacuzzi; outdoor pool; room service. *In room:* A/C, TV, fridge, hair dryer, MP3 docking station, free Wi-Fi.

Moderate

Courtyard Seattle Downtown/Pioneer Square ★ Although the building housing this hotel dates to 1904, it isn't as impressive an edifice as the nearby Arctic Club Seattle. However, the Courtyard is equally well placed, close to historic Pioneer Square, yet far enough away that the immediate neighborhood isn't as boisterous after dark. Opened in 2010, this hotel feels very modern, and while it is obviously designed with corporate travelers in mind, the contemporary furnishings are very attractive and comfortable. The location, however, is this hotel's real selling point.

612 Second Ave., Seattle, WA 98104. www.marriott.com/seaps. ✆ **888/236-2427** or 206/625-1111. Fax 206/625-3270. 262 units. Summer $199–$249 double, $229–$259 suite; other months $119–$199 double, $169–$219 suite. AE, DC, DISC, MC, V. Children 17 and under stay free in parent's room. AE, DC, DISC, MC, V. Valet parking $26. **Amenities:** Restaurant, lounge; exercise room; indoor pool; room service. *In room:* A/C, TV, fridge, hair dryer, free Wi-Fi.

SEATTLE CENTER & QUEEN ANNE

The Queen Anne neighborhood is divided into upper Queen Anne and lower Queen Anne. The lower section surrounds Seattle Center and is mostly a busy commercial district, where you'll find several moderately priced hotels. Upper Queen Anne is an upscale residential area with an attractive shopping district.

Best For: Convenience to Seattle Center (and the monorail to downtown), makes this neighborhood a good choice for families. A plethora of inexpensive restaurants and the many moderately priced hotels also make this area a good choice for budget-conscious travelers.

Drawbacks: The lower Queen Anne commercial district is a bit seedy, and the upper Queen Anne shopping district is a steep walk (or short bus or car ride) up to the top of the hill.

Moderate

Comfort Suites Downtown Seattle Center ★ ☺ Although it's none too easy to find this place (call and get directions), the bargain rates and spacious rooms make the Comfort Suites worth searching out. Because it's only 3 blocks from Seattle Center, you could feasibly leave your car parked at the hotel for most of your stay and walk or use public transit to get around. If you've brought the family, the suites are a good deal, and the proximity to Seattle Center will help moms and dads keep the kids entertained. Ask for a room away from the highway that runs past the hotel.

601 Roy St., Seattle, WA 98109. www.comfortsuites-seattle.com. ✆ **800/517-4000** or 206/282-2600. Fax 206/282-1112. 158 units. $140–$200 double. Call or check website for seasonal specials. Rates include continental breakfast. Children 17 and under stay free in parent's room. AE, DC, DISC, MC, V. Free parking. **Amenities:** Exercise room. *In room:* A/C, TV, fridge, hair dryer, free Internet.

Hampton Inn & Suites Seattle Downtown/Seattle Center Step out the front door of this hotel and you're staring straight at the Space Needle, which is only about 5 blocks away. That view and the convenient location within blocks of Seattle Center are the main reasons to stay here, and numerous good restaurants and cafes are also nearby. The standard rooms are comfortable enough, but if you plan to stay for more than a few days, consider one of the suites, which have fireplaces and balconies.

700 Fifth Ave. N., Seattle, WA 98109. www.hamptoninnseattle.com. ✆ **800/426-7866** or 206/282-7700. Fax 206/282-0899. 198 units. Summer $169–$209 double, $199–$309 suite; other months $129–$209 double, $169–$319 suite. Rates include continental breakfast. Children 18 and under stay free in parent's room. AE, DC, DISC, MC, V. Self-Parking $15. **Amenities:** Exercise room. *In room:* A/C, TV, fridge, hair dryer, free Internet.

MarQueen Hotel ★ ☺ This Lower Queen Anne hotel is in a renovated 1918 brick building that will appeal to travelers who enjoy lodgings with historic character. Seattle Center, with its many performance venues and family-oriented attractions, is only 3 blocks away, and from there you can take the monorail into downtown. Although the MarQueen's many high-tech amenities are geared toward business travelers, it's a good choice for vacationers as well. Guest rooms are spacious, although furnished very traditionally and a bit oddly laid out due to the hotel's previous incarnation as an apartment building. Many units have separate seating areas and full kitchens. The hotel is adjacent to both an excellent espresso bar and several good restaurants.

600 Queen Anne Ave. N., Seattle, WA 98109. www.marqueen.com. ✆ **888/445-3076** or 206/282-7407. Fax 206/283-1499. 59 units. Summer $169–$185 double, $189–$235 suite; other months $129–$135 double, $169–$225 suite. Rates include continental breakfast. Children 17 and under stay free in parent's room. AE, DC, DISC, MC, V. Valet parking $25. **Amenities:** Access to nearby health club; room service; spa. *In room:* A/C, TV, hair dryer, kitchen, free Wi-Fi.

The Maxwell Hotel ★ With its theatrical decor, this hotel across the street from Seattle Center plays up its local arts connection; and, with several theaters across the street, it does make a great choice for a theater-focused Seattle vacation. Rooms are like little stage sets, with lots of bright colors and bold patterns, and they go by such names as Aria, Duet, Ensemble, and Prima Donna. The Maxwell is affiliated with the Watertown and the University Inn, two of my favorite north Seattle hotels. However, the Maxwell is in a better neighborhood and is a much more convenient option.

300 Roy St., Seattle, WA 98109. www.themaxwellhotel.com. ✆ **877/298-9728** or 206/286-0629. Fax 206/285-0476. 139 units. Summer $159–$249 double, $219–$269 suite; other months $119–$189 double, $179–$209 suite. Children 17 and under stay free in parent's room. AE, DC, DISC, MC, V. Parking $15. Pets accepted ($20 per night). **Amenities:** Bikes; exercise room; indoor pool. *In room:* A/C, TV/DVD, fridge, hair dryer, MP3 docking station, free Wi-Fi.

Mediterranean Inn Don't be fooled by the name: This is not a bed-and-breakfast-type inn. But this modern apartment-hotel, in the Lower Queen Anne neighborhood, is just a couple of blocks from Seattle Center and is an ideal choice for extended stays. Because the Mediterranean Inn was designed with longer stays in mind, its rooms are much more comfortable than those at the nearby Inn at Queen Anne. With the exception of the least expensive rooms, you'll get plenty of space and a kitchenette. In summer, be sure to opt for a unit with air-conditioning.

425 Queen Anne Ave. N., Seattle, WA 98109. www.mediterranean-inn.com. ✆ **866/525-4700** or 206/428-4700. Fax 206/428-4699. 180 units. Summer $149–$189 double; other months $129–$169 double. Children may stay in parents' room ($10 additional per night). AE, DC, DISC, MC, V. Self-Parking $15. **Amenities:** Exercise room. *In room:* TV/DVD, hair dryer, kitchenette, Wi-Fi ($7/day).

Inexpensive

Inn at Queen Anne In the Lower Queen Anne neighborhood, close to Seattle Center and numerous restaurants and espresso bars, this hotel is housed in a converted older apartment building. Though the rooms here aren't as nice as those at the nearby MarQueen, they're comfortable enough, albeit sometimes a bit cramped and not entirely modern. The convenient location and economical rates are the big pluses here, but there's also a pleasant garden surrounding the hotel.

505 First Ave. N., Seattle, WA 98109. www.innatqueenanne.com. ✆ **800/952-5043** or 206/282-7357. Fax 206/217-9719. 68 units. Summer $119–$139 double; other months $99–$129 double. Rates include continental breakfast. Children 17 and under stay free in parent's room. AE, DC, DISC, MC, V. Limited self-parking $15. *In room:* A/C, TV, kitchenette, free Wi-Fi.

SOUTH LAKE UNION & LAKE UNION

Stretching from downtown to the southern shores of Lake Union, this is the city's newest neighborhood, a modern urban village that is also home to Amazon's corporate headquarters. The SLU, as it's known, is where everything is happening in Seattle these days. Along the lake, there are houseboats, marinas, and waterfront restaurants. Floatplanes use the lake as a runway, and you can rent kayaks from several places around the lake.

Best For: Feeling like you're a part of Seattle's future. Traveling techies will want to park themselves here.

Drawbacks: The neighborhood is still a bit top heavy with 9-to-5ers, so the streets get pretty quiet after quitting time.

Expensive

Pan Pacific Hotel Seattle ★★ This hotel, 4 long blocks north of the downtown shopping district and feeling entirely removed from the streets of Seattle, is a stylish, contemporary hotel that opens onto a central courtyard surrounded by condominium towers. Although primarily a business hotel, the Pan Pacific's rooms are such plush retreats that they rightfully belong at some luxury resort, not at a business hotel. Rooms here are larger than at most Seattle downtown hotels, and even standard rooms have soaking tubs with pocket doors that open onto the bedroom area. Decor is minimalist and sleek, though with a soft edge, and walls of glass flood the rooms with light. Be sure to ask for a room with a view of the Space Needle.

2125 Terry Ave., Seattle, WA 98121. www.panpacific.com/seattle. ✆ **877/324-4856** or 206/264-8111. Fax 206/654-5049. 160 units. Summer $250–$400 double, $2,000 suite; other months $209–$309 double, $2,000 suite. Children 18 and under stay free in parent's room. AE, DC, DISC, MC, V. Valet parking $39. Pets accepted ($50 fee). **Amenities:** Restaurant, 2 lounges; babysitting; concierge; executive-level rooms; health club; Jacuzzi; room service; sauna; full-service spa. *In room:* A/C, TV, hair dryer, minibar, MP3 docking station, free Wi-Fi.

Residence Inn Seattle Downtown/Lake Union ★★ Right across the street from Lake Union, Marriott's Residence Inn is a good bet that's slightly removed from the city center. A seven-story atrium floods the hotel's plant-filled lobby with light, while the sound of a waterfall soothes traffic-weary nerves. All accommodations here, done in a bright, modern style, are suites, so you get more space for your money than you do at downtown hotels. Suites have full kitchens, so you can prepare your own meals if you like (though breakfast is provided). There's no restaurant on the premises, but several options are right across the street. Amenities include guest receptions 3 nights per week and a grocery-shopping service.

800 Fairview Ave. N., Seattle, WA 98109. www.marriott.com/sealu. ✆ **800/331-3131** or 206/624-6000. Fax 206/223-8160. 234 units. Summer $219–$229 1-bedroom suite, $309–$339 2-bedroom suite; other months $139–$179 1-bedroom suite, $199–$289 2-bedroom suite. Rates include full breakfast. Children 18 and under stay free in parent's room. AE, DC, DISC, MC, V. Parking $21. Pets accepted ($10 per night). **Amenities:** Exercise room; Jacuzzi; indoor lap pool; room service; sauna. *In room:* A/C, TV, hair dryer, kitchen, free Wi-Fi.

Moderate

Courtyard Seattle Downtown/Lake Union ★ ☺ On the southwest side of Lake Union, at the edge of the South Lake Union neighborhood, this business hotel has both a convenient location and great lake views from many of its rooms. Guest rooms are modern and quite comfortable, and some rooms have both refrigerators and microwaves. With an indoor pool, a park across the street, proximity to Seattle Center, and special goodies for kids, this hotel is an excellent choice for families. The diverse assortment of restaurants in the South Lake Union neighborhood also make the Courtyard a good choice for grown-ups.

925 Westlake Ave. N., Seattle, WA 98109. www.marriott.com/courtyard. ✆ **800/321-2211** or 206/213-0100. Fax 206/213-0101. 250 units. Summer $159–$219 double; other months $99–$179 double. Children 18 and under stay free in parent's room. AE, DC, DISC, MC, V. Self-parking $20. **Amenities:** Restaurant, lounge; concierge; exercise room; Jacuzzi; indoor pool; room service. *In room:* A/C, TV, fridge, hair dryer, free Wi-Fi.

Hyatt Place Seattle/Downtown ★ Although this hip business hotel is on a busy intersection, it is within 4 blocks of Seattle Center and the Space Needle, and 4 blocks from the new South Lake Union neighborhood, which is home to several excellent restaurants and is served by the Seattle Streetcar. If you're looking for a large room close to downtown, this is the place. The guest rooms, done in a tasteful contemporary style, are all junior suites with separate seating and sleeping areas, and the 42-inch TVs swivel, so you can watch from the bed or the sofa bed. The lobby cafe is open 24 hours a day for grab-and-go light meals—a real plus if you're a night owl—and also serves espresso and hot breakfasts for a charge.

110 Sixth Ave. N., Seattle, WA 98109. http://seattledowntown.place.hyatt.com. ✆ **888/492-8847** or 206/441-6041. Fax 206/441-6042. 160 units. Summer $161–$224 double; other months $121–$174 double. Rates include continental breakfast. Children 17 and under stay free in parent's room. AE, DC, DISC, MC, V. Self-parking $15. **Amenities:** Cafe, lounge; exercise room; indoor pool. *In room:* A/C, TV, fridge, hair dryer, free Wi-Fi.

Silver Cloud Inn–Lake Union ★ ☺ Across the street from Lake Union, this hotel offers good views (some of which take in the Space Needle). The rooms are big and filled with lots of amenities, which make them convenient for long stays and family vacations. Although the hotel doesn't have a restaurant of its own, plenty of waterfront options are within walking distance. The indoor swimming pool appeals to kids, and floatplane tours leave from right across the street. This is a good value for such a great location. Lower rates are almost always available on this hotel's website.

1150 Fairview Ave. N., Seattle, WA 98109. www.silvercloud.com/seattlelakeunion. ✆ **800/330-5812** or 206/447-9500. Fax 206/812-4900. 184 units. $199–$219 double, $219–$249 suite. Call or check website for seasonal specials. Rates include full breakfast. Children 18 and under stay free in parent's room. AE, DC, DISC, MC, V. Free parking. **Amenities:** Exercise room; Jacuzzi; indoor pool. *In room:* A/C, TV, fridge, hair dryer, free Wi-Fi.

The Sixth Avenue Inn ★ It's never easy finding a decent budget hotel in a major city, but to find one within blocks of the main shopping district and almost as close to one of the city's top attractions is a real find. This older low-rise hotel has been around for years and is still worth a stay. Pike Place Market is 6 blocks away, and Nordstrom and two other shopping centers are even closer. Rooms aren't fancy, but they're comfortable and functional.

2000 Sixth Ave., Seattle, WA 98121. www.sixthavenueinn.com. ✆ **800/648-6440** or 206/441-8300. Fax 206/441-9903. 167 units. Summer $145–$180 double; other months $85–$140 double. Children 17 and under stay free in parent's room. AE, DC, DISC, MC, V. Parking $15. **Amenities:** Restaurant, lounge; concierge; exercise room; room service. *In room:* A/C, TV, hair dryer, free Wi-Fi.

CAPITOL HILL & FIRST HILL

This pair of hills lie just to the east of downtown Seattle. First Hill, known locally as Pill Hill due to its many hospitals, begins just across I-5 from downtown. Capitol Hill, Seattle's main gay neighborhood, lies a mile or so uphill and to the east of downtown. It features both a busy commercial district and pleasant residential streets, where you'll find a few B&Bs in restored historic homes.

Best For: Gay travelers and those wanting to stay close to downtown without staying in a corporate high-rise. Capitol Hill also has one of the city's best restaurant districts.

Drawbacks: While new condominiums and restaurants are slowly upgrading the character of Capitol Hill, it still is frequented primarily by the young and the gay. Consequently, there are lots of bars and nightclubs, and shops cater to a youthful clientele.

Moderate

The Baroness Hotel Affiliated with the Inn at Virginia Mason and located right across the street, the Baroness is an apartment hotel that is primarily used by people in Seattle for medical reasons. That said, it is a great value if you are not a demanding traveler. Rooms, though a bit dowdy, are comfortable, and some have kitchens. The surrounding neighborhood (aside from the hospital) is quite pretty. Downtown Seattle starts 4 blocks downhill from the Baroness. Although the rooms are not centrally air-conditioned, air conditioners can be requested.

1005 Spring St., Seattle, WA 98104. www.baronesshotel.com. ✆ **800/283-6453** or 206/583-6453. Fax 206/223-6771. 58 units. Summer $127–$134 double, $134–$142 suite; other months $117–$124 double, $124–$132 suite. Children 18 and under stay free in parent's room. AE, DISC, MC, V. Parking $20. *In room:* TV, kitchenette, free Wi-Fi.

Shafer Baillie Mansion Bed & Breakfast ★★ Be sure to bring your top hat and tails if you plan to stay at this 1914 Tudor-revival mansion a block from Volunteer Park. You'll feel like puttin' on the Ritz as soon as you step through the front door and find yourself surrounded by mahogany paneling, stained-glass windows, and antique furnishings. Set on what was once known as Millionaire's Row, this mansion envelops guests in the luxurious lifestyles of the rich and famous, circa 1920. There's a huge entrance hall, a dark-and-masculine library, a lovely light-filled sunroom, and, of course formal dining and living rooms. Up the wide, curving staircase, you'll find large guest rooms with antique beds, including a few four-posters. Some rooms have refinished original bathtubs, while others have modern showers. For the ultimate shower, opt for the master suite, which has the original 450-jet "ribcage shower."

907 14th Ave. E., Seattle, WA 98112. http://sbmansion.com. ✆ **800/985-4654** or 206/322-4654. Fax 206/329-4654. 8 units. $139–$149 double; $159–$219 suite. Call or check website for seasonal specials. Children by arrangement; $20 per child extra to stay in parents' room. 2-night minimum weekends, 3-night minimum holidays. AE, DISC, MC, V. **Amenities:** Concierge. *In room:* A/C, TV, hair dryer, free Wi-Fi.

Silver Cloud Hotel–Broadway ★ At the "Pill Hill" end of Capitol Hill, this hotel is comfortable, reasonably priced, and close enough to downtown that anyone in good condition can walk there. (Although it's only a 10- to 15-min. walk, be forewarned that the way back is all uphill.) The Silver Cloud is a good bet if you want to check out the Capitol Hill nightlife scene, which is dominated by gay bars and clubs. There's even a hip bowling alley next door. Rooms are all attractively decorated; my favorites have in-room whirlpool tubs.

1100 Broadway, Seattle, WA 98122. www.silvercloud.com/seattlebroadway. ✆ **800/590-1801** or 206/325-1400. Fax 206/324-1995. 179 units. $199–$249 double; $249–$259 suite. Call or check website for seasonal specials. Rates include continental breakfast. Children 18 and under stay free in parent's room. AE, DC, DISC, MC, V. Parking $16. **Amenities:** Restaurant, lounge; concierge; exercise room; Jacuzzi; indoor pool; room service. *In room:* A/C, TV, fridge, hair dryer, free Wi-Fi.

Sorrento Hotel ★★ With its wrought-iron gates, courtyard of palm trees, and plush seating in the octagonal **Fireside Room**, the Sorrento, which first opened in 1909, has a classic charm. The guest rooms are among the finest in the city: No two are alike; and, while most are set up for business travelers, this hotel also makes a great choice for vacationers. Although more than half the units are suites, many provide little more space than you get in a standard room, so you may not want to splurge on an upgrade. The hotel is set high on First Hill, yet downtown is only a few (steep) blocks away. If you'd rather not walk, there's a complimentary shuttle service. The hotel's dining room has the feel of a 1950s supper club, and in the **Fireside Room,** you can get afternoon tea and catch live jazz on weekend evenings.

900 Madison St., Seattle, WA 98104. www.hotelsorrento.com. ✆ **800/426-1265** or 206/622-6400. Fax 206/343-6155. 76 units. Summer $176–$259 double, $243–$339 suite; other months $155–$219 double, $205–$319 suite. Children 17 and under stay free in parent's room. AE, DC, DISC, MC, V. Valet parking $32. Pets accepted ($60 fee). **Amenities:** Restaurant, 2 lounges; concierge; exercise room and access to nearby health club; room service. *In room:* A/C, TV, fridge, hair dryer, minibar, MP3 docking station, free Wi-Fi.

Inexpensive

The Bacon Mansion Bed & Breakfast ★ As the name implies, the Bacon Mansion is a big place—an 8,000-square-foot Tudor, built in 1909, to be precise—and has all the accoutrements of a mansion: crystal chandelier, grand piano, huge dining room table, and library. Located on a shady stretch of Broadway, 2 blocks beyond Capitol Hill's busy commercial area, the inn combines a quiet residential feel with proximity to an evolving and ever-more-sophisticated shopping and dining scene. Decor includes a mix of antiques and reproductions, with an abundance of floral prints. Although during the winter you may catch a glimpse of the Space Needle from the Capitol Suite, other rooms lack views. Two units are in the original carriage house.

959 Broadway E., Seattle, WA 98102. www.baconmansion.com. ✆ **800/240-1864** or 206/329-1864. Fax 206/860-9025. 11 units, 2 with shared bathroom. $99–$129 double with shared bathroom; $119–$239 double with private bathroom. Call or check website for seasonal specials. Rates include expanded continental breakfast. AE, DC, DISC, MC, V. Pets accepted in carriage house ($10 per night). **Amenities:** Concierge. *In room:* TV, hair dryer, free Wi-Fi.

Gaslight Inn ★ Anyone enamored of Craftsman bungalows and the Arts and Crafts movement of the early 20th century should enjoy a stay in this 1906 home. Throughout the inn are numerous pieces of Stickley furniture, and everywhere you turn you'll see oak trim framing the doors and windows. In summer, guests can swim in the backyard pool or lounge on the deck. Guest rooms continue the design themes of the common areas, with lots of oak furnishings and peeled-log beds in some units. The innkeepers can provide a wealth of information about the surrounding Capitol Hill neighborhood, the center of Seattle's gay community. The Gaslight also manages three apartments at the nearby **Squire Park Guest House** (www.squireparkguest.com).

1727 15th Ave., Seattle, WA 98122. www.gaslight-inn.com. ✆ **206/325-3654.** Fax 206/328-4803. 8 units, 3 with shared bathroom. $98–$118 double with shared bathroom; $128–$168 double with

family-friendly HOTELS

Best Western Plus Bainbridge Island Suites (p. 68) Rooms here are primarily large suites with kitchenettes and are ideal for trips with the family or for longer stays.

Comfort Suites Downtown Seattle Center (p. 57) The suites make this a good family choice, and the location near the Seattle Center will make the kids happy.

MarQueen Hotel (p. 57) A few blocks from Seattle Center and its many attractions is this converted apartment building, which provides a convenient location for families, as well as spacious suites with kitchenettes.

Seattle Airport Marriott (p. 66) With a huge jungle-y atrium containing a swimming pool and whirlpool spas, kids can play Tarzan and never leave the hotel.

Silver Cloud Hotel–Stadium (p. 56) Adjacent to Qwest Field, where the Seattle Seahawks football team plays, this is one of few hotels in the area that has a swimming pool.

Silver Cloud Inn–Lake Union (p. 60) Right across the street from Lake Union and several reasonably priced restaurants, this modern hotel has an indoor pool and spacious rooms.

The Westin Seattle (p. 52) Parents will love the views from the tallest hotel in Seattle, while the kids will enjoy the pool—a rarity in downtown hotels.

private bathroom. Call or check website for seasonal specials. Rates include continental breakfast. AE, MC, V. No children allowed. **Amenities:** Concierge; small seasonal heated outdoor pool. *In room:* TV, hair dryer, MP3 docking station, free Wi-Fi.

The Inn at Virginia Mason You may think I've sent you to a hospital rather than a hotel when you arrive at this older establishment on "Pill Hill"—but this is definitely a hotel, though it is adjacent to and managed by the Virginia Mason Hospital. Despite the fact that most guests are here because of the hospital, the hotel is a good choice for vacationers as well. Rates are economical, the location is quiet, and you're close to downtown. There's a rooftop deck and a shady little courtyard just off the lobby. Although the carpets and furniture here are in need of replacement, the rooms are still serviceable. Because this is an old building, room sizes vary. Deluxe rooms and suites can be quite large, and some have whirlpool tubs and fireplaces.

1006 Spring St., Seattle, WA 98104. www.innatvirginiamason.com. ✆ **800/283-6453** or 206/583-6453. Fax 206/223-6771. 79 units. Summer $119–$149 double, $139–$199 suite; other months $109–$139 double, $129–$199 suite. Children 18 and under stay free in parent's room. AE, DISC, MC, V. Parking $20. **Amenities:** Restaurant; room service. *In room:* TV, free Wi-Fi.

THE UNIVERSITY DISTRICT (NORTH SEATTLE)

About 15 minutes north of downtown, the University District (more commonly known as the U District) appeals primarily to younger travelers, but it does offer less expensive accommodations than downtown and is still fairly convenient to Seattle's major attractions. Also nearby are the Burke Museum, Henry Art

Gallery, Museum of History and Industry, Woodland Park Zoo, and, of course, the University of Washington.

Best For: Budget-conscious travelers in search of affordable, yet hip, accommodations.

Drawbacks: Neighborhood restaurants cater to college students craving quantity over quality.

Moderate

Chambered Nautilus Bed & Breakfast Inn ★ This Georgian Colonial inn sits high above an apartment-lined street atop an ivy-covered embankment, out of view of the sidewalk. Because the surrounding shady forest gives it a secluded feel, you'll hardly realize you're in the middle of the city. The antiques-filled B&B, which dates from 1915, has a homey feel, and innkeeper Joyce Schulte makes sure guests are comfortable and well fed. Four of the rooms have porches; some have mountain views. Third-floor units have fireplaces and the best views. Be advised that this inn is not recommended for anyone who has trouble climbing stairs. Four suites, with DVD players, kitchens, and porches, are in an adjacent house, where children are welcome.

5005 22nd Ave. NE, Seattle, WA 98105. www.chamberednautilus.com. ✆ **800/545-8459** or 206/522-2536. Fax 206/528-0898. 10 units. Summer $149–$189 double, $179–$214 suite; other months $124–$164 double, $149–$184 suite. Rates include full breakfast. AE, MC, V. Pets accepted in suites ($20 per night). Children 8 and over welcome in main house; children of all ages welcome in suites for an additional $20 a night. Free parking. **Amenities:** Concierge; access to nearby health club. *In room:* TV, CD player, hair dryer, MP3 docking station, free Wi-Fi.

Hotel Deca ★★ The 16-story Hotel Deca is one of Seattle's hippest hotels, and it offers excellent value. Consequently, it's one of my favorite hotels in the city. You'll be surrounded by modern Art Deco style as soon as you arrive, and the retro look is elegant, playful, and reminiscent of the 1930s. You'll also enjoy views of downtown Seattle, distant mountains, and various lakes and waterways. Every room is a corner unit, which means plenty of space to spread out. Small bathrooms are the biggest drawback. Hotel Deca is considerably cheaper than comparable downtown options, and if you need to be near the university, it's definitely the top choice in the neighborhood.

4507 Brooklyn Ave. NE, Seattle, WA 98105. www.hoteldeca.com. ✆ **800/899-0251** or 206/634-2000. Fax 206/547-6029. 158 units. Summer $149–$249 double; other months $119–$189 double. Children 18 and under stay free in parent's room. AE, DC, DISC, MC, V. Parking $12. **Amenities:** Restaurant, lounge, coffee shop; concierge; exercise room; room service. *In room:* A/C, TV/DVD, CD player, hair dryer, MP3 docking station, free Wi-Fi.

University Inn ★ Within easy walking distance of the university, this hotel offers surprisingly attractive rooms. Although the least expensive units (called "traditional rooms") have bathrooms with showers but no tubs, small balconies and attractive furnishings make up for this shortcoming. The deluxe rooms, which have refrigerators and microwaves, are more spacious. For more space and the best views, opt for one of the "premier rooms," which have large windows and extra-comfy beds (ask for no. 331, which has a view of Mount Rainier). The upgraded rooms are worth the extra money.

4140 Roosevelt Way NE, Seattle, WA 98105. www.universityinnseattle.com. ✆ **800/733-3855** or 206/632-5055. Fax 206/547-4937. 102 units. $139–$229 double. Call or check website for seasonal specials. Rates include full breakfast. Children 18 and under stay free in parent's room. AE, DC, DISC, MC, V. Parking $10. Pets accepted ($20 per night). **Amenities:** Restaurant; concierge; access to exercise room at nearby sister hotel; small outdoor pool. *In room:* A/C, TV, hair dryer, free Wi-Fi.

Watertown ★★ Watertown is one of Seattle's U District entries in the hip boutique-hotel market. Only blocks from the University of Washington, this beautifully designed hotel is definitely well placed for a trendy clientele. If you're into contemporary styling, you'll love it, even if you aren't in town on university business. Platform beds, streamlined built-ins, desks with frosted-glass tops and ergonomic chairs, and huge full-length mirrors are just a few of the interesting features in the guest rooms.

4242 Roosevelt Way NE, Seattle, WA 98105. www.watertownseattle.com. ✆ **866/944-4242** or 206/826-4242. Fax 206/315-4242. 100 units. Summer $149–$199 double, $209–$259 suite; other months $119–$179 double; $179–$239 suite. Rates include full breakfast. Children 17 and under stay free in parent's room. AE, DC, DISC, MC, V. Parking $10. **Amenities:** Bikes; concierge; exercise room. *In room:* A/C, TV, CD player, fridge, hair dryer, free Wi-Fi.

Inexpensive

The College Inn Built in 1909 for the Alaska-Yukon Exposition, this Tudor Revival building has loads of character and a great location right across the street from the University of Washington campus. That said, I really only recommend the College Inn for young travelers. All its rooms have shared bathrooms, and the inn itself, as with many budget accommodations in Europe, is up a couple of steep flights of stairs. The decor is a bit funky, but guests don't seem to mind. Rooms range from tiny to spacious, and all have wash basins. Parking can be a problem, so this is a good bet for anyone traveling without a car; there's good bus service into downtown.

4000 University Way NE, Seattle, WA 98105. www.collegeinnseattle.com. ✆ **206/633-4441.** Fax 206/547-1335. 27 units, all with shared bathroom. Summer $85–$105 double; other months $75–$95 double. Rates include continental breakfast. MC, V. **Amenities:** Restaurant, lounge; free Internet. *In room:* Free Wi-Fi.

NEAR SEA-TAC AIRPORT

The airport is 30 to 45 minutes south of downtown by car (depending on the traffic) or 40 minutes on the Central Link light-rail line. Adjacent to the airport are numerous conference, business, and budget hotels.

Best For: Anyone arriving late or leaving especially early in the morning.

Drawbacks: There's little to recommend this area besides its proximity to the airport.

Moderate

Cedarbrook Lodge ★★ In most cases, I wouldn't choose to stay at an airport-area hotel for any other reason than convenience or price, but Cedarbrook Lodge is such a quintessentially northwestern luxury lodge that it is worth considering, especially if you have a car with you. While the lodge is barely a half-mile from the airport, the woodsy, garden setting makes it seems as if it were out in the country. Inside, you'll find contemporary lodge styling. Guest rooms have lots of exposed wood, yet are modern in their design, and the floor-to-ceiling windows take in views of the manicured grounds. A short walking path meanders through the grounds, which include a wetland area. Other pluses here include a lower room tax, free parking, and a free shuttle to the nearby light-rail station.

18525 36th Ave. S., Seattle, WA 98188. www.cedarbrooklodge.com. ✆ **877/515-2176** or 206/901-9268. Fax 206/901-9269. 110 units. $159–$249 double. Call or check website for seasonal specials. Rates include continental breakfast. Children 17 and under stay free in parent's room. AE, DC, DISC, MC, V. Pets accepted ($50 fee). Free parking. **Amenities:** Restaurant, lounge; free airport transfers; exercise room; room service. *In room:* A/C, TV, hair dryer, MP3 docking station, free Wi-Fi.

Seattle Airport Marriott ★ ☺ With a steamy atrium garden in which you'll find plenty of tropical plants, a swimming pool, and two whirlpool tubs, this resortlike hotel is an excellent choice if you're visiting during the rainy season. There are even waterfalls and totem poles for that Northwest outdoorsy feeling; best of all, it's always sunny and warm in here (which is more than you can say for the real Northwest outdoors). Guest rooms are attractively furnished and comfortable, with good beds and great pillows. Ask for one of the rooms with a view of Mount Rainier.

3201 S. 176th St., Seattle, WA 98188. www.seattleairportmarriott.com. ✆ **800/314-0925** or 206/241-2000. Fax 206/248-0789. 459 units. Summer $129–$239 double; other months $99–$219 double. Children 18 and under stay free in parent's room. AE, DC, DISC, MC, V. Valet parking $24; self-parking $19. **Amenities:** 2 restaurants, lounge; free airport transfers; concierge; executive-level rooms; exercise room and access to nearby health club; 2 Jacuzzis; indoor atrium pool; room service; sauna. *In room:* A/C, TV, hair dryer, MP3 docking station, Wi-Fi ($13/day).

THE EASTSIDE

The Eastside (a reference its location on the east side of Lake Washington) is Seattle's main high-tech suburb and comprises the cities of Bellevue, Kirkland, Issaquah, and Redmond. Two of the most luxurious hotels in the metropolitan area are here on this side of the lake.

Best For: Travelers out this way on business. An Eastside hotel may be more convenient than one in downtown Seattle.

Drawbacks: During rush hour, the commute between Seattle and the eastside can be 45 minutes or more. If it isn't rush hour, you can usually get from the Eastside to downtown in about 20 minutes via the I-90 or Wash. 520 floating bridges.

Expensive

Woodmark Hotel, Yacht Club & Spa on Lake Washington ★★★ This resortlike hotel is so luxurious and in such a beautiful setting that it is the metro area's premier waterfront lodging—and well worth the 20-minute drive from downtown Seattle. Surrounded by a luxury residential community, the Woodmark has the feel of a beach resort and looks out over the very same waters that Bill Gates sees from his nearby Xanadu. There are plenty of lakeview rooms here, although you will pay a premium for them. For less expensive lodging, try the marina-view rooms. In addition to the hotel's dining room, several other restaurants are in the area. With advance reservations, guests can go out for a 2-hour cruise on the hotel's restored 1956 Chris-Craft boat. Beautiful surroundings, luxurious rooms, and boat tours all add up to one of Seattle's best hotel values.

1200 Carillon Point, Kirkland, WA 98033. www.thewoodmark.com. ✆ **800/822-3700** or 425/822-3700. Fax 425/822-3699. 100 units. $200–$300 double, $250–$420 suite. Call or check website for seasonal specials. Children 17 and under stay free in parent's room. AE, DC, MC, V. Valet parking $15; self-parking $12. Pets accepted ($25 fee). **Amenities:** 2 restaurants, 2 lounges; babysitting; concierge; exercise room and access to nearby health club; room service; full-service spa; watersports equipment/rentals. *In room:* A/C, TV, hair dryer, minibar, free Wi-Fi.

Moderate

Hotel Bellevue ★★★ 🎁 In its gardens, architecture, and interior design, this hotel epitomizes contemporary Northwest style. Beautiful landscaping surrounds the entrance, and works of contemporary art are found throughout the public areas. The hotel is affiliated with a state-of-the-art health club that has everything from an indoor running track and three pools to indoor squash and outdoor tennis courts (there's also a full-service spa). But even if you aren't into aerobic workouts, this hotel has much to offer. You won't find more elegant rooms anywhere in the Seattle area. Accommodations are plush, with the high-ceilinged club rooms among my favorites; these have floor-to-ceiling walls of glass, massive draperies, and private patios facing a garden. European fabrics are everywhere, giving rooms a romantic feel. Bathrooms are resplendent in granite and glass, and most have whirlpool tubs.

11200 SE Sixth St., Bellevue, WA 98004. www.thehotelbellevue.com. ✆ **800/579-1110** or 425/454-4424. Fax 425/688-3197. 67 units. Summer $179–$279 double, $645–$1,545 suite; other months $149–$259 double; $645–$1,545 suite. Children 17 and under stay free in parent's room. AE, DC, DISC, MC, V. Valet parking $12. Pets accepted ($30 fee). **Amenities:** 3 restaurants, lounge; babysitting; children's programs; concierge; expansive health club w/Jacuzzis, saunas, and steam rooms; 2 indoor pools and 1 outdoor pool; room service; full-service spa; 10 tennis courts. *In room:* A/C, TV, CD player, hair dryer, minibar, free Wi-Fi.

Inexpensive

Extended StayAmerica Seattle–Bellevue Just off I-405 near downtown Bellevue, this modern off-ramp motel caters primarily to long-term guests. To this end, the rooms are all large and have kitchenettes. However, you won't get daily maid service unless you are staying only a few days and pay extra for it. If you stay for a week, rates drop considerably.

11400 Main St., Bellevue, WA 98004. www.extendedstay.com. ✆ **800/804-3724** or 425/453-8186. Fax 425/453-8178. 148 units. Summer $85–$115 double; other months $70–$105 double. Children 17 and under stay free in parent's room. AE, DC, DISC, MC, V. Free parking. Pets accepted ($25 per day, $150 maximum). *In room:* A/C, TV, kitchen, Wi-Fi ($5/stay).

La Quinta Inn & Suites Bellevue/Kirkland This budget chain hotel is just across the Wash. 520 floating bridge (Evergreen Point Bridge), and while traffic is heavy during rush hour, the location is surprisingly convenient. If traffic is light, you're only 15 minutes from downtown or the Seattle Center area. Guest rooms are basic but serviceable. Pluses include an outdoor pool, an exercise room, and a couple of casual restaurants right next door.

10530 NE Northup Way, Kirkland, WA 98033. www.lq.com. ✆ **800/753-3757** or 425/828-6585. Fax 425/822-8722. 121 units. Summer $95–$145 double, $135–$155 suite; other months $82–$132 double, $122–$142 suite. Rates include continental breakfast. Children 17 and under stay free in parent's room. AE, DC, DISC, MC, V. Free parking. Pets accepted (no fee). **Amenities:** Exercise room; seasonal outdoor pool; Wi-Fi. *In room:* A/C, TV, hair dryer, free Internet.

Red Lion Hotel Bellevue ★ ☺ The Red Lion Hotel Bellevue is one of the few hotels in the Seattle area that captures the feel of the Northwest in its design and landscaping. The sprawling two-story property is roofed with cedar-shake shingles, while the grounds are lushly planted with rhododendrons, ferns, azaleas, and fir trees. Guest rooms here are quite sophisticated and upscale, with elegant country French furnishings and decor. Parents take note: Kids 10 and under eat free in this hotel's restaurant.

11211 Main St., Bellevue, WA 98004. www.redlion.com. ✆ **800/733-5466** or 425/455-5240. Fax 425/455-0654. 181 units. $84–$149 double. Children 17 and under stay free in parent's room. AE, DC, DISC, MC, V. Free parking. Pets accepted ($20 fee). **Amenities:** Restaurant, lounge; exercise room and access to nearby health club; seasonal outdoor pool; room service. *In room:* A/C, TV, fridge, hair dryer, MP3 docking station, free Wi-Fi.

BAINBRIDGE ISLAND

Bainbridge Island is an idyllic bedroom community a 30-minute ferry ride from Seattle, and within a mile of the ferry landing, there are several lodging options. The ease of the commute makes island inns and hotels eminently recommendable. Riding the ferry between city and island captures the essence of the Seattle experience.

Best For: Those who want to explore the city, but who don't want to deal with noisy urban nights.

Drawbacks: The lodgings listed are within a short taxi or bus ride of the ferry terminal. However, you'll need to factor in the cost and the time requirements of the ferry commute. If you're exploring by car, it adds up.

Moderate

Best Western Plus Bainbridge Island Suites ★ ☺ This is an all-suites hotel—a bit removed from downtown Bainbridge Island, but still within walking distance of the ferry. Rooms are primarily large suites with kitchenettes and are ideal for trips with the family or for longer stays. By staying here, you get loads more space than you would in Seattle, and even when you add in the cost of taking the ferry, rates are still very reasonable.

350 NE High School Rd., Bainbridge Island, WA 98110. www.bestwestern.com/bainbridgeislandsuites. ✆ **866/396-9666** or 206/855-9666. Fax 206/855-9790. 51 units. $130–$170 double. Rates include continental breakfast. Children 12 and under stay free in parent's room. AE, DC, DISC, MC, V. Free parking. Pets accepted ($20 per night). **Amenities:** Concierge; exercise room. *In room:* A/C, TV, fridge, hair dryer, free Wi-Fi.

The Eagle Harbor Inn ★ This inn, a block from the water in downtown Bainbridge Island, is the prettiest and most convenient inn on the island. You can easily walk between the inn and the ferry, and across the street are a waterfront trail, a coffeehouse, a tavern, and a marina. This corner of town is quintessentially Bainbridge Island. With its colorful facade, varied rooflines, and residential feel, the Eagle Harbor Inn conjures up inns in a small town in Tuscany. Guest rooms, which vary in size and are done in a luxurious contemporary island-cottage style, are built around a small, attractively landscaped courtyard that is a pleasant place to sit in the sun with a cup of coffee. Keep in mind that this place is geared toward self-sufficient travelers, as there is no front desk—it feels more like renting an apartment than staying in a hotel.

291 Madison Ave. S. (P.O. Box 10386), Bainbridge Island, WA 98110. www.theeagleharborinn.com. ✆ **206/842-1446.** Fax 206/780-1715. 8 units. $149–$199 double; $169–$179 suite; $349–$499 town house. Call or check website for seasonal specials. AE, MC, V. Free parking. *In room:* A/C, TV, free Internet (some units), free Wi-Fi (some units).

PRACTICAL INFORMATION

The Big Picture

As one of the high-tech capitals of North America, Seattle is packed with high-end corporate business hotels. These hotels tend to be quite expensive, and often, despite being packed with high-tech features, the rooms can be depressingly small. Likewise, the city's few historic hotels, situated around downtown and the Pioneer Square neighborhood, also tend to have small rooms. In other words, unless you plan to pay top dollar (and sometimes even if you do pay top dollar), you're going to be a bit cramped. If you need plenty of space and don't want to pay a fortune for it, head out from downtown to some of the outlying neighborhoods.

Despite all the water in and around Seattle, the city has only a handful of waterfront hotels, and of these, only two are right on the water. **The Edgewater** is in Seattle proper, while the **Woodmark** is on the east side of Lake Washington in Kirkland. For the quintessential Seattle experience, I highly recommend staying at one of the hotels. Just be sure to plan far in advance; these places tend to be very popular, especially in the summer.

Seattle is a city of diverse neighborhoods, many of which have fine B&Bs. Often less expensive than downtown hotels, B&Bs provide an opportunity to see what life is like for the locals. I've listed some of my favorites, but to find other good options, contact the **Seattle Bed & Breakfast Association** (✆ **206/547-1020;** www.lodginginseattle.com). Capitol Hill has the largest concentration of B&Bs and among my favorite neighborhood inns are the **Gaslight Inn, Bacon Mansion,** and the **Shafer Baillie Mansion.** These inns offer both historic settings and proximity to some of the city's best restaurants.

A few hotels include breakfast in their rates; others provide complimentary breakfast only on certain deluxe floors. All Seattle hotels offer nonsmoking rooms, while most bed-and-breakfast inns and many new business hotels are exclusively nonsmoking. The majority of hotels, but few inns, offer wheelchair-accessible rooms.

Be sure to make reservations as far in advance as possible, especially if you plan to visit during Seafair or another major festival. See "Seattle Calendar of Events" (p. 22) for the dates of all the big festivals.

Getting the Best Deal

If you're looking to save money, you're likely going to have to visit in the rainy season (Oct–Apr), when rates are sometimes half of what they are in summer; or book a room somewhere other than downtown Seattle. If you must stay downtown, or prefer to visit during the glorious summer weather instead of during the dreary gray of the rainy season, be sure to compare weekend rates (Fri, Sat, Sun) with weekday rates. Downtown hotels often charge less on weekends. Budget hotels, on the other hand, generally charge more on weekends.

My favorite places to look for good values are near Seattle Center, on the shores of Lake Union, and in the University District. Seattle Center–area hotels have the convenience of being connected to downtown Seattle by the monorail, while Lake Union hotels have access to downtown via streetcar. The University District is a bit less convenient to downtown but is accessible by bus. If you long for that quintessential waterview room but don't want to blow your vacation budget, consider Lake Union's **Courtyard, Residence Inn,** or **Silver Cloud Inn.**

When planning your trip, you might also want to check with **Seattle Super Saver** (✆ **866/285-2535;** www.seattlesupersaver.com), a reservations service operated by Seattle's Convention and Visitors Bureau. Rates are comparable to what you might find at such sites as Orbitz, Expedia, Hotwire, or Priceline.

Reservation Services

If you want to get a great deal on a great hotel (don't we all?), get in touch with Sheri Doyle at **Pacific Northwest Journeys** (✆ **800/935-9730** or 206/935-9730; www.pnwjourneys.com). This company specializes in itinerary planning and also offers a reservations service. The charge is $45 per reservation, but you can usually make that up in savings on just a 2-night stay; if you're going to be in town for longer than that, you'll definitely save money. Last-minute reservations are often possible, too. A consultation service is also available for people who would like assistance with itinerary planning. **A Pacific Reservation Service** (✆ **800/684-2932** or 206/439-7677; www.seattlebedandbreakfast.com) is a reservations service that books rooms at dozens of accommodations in the Seattle area. A wide range of rates is available.

WHERE TO EAT

5

That Pike Place Market, with its produce stalls, bakeries, gourmet food shops, and restaurants, is one of Seattle's top attractions is a good indicator of how seriously this city takes food. The market overflows with a bounty of wild-caught salmon, Dungeness crabs, local oysters, artisanal cheeses, Northwest berries, organic vegetables, wild mushrooms, and Washington wines. You'll find this plethora of produce on restaurant menus all around the city, which is what makes dining out in Seattle such a memorable experience. That salmon you photographed in the market in the morning might be your entree at dinner.

---

best BETS FOR EATING

- **Best Taste of Seattle: Dahlia Lounge:** You can't say that you've "done" Seattle if you haven't eaten at a Tom Douglas restaurant, and for my money, Dahlia Lounge is the place to go if you're going to dine at only one. A dinner of crab cakes followed by coconut-cream pie captures the absolute essence of this place. See p. 83.
- **Best for Families: Ivar's Salmon House** resembles a Native American longhouse and is filled with cool stuff sure to fascinate kids. In sunny weather, the waterfront deck has a great view of Lake Union and the Seattle skyline. See p. 100.
- **Best Value:** Of course you could shell out big bucks to dine at Salty's on Alki Beach (see below), but you can get the same view at a fraction of the cost at the adjacent **Alki Crab & Fish Co.** Okay, so the menu is pretty limited, but the fish and chips are excellent, and that view—wow! See p. 106.
- **Best Splurge:** The Seattle area's best splurge restaurant is actually a 30-minute drive away. **The Herbfarm,** in Woodinville—the Seattle-area's wine country—puts on lavish nine-course dinners that celebrate fresh Northwest flavors. See p. 292, in chapter 10.

For good value eats with a million dollar view, head for Alki Crab & Fish Co.

PREVIOUS PAGE: Locally sourced food served in a gracious atmosphere is one of the hallmarks of Seattle dining at restaurants like Tilth.

- **Most Romantic:** There's no denying that Tuscany is one of the world's most romantic destinations, so it isn't surprising that **Volterra,** an Italian restaurant on a shady street in the historic Ballard neighborhood, is the perfect place for a romantic dinner. See p. 104.
- **Best Service: Canlis** is a Seattle tradition, the perfect place to close a big deal or celebrate a special occasion. When you want to feel pampered, this is the place to dine. See p. 90.
- **Best View:** Without a doubt, **SkyCity** has the best views in Seattle—360 degrees worth of them. Sure, it's expensive, but there's no place in town with views to rival these. See p. 88.
- **Best Northwest Cuisine:** At **Rover's,** Chef Thierry Rautureau combines his love of local ingredients with classic French training to produce a distinctive take on Northwest cuisine. See p. 99.

You might find yourself in need of a "lunar orbiter" at the top of the Space Needle, at SkyCity.

Alfresco All Summer Long in Seattle

Eight to nine months of rain and cloudy skies is a heavy price to pay for long summer days and sunsets that linger until almost 10pm. So can you blame Seattle's residents if they just won't go inside during the summer? The thought of eating indoors on a summer evening can be just too depressing to contemplate. If you happen to be here in the rain-free months (July, Aug, and Sept), and just don't want to eat indoors, here are some suggestions for alfresco meals.

If you got any closer to the water than the narrow deck at the **Six-Seven** (p. 74), you'd need a wet suit. No deck in Seattle has a better view. Want a million-dollar view for pennies? Take the water taxi to Alki Beach and have fish and chips on the patio at **Alki Crab & Fish Co.** (p. 106). You can get the same view and dine on more creative (and expensive) fare down the street at **Salty's on Alki** (p. 105). There's more high-end fish to be had with your views at **Ray's Boathouse/Ray's Cafe** (p. 103), a restaurant with a split personality and killer views. Keep an eye out for bald eagles.

If you don't have to have a view with your meal, try the shady courtyard patio at **Volterra** (p. 104), in the Ballard neighborhood. **Serafina** (p. 94), not far from the east shore of Lake Union, is another good Italian restaurant with a garden patio. There's still more alfresco Italian at **The Pink Door** (p. 81), Seattle's favorite "secret" Pike Place Market restaurant, which has a big deck with a big view. If you're more in the mood for an urban sidewalk-table experience, head to the **Virginia Inn** (p. 85) near Pike Place Market. For a thoroughly Pike Place Market experience, grab a table at **El Puerco Llorõn** (p. 82), an inexpensive Mexican place on the Pike Street Hill Climb.

- **Best Steaks: Metropolitan Grill** in downtown Seattle, serves corn-fed, aged beef grilled over mesquite charcoal. Steaks just don't get any better than this. See p. 78.
- **Best Cured Meats:** At **Salumi,** you'll stand in line on the sidewalk, then squeeze your way into this Pioneer Square hole-in-the-wall, where you'll savor the finest, freshest artisan-made salami in the Northwest. See p. 86.
- **Best Sushi:** If the sight of so much fresh fish in Pike Place Market has you craving sushi, then head up to the north end of Belltown to **Shiro's Sushi Restaurant.** All the Japanese businessmen here should give you a clue that this place is the real deal. See p. 85.
- **Best Waterfront Dining:** The best waterfront dining experience is in the Edgewater hotel. **Six-Seven** can claim not only superb food, but also cool decor, a fabulous deck, and one of the best views from any restaurant in the city. See p. 74. The Northwest produces an astonishing variety of oysters, and locals are almost as obsessive about their bivalves as they are about coffee and beer. For the best selection, head to **Elliott's Oyster House.** See p. 75.

THE WATERFRONT

Expensive

Six-Seven ★★ NEW AMERICAN This stylish waterfront restaurant in the Edgewater hotel has more than just superb food to recommend it; the views of Elliott Bay and the Olympic Mountains are also a feast for the eyes. Throw in the restaurant's distinctive "robo-trees," which are a curious blend of rustic and high-tech, and you have an all around unforgettable dining experience. If the weather is warm, try to get a seat on the narrow little deck; it's the best waterfront deck in Seattle. The menu changes regularly, so you never know what to expect, but the kitchen always does a great job with both halibut and salmon. Entrees are available in economical half portions.

The Edgewater, Pier 67, 2411 Alaskan Way. ✆ **206/269-4575.** www.edgewaterhotel.com. Reservations recommended. Main courses $8–$19 lunch, $29–$48 dinner. AE, DC, DISC, MC, V. Sun–Thurs 6:30am–9pm; Fri–Sat 6:30am–10pm.

Moderate

Anthony's Pier 66 and Bell Street Diner ★ SEAFOOD The Anthony's chain has several outposts around the Seattle area, but this complex is the most convenient and versatile. It has not only an upper-end, stylish seafood restaurant with good waterfront views, but also a moderately priced casual restaurant and a walk-up counter. The bold contemporary styling and abundance of art glass set Anthony's apart from most waterfront restaurants. The upscale crowd heads upstairs for steaks and creative seafood dishes, while the more cost-conscious stay downstairs at the Bell Street Diner, where meals are easier on the wallet. For the higher prices, you get better

Price Categories

Prices are for a three-course dinner (alcoholic beverages and tip not included).

Very Expensive	$80 and up
Expensive	$40–$79
Moderate	$20–$39
Inexpensive	Under $20

views. In summer, the decks are the place to be. You can save money with the $20 "Sunset Dinners" that are served Monday through Friday between 3 and 6pm.

2201 Alaskan Way. ✆ **206/448-6688.** www.anthonys.com. Reservations recommended at Pier 66, not taken at Bell Street Diner. Pier 66 main courses $19–$47; Bell Street Diner main courses $11–$36. AE, DISC, MC, V. Pier 66 Mon–Thurs 5–9:30pm; Fri–Sat 5–10pm; Sun 5–9pm. Bell Street Diner Mon–Thurs 11am–10pm; Fri–Sat 11am–10:30pm; Sun 11am–9pm.

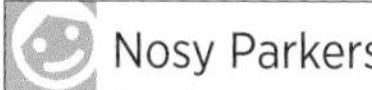

Nosy Parkers

Many waterfront restaurants offer free or validated parking. When you make a reservation, be sure to ask where to park.

Elliott's Oyster House ★★ SEAFOOD While most of its neighbors are content to coast along on tourist business, Elliott's actually aims to keep the locals happy by serving some of the best seafood in Seattle. Although the restaurant is right on the waterfront, the view isn't that great, which, I think, is partly why the food is good: Elliott's tries a little harder. Salmon and Dungeness crab are prepared several different ways and are always a good bet here. However, the oyster bar, which can have more than 25 varieties, is the real reason to eat here. This is definitely the place to get to know your Northwest oysters. Monday through Friday from 3 to 6pm, they have an "oyster happy hour"; arrive early to get the best price.

Pier 56, 1201 Alaskan Way. ✆ **206/623-4340.** www.elliottsoysterhouse.com. Reservations recommended. Main courses $11–$19 lunch, $16–$42 dinner. AE, DISC, MC, V. Sun–Thurs 11am–10pm; Fri–Sat 11am–11pm.

Inexpensive

The Old Spaghetti Factory ☺ ITALIAN The Old Spaghetti Factory is a chain restaurant, which I don't normally recommend, but kids wandering the waterfront with their parents may be relieved to know that here at this palace of pasta, they won't have to try raw oysters, clam chowder, or any of that other icky stuff grown-ups eat at seafood restaurants. Anyone who's been to an Old Spaghetti Factory knows what to expect. If you haven't dined at one of the antiques-filled restaurants, I have two words for you—cheap pasta—and two other words for the kids—yummy noodles. Enough said? You'll find this place across from Pier 70 at the north end of the waterfront.

2801 Elliott Ave. ✆ **206/441-7724.** www.osf.com. Reservations not accepted. Main courses $8–$13. AE, DISC, MC, V. 1st Mon in July to Labor Day Mon–Thurs 11:30am–10pm, Fri 11:30am–10:30pm, Sat noon–10:30pm, Sun noon–9:30pm; Labor Day to 1st Mon in July Mon–Thurs 11:30am–2pm and 4:30–9:30pm, Fri 11:30am–2pm and 4:30–10:30pm, Sat noon–10:30pm, Sun noon–9:30pm.

DOWNTOWN

Very Expensive

The Georgian ★★★ 📷 CONTINENTAL/NORTHWEST The Georgian is as grand as they come, and if you're looking for haute cuisine, palatial surroundings, and superb service, no other restaurant in Seattle comes close. This is by far the most traditional and formal restaurant in the city. For the full Georgian experience, I recommend opting for the three-course or the seven-course dinner. The latter might include seared foie gras with pressed cherries, oysters with caviar and horseradish foam, seared scallops with truffle-bacon butter sauce,

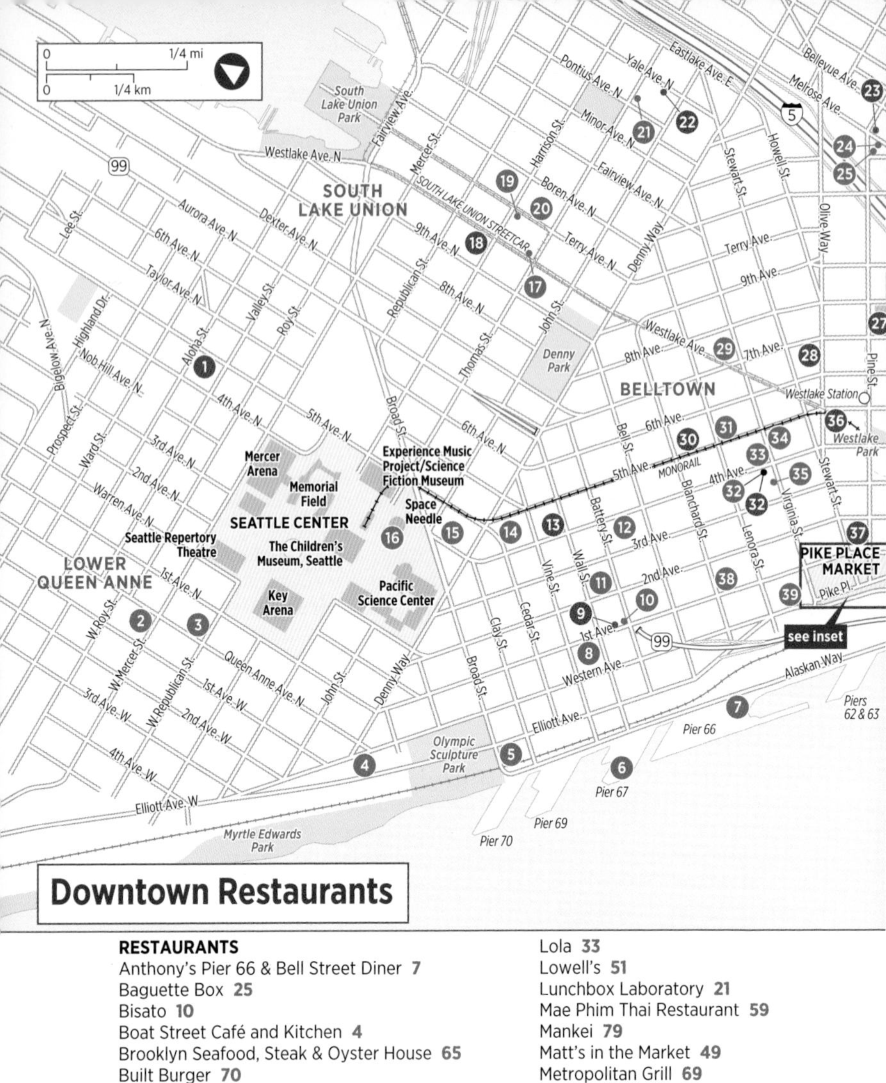

Downtown Restaurants

RESTAURANTS

Anthony's Pier 66 & Bell Street Diner **7**
Baguette Box **25**
Bisato **10**
Boat Street Café and Kitchen **4**
Brooklyn Seafood, Steak & Oyster House **65**
Built Burger **70**
Café Champagne **46**
Cuoco **20**
Dahlia Lounge **32**
Dick's **3**
El Gaucho **8**
El Puerco Lloron **54**
Elliott's Oyster House **62**
Elysian Fields **76**
Etta's Seafood **39**
Flying Fish **17**
The Georgian **67**
Icon Grill **34**
Il Bistro **56**
Jade Garden Restaurant **81**
Le Pichet **41**
Lecosho **63**
Lola **33**
Lowell's **51**
Lunchbox Laboratory **21**
Mae Phim Thai Restaurant **59**
Mankei **79**
Matt's in the Market **49**
Metropolitan Grill **69**
Mistral Kitchen **29**
The Old Spaghetti Factory **5**
Palace Kitchen **31**
Pike Place Chowder **48**
The Pink Door **42**
Portage Bay Café **19**
Purple Café and Wine Bar **66**
Salumi **75**
Samurai Noodles **78**
Serious Pie **35**
Shiro's Sushi Restaurant **11**
Sitka & Spruce **24**
Six-Seven Restaurant & Lounge **6**
SkyCity at the Needle **16**
Sport Restaurant & Bar **15**
Spur Gastropub **38**

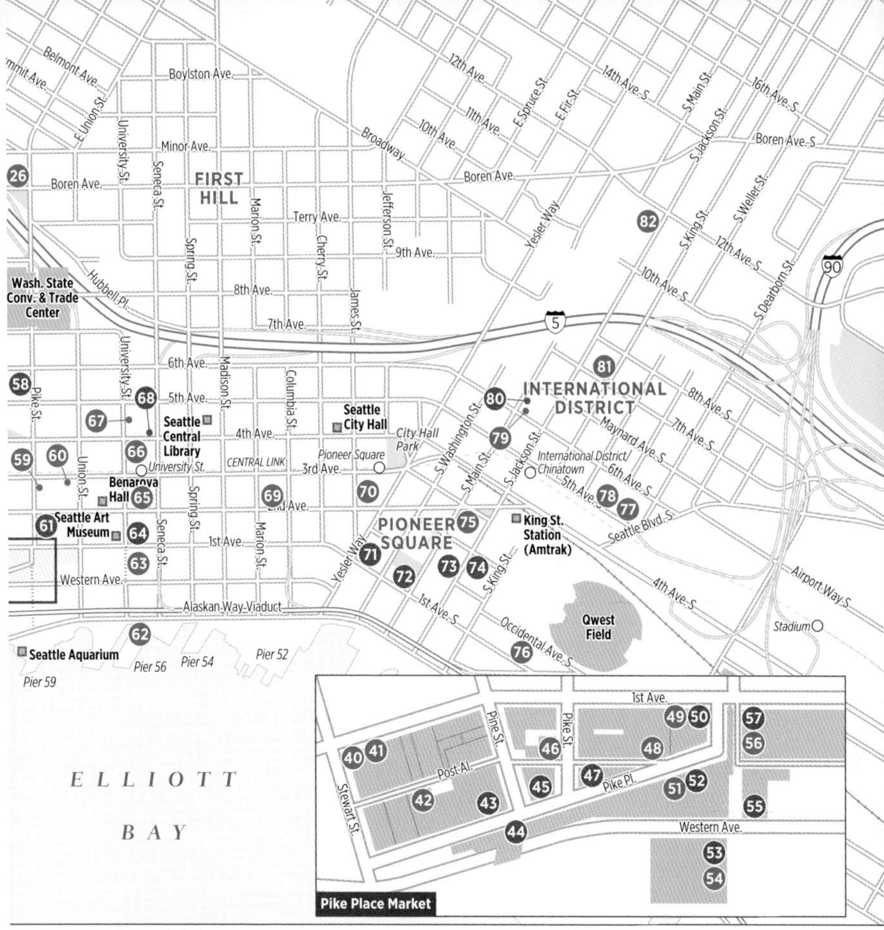

Tamarind Tree **82**
Tango Restaurant & Lounge **26**
Tilikum Place Café **14**
Ting Momo **20**
Toulouse Petit **2**
Two Bells Bar & Grill **12**
Uwajimaya **77**
Virginia Inn **40**
Wild Ginger Asian Restaurant & Satay Bar **60**

COFFEE, TEA, BAKERIES & PASTRY SHOPS
Ancient Grounds **64**
Bauhaus Books & Coffee **23**
Beecher's Handmade Cheese **45**
Belle Epicurean **68**
Bottega Italiana **57**
Caffe Ladro **27**
Caffe Senso Unico **28**
Caffe Umbria **73**
Caffe Vita **1**
Chocolate Box **37**
City Fish Co. **44**
The Confectional **47**
Cow Chip Cookies **61, 71**
Crumpet Shop **50**
Dahlia Bakery **32**
Dahlia Workshop **18**
Daily Dozen Doughnut Company **57**
DeLaurenti **57**
Espresso Vivace Alley 24 **22**
Grand Central Baking Company **72**
Le Panier **43**
Local Color **45**
Macrina **9**
Monorail Espresso **58**
Panama Hotel Tea & Coffee House **80**
Piroshky, Piroshky **43**
Procopio **53**
Spanish Table **55**
Starbucks **43**
Top Pot Doughnuts **30**
Uli's Famous Sausage **52**
Uptown Espresso **13**
Westlake Center **37**
Zeitgeist Art/Coffee **74**

Dungeness crab bisque, bacon-wrapped pheasant with black trumpet mushrooms, a local cheese served with huckleberries, and a trio of small cakes. The wine list is superb, and service is so attentive that you will likely feel as though yours is the only table in the restaurant.

The Fairmont Olympic Hotel, 411 University St. ✆ **206/621-7889.** www.fairmont.com/seattle. Reservations highly recommended. Main courses $12–$18 lunch, $30–$46 dinner; 3-course prix-fixe menu $49 ($69 with wine); 7-course tasting menu $90 ($145 with wine). AE, DC, DISC, MC, V. Mon 6:30–11am and 11:30am–2:30pm; Tues–Fri 6:30–11am, 11:30am–2:30pm and 5:30–10pm (Fri until 10:30pm); Sat 7am–2:30pm and 5:30–10:30pm; Sun 7am–2:30pm.

Expensive

The Brooklyn Seafood, Steak & Oyster House ★ SEAFOOD This classic seafood restaurant in the middle of the financial district looks as if it's been here since the Great Seattle Fire and is housed in one of the city's oldest buildings. The specialty is oysters, with close to a dozen different types piled up at the oyster bar on any given night. Other tempting appetizers range from a cilantro-battered calamari steak to Dungeness crab cakes with wasabi aioli. The wild salmon (roasted on a slab of alder wood) is a Northwest classic and is your best bet if you aren't having oysters.

1212 Second Ave. ✆ **206/224-7000.** www.thebrooklyn.com. Reservations recommended. Main courses $13–$16 lunch, $22–$42 dinner. AE, DC, DISC, MC, V. Mon–Thurs 11am–3pm and 5–10pm; Fri 11am–3pm and 5–10:30pm; Sat 4:30–10:30pm; Sun 4–10pm.

Lecōsho ★★ NEW AMERICAN Matt Janke, who for many years ran Matt's in the Market, has long been one of my favorite Seattle chefs, and here at his latest restaurant, on the pretty Harbor Steps, he continues to impress me with his simple yet creative cuisine. On a recent visit, I had the best grilled octopus I've had since the first time I had it decades ago in Greece. A house-made sausage, flavored with caraway rather than fennel, and served atop creamy lentils was equally delicious. The name Lecōsho means pig in the Chinook jargon once used by the region's Native Americans, and you'll find plenty of pork dishes on the menu, including pork belly stuffed with pork tenderloin and served with white beans and turnips, a braised pork belly terrine, and pork chops with potato-parsnip puree and sherry-braised shallots. Happy hour features lots of creative dishes, too.

89 University St. ✆ **206/623-2101.** www.lecosho.com. Reservations recommended. Main courses $10–$16 lunch, $17–$32 dinner. AE, DISC, MC, V. Mon–Thurs 11am–3pm and 5–10pm; Fri–Sat 11am–3pm and 5–10pm; Sun 5–10pm.

Metropolitan Grill ★ STEAK Fronted by massive granite columns that make it look more like a bank than a restaurant, the Metropolitan Grill is a traditional steakhouse that attracts a well-heeled clientele, primarily men in suits. If you have any doubt about how seriously this place takes beef, just steal a glance at the display case full of beef just inside the front door; the pieces of meat are displayed as if they were rare jewels. Perfectly cooked dry-aged steaks are the primary attraction; a baked potato and a pile of thick-cut onion rings complete the ultimate carnivore's dinner. Financial matters are a frequent topic of discussion here, and the bar even has a "Guess the Dow" contest. I hope you sold high, as it'll take some capital gains to finance a dinner for two here.

820 Second Ave. ✆ **206/624-3287.** www.themetropolitangrill.com. Reservations recommended. Main courses $12–$60 at lunch, $20–$75 at dinner. AE, DISC, MC, V. Mon–Thurs 11am–3pm and 5–10pm; Fri 11am–3pm and 5–10:30pm; Sat 4–11pm; Sun 4–9pm.

family-friendly RESTAURANTS

Ivar's Salmon House (p. 100) is built to resemble a Northwest Coast Native American longhouse and is filled with artifacts that kids find fascinating. If they get restless, they can go out to the floating patio and watch the boats passing by.

At a marina overlooking Elliott Bay and downtown Seattle, economical **Maggie Bluffs Marina Grill** (p. 91) has food the kids will enjoy and provides crayons to keep them occupied while they wait. Before or after a meal, you can take a free boat ride across the marina to an observation deck atop the breakwater.

The Old Spaghetti Factory (p. 75) may be part of a chain, but with cheap food, a convenient location across the street from the waterfront, and loads of kid-friendly noodle dishes, this place is a good bet when you've worked up an appetite walking the length of the Seattle waterfront.

If you've got a young sports fan in your family, don't miss **Sport Restaurant & Bar** (p. 89), across the street from the Space Needle. If you aren't too hungry to wait, try to get one of the booths that has its own private wall-hung TV. You'll be so close to the on-screen action, you'll be able to make the calls before the refs do.

Moderate

Purple Café and Wine Bar ★ AMERICAN REGIONAL Seattleites love this big, loud wine bar near Benaroya Hall and the Seattle Art Museum. The beautiful bi-level dining room has tall walls of glass that let in lots of precious light and let diners see and be seen. However, the restaurant's real centerpiece is its curving staircase that wraps around a towering column of wine bottles. The menu is almost intimidatingly long, and everything sounds so good that you won't know where to start or finish. If you have a hard time making decisions, just start ordering little bites off the tapas-style tasting menu. Portions are tiny, so you can sample lots of different flavors—maybe some beef carpaccio with a quail egg and truffle oil, lamb chili with polenta croutons, Gorgonzola-stuffed dates, or country-style pâté.

1225 Fourth Ave. ✆ **206/829-2280.** www.thepurplecafe.com. Reservations recommended. Small plates $3–$14, main courses $12–$28. AE, DISC, MC, V. Mon–Thurs 11am–11pm; Fri 11am–midnight; Sat noon–midnight; Sun noon–11pm.

Wild Ginger ★★ PAN-ASIAN This Pan-Asian restaurant has long been a Seattle favorite, and because it's across the street from Benaroya Hall, it's perfect for a pre-symphony dinner. I like to pull up a stool at the large satay bar and watch the cooks grill little skewers of everything from chicken to scallops to prawns to lamb. Every skewer is served with a small cube of sticky rice and pickled cucumber; order three or four satay sticks and you have yourself a meal. Of course, you can also sit at a table and have a more traditional dinner. The Panang beef curry (prime rib-eye steak in pungent curry sauce of cardamom, coconut milk, Thai basil, and peanuts) is one of my favorites, but there are loads of good dishes. The restaurant is upstairs from the **Triple Door,** a classy live-music club; be sure to check the performance schedule. There's a second Wild Ginger, in Bellevue at 11020 NE Sixth St., Ste. 90 (✆ **425/495-8889**).

1401 Third Ave. ✆ **206/623-4450.** www.wildginger.net. Reservations recommended. Satay sticks $3.50–$6.50; main courses $9–$20 lunch, $13–$30 dinner. AE, DISC, MC, V. Mon–Fri 11:30am–3pm and 5–11pm; Sat 11:30am–3pm and 4:30pm–11pm; Sun noon–3pm and 4–11pm.

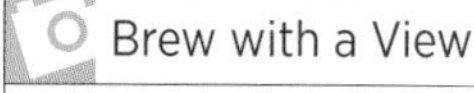

Brew with a View

With a Starbucks on every corner, how special can a grande latte really be? Well, at this particular Seattle Starbucks, you get more than your money's worth. Up on the 40th floor of downtown's Columbia Center, at the corner of Fifth Avenue and Columbia Street, you can soak up the city views as you sip your espresso. Take the elevator to the 40th floor Sky Lobby. Want a better view? Head to the 73rd floor observation deck. **See p. 133 for details.**

Inexpensive

Mae Phim Thai Restaurant THAI Both my brother, who was born in Thailand, and my sister, who lived there for 12 years, love this restaurant. While the setting is as basic as it gets, the flavors are authentic and the prices are great. It's hard to go wrong here with any of the Thai classic dishes. Mae Phim is less than 2 blocks from Pike Place Market, but the tourist crowds rarely discover this great hole in the wall. That said, this place is immensely popular at lunch and usually has a line of locals out the door. Try coming for an early dinner to avoid the crowds.

213 Pike St. ✆ **206/623-7453.** www.maephimpike.com. Main courses $8–$16. Reservations not taken. MC, V. Daily 11am–9pm.

PIKE PLACE MARKET

Expensive

Il Bistro ★★ ITALIAN With the fishmongers and crowds of tourists, Pike Place Market might not seem like the place for a romantic candlelit dinner, but romantic dinners are what Il Bistro is all about. This basement trattoria takes Italian cooking very seriously, and in doing so also puts the Northwest's bountiful ingredients to good use. The menu includes such mouthwatering starters as calamari sautéed with fresh basil, garlic, vinegar, and tomatoes. Hundreds of loyal fans insist that Il Bistro's rack of lamb with red-wine reduction sauce is the best in Seattle, and I'd have to agree. The pasta here can also be a true delight. You'll find Il Bistro tucked away down the cobblestone alley beside the market information kiosk.

93A Pike St. (at First Ave.). ✆ **206/682-3049.** www.ilbistro.net. Reservations recommended. Main courses $17–$44. AE, DC, DISC, MC, V. Sun–Thurs 5:30–10pm; Fri–Sat 5:30–11pm; late-night menu until 1am.

Matt's in the Market ★ AMERICAN REGIONAL/FRENCH This casual gourmet restaurant boasts the best location in Pike Place Market. It's on the third floor of the Corner Market Building facing the big neon clock that is the quintessential symbol of the market. Not surprisingly, the menu at Matt's changes regularly, with an emphasis on fresh ingredients from the market stalls only steps away. Of course, the latest culinary trends are always well represented as well. Recent starters included foie gras–lardon sliders as well as pork belly served two ways (as pâté and as confit). The confit here, whether duck or pork, is always a good choice, as are lamb shanks if they're on the menu. There's also a good selection of reasonably priced wines.

Corner Market Building, 94 Pike St., Ste. 32. ✆ **206/467-7909.** www.mattsinthemarket.com. Reservations highly recommended. Main courses $13–$23 lunch, $24–$33 dinner. AE, MC, V. Mon–Sat 11:30am–2:30pm and 5:30–10pm.

Moderate

Cafe Campagne ★★ FRENCH This little cafe is an offshoot of the popular Campagne, a much more formal French restaurant, and though it's in the heart of the Pike Place Market neighborhood, it's a world away from the market madness. I like to duck in here for lunch and escape the crowds. What a relief—so civilized, so very French. Most people leave this dark, cozy place feeling that they've discovered some secret hideaway. The menu changes with the seasons, but the roast chicken is always on the menu and is a favorite of mine. The cafe also doubles as a wine bar.

1600 Post Alley. ✆ **206/728-2233.** www.campagnerestaurant.com. Reservations recommended. Main courses $13–$23 lunch, $15–$23 dinner. AE, DC, DISC, MC, V. Mon–Thurs 11am–10pm; Fri 11am–5pm and 5:30–11pm; Sat 8am–4pm and 5:30–11pm; Sun 8am–4pm and 5:30–10pm.

Etta's ★ SEAFOOD Seattle chef Tom Douglas's strictly seafood (well, almost) restaurant, Etta's, is smack in the middle of the Pike Place Market neighborhood and, of course, serves Douglas's signature crab cakes (crunchy on the outside, creamy on the inside), which are not to be missed (and if they're not on the menu, just ask). Don't ignore your side dishes, either; they can be exquisite and are usually enough to share around the table. In addition to the great seafood, the menu always has a few other fine options. Stylish contemporary decor sets the mood, making this place as popular with locals as it is with tourists.

2020 Western Ave. ✆ **206/443-6000.** www.tomdouglas.com. Reservations recommended. Main courses $10–$29 lunch, $14–$30 dinner. AE, DC, DISC, MC, V. Mon–Thurs 11:30am–9:30pm; Fri 11:30am–10pm; Sat 9am–3pm and 4–10pm; Sun 9am–3pm and 4–9pm.

Le Pichet ★★ FRENCH You would be hard pressed to find a more authentic French bistro in Seattle, and this is a city that seems to have a thing for French restaurants. The name is French for "pitcher" and refers to the traditional ceramic pitchers used for serving inexpensive French wines. This should clue you in to the casual nature of the place, the sort of spot where you can drop by any time of day, grab a stool at the bar, and have a light meal. The menu is rustic French, and almost everything is made fresh on the premises. With lots of small plates and appetizers, it's fun and easy to piece together a light meal of shareable dishes. I like the country-style pâté, which is served with honey and walnuts. On Sunday afternoons, there's live music. Le Pichet also operates Capitol Hill's **Café Presse,** 1117 12th Ave. (✆ **206/709-7674;** www.cafepresseseattle.com).

1933 First Ave. ✆ **206/256-1499.** www.lepichetseattle.com. Dinner reservations recommended. Small plates $6–$17; main courses $17–$19. DISC, MC, V. Daily 8am–midnight.

The Pink Door ★ ITALIAN/LATE-NIGHT Pike Place Market's better restaurants tend to be well hidden, and if I didn't tell you about this one, you'd probably never find it. There's no sign out front—only the pink door for which the restaurant is named (look for it between Stewart and Virginia). On the other side of the door, stairs lead to a cellarlike space, which is almost always empty on summer days when folks forsake it to dine on the deck with a view of Elliott Bay. What makes this place so popular is as much the fun atmosphere as the reliable Italian food. You might encounter a tarot-card reader or a magician, and most nights in the bar there's some sort of Felliniesque cabaret performer (accordionists, trapeze artists, and the like). The lasagna is always reliable, as are seafood dishes with fresh market seafood.

1919 Post Alley. ✆ **206/443-3241.** www.thepinkdoor.net. Reservations recommended. Main courses $8–$18 lunch, $13–$24 dinner. AE, DISC, MC, V. Mon–Thurs 11:30am–10pm; Fri–Sat 11:30am–11pm; Sun 4–10pm.

Inexpensive

El Puerco Llorón MEXICAN On one of the terraces of the Pike Street Hill Climb—a stairway that connects the waterfront with Pike Place Market—this fast-food place has a genuinely Mexican feel, in large part because of the battered south-of-the-border tables and chairs. The menu is limited, but the food is as authentic as it gets. While you wait to place your order, you can watch tortillas being made by hand. A little patio seating area is very popular in summer.

1501 Western Ave. ✆ **206/624-0541.** www.elpuercolloron.com. Main courses $6.50–$9. Reservations not taken.. MC, V. Sun–Thurs 11am–7pm; Fri–Sat 11am–8pm.

Lowell's Restaurant AMERICAN Everyone in Seattle seems to have a favorite budget place to eat at Pike Place Market. Most of the time, I like to grab little bites here and there and savor lots of flavors, but when I've been on my feet for too many hours and just have to sit down, I head to Lowell's. Although the counter-service restaurant is nothing to e-mail home about, this place is an institution. I like the fish tacos, but there are also good steamer clams, decent fish and chips, salmon dishes, chowder, and burgers. However, what makes this place truly special is the view. Big walls of glass look out to Elliott Bay and the Olympic Mountains. It's so quintessentially Seattle and so unforgettable that you can't help wondering why you aren't being asked to pay a king's ransom to eat with this view. Altogether Lowell's has three floors (with a bar on the second floor), all of which have those same superb views.

Main Arcade, 1519 Pike Place. ✆ **206/622-2036.** www.eatatlowells.com. Reservations not accepted. Main courses $10–$28. AE, DISC, MC, V. Mon–Thurs 7am–6pm, Fri–Sat 7am–7pm (open 1 hour later in summer).

Pike Place Chowder SEAFOOD This place does chowder, pure and simple. And while its great New England–style clam chowder has won a national award, it also does Manhattan clam chowder, smoked-salmon chowder, mixed-seafood chowder, and even a Southwestern-style chowder with chicken and corn. Can't decide which to get? Try the four-cup sampler and decide for yourself which is the best. You'll find this tiny place tucked away in Pike Place Market's Post Alley. There's a second restaurant in Pacific Place shopping center, 600 Pine St. (✆ **206/838-5680**).

When you're on Post Alley, duck into Pike Place Chowder for some of their award-winning fare.

1530 Post Alley. ✆ **206/267-2537.** www.pikeplacechowder.com. Reservations not accepted. Main courses $6.50–$12. AE, DISC, MC, V. Daily 11am–5pm.

BELLTOWN

Very Expensive

El Gaucho ★★ STEAK/LATE-NIGHT Conjuring up the ghosts of dinner clubs of the 1930s and 1940s, this Belltown spot looks as though it could be a Fred Astaire film set. Okay, you may find a better steak at one of the other high-end steakhouses in town, but you just can't duplicate the purely theatrical experience of dining at El Gaucho. Stage-set decor aside, the real stars of the show here are the 28-day dry-aged Angus beef steaks. All the classics are here, too, including Caesar salad tossed tableside and chateaubriand carved before your eyes. Not a steak eater? How about venison chops, rack of lamb, or baby back ribs? There's also a classy bar off to one side and a separate cigar lounge.

2505 First Ave. ✆ **206/728-1337.** www.elgaucho.com. Reservations recommended. Main courses $27–$68. AE, DISC, MC, V. Sun–Thurs 5–11pm; Fri–Sat 5pm–1am.

Expensive

Bisato ★★ ITALIAN A restaurant where the most expensive dish is only $12 wouldn't normally be considered an expensive restaurant, but in order to fill up at this beautiful little Belltown restaurant, you'll need to order at least five or so dishes. Those dishes, though small, are veritable works of art that are bursting with flavor. Just to give you an idea of how complex food here can be, I once had a bowl of chilled pea-and-mint soup that was accompanied by a tiny savory popsicle, black-olive pâté, and chopped ham; it was a medley of flavors that I wanted to savor for far longer than the bowl lasted. There can be occasional misses, but overall, a meal here can be a revelation. Although it seems a bit odd, this restaurant is officially considered a bar, and consequently, minors are not permitted.

2400 First Ave. ✆ **206/443-3301.** www.bisato.com. Reservations only for parties of 5 or more. Small plates $8.50–$12. AE, MC, V. Tues–Sat 5–10:30pm; Sun 5–10pm.

Dahlia Lounge ★★★ NORTHWEST Out front, the neon chef holding a flapping fish may suggest that the Dahlia is little more than a roadside diner. However, a glimpse of the stylish interior will quickly convince you otherwise, and a single bite of any dish will assure you that this is one of Seattle's finest restaurants. Mouthwatering Dungeness crab cakes, a bow to Chef Tom Douglas's Delaware roots, are the house specialty and should not be missed. The menu—influenced by both the Mediterranean and the far side of the Pacific Rim—changes regularly, with the lunch menu featuring some of the same offerings available at night but at lower prices. It's way too easy to fill up on the restaurant's breads, which are baked in the adjacent Dahlia Bakery, and for dessert, it takes a Herculean effort to resist the crème caramel and the coconut-cream pie.

2001 Fourth Ave. ✆ **206/682-4142.** www.tomdouglas.com. Reservations highly recommended. Main courses $12–$29 lunch, $27–$38 dinner. AE, DC, DISC, MC, V. Mon–Thurs 11:30am–2:30pm and 5–10pm; Fri 11:30am–2:30pm and 5–11pm; Sat 9am–2pm and 5–11pm; Sun 9am–2pm and 5–9pm.

Lola ★★ GREEK Local chef Tom Douglas celebrates his wife's Greek heritage with this restaurant in the hip Hotel Ändra. More akin to Douglas's Palace Kitchen than his plush Dahlia Lounge, Lola is a loud, lively, casual spot. Other than the words *kebab, tzatziki,* and *dolmades,* you won't find much common ground here with other Greek restaurants. Start things out with the super-garlicky *skordalia* spread and pita bread. I also recommend the salmon kebabs and the lamb burger, which is absolutely fabulous. For a classic family dinner, Greek-style, order Tom's Big Dinner ($45).

2000 Fourth Ave. ✆ **206/441-1430.** www.tomdouglas.com. Reservations highly recommended. Main courses $13–$16 lunch, $15–$32 dinner. AE, DC, DISC, MC, V. Mon–Thurs 6am–midnight; Fri 6am–2am; Sat 7am–2am; Sun 7am–midnight.

Restaurant Zoë ★★ NORTHWEST Although Belltown has lost its shine in recent years, the neighborhood still has a few upscale restaurants that hard-core foodies will want to frequent, and this is one of the best. The decor is subtly stylish, and the waitstaff is gracious and helpful. Chef/owner Scott Staples mines the bounties of the Northwest to prepare his seasonal fare, preparing such dishes as wild-boar Bolognese with arugula pappardelle pasta, as well as reliably tasty risottos that change with the seasons. The menu here is long on small plates, and the menu descriptions hardly hint at the complex flavors you can expect. For dessert, try one of the tarts with seasonal fruit, and if you appreciate a creative cocktail, be sure to peruse the list of specialty drinks. In July 2011, the restaurant closed in anticipation of a move to the corner of 14th and Union, and is set to reopen in January 2012. Because Zoë has always been such a reliable favorite of mine, I encourage you to check their website to find out if they have reopened by the time you visit. If so, be sure to give them a try in their new location.

2137 Second Ave. ✆ **206/256-2060.** www.restaurantzoe.com. Reservations highly recommended. Main courses $10–$33. AE, MC, V. Sun–Thurs 5–10pm; Fri–Sat 5–11pm.

Spur Gastropub ★★ NEW AMERICAN Set on one of the prettiest streets in Belltown, this restaurant serves high-style food in a casual setting. The menu includes some of the most daring dishes in Seattle, yet service is laid-back and there is a pronounced emphasis on the drinks served at the bar. Sustainability and the farm-to-table connection are emphasized here, with perfectly prepared dishes highlighting fresh, seasonal flavors. Dishes are simple and meant to be shared; however, portions are small, so to make a meal, you'll want to order several dishes. In the spring, you might find wonderfully crunchy veal sweetbreads served with rutabaga and mustard, or tagliatelle pasta with a duck egg, oyster mushrooms, and pine nuts. Note that because this is officially a pub, you must be 21 or over to dine here. And by the way, the cocktails are outstanding.

113 Blanchard St. ✆ **206/728-6706.** www.spurseattle.com. Reservations recommended. Main courses $10–$30; 5-course dinner $80. AE, DC, DISC, MC, V. Daily 5pm–2am.

Moderate

Icon Grill ★ AMERICAN With colorful art glass hanging from chandeliers, overflowing giant vases, and every inch of wall space covered with framed artwork, the decor at the Icon Grill is overboard, but that's what makes it so much fun. Basically, it's an over-the-top

Rainy Season Dining Deals

While spring and fall can be dreary and drizzly in Seattle, anyone visiting during these times of year has a consolation prize for putting up with the rainy weather—Seattle Restaurant Week. During this event, which actually spans two weeks in April and October, more than 100 restaurants offer three-course dinners for $28 and three-course lunches for $15. Actually these "weeks" only span Sunday through Thursday, but it's still a great deal. For more information, visit www.theseattlerestaurantweek.com.

rendition of a Victorian setting gone 21st century. The menu leans heavily toward well-prepared comfort foods, such as a molasses-glazed meatloaf (which locals swear by), and a macaroni and cheese unlike anything your mother ever made. Liven things up with a grilled pear salad. The food here is usually consistent, but the Icon is as much a Seattle experience as a culinary experience.

1933 Fifth Ave. ✆ **206/441-6330.** www.icongrill.net. Reservations recommended. Main courses $12–$21 lunch, $14–$34 dinner. AE, DISC, MC, V. Mon–Thurs 11am–11pm; Fri 11am–midnight; Sat 10am–midnight; Sun 10am–11pm.

Palace Kitchen ★ AMERICAN REGIONAL/LATE-NIGHT/MEDITERRANEAN Aside from Serious Pie, Tom Douglas's pizza place, this is the most casual of Douglas's Seattle restaurants. The atmosphere is urban chic, with cement pillars, simple wood booths, and a few tables in the front window, which overlooks the monorail tracks. The menu is short and features a nightly selection of unusual cheeses and different preparations from the apple-wood grill (flat-iron steak with pickled peppers, rotisserie chicken with bacon-date jam, whole trout with herbs and *casteltrevano* olives). I like to begin a meal with the lavender-scented goat-cheese fondue. Entrees are usually simple and delicious, and the Palace burger royale is a strong contender for best burger in Seattle. For dessert, the coconut-cream pie is an absolute must.

2030 Fifth Ave. ✆ **206/448-2001.** www.tomdouglas.com. Reservations accepted only for parties of 6 or more. Main courses $15–$29. AE, DC, DISC, MC, V. Daily 5pm–1am.

Serious Pie ★★ PIZZA Serious Pie, local celeb-chef Tom Douglas's little pizza place around the corner from his flagship Dahlia Lounge, makes the best pizza in Seattle. With the feel of a *Ratskeller* (a basement tavern in Germany), Serious Pie bakes beautiful crunchy-chewy crusts topped with the likes of chanterelle mushrooms and truffle cheese, or red peppers and fennel sausage. The pizza list is short, and the pies are small enough that you can order several for your table. Top it all off with some Italian wine from the short wine list. Be sure to save room for dessert.

316 Virginia St. ✆ **206/838-7388.** www.tomdouglas.com. Reservations not accepted. Main courses $15–$17. AE, DC, DISC, MC, V. Daily 11am–11pm.

Shiro's Sushi Restaurant ★★ JAPANESE If ogling all the fish at Pike Place Market puts you in the mood for some sushi, then this is the place for you. Shiro's serves the best sushi in the city; it's fresh, flavorful, and perfectly prepared. Eat at the sushi bar and you'll be rubbing shoulders with locals and visiting Japanese businessmen, all of whom know that sushi master Shiro Kashiba has a way with raw fish. Be sure to order at least one of Shiro's special rolls. Also, the broiled black-cod *kasuzuke* should not be missed.

2401 Second Ave. ✆ **206/443-9844.** www.shiros.com. Reservations recommended. Sushi $2.50–$15; main courses $25–$50. AE, DISC, MC, V. Daily 5:30–10:30pm.

Virginia Inn ★ FRENCH/NORTHWEST In business for more than a century, the Virginia Inn is a cozy spot for lunch or a cheap dinner in the Pike Place Market area. This place has long been a favorite local hangout, though today it is more bistro than bar. The menu includes lots of interesting small plates (grilled duck sausage, house-made pâté, cider-braised pork belly) for light eaters, as well as the likes of *moules frites,* hangar steak with the sauce of the moment, and bourbon-glazed chicken breast. Big windows let lots of light into the dining room, but if the sun is shining, most people try to get a seat on the sidewalk patio.

1937 First Ave. ✆ **206/728-1937.** www.virginiainnseattle.com. Reservations recommended. Main courses $9–$13 lunch, $13–$22. DISC, MC, V. Sun–Thurs 11:30am–10pm; Fri–Sat 11:30am–11pm.

Inexpensive

Two Bells Bar & Grill 🎁 AMERICAN Looking for the best burger in Seattle? Give the patties here a try. Although this is little more than an old tavern and a hangout for Belltown residents who can still remember the days before all the condos went up, the burgers are superb. They're thick, hand-formed, and served on chewy sourdough rolls. You can get yours with grilled onions and bacon, with blue cheese, or a few other ways. Accompany your burger with a pint of local beer and some mustardy coleslaw for the perfect burger-and-beer indulgence.

2313 Fourth Ave. ✆ **206/441-3050.** www.thetwobells.com. Reservations not accepted. Main courses $8–$10. AE, MC, V. Mon–Fri 11am–10pm; Sat 1–10pm; Sun 11:30am–10pm.

PIONEER SQUARE & SODO

Inexpensive

BuiltBurger AMERICAN In 2011, Seattle became embroiled in a burger battle with high-end burger joints opening all over the city. With so much high-caliber competition, it's now impossible to decide who makes the best burger in town. Suffice it to say that the burgers at this minimalist, modern restaurant are among the best. The basic burger is made from three cuts of natural beef and is packed with flavor. BuiltBurger stretches the definition of burger a bit with burgers made from chicken (and topped with cilantro-lime slaw), a barbecued pork burger, a spicy chorizo sausage burger, and even a veggie burger. Can't decide? Try a trio of sliders and sample several burgers. By the way, this place started out as a mail-order burger business.

217 James St. ✆ **206/724-0599.** www.builtburger.com. Reservations not accepted. Main courses $7.50–$12. AE, MC, V. Mon–Wed and Fri 11am–4pm; Thurs 11am–8pm; Sat 11am–3pm; Sun 10am–3pm.

Elysian Fields AMERICAN This outpost of my favorite Seattle brewpub chain is across the street from Qwest Field and 3 blocks from both Safeco Field and the heart of the Pioneer Square historic neighborhood. Not only can you get great beers here, but they also do decent stick-to-your-ribs dishes (shepherd's pie, local sausage plates, wine-braised beef). For starters, they have steamed clams and steamed mussels, as well as smoked salmon and seasonal cured meats.

542 First Ave. S. ✆ **206/382-4498.** www.elysianbrewing.com. Reservation accepted for large groups only. Main courses $8–$17. AE, DISC, MC, V. Daily 11:30am–11pm.

Salumi ★★ 🎁 ITALIAN Raise the bar on salami, and you have the artisan-cured meats of this closet-size eatery. The owner, Armandino Batali—who happens to be the father of New York's famous chef Mario Batali—makes all his own salami (as well as traditional Italian-cured beef tongue and other meaty delicacies). Order up a meat plate with a side of cheese, some roasted red bell peppers, and a glass of wine, and you have a perfect lunchtime repast in the classic Italian style. Did I mention the great breads and tapenades? Wow! If you're down in the Pioneer Square area at lunch, don't miss Salumi (even if there's a long line).

309 Third Ave. S. ✆ **206/621-8772.** www.salumicuredmeats.com. Reservations not accepted. Main courses $7.50–$10. MC, V. Tues–Fri 11am–4pm.

THE INTERNATIONAL DISTRICT

In addition to the International District restaurants listed below, you'll find a large food court at **Uwajimaya ★**, 600 Fifth Ave. S. (✆ **206/624-6248;** www.uwajimaya.com), a huge Asian supermarket. Its stalls serve foods from various Asian countries. It all smells great, and everything is inexpensive, which makes it a great place for a quick meal.

Moderate

Maneki ★ JAPANESE This family-run restaurant in the Chinatown/International District may look neither historic nor very large from the outside, but it is actually both. In business since 1904, Maneki is one of Seattle's oldest restaurants. The original restaurant building was ransacked and destroyed while Japanese-Americans were interned in camps during World War II. However in the years since that time, Maneki has given Seattle its first taste of sushi, its first tatami rooms, and even its first karaoke bar. Don't be discouraged by the tiny space just inside the front door; in addition to the front dining room, there's a small bar, a sushi bar, a regular dining room, and tatami rooms for special dinners with friends and family. The menu is very reasonably priced, but as you probably already know, when you eat sushi, the bill can add up.

304 Sixth Ave. S. ✆ **206/622-2631.** www.manekirestaurant.com. Reservations recommended. Main courses $11–$15. MC, V. Tues–Sun 5:30–10:30pm.

Tamarind Tree ★★ VIETNAMESE This restaurant is a bit hard to find but is well worth searching out. It's in the back corner of the dingy Asian Plaza strip mall at the northwest corner of South Jackson Street and 12th Avenue South. Step through the door and glance around at the packed tables, and you'll immediately get the idea that lots of Seattleites are in the know. Now take a deep breath and let the aromas of Vietnam fill your nose. Immediately order the fresh spring rolls, which are packed with great flavors and textures. The ultimate dinner here is the "seven courses of beef," and each course is packed with the zesty flavors that imbue all the dishes here with such exotic character. By the way, this place is way more stylish than the location would suggest.

1036 S. Jackson St., Ste. A. ✆ **206/860-1404.** www.tamarindtreerestaurant.com. Reservations recommended. Main courses $4.75–$9.50 lunch, $9–$19 dinner. MC, V. Sun–Thurs 10am–10pm; Fri–Sat 10am–midnight.

Inexpensive

Jade Garden Restaurant CHINESE It doesn't look like much from the outside (or from the inside, for that matter), but the Jade Garden is considered by many to have the best dim sum in Seattle. Dim sum, if you aren't familiar, is a Chinese fast food that features little plates of steamed or fried dishes served from carts that are wheeled around the restaurant; pick a few plates and eat your fill. See something you like? Order some more. Pace yourself; it all looks so tempting, it's easy to order too many plates. Dim sum is served daily between 9am and 3pm.

424 Seventh Ave. S. ✆ **206/622-8181.** Reservations not necessary. Main courses $4.50–$13; dim sum $2.50–$4. MC, V. Mon–Thurs 9am–2:30am; Fri–Sat 9am–3:30am; Sun 9am–1am.

Samurai Noodle JAPANESE If you're looking for someplace in the International District for a quick lunch or dinner, duck into this tiny noodle shop in the same building that houses the huge Uwajimaya Asian supermarket. The menu is short, with just a dozen or so noodle soups, but they're all packed with flavor and are filling and inexpensive. The *tonkotsu* is a delicious pork broth with sliced pork, green onions, and black mushrooms, and the miso ramen, topped with a pat of butter, is the richest of the broths. They even have gluten-free noodles. All the Japanese families eating here should convince you that these noodles are the best. There's a second Samurai Noodle in the University District at 4138 University Way NE (✆ **206/547-1774**).

606 Fifth Ave. S. ✆ **206/624-9321.** www.samurainoodle.com. Reservations not accepted. Main courses $6.75–$8. AE, MC, V. Sun–Wed 10am–8:30pm; Thurs–Sat 10am–9:30pm.

SEATTLE CENTER & LOWER QUEEN ANNE

Very Expensive

SkyCity ★ NORTHWEST Both the restaurant and the prices are sky high at this revolving restaurant, located just below the observation deck at the top of Seattle's famous Space Needle. However, because you don't have to pay extra for the elevator ride if you dine here, the charges start to seem a little bit more in line with those at other Seattle splurge restaurants. Okay, so maybe you can get better food elsewhere, but you won't get a more spectacular panorama anywhere else. Simply prepared steaks and seafood make up the bulk of the offerings, with a couple of vegetarian options and some Northwest favorites thrown in. I recommend coming here for lunch; the menu includes some of the same dishes, prices are more reasonable, and the views, encompassing the city skyline, Mount Rainier, and the Olympic Mountains, are unsurpassed.

Space Needle, 400 Broad St. ✆ **800/937-9582** or 206/905-2100. www.spaceneedle.com. Reservations highly recommended. Main courses $23–$35 lunch, $35–$58 dinner; weekend brunch $46 adults, $16 children 10 and under. AE, DISC, MC, V. Mon–Thurs 11:30am–2pm and 5–8:45pm; Fri 11:30am–2pm and 5–9:45pm; Sat 10am–2:45pm and 5–9:45pm; Sun 10am–2:45pm and 5–8:45pm.

Moderate

Boat Street Café and Kitchen ★★ FRENCH At the north end of Belltown, 2 blocks north of the Olympic Sculpture Park, you'll find this hidden gem, which is one of my favorite Seattle restaurants. The setting, with its Japanese lanterns and rice-paper umbrellas hanging from the ceiling, is quintessential Seattle casual, while the menu is superbly prepared French cuisine at reasonable prices. Attention to the tiniest of details is what makes this place so special. I like to start with the pickle plate, which consists of an assortment of house-made pickled vegetables and fruits. Salads are often artfully composed and packed with distinctive flavors. Entrees lean toward hearty farmhouse French such as roast chicken with pickled raisins and preserved Meyer lemon relish. Crab cakes and the savory flan (maybe mushroom, maybe asparagus) are two other good bets.

3131 Western Ave. ✆ **206/632-4602.** www.boatstreetcafe.com. Reservations recommended. Main courses $6.50–$12 lunch, $15–$28 dinner. MC, V. Sun–Mon 10:30am–2:30pm; Tues–Sat 10:30am–2:30pm and 5–10pm.

Tilikum Place Café NEW AMERICAN Conveniently located about halfway between the Space Needle and the Olympic Sculpture Park, this restaurant is on one of the few remaining historic blocks in Belltown. The Tilikum, a cozy old-fashioned place that feels a bit like a Parisian backstreet cafe, is most popular as a weekend brunch spot, but even during weekday lunches you can get its popular breakfast dishes, including both sweet and savory Dutch babies (puffy baked pancakes) and some interesting egg dishes. While the dinner menu is short, it features such creative dishes as nettle ravioli and pork tenderloin with smoked yams, clams, and pickled pepper. Before or after a meal, be sure to admire the statue of Chief Sealth on the restaurant's namesake plaza.

407 Cedar St. ✆ **206/282-4830.** www.tilikumplacecafe.com. Reservations recommended. Main courses $8–$14 lunch, $18–$23 dinner. MC, V. Mon–Fri 11am–3am and 4–10pm; Sat–Sun 8am–3pm and 4–10pm.

Toulouse Petit ★ CAJUN/CREOLE This lively restaurant in Lower Queen Anne is a celebration of New Orleans, the French Quarter, and Cajun cooking. To that end, a party atmosphere prevails, and the happy hour, with its list of 75 discounted dishes and tasty cocktails, is a huge hit with locals. Likewise, the breakfast happy hour (Mon–Fri 9–11am, $6) and weekend brunch are immensely popular, not only for the assortment of well-prepared dishes but also for the low prices. Throw in a pretty dining room, with 10-foot-tall windows and a view of the Space Needle from some tables, and you have the sort of place you'll want to come back to again.

601 Queen Anne Ave. N. ✆ **206/432-9069.** www.toulousepetit.com. Reservations recommended. Main courses $13–$49. AE, MC, V. Daily 9am–1am.

Inexpensive

Dick's AMERICAN If you're like me, sometimes you just have to have a burger. I don't mean one of those fancy-shmancy Kobe beef burgers on an artisan focaccia roll; I mean a good, old-fashioned two-napkin fast-food burger. If that craving should strike while you're in Seattle Center, head to this classic fast-food joint in the Lower Queen Anne neighborhood. Dick's has been a local favorite for decades. In addition to burgers and shakes, they serve ice cream here.

500 Queen Anne Ave. N. ✆ **206/285-5155.** www.ddir.com. Reservations not accepted. Main courses $1.20–$2.50. No credit cards. Daily 10:30am–2am.

Sport Restaurant & Bar ☺ AMERICAN If you've got sports fans for kids (or you're one yourself), this big restaurant right across the street from the Space Needle is a must. While the food is decent enough (especially the chili and the burgers), it's the in-booth plasma-screen TVs that make this place such a hit with sports fans. Be forewarned, however, that you can't reserve these way-cool booths, so arrive early or plan on a wait for one of these in-demand tables. For adults, there's a bar with a huge wall-hung TV, in addition to plenty of other standard-size screens.

140 Fourth Ave. N., Ste. 130. ✆ **206/404-7768.** www.sportrestaurant.com. Reservations accepted only for parties of 6 or more. Main courses $7–$21. AE, DISC, MC, V. Sun–Thurs 11:30am–11pm; Fri–Sat 11:30am–1am.

UPPER QUEEN ANNE & MAGNOLIA

Very Expensive

Canlis ★★★ CONTINENTAL/NORTHWEST A local institution, Canlis has been in business since 1950 and yet still manages to keep up with the times. Its stylish interior mixes contemporary decor with Asian antiques, and its Northwest cuisine, with Asian and Continental influences, keeps both traditionalists and more adventurous diners content. Steaks from the copper grill are perennial favorites, as are the Canlis salad and the spicy Peter Canlis prawns. To finish, why not go all the way and have the Grand Marnier soufflé? Canlis also has one of the best wine lists in Seattle. This is one of Seattle's most formal and traditional restaurants, the perfect place to celebrate a very special occasion.

2576 Aurora Ave. N. ✆ **206/283-3313.** www.canlis.com. Reservations highly recommended. Main courses $36–$68; chef's tasting menu $95–$115 ($150–$210 with wines). AE, DC, DISC, MC, V. Mon–Thurs 5:30–9pm; Fri 5:30–10pm; Sat 5–10pm.

Expensive

Palisade ★★ NORTHWEST With a panorama that sweeps from downtown to West Seattle and across the sound to the Olympic Mountains, Palisade has one of the best views of any Seattle waterfront restaurant and is one of my top choices for a splurge waterfront dinner. It also happens to have fine food and inventive interior design (incorporating a saltwater pond, with fish, sea anemones, and starfish, in the middle of the dining room). The menu features a good mix of fish and meats prepared in both a wood-fired oven and a wood-fired rotisserie. The three-course sunset dinners, served before 6pm (before 5pm on weekends), cost $29 and are a great way to enjoy this place on a budget. Palisade also has an excellent and very popular Sunday brunch. ***Note:*** The restaurant is not easy to find; call for directions.

Elliott Bay Marina, 2601 W. Marina Place. ✆ **206/285-1000.** www.palisaderestaurant.com. Reservations recommended. Main courses $12–$17 at lunch, $19–$59 at dinner; Sun brunch $27–$38. AE, DC, DISC, MC, V. Mon–Thurs 11:30am–2pm and 5–9pm; Fri 11:30am–2pm and 5–10pm; Sat 4–9pm; Sun 9:30am–2pm and 4–9pm.

Inexpensive

5 Spot ★ AMERICAN REGIONAL/LATE-NIGHT Every 3 months or so, this restaurant, one of Seattle's favorite diners, changes its menu to reflect a different regional U.S. cuisine. You might find spicy Southwestern food featured, or Cuban-influenced Miami-style meals, but you can bet that whatever's on the menu will be filling and fun. The atmosphere here is pure kitsch—whenever the theme is Florida, the place is adorned with palm trees and flamingos and looks like the high-school gym done up for prom night. This bustling diner is popular with all types who appreciate the fact that you won't go broke eating here. To find it, look for the neon sign of coffee pouring into a giant cup, right at the top of Queen Anne Hill.

1502 Queen Anne Ave. N. ✆ **206/285-7768.** www.chowfoods.com. Reservations recommended. Main courses $11–$17. MC, V. Mon–Fri 8:30am–midnight; Sat–Sun 8:30am–3pm and 5pm–midnight.

Maggie Bluffs Marina Grill ☺ AMERICAN It's never easy to find affordable waterfront dining in any city, and Seattle is no exception. However, if you're willing to drive a few miles, you can save a few bucks at this casual marina restaurant at the foot of Magnolia Bluff (northwest of downtown Seattle). The menu is simple for the most part, offering the likes of burgers and fish and chips, but also includes a few more creative dishes. The restaurant overlooks a marina full of boats, and though the view is partially obstructed by a breakwater, you can also see Elliott Bay, West Seattle, downtown, and even the Space Needle. On sunny summer days, it's worth waiting for a patio table. Crayons keep the kids entertained, and after your meal, you can walk out on Pier G and take a free shuttle boat a few yards through the marina to an observation deck atop the breakwater.

Elliott Bay Marina, 2601 W. Marina Place. ✆ **206/283-8322.** www.maggiebluffs.com. Reservations recommended. Main courses $10–$14. AE, DISC, MC, V. Mon–Thurs 11am–8pm; Fri 11am–9pm; Sat 9am–9pm; Sun 9am–8pm.

SOUTH LAKE UNION & LAKE UNION

Expensive

Mistral Kitchen ★★ NORTHWEST From its humble former Belltown space (now occupied by Spur Gastropub), Mistral has morphed into the South Lake Union neighborhood's grand Mistral Kitchen, a hot hangout for beautiful, well-heeled Seattle foodies. With a bustling bar and a couple of dining rooms across two levels, Mistral covers a lot of bases. If you're in the mood for an unforgettable multicourse tasting menu, dine in the formal Jewel Box dining room. Then again, if you just want one of Seattle's most creative cocktails and perhaps some sushi, there's the bar area and a couple of quiet lounges. In between these extremes is the main dining room, where you can get the likes of clay-oven roasted rib-eye, seared foie gras with sauternes gelée, or salmon with nasturtium-and-lemon butter.

2020 Westlake Ave. ✆ **206/623-1922.** http://mistral-kitchen.com. Reservations highly recommended. Main courses $12–$19 lunch, $21–$34 dinner; multicourse tasting menus $60–$90 ($120–$250 with wine). AE, DC, DISC, MC, V. Sun–Thurs 11am–2pm and 5–10pm; Fri–Sat 11am–2pm and 5–midnight.

Moderate

Cuoco ★★ ITALIAN Tom Douglas, one of Seattle's top chefs, has opened five restaurants in the neighborhood, and this is the most sophisticated. In one of the few older buildings that has survived Paul Allen's extreme makeover of the area, Cuoco (Italian for "cook") specializes in house-made pastas. As you enter, you'll pass the counters where the pastas are made, so take a moment to marvel at the making of your meal. Dishes here tend to be simply prepared, which allows the flavors of fresh pasta and seasonal ingredients to express themselves. Imagine pillow soft gnocchi with pancetta and hazelnuts atop dark green nettle pesto or lamb ravioli with green garlic, peas, and pecorino cheese. The antipasti list is long and includes such dishes as crostini topped with flavorful *lardo* (herbed Italian pork fat) and sweetbreads with porcini, peas, turnips, and goat cheese.

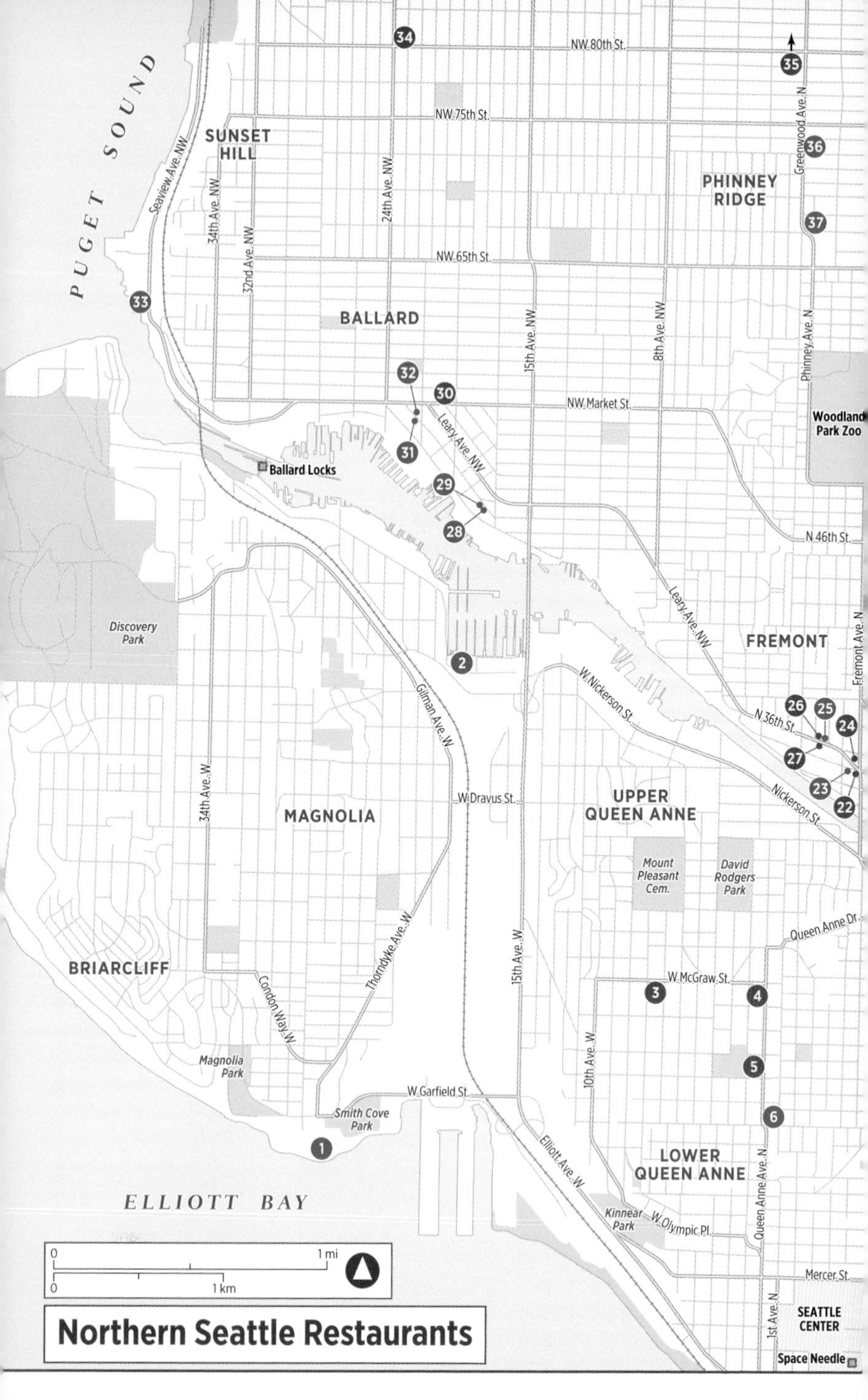
PUGET SOUND
NW 80th St.
NW 75th St.
SUNSET HILL
Seaview Ave. NW
34th Ave. NW
32nd Ave. NW
24th Ave. NW
Greenwood Ave. N
PHINNEY RIDGE
NW 65th St.
BALLARD
15th Ave. NW
8th Ave. NW
Phinney Ave. N
NW Market St.
Leary Ave. NW
Woodland Park Zoo
Ballard Locks
N 46th St.
Discovery Park
FREMONT
Fremont Ave. N
Gilman Ave. W
W. Nickerson St.
N 36th St.
Nickerson St.
34th Ave. W
W Dravus St.
MAGNOLIA
UPPER QUEEN ANNE
Mount Pleasant Cem.
David Rodgers Park
Queen Anne Dr.
Thorndyke Ave. W
15th Ave. W
BRIARCLIFF
Condon Way W
W McGraw St.
10th Ave. W
Magnolia Park
W Garfield St.
Smith Cove Park
Elliott Ave. W
LOWER QUEEN ANNE
Queen Anne Ave. N
ELLIOTT BAY
Kinnear Park
W Olympic Pl.
0
1 mi
0
1 km
Mercer St.
1st Ave. N
SEATTLE CENTER
Space Needle
Northern Seattle Restaurants

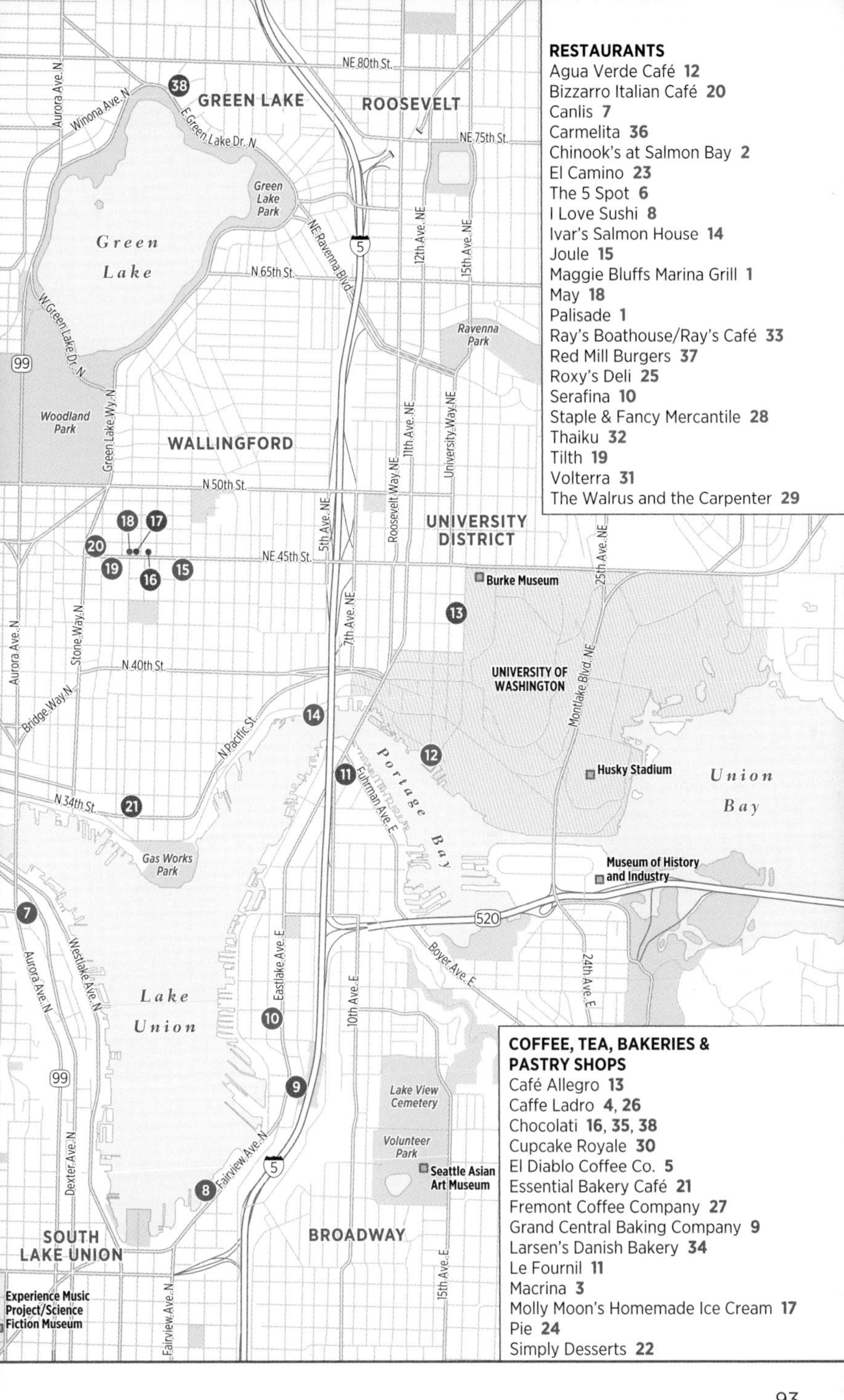
RESTAURANTS
Agua Verde Café 12
Bizzarro Italian Café 20
Canlis 7
Carmelita 36
Chinook's at Salmon Bay 2
El Camino 23
The 5 Spot 6
I Love Sushi 8
Ivar's Salmon House 14
Joule 15
Maggie Bluffs Marina Grill 1
May 18
Palisade 1
Ray's Boathouse/Ray's Café 33
Red Mill Burgers 37
Roxy's Deli 25
Serafina 10
Staple & Fancy Mercantile 28
Thaiku 32
Tilth 19
Volterra 31
The Walrus and the Carpenter 29
COFFEE, TEA, BAKERIES & PASTRY SHOPS
Café Allegro 13
Caffe Ladro 4, 26
Chocolati 16, 35, 38
Cupcake Royale 30
El Diablo Coffee Co. 5
Essential Bakery Café 21
Fremont Coffee Company 27
Grand Central Baking Company 9
Larsen's Danish Bakery 34
Le Fournil 11
Macrina 3
Molly Moon's Homemade Ice Cream 17
Pie 24
Simply Desserts 22
GREEN LAKE
ROOSEVELT
Green Lake
Green Lake Park
WALLINGFORD
UNIVERSITY DISTRICT
Woodland Park
Ravenna Park
Burke Museum
UNIVERSITY OF WASHINGTON
Husky Stadium
Union Bay
Portage Bay
Museum of History and Industry
Gas Works Park
Lake Union
Lake View Cemetery
Volunteer Park
Seattle Asian Art Museum
SOUTH LAKE UNION
BROADWAY
Experience Music Project/Science Fiction Museum
NE 80th St.
NE 75th St.
N 65th St.
N 50th St.
NE 45th St.
N 40th St.
N 34th St.
Winona Ave. N
E Green Lake Dr. N
W Green Lake Dr. N
NE Ravenna Blvd.
Aurora Ave. N
Green Lake Wy. N
Stone Way N
Bridge Way N
N Pacific St.
5th Ave. NE
7th Ave. NE
Roosevelt Way NE
11th Ave. NE
12th Ave. NE
15th Ave. NE
University Way NE
25th Ave. NE
Montlake Blvd. NE
Fuhrman Ave. E
Boyer Ave. E
24th Ave. E
Eastlake Ave. E
10th Ave. E
15th Ave. E
Westlake Ave. N
Dexter Ave. N
Fairview Ave. N
5
99
520

310 Terry Ave. N. ✆ **206/971-0710.** www.cuoco-seattle.com. Reservations recommended. Main courses $12–$25 lunch, $15–$25 dinner. AE, DC, DISC, MC, V. Mon–Fri 11am–2pm and 4–10pm; Sat 9am–2pm and 4–10pm; Sun 9am–2pm and 4–9pm.

Flying Fish ★★ NORTHWEST/SEAFOOD Flying Fish, the main stage for local celebrity chef Christine Keff, offers bold combinations of vibrant flavors and serves some of the best seafood dishes in Seattle. Every dish is a work of art, and with small plates, large plates, and platters for sharing, diners can sample a variety of the kitchen's creations. The menu changes daily, so you can be sure that the latest seasonal ingredients will show up on the tables. Desserts are festive little parties on each plate, and the wine list is vast. In keeping with the upscale character of the South Lake Union neighborhood, Flying Fish is designed to appeal to a well-heeled clientele.

300 Westlake Ave. N. ✆ **206/728-8595.** www.flyingfishrestaurant.com. Reservations recommended. Main courses $7–$13 lunch, $14–$26 dinner. AE, DISC, MC, V. Mon–Fri 11:30am–2pm; daily 5–11pm.

I Love Sushi ★ JAPANESE This local's-favorite sushi bar is on Lake Union at the south end of the lake, and although it's a bit difficult to find, it's worth searching out. Not only is the sushi excellent, but there are some tasty, exotic cocktails. The views of the lake are limited, which is probably why the food is so good. Be sure to try the Seattle roll, which is made with flying fish roe and salmon (a nod to the flying fish at Pike Place Market perhaps). If you're not a fan of sushi, try the black cod *kasuzuke,* which is marinated in sake curd.

1001 Fairview Ave. N. ✆ **206/625-9604.** www.ilovesushi.com. Reservations recommended. Main courses $9.50–$27 lunch, $16–$30 dinner. AE, MC, V. Mon–Thurs 11:30am–2pm and 4–10pm; Fri 11:30am–2pm and 4–10:30pm; Sat noon–2:30pm and 5–10:30pm; Sun noon–9:30pm.

Serafina ★ 🎁 ITALIAN A bit off the beaten track but close to downtown, Serafina is one of my favorite Seattle dining spots. It has a nice touch of sophistication, but overall it's a relaxed neighborhood place where the rustic, romantic atmosphere underscores the earthy, country-style dishes. It's hard to resist ordering at least one of the bruschetta appetizers, which come with any of three different toppings. Among the pasta offerings, don't pass up the delicious veal meatballs in a green-olive tomato sauce served over penne. Also be sure not to miss the *melanzane alla Serafina* (thinly sliced eggplant rolled with ricotta cheese, basil, and Parmesan and baked in tomato sauce). Live music (mostly jazz and Latin) plays Friday through Sunday nights and for Sunday brunch.

2043 Eastlake Ave. E. ✆ **206/323-0807.** www.serafinaseattle.com. Reservations recommended. Main courses $10–$15 lunch, $19–$27 dinner. AE, MC, V. Mon–Thurs 11:30am–2:30pm and 5–10pm; Fri 11:30am–2:30pm and 5–11pm; Sat 5–11pm; Sun 10am–2:30pm and 5–10pm.

Inexpensive

Lunchbox Laboratory AMERICAN This kitschy restaurant, immensely popular with nerds from Amazon, just may represent the comfort food of the future. Think nostalgia food for grown-up nerdy latchkey kids and you'll begin to get an idea of what to expect at this burger joint. Old Saturday-morning cartoons play on the TV over the bar, old metal lunch boxes serve as room dividers, and on the walls there are paintings based on 1960s sci-fi TV shows. The menu here is all about burgers, and they're creative, amply proportioned, and made from Kobe beef. Try one with blue cheese, balsamic onions, and creamy gorgonzola sauce or one with onions, bacon, Swiss cheese, and truffle mayo. Not a beef person? Try the dork; it's made with duck and pork. Alternatively, you can build your own burger from the long list of ingredients.

1253 Thomas St. ✆ **206/621-1090.** http://lunchboxlaboratory.com. Reservations accepted for parties of 8 or more. Main courses $13–$15. AE, DISC, MC, V. Daily 11am–11pm.

Portage Bay Cafe ★ AMERICAN This restaurant, right on the streetcar line through the developing South Lake Union neighborhood, is my favorite neighborhood breakfast spot. Local, organic, and sustainable ingredients are used as much as possible, and the portions at breakfast are huge. Order pancakes, waffles, or French toast, and you'll get to make a trip to the toppings bar, which is loaded with fresh fruit, organic maple syrup, nuts, and other goodies. There are even breakfast choices for the gluten-intolerant (buckwheat pancakes and rice-flour pancakes). At lunch you can get sandwiches and burgers, but this place is really all about breakfast, which is served all day.

391 Terry Ave. N. ✆ **206/462-6400.** www.portagebaycafe.com. Reservations not accepted. Main courses $8–$15. AE, DISC, MC, V. Daily 7:30am–2:30pm.

Ting Momo ★ TIBETAN Despite the widespread interest in Tibetan Buddhism and the Dalai Lama, Tibetan food is a rarely encountered ethnic fare. During many visits to Nepal to research the *Frommer's Nepal* book, I often ate Tibetan food, but I've never had Tibetan food as good as that served here at Ting Momo, another of local chef Tom Douglas's restaurants. Ting Momo is a primarily a lunch spot, and the specialties are *momos* (steamed dumplings) and *samos* (fried dumplings). These are similar to Chinese pot-stickers or Japanese *gyoza* and come stuffed with such fillings as yak meat with star anise, bay leaf, and cranberry; potatoes, peas, oyster mushrooms, and orange zest; or pork, cumin, coriander, and apricot. I recommend ordering the *azag azog* plate, which includes samples of various dumplings. Get it with the tasty *thenthuk* soup for a delicious and filling lunch.

310 Terry Ave. N. ✆ **206/971-0720.** http://tingmomo.com. Reservations not accepted. Main courses $8–$13. AE, DISC, MC, V. Mon–Fri 11am–3pm.

CAPITOL HILL

The section of Capitol Hill near the intersection of 12th Avenue and Pike Street has become Seattle's hottest restaurant neighborhood. I've listed some of my favorite neighborhood restaurants (Anchovies & Olives, Café Presse, Cascina Spinasse, Lark, Osteria La Spiga, Quinn's), but there are plenty of others worth trying. If you feel like finding your own favorite restaurant, stroll around this neighborhood and check out the menus.

Expensive

Anchovies & Olives ★★ ITALIAN Ethan Stowell is one of Seattle's top chefs, and here on Capitol Hill, in a bright, minimally decorated urban-hip dining room, he focuses on simple, seasonal Italian food with the emphasis on seafood. Not surprisingly, as the restaurant name implies, anchovies show up in quite a few dishes. I know, I know, either you love 'em or you hate 'em. Personally, I fall into the former camp, which is why I like this restaurant so much. The menu also includes several *crudos,* which are the Italian version of sashimi or ceviche. Because the portions here are all quite small, you can get a lot of great tastes over the course of a meal; however, if you have a big appetite, your bill can really add up.

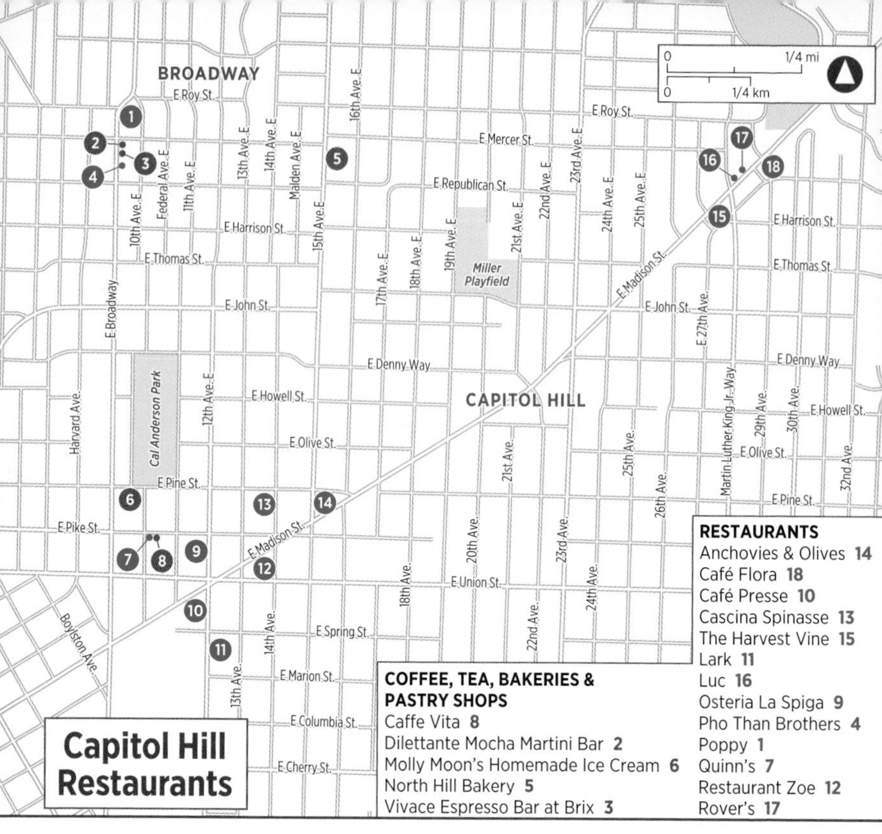

1550 15th Ave. ✆ **206/838-8080.** www.anchoviesandolives.com. Reservations recommended. Main courses $10–$20. AE, DC, DISC, MC, V. Sun–Thurs 5–11pm; Fri–Sat 5pm–midnight.

Cascina Spinasse ★★ ITALIAN This little hole in the wall on Capitol Hill is the most authentic-feeling Italian restaurant in Seattle. The menu is written in Italian on a blackboard (though with English translations on the paper menu), candles light the dining room, and a long wooden table down one side of the restaurant provides communal seating. Highlighting the cuisine of Italy's Piedmont region, the menu lets the simple flavors of each ingredient shine through. You might start your meal with a poached egg served with local black truffles and *fonduta* (Italian fondue) or a roasted leek flan with garlic cream and smoked steelhead roe. Pastas are made in-house (all the pasta-making equipment is on view at dinner), so be sure to have a pasta course, perhaps Jerusalem-artichoke ravioli topped with crushed amaretti cookies.

1531 14th Ave. ✆ **206/251-7673.** www.spinasse.com. Reservations recommended. Main courses $17–$26; tasting menu $90. AE, DISC, MC, V. Sun–Mon and Wed–Thurs 5–10pm; Fri–Sat 5–11pm.

Osteria La Spiga ★★ ITALIAN Italian restaurants all over Seattle serve a wide range of regional Italian dishes that do *not* include tomato sauce, and here at La Spiga, you can sample the cuisine of Italy's Emilia-Romagna region. The restaurant is a big, contemporary space in the heart of Capitol Hill's restaurant district, and on warm summer days, the tables on the sidewalk patio are the place to be. Be sure to start a meal with the *piadina,* a flatbread made from faro (an ancient wheat-like grain); the bread is served with a variety of meats and cheeses. There are always lots of interesting pasta dishes and a short list of more substantial entrees.

1429 12th Ave. ✆ **206/323-8881.** www.laspiga.com. Reservations highly recommended. Main courses $13–$24. AE, DISC, MC, V. Mon–Thurs 5–10pm; Fri–Sat 5pm–11pm; Sun 5–9pm.

Poppy ★★★ NORTHWEST When Chef Jerry Traunfeld, long head of the kitchen at the fabled **Herbfarm** restaurant (p. 292) in the nearby wine-country town of Woodinville, struck out on his own, he did not go the expected route of opening a French restaurant or a trendy tapas place. Instead, he took as inspiration the compartmentalized platters that are common in India and are known as *thalis.* That is where the similarity to Indian food begins and ends. Your thali here might include beef-coriander-yoghurt soup; striped bass with carrot and fennel; shaved cauliflower salad with sumac; yams with sour orange; tandoori-smoked quail with mandarinquats and warm potato salad; and rhubarb pickles. The flavors are reminiscent of dishes at the Herbfarm, but the presentation is very casual.

622 Broadway E. ✆ **206/324-1108.** http://poppyseattle.com. Reservations highly recommended. Prix-fixe dinner $22–$32. AE, DISC, MC, V. Sun–Thurs 5:30–10pm; Fri–Sat 5:30–11pm.

Sitka & Spruce ★★ NEW AMERICAN Melrose Market, just across I-5 from downtown Seattle's convention center, is a locals' alternative to Pike Place Market. Inside the market are a butcher shop, wine shop, cheese shop, flower shop, a bar, and two restaurants, including Sitka & Spruce, which is one of the best and most memorable eateries in the city. With its brick walls and old-fashioned windows used as a partition, this restaurant feels like a back-street discovery. Chef Matt Dillon is a master of creative flavor combinations and dishes here can be deceptively simple yet packed with unexpected flavors. A halibut-and-prawn salad might rest atop foraged greens and fresh herbs on bed of walnut sauce, while steamed clams might be served with nettles, black rice, and aioli. The menu emphasizes local produce, seafood, and foraged foods, and the many small plates make this a great place to sample a lot of regionally-inspired dishes.

1531 Melrose Ave. E. ✆ **206/324-0662.** www.sitkaandspruce.com. Reservations recommended. Main courses $10–$15 lunch, $22–$24 dinner. MC, V. Mon 11:30am–2pm and 5:30–9:30pm; Tues–Thurs 11:30am–2pm and 5:30–10pm; Fri 11:30am–2pm and 5:30–11pm; Sat 10am–2pm and 5:30–11pm; Sun 10am–2pm.

Moderate

Lark ★ MEDITERRANEAN/NORTHWEST You wouldn't think to look at it, but this little neighborhood restaurant on a somewhat run-down back street on Capitol Hill has an impressive pedigree. Chef John Sundstrom formerly headed the kitchen at the W Seattle's Earth & Ocean restaurant, but Sundstrom fled the financial district in favor of the 'hoods and opened this far more casual bistro. The menu consists of dozens of small plates that you assemble into a meal to fit your appetite. The menu changes with the seasons, and it pays to be adventurous. You might try carpaccio of yellowtail with preserved lemons and green olives; squab with pomegranate glaze and pistachio couscous; or sunchoke soup with chestnuts and duck confit. Cheese lovers take note: The cheese list is one of the best in the city, so be sure to try something off this list.

926 12th Ave. ✆ **206/323-5275.** www.larkseattle.com. Online reservations available. Main courses $8–$20. MC, V. Tues–Sun 5–10:30pm.

Quinn's ★ NEW AMERICAN Patterned after the much-lauded gastropubs of London, Quinn's is the second Seattle restaurant for local kitchen legend Scott Staples, whose **Restaurant Zoë** (p. 84) is one of my favorite Belltown eateries. This place is casual and boisterous, but the food, made from top ingredients, is great, and the beer list, heavy on Belgian beers, is one of the best in the city. If you're looking for simple comfort food, go for the wild-boar sloppy joe or the fish and chips. Foodies looking for something more interesting might want to opt for the foie gras, the escargot with marrow bones, or a selection of artisan cheeses. Be forewarned: This is a mix-and-match small-plates sort of place, and your tab will add up quickly.

1001 E. Pike St. ✆ **206/325-7711.** www.quinnspubseattle.com. Reservations not accepted. Main courses $9–$19. AE, DISC, MC, V. Mon–Thurs 5pm–midnight; Fri–Sat 5pm–1am; Sun 5–10pm.

Tango Restaurant & Lounge ★ PAN-LATIN In Spain the appetizer-size plates of food known as tapas are traditionally served with drinks in bars. Here at Tango, however, tapas are front and center, taking inspiration from both classic and contemporary Spanish and Latin cuisine. Many of the items on the menu are substantial enough to serve as entrees, but you'll be much happier if you order lots of different plates and share everything with your dinner companions. Don't miss the *gambas picantes* (chipotle-pepper-flavored tiger prawns with a sauce made from pumpkin seeds and cilantro). On Monday nights, all wines by the bottle are half-price, and every night discounted tapas are served in the lounge between 4:30 and 6pm. This restaurant is conveniently located just across I-5 from downtown.

1100 Pike St. ✆ **206/583-0382.** www.tangorestaurant.com. Reservations recommended. Tapas $1.75–$14; main courses $12–$25. AE, MC, V. Sun–Thurs 5–10:30pm; Fri–Sat 5pm–midnight.

Inexpensive

Baguette Box INTERNATIONAL Sandwiches served on crunchy slices of baguette are the specialty of this casual restaurant just a few blocks uphill from the convention center. The crispy drunken chicken sandwich, served with caramelized onions, cilantro, and a sweet-and-sour sauce, was inspired by a Vietnamese dish and is the house favorite, but I also like the grilled lemongrass steak sandwich, which is also inspired by an Asian dish. Baguette Box has a second location, in the Fremont neighborhood at 626 N. 34th St. (✆ **206/632-1511**).

1203 Pine St. ✆ **206/332-0220.** www.baguettebox.com. Reservations not taken. Main courses $6.50–$13. MC, V. Daily 11am–8pm.

Café Presse ★ FRENCH Under the same ownership as Belltown's **Le Pichet** (my favorite Seattle French cafe, p. 81), Café Presse is modeled after a traditional Parisian bar-cafe. This is an all-day sort of place. You can start with eggs or a pastry for breakfast, get a *croque monsieur* ham sandwich for lunch, and at dinner order steak *frites* or a whole roasted chicken for two. At the end of the day, you can wind down with a drink at the bar. This is a casual neighborhood place that's popular with students from Seattle University, which is only half a block away. There's even a newsstand with imported magazines, and you'll often see international soccer games on the TV.

1117 12th Ave. ✆ **206/709-7674.** www.cafepresseseattle.com. Reservations not accepted. Main courses $5–$16. DISC, MC, V. Daily 7am–2am.

Pho Than Brothers VIETNAMESE Seattleites are crazy about Vietnamese food, and restaurants serving traditional *pho* (noodle soup) can be found all over the city. The Pho Than Brothers chain, which has 13 restaurants around the region, is one of the most reliable of these. Try the *chin nam,* which is made with beef brisket and flank steak. Be sure to finish your meal with a custard puff. Other convenient Pho Than Brothers restaurants are in Ballard at 2021 NW Market St. (© **206/782-5715**), and in the University District at 4207 University Way NE (© **206/632-7272**).

516 Broadway E. © **206/568-7218.** www.thanbrothers.com. Reservations not taken. Main courses $5–$7. MC, V. Daily 11am–9pm.

MADISON VALLEY

This shady neighborhood lies to the east and downhill from Capitol Hill. In the main commercial district, which is just south of the Washington Park Arboretum, there are numerous restaurants and shops. Madison Park, a second commercial district farther along Madison Street, has still more restaurants and is close to the waters of Lake Washington.

Very Expensive

Rover's ★★★ NORTHWEST/VEGETARIAN Tucked away in a quaint clapboard house behind a chic little shopping center in the Madison Valley neighborhood, east of downtown, Rover's is one of Seattle's most acclaimed restaurants. Thierry Rautureau, the restaurant's award-winning chef, received classical French training before falling in love with the Northwest and all the wonderful ingredients it has to offer. The delicacies on the frequently changing menu are enough to send the most jaded of gastronomes into fits of indecision. Luckily, you can simply opt for one of the fixed-price dinners and leave the decision making to a professional. Notable creations include scrambled eggs with lime crème fraîche; foie gras with a savory profiterole, chai-tea foam, and Madeira gastrique (sweet-and-sour sauce); and venison medallions, perhaps with a salsify tartlet. ***Vegetarians, take note:*** You won't find many vegetarian feasts to compare with what's served here.

2808 E. Madison St. © **206/325-7442.** http://thechefinthehat.com/rovers. Reservations required. Main courses $19–$24 lunch, prix-fixe menus $59–$135 ($99–$210 with wine). AE, MC, V. Tues–Thurs 6–8:30pm; Fri noon–1:30pm and 5:30–10pm; Sat 5:30–10pm; Sun 5–9pm.

Moderate

The Harvest Vine ★★ SPANISH From the sidewalk, the Harvest Vine, the most authentic tapas restaurant in the city, appears to be little more than a tiny bar, but downstairs is a cozy wine-cellar-like dining room. The menu consists exclusively of traditional Spanish small plates, and though prices can sometimes be quite high, it's still possible to piece together a very satisfying and economical meal. The menu changes daily, but you can always count on the cured meat plates and assorted cheeses. Also keep an eye out for such delicacies as cured tuna loin with caramelized onion and salmon caviar and grilled venison with licorice root and oyster mushrooms.

2701 E. Madison St. © **206/320-9771.** www.harvestvine.com. Reservations recommended. Tapas $6.50–$38. AE, MC, V. Mon–Fri 5–10pm; Sat–Sun 10am–2pm and 5–10pm.

Luc ★★ FRENCH At this casual neighborhood cafe, local celebrity chef Thierry Rautureau, known around town as the "Chef in the Hat," is up to his old tricks. He has once again melded French aesthetics and American tastes to create a casual, less-expensive version of his ever-popular Rover's restaurant, which is on the same block. Luc has an authentically French feeling, yet also feels like the sort of place you would want to have within walking distance of your house. It's the sort of place where you're welcome to stop in for coffee or a cocktail, a burger or boeuf bourguignon. There are grilled lamb sausages and pizzas, trout amandine, steaks, and couscous. Every night of the week, there's also a special that's meant to be shared (leg of lamb, pork shoulder roast, whole salt-crusted chicken). The neighborhood is beautiful, and Washington Park Arboretum and the Japanese Garden are nearby.

2800 E. Madison St. ✆ **206/328-6645.** http://thechefinthehat.com/luc. Reservations recommended. Main courses $11–$19. AE, DISC, MC, V. Mon–Thurs 4:30pm–10:30pm; Fri–Sat 4:30pm–midnight; Sun 10am–1:30pm and 4:30–10:30pm.

Inexpensive

Cafe Flora ★ VEGETARIAN Big, bright, and airy, this Madison Valley cafe will dispel any ideas you might have about vegetarian food being boring. Meatless gourmet cooking draws on influences from around the world, which makes this a vegetarian's dream come true. One of the house specialties is a portobello Wellington made with mushroom-pecan pâté and sautéed leeks in a puff pastry. Keep an eye out for unusual pizzas, some of which are vegan and can be made with a gluten-free crust. On weekends a casual brunch features interesting breakfast fare.

2901 E. Madison St. ✆ **206/325-9100.** www.cafeflora.com. Reservations accepted only for parties of 6 or more. Main courses $10–$18. MC, V. Mon–Thurs 9am–9pm (until 10pm spring and summer); Fri 9am–10pm; Sat 9am–2pm and 5–10pm; Sun 9am–2pm and 5–9pm.

THE UNIVERSITY DISTRICT

Moderate

Ivar's Salmon House ★ ☺ SEAFOOD With a view of the Space Needle on the far side of Lake Union, flotillas of sea kayaks silently slipping by, sailboats racing across the lake, and powerboaters tying up at the dock out back, this restaurant on the north side of Lake Union is quintessential Seattle. Add a building designed to resemble a Northwest Coast Indian longhouse, and you have what just might be the best place in town for a waterfront meal. This place is a magnet for weekend boaters who abandon their own galley fare in favor of Ivar's clam chowder and famous alder-grilled salmon. Lots of artifacts, including long dugout canoes and historic photos of Native American chiefs, make Ivar's a hit with both kids and adults. Bear in mind that this restaurant's popularity means that service can be slow; just relax and keep enjoying the views.

401 NE Northlake Way. ✆ **206/632-0767.** www.ivars.com. Reservations recommended. Main courses $9–$20 lunch, $16–$30 dinner. AE, DC, DISC, MC, V. Mon–Thurs 11am–9pm; Fri–Sat 11am–10pm; Sun 9:30am–2pm and 3:30–9pm.

Inexpensive

Agua Verde Cafe ★ 🎁 MEXICAN Set on the shore of Portage Bay, which lies between Lake Union and Lake Washington, this casual Mexican restaurant is a hit with college students from the University of Washington. Consequently, there's often a line. The menu is limited to tacos, burritos, *tortas* (Mexican-style sandwiches), quesadillas, and, at dinner, a handful of more substantial entrees. I recommend the tacos, which come three to an order. Try the smoked-salmon or yam versions, both of which are topped with a delicious avocado cream sauce. Add a couple of sides—cranberry slaw, pineapple-jicama salsa, or creamy chile-mashed potatoes—for a filling and inexpensive meal. Agua Verde also serves good margaritas and rents kayaks for $15 to $20 per hour. This is Mexican food with a conscience: Agua Verde uses wild-caught fish, free-range chickens, and shade-grown coffee.

1303 NE Boat St. ✆ **206/545-8570.** www.aguaverde.com. Dinner reservations accepted for parties of 8 or more. Main courses $6–$10 lunch; $7.75–$17 dinner. AE, DISC, MC, V. Mon–Fri 11am–3:30pm and 4–9pm; Sat 9am–3:30pm and 4–9pm; Sun 9am–3:30pm (closed Sun in winter). Takeout window Mon–Fri 7:30am–2:30pm.

WALLINGFORD, FREMONT & PHINNEY RIDGE

Expensive

Joule ★★ FRENCH-KOREAN FUSION With a casual, laid-back urban feel, this little restaurant brings a bit of Belltown vibe to the family-oriented Wallingford neighborhood and is worth an excursion out from downtown Seattle. The menu, an eclectic blend of Korean dishes and flavors from around the world, is divided into broad flavor categories: abroad, native, and collected. Under flavors from abroad, you'll find various *kimchis.* Flavor combinations may at first seem bizarre but are often truly inspired. There's even bacon butter to go with the bread. Obviously, this restaurant is for adventurous eaters, but if you're the been-there, done-that sort of culinary explorer, Joule should not be missed.

1913 N. 45th St. ✆ **206/632-1913.** www.joulerestaurant.com. Reservations recommended. Main courses $10–$24. AE, DISC, MC, V. Tues–Thurs and Sun 5–10pm; Fri–Sat 5–11pm.

Tilth ★★ NEW AMERICAN Tilth is one of the nation's only restaurants to receive organic certification from Oregon Tilth (an organization that sets organic standards), but don't confuse organic with granola-crunchy hippie food. Chef Maria Hines, one of Seattle's most creative chefs, oversaw the kitchen at the W Seattle's acclaimed Earth & Ocean before opening this restaurant in a little cottage in Wallingford. The menu emphasizes fresh, seasonal ingredients in dishes that seem simple yet are packed with flavor. While the menu changes with the seasons, you can almost always count on finding the mini duck burgers on the menu. One of my favorite aspects of the menu here is that most dishes are available as appetizers or entrees, so if you want to try several dishes, you can.

1411 N. 45th St. ✆ **206/633-0801.** www.tilthrestaurant.com. Reservations recommended. Main courses $25–$29. MC, V. Mon–Thurs 5–10pm; Fri 5–10:30pm; Sat 10am–2pm and 5–10:30pm; Sun 10am–2pm and 5–10pm.

Moderate

Bizzarro Italian Cafe ★ 🎁 ITALIAN The name neatly sums up this casual Italian restaurant, where a party atmosphere reigns most nights. The tiny room is filled with mismatched thrift-store furnishings, and strange things hang from the walls and ceiling. The food usually changes with the seasons and emphasizes pasta dishes. Expect to find the likes of elk bolognese; wine-braised lamb shank with lamb-and-fig demiglace; and pappardelle pasta with wild mushrooms, walnuts, and sherry cream sauce. Bizzarro is at the west end of Wallingford, just off Stone Way North.

1307 N. 46th St. ✆ **206/632-7277.** www.bizzarroitaliancafe.com. Reservations accepted only for parties of 6 or more Sun–Thurs; reservations not accepted Fri–Sat. Main courses $15–$20. MC, V. Daily 5–10pm.

Carmelita ★★ VEGETARIAN Who says vegetarianism and decadence have to be mutually exclusive? Here at Carmelita's, the two coexist quite nicely. In the Phinney Ridge neighborhood north of Woodland Park Zoo, this very Northwestern restaurant features lots of natural woods, a relaxed ambience, and a seasonal menu that incorporates the best local ingredients. In warm weather, there's seating out on the lovely garden patio. Main courses might include pizza with basil-arugula pesto, port-caramelized onions, and roasted garlic; or chestnut-and-manchego cheese spaetzle with caramelized salsify, kale, sun-dried tomatoes, and apple-balsamic brown-butter sauce. And for dessert, definitely go for the warm chocolate "muck muck" (a fallen chocolate cake with whipped cream and seasonal compote).

7314 Greenwood Ave. N. ✆ **206/706-7703.** www.carmelita.net. Reservations recommended. Main courses $16–$18. MC, V. Sun and Tues–Thurs 5–9pm; Fri–Sat 5–10pm.

El Camino ★ MEXICAN Maybe it's the implied promise of sunshine and warm weather in every bite, but Seattle seems to have an obsession with Southwestern and Mexican food. If you, too, need a dose of spicy flavors, hit the road *(el camino)* in the Fremont neighborhood. As soon as you sit down, order a margarita; the house margarita here is the best I've had north of Tucson. As you sip your cocktail, you'll notice that the menu is unlike just about any Mexican restaurant menu you've ever seen. Forget the cheesy chalupas—here you might find salmon in tart tamarind sauce or enchiladas in *pipian* (pumpkin-seed sauce). Daily fresh-fish specials are available, and the fish of the day also goes into the delicious fish tacos.

607 N. 35th St. ✆ **206/632-7303.** www.elcaminorestaurant.com. Reservations recommended. Main courses $12–$22. AE, MC, V. Tues–Thurs and Sun 5–10pm; Fri–Sat 5–11pm (late-night menu until midnight).

May ★ THAI I've spent a lot of time in Thailand, and even if the food at this second-floor Wallingford restaurant wasn't some of the best Thai food in Seattle, I would love May for its architecture. From the outside it looks just like a Thai Buddhist temple, complete with shiny blue glass along the steeply pitched eaves; from the inside, it duplicates the old teak houses that are so rare in Thailand in the 21st century. Throw in a street-level bar lifted straight off a beach on the Gulf of Siam, and you have a fun restaurant in a pleasant Seattle neighborhood. The *phad Thai,* made the traditional way (with tamarind sauce, not ketchup), is a must, as is the grilled squid appetizer. Seafood dishes, such as the *phad grapao Samui* (made with scallops, prawns, and squid), are a highlight here.

1612 N. 45th St. ✆ **206/675-0037.** www.maythaiseattle.com. Reservations recommended. Main courses $10–$22. AE, DISC, MC, V. Daily 11:30am–1am.

Inexpensive

Red Mill Burgers AMERICAN Just a little north of Woodland Park Zoo, this retro burger joint is tiny and always hoppin' because everyone knows it does one of the best burgers in Seattle. Try the *verde* burger, made with Anaheim peppers for just the right amount of fire. Don't miss the onion rings. And don't come dressed in your finest attire—burgers here are definitely multi-napkin affairs.

A second Red Mill Burgers is at 1613 W. Dravus St. (✆ **206/284-6363**), which is midway between downtown Seattle and Ballard. Lines often seem to be shorter here.

312 N. 67th St. ✆ **206/783-6362.** www.redmillburgers.com. Reservations not taken. Burgers $3.50–$6.50. No credit cards. Tues–Sat 11am–9pm; Sun noon–8pm.

Roxy's Diner ★ DELI With pastrami and corned-beef sandwiches that come in regular and New York sizes, Roxy's takes the concept of traditional New York Jewish deli seriously. Lucky Seattle! Only the best pastrami and corned beef are used here, and if you're a fan of hot pastrami sandwiches, you'll want to be sure to search out this little gem. Also, if you've dedicated your life to the quest for the perfect Reuben sandwich, be sure to try Roxy's. Definitely a contender for best in Seattle. Breakfast is served all day.

462 N. 36th St. ✆ **206/632-3963.** www.pastramisandwich.com. Reservations not taken. Main courses $5.25–$16. AE, MC, V. Daily 7am–7pm.

BALLARD

Expensive

Ray's Boathouse/Ray's Cafe ★★ SEAFOOD When Seattleites want to impress visiting friends and relatives, this restaurant often ranks right up there with the Space Needle, the ferries, and Pike Place Market. The view across Puget Sound to the Olympic Mountains is guaranteed to impress out-of-towners. You can watch the boat traffic coming and going from the Lake Washington Ship Canal, and bald eagles are often seen fishing just offshore. Then there's Ray's dual personality: Ray's Cafe upstairs is a lively (and loud) cafe and lounge, while Ray's Boathouse downstairs is a much more formal, sedate scene. The downstairs menu is more creative, the upstairs menu less expensive (but even upstairs you can order from the downstairs menu). The crab cakes here are a must; they're delicious and packed full of crab. Also, if you see any sort of fish in *sake kasu* (a typically Northwest/Pacific Rim preparation), order it.

6049 Seaview Ave. NW. ✆ **206/789-3770** for Boathouse or 206/782-0094 for Cafe. www.rays.com. Reservations recommended. Main courses $25–$58 at Boathouse, $12–$23 at Cafe. AE, DC, DISC, MC, V. Boathouse Mon–Fri 5–9pm; Sat–Sun 4:30–9pm. Cafe Sun–Thurs 11:30am–9:30pm; Fri–Sat 11:30am–10pm.

Staple & Fancy Mercantile ★★ 🎁 NEW AMERICAN I am not a picky eater. Given the option, I will almost always order something I've never had before. If this describes you, you must eat at Chef Ethan Stowell's Staple & Fancy Mercantile, and the best way to enjoy a meal here is to opt for the chef's-choice menu. You won't know what you're getting until it arrives at your table, but, I can assure you, you won't be disappointed. You might wind up with a half dozen flavorful little starters such as cold asparagus soup, fried anchovies, or crostini with halibut. Other courses might include gnocchi with sausage, pork loin with capers, or a whole grilled fish. With its battered wood floors and faded advertising on the exposed brick walls, this Ballard restaurant seems barely changed from its former industrial days, definitely a diamond in the rough.

4739 Ballard Ave. NW. ✆ **206/789-1200.** www.ethanstowellrestaurants.com. Reservations recommended. Main courses $16–$24; 4-course dinner $45. AE, DC, DISC, MC, V. Daily 5–11pm.

Volterra ★★ ITALIAN It would be hard to imagine a more picture-perfect little restaurant than Volterra. Set on a shady tree-lined street of historic brick buildings, this place is made for romantic dinners. It's also a wonderful place for a weekend brunch. Rest assured that this is not your typical southern-Italian joint. Start your meal with polenta stuffed with fontina cheese and served with truffle-scented wild-mushroom ragu, and then move on to the wild-boar tenderloin with Gorgonzola sauce. At brunch be sure you order something with hash browns—they're to die for. Whenever you come here to dine, be sure to do a little shopping along Ballard Avenue before or after your meal.

5411 Ballard Ave. NW. ✆ **206/789-5100.** www.volterrarestaurant.com. Reservations recommended. Main courses $15–$29. AE, DISC, MC, V. Mon–Thurs 5–10pm; Fri 5–11pm; Sat 9am–2pm and 5–11pm; Sun 9am–2pm and 5–9pm.

Moderate

Chinook's at Salmon Bay ★ SEAFOOD Fishermen's Terminal, the winter home of the Alaska fishing fleet, is just across the Lake Washington Ship Canal from the Ballard neighborhood, and overlooking all of the moored commercial fishing boats is one of Seattle's favorite seafood restaurants. This big, boisterous place has walls of windows looking out onto the marina and a long menu featuring seafood fresh off the boats. My favorite meal here is a cup of the oyster stew followed by the alder-plank-roasted salmon.

The only problem with Chinook's is that it isn't very easy to reach. Take Elliott Avenue north from the downtown waterfront, continue north on 15th Avenue West, take the last exit before crossing the Ballard Bridge, and follow the signs to Fishermen's Terminal. Before or after a meal, you can stroll around the marina and have a look at all the fishing boats.

1900 W. Nickerson St. ✆ **206/283-4665.** www.anthonys.com. Reservations not accepted. Main courses $7–$30. AE, DISC, MC, V. Mon–Thurs 11am–10pm; Fri 11am–11pm; Sat 7:30am–11pm; Sun 7:30am–10pm.

The Walrus and the Carpenter ★ SEAFOOD Taking its name from the Lewis Carroll poem and set at the back of a converted commercial building on shady Ballard Avenue, this oyster bar has the look and feel of someplace that catered to walrus-mustached fisherman and carpenters a century ago. The casual, cozy restaurant does plenty of seafood dishes, but the main reason to eat here is for fresh oysters on the half shell. On any given night, expect a dozen varieties of oysters on the menu, and with most of these from Washington state. To go with your oysters, there are lots of other small plates such as smoked trout, fried oysters, and salmon tartare. Add a vegetable side dish such as nettle soup, asparagus with anchovies and bread crumbs, or chilled pea soup and a selection from the cheese menu for a simple yet sophisticated repast.

4743 Ballard Ave. NW. ✆ **206/395-9227.** http://thewalrusbar.com. Reservations not accepted. Small plates $8–$12. AE, DISC, MC, V. Daily 4–11pm.

Inexpensive

Thaiku ★ 🎁 THAI Ballard Avenue is one of the prettiest streets in Seattle: Its sidewalks are shaded by trees, and the old brick commercial buildings have been converted into boutiques, galleries, restaurants, and nightclubs. Amid these pleasant historic surroundings, you'll find my favorite Thai restaurant in town. Known to locals as the Noodle House, Thaiku is a dark place with lots of wooden Asian antiques hanging from the walls and ceilings. The fun atmosphere is just a bonus, though, as it's the great noodle dishes that are the main attraction. I don't think you'll find a better *phad Thai* anywhere in Seattle. The bar here, which is known for its unusual herb-infused cocktails, gets lively on weekends, and there's even live jazz on Wednesday and Thursday nights.

5410 Ballard Ave. NW. ✆ **206/706-7807.** www.thaiku.com. Reservations not necessary. Main courses $7–$13. AE, DISC, MC, V. Mon–Thurs 11:30am–9:30pm; Fri 11:30am–10:30pm; Sat noon–10:30pm; Sun noon–9:30pm.

WEST SEATTLE

Expensive

Salty's on Alki Beach ★★ SEAFOOD Although the prices here are almost as out of line as those at the Space Needle, and the service is unpredictable, this restaurant has *the* waterfront view in Seattle, and the food is usually pretty good. Because Salty's is on the northeast side of the Alki Peninsula, it faces downtown Seattle on the far side of Elliott Bay. Come for a sunset dinner, and watch the setting sun sparkle off skyscraper windows as the lights of the city begin to twinkle. On sunny summer days, lunch on one of the two decks is a sublimely Seattle experience. Don't be discouraged by the ugly industrial/port area you drive through to get here; Salty's marks the start of Alki Beach, the closest Seattle comes to a Southern California beach scene. Watch for the giant rusted salmon sculptures swimming amid rebar kelp beds and the remains of an old bridge (hey, Seattle even recycles when it comes to art).

1936 Harbor Ave. SW. ✆ **206/937-1600.** www.saltys.com/seattle. Reservations recommended. Main courses $10–$28 lunch, $16–$50 dinner. AE, DC, DISC, MC, V. Mon–Thurs 11am–8:45pm (9pm in summer); Fri 11am–9pm; Sat 9:30am–1pm and 3–9pm (9:30pm in summer); Sun 8:45am–1:30pm and 3–8:30pm (9pm in summer).

Moderate

Cactus ★ MEXICAN Maybe you're not a fish-and-chips kind of person, or maybe long sandy beaches remind you of Mexico. If either of these describe you and you happen to be hungry and out Alki Beach way, check out this modern Mexican restaurant. It's a big, colorful place with glass garage doors that open to the fresh air on warm summer days (perfect for sipping a margarita or a cold beer). The blue-corn calamari and wild-mushroom quesadillas are good bets for starters. Personally, I like the soft-shell *carnitas* (pork) tacos, but you should also consider the Chimayo enchilada and the chile relleno. If you've never had it, try the Navajo fry bread. There are other Cactus restaurants: in the Madison Park neighborhood at 4220 E. Madison St. (✆ **206/324-4140**); and in Kirkland at 121 Park Lane (✆ **425/893-9799**).

2820 Alki Ave. SW. ✆ **206/933-6000.** www.cactusrestaurants.com. Reservations accepted for parties of 6 to 8. Main courses $9.50–$13 lunch, $11–$18 dinner. AE, DISC, MC, V. Sun–Thurs 11:30am–10pm; Fri–Sat 11:30am–11pm.

Inexpensive

Alki Crab & Fish Co. ★ SEAFOOD Sure, there are plenty of places on the Seattle waterfront where you can get fish and chips, but for an unforgettable cheap meal, catch the water taxi over to Alki Beach. Right at the dock, you'll find this little fish-and-chips joint that boasts one of the best views in Seattle. In fact, next-door neighbor Salty's on Alki Beach has made its reputation almost solely based on this vista. So if you want the city's best view of the Seattle skyline but don't want to blow your budget, this is the place. The cost of the water taxi from the Seattle waterfront plus the halibut and chips doesn't even come close to what you would spend at Salty's.

1660 Harbor Ave. SW. ✆ **206/938-0975.** Reservations not accepted. Main dishes $4–$15. MC, V. Sun–Thurs 9am–9pm; Fri–Sat 9am–10pm.

THE EASTSIDE

The Eastside, the high-tech suburb on the east side of Lake Washington, includes the cities of Bellevue, Kirkland, Issaquah, and Redmond.

Moderate

Beach Cafe ★ INTERNATIONAL This casual waterfront cafe is the Eastside's best bet for an economical and creative meal with a view. In summer, the patio dining area just can't be beat. The menu focuses on comfort foods as well as popular dishes from around the world. In other words, you can get fish and chips or salmon with roasted-garlic polenta, gumbo or fish tacos, and chicken pot pie or sweet-potato fries with chipotle aioli.

1170 Carillon Point, Kirkland. ✆ **425/889-0303.** www.beachcafekirkland.com. Reservations recommended. Main courses $12–$28. AE, DC, MC, V. Mon–Fri 6:30am–10:30am and 11am–10:30pm; Sat 7am–10:30pm; Sun 7am–9:30pm.

Chantanee Thai Restaurant ★★ THAI The first time I ate at this stylishly modern Thai restaurant in downtown Bellevue, my dinner companions and I were all transported to Thailand. The flavors at Chantanee were simply the most authentic any of us had tasted on this side of the Pacific. So if you want to find out what Thai food tastes like in Thailand, search out this restaurant. The bar here also happens to serve the most creative cocktails in town. You'll find this eatery in the building opposite the Bellevue Transit Center; parking in the Key Center Building is free in the evening and on weekends with validation.

Key Center Building, 601 108th Ave. NE, Ste. 100A, Bellevue. ✆ **425/455-3226.** www.chantanee.com. Reservations recommended. Main courses $9–$18. AE, MC, V. Sun–Wed 11am–10pm; Thurs–Sat 11am–11pm.

COFFEE, TEA, BAKERIES & PASTRY SHOPS

You may perhaps be aware that Seattle is the espresso capital of America. Seattleites are positively rabid about coffee, which isn't just a hot drink or a caffeine fix anymore, but rather a way of life. Wherever you go in Seattle, you're rarely more than a block from your next cup. There are espresso carts on the sidewalks, drive-through espresso windows, espresso bars, espresso counters at gas stations, espresso milkshakes, espresso chocolates, even eggnog lattes at

Christmas. Here I'll list some of my favorite coffee spots, as well as places where you can get a great cup of tea, and maybe something for your sweet tooth.

Coffee Shops & Cafes

Starbucks (www.starbucks.com), the ruling king of coffee, is seemingly everywhere you turn. It sells some 30 types and blends of coffee beans. Close on the heels of Starbucks in popularity and citywide coverage is the **Tully's Coffee** (www.tullys.com) chain, which seems to have an espresso bar on every corner that doesn't already have a Starbucks. Serious espresso junkies, however, swear by **Caffe Ladro** (www.caffeladro.com) and **Caffé Vita** (www.caffevita.com). If you see one of either of these chains, check it out and see what you think.

As places to hang out and visit with friends, coffeehouses and cafes are as popular as bars and pubs. Among my favorite Seattle cafes and espresso bars are the following (organized by neighborhood):

DOWNTOWN If you're a total espresso fanatic and want to sip a triple latte where it all started, head to **Monorail Espresso,** a walk-up window at the northeast corner of Fifth Avenue and Pike Street. Although this is not the espresso stand's original location, in its previous incarnation (way back in 1980), Monorail was the very first espresso cart in Seattle.

Ancient Grounds ★, 1220 First Ave. (✆ **206/749-0747**), is hands down the coolest and most unusual espresso bar in Seattle. This coffeehouse doubles as an art gallery specializing in antique Mexican, Japanese, and Northwest Coast Indian masks, and ethnic artifacts from around the world. Cases are full of colorful minerals and insects in glass boxes. It's all very dark and Victorian.

Caffe Ladro, a small local chain of espresso bars, is one of my favorite places to get coffee in Seattle. Downtown you'll find cafes at 801 Pine St. (✆ **206/405-1950**) and 108 Union St. (✆ **206/267-0600**). The coffee served here is 100% fair-trade, organic, and shade grown.

If you're getting tired from shopping all day, head to **Caffè Senso Unico,** 622 Olive Way (✆ **206/264-7611;** www.caffesensounico.com), which is right across the street from the Pacific Place shopping mall, yet has a very Italian feel.

PIKE PLACE MARKET, BELLTOWN & THE WATERFRONT Seattle is legendary as a city of coffeeholics, and Starbucks is the main reason. This company has coffeehouses all over town (and all over the world), but the **Starbucks** in Pike Place Market, at 1912 Pike Place (✆ **206/448-8762**), was once the only Starbucks anywhere. Today it is the only chain store allowed in the market. Although you won't find any tables or chairs, Starbucks fans shouldn't miss an opportunity to get their coffee at the "source." Be sure to notice the bare-breasted-mermaid sign out front, which is how the Starbucks logo started out before becoming modest enough for mass-market advertising.

If you need to sit down while you drink your latte, or simply don't want to drink a Starbucks, then try **Local Color,** 1606 Pike Place (✆ **206/728-1717;** www.localcolorseattle.com), a combination cafe and art gallery.

If you're wandering around checking out the hip shops in Belltown and need a pick-me-up, head over to **Uptown Espresso,** 2504 Fourth Ave. (✆ **206/441-1084;** www.uptownespresso.net). Down on the waterfront, try the branch at Pier 70, 2801 Alaskan Way (✆ **206/770-7777**).

Pioneer Square's Caffè Umbria offers a taste of the Seattle scene.

For hot chocolate, sipping chocolate (basically warm liquid chocolate), and a wide variety of chocolates and chocolate confections, don't miss **Chocolate Box,** 108 Pine St. (✆ **888/861-6188** or 206/443-3900; www.sschocolatebox.com), which is just a half block from Pike Place Market.

PIONEER SQUARE & THE INTERNATIONAL DISTRICT **Zeitgeist Art/Coffee** ★, 171 S. Jackson St. (✆ **206/583-0497;** www.zeitgeistcoffee.com), with its big windows and local artwork, is popular with the Pioneer Square art crowd. For a classically Italian cafe experience, sit and sip at **Caffè Umbria,** 320 Occidental Ave. S. (✆ **206/624-5847;** www.caffeumbria.com), which is on a pretty, shady plaza.

In the International District, don't miss the atmospheric **Panama Hotel Tea & Coffee House** ★, 607 S. Main St. (✆ **206/515-4000;** www.panamahotelseattle.com), which is filled with historic photos and offers a fascinating glimpse into the neighborhood's past. This is a great place to relax over a pot of rare Chinese tea.

SEATTLE CENTER & QUEEN ANNE **Caffé Vita** is one of Seattle's finest coffee roasters. In the Lower Queen Anne neighborhood, you can sample these superb coffees at Caffé Vita's own coffeehouse, at 813 Fifth Ave. N. (✆ **206/285-9662**). Grab a table on the sidewalk here, and you can even sip your espresso with a view of the Space Needle.

In the heart of the pleasant Upper Queen Anne area, **Caffe Ladro,** 2205 Queen Anne Ave. N. (✆ **206/282-5313**), has the feel of a cozy neighborhood coffeehouse. There's another Caffe Ladro in the MarQueen Hotel building in Lower Queen Anne, at 600 Queen Anne Ave. N. (✆ **206/282-1549**).

If you've tired of double-tall raspberry mochas and are desperately seeking a new coffee experience, make a trip to Upper Queen Anne's **El Diablo Coffee Co.,** 1811 Queen Anne Ave. N. (✆ **206/285-0693;** www.eldiablocoffee.com), a Latin-style coffeehouse. The Cubano, made with two shots of espresso and caramelized sugar, and the café con leche (a Cubano with steamed milk) are both devilishly good drinks. *¡Viva la revolución!*

SOUTH LAKE UNION & LAKE UNION A Seattle friend insists that the espresso at **Espresso Vivace** ★, 227 Yale Ave. N. (✆ **206/388-5164;** www.espressovivace.com), across the street from the R.E.I flagship store, is the best in Seattle. Give it a try and see if you agree.

CAPITOL HILL On the downtown edge of Capitol Hill, **Bauhaus Books & Coffee,** 301 E. Pine St. (✆ **206/625-1600;** www.bauhauscoffee.net), is a great place to hang out and soak up the atmosphere of Seattle's main gay neighborhood. You can always find lots of interesting 30-something types (mostly men) hanging out and reading or carrying on heated discussions.

Caffé Vita, 1005 E. Pike St. (✆ **206/709-4440**), has a devoted following of espresso fanatics who swear by the perfectly roasted coffee beans and lovingly crafted lattes served here.

Capitol Hill has two outposts of Espresso Vivace, a locals' favorite. There's **Vivace Espresso Bar at Brix ★**, 532 Broadway Ave. E. (✆ **206/860-2722**), a curved marble bar; and a sidewalk cart at 321 Broadway Ave. E. By the way, this coffee roastery participates in a carbon-sequestration program.

If hot chocolate and chocolate cake are more your style, stop in at **Dilettante Mocha Cafe & Chocolate Martini Bar,** 538 Broadway Ave. E. (✆ **206/329-6463;** www.dilettante.com), which is located in a modern space at the north end of the Capitol Hill commercial district, not far from Volunteer Park.

Read or have a chat and a latte at Bauhaus Books & Coffee.

NORTH SEATTLE In the U District, you'll find Seattle's oldest coffeehouse: **Cafe Allegro,** 4214 University Way NE (✆ **206/633-3030;** www.seattleallegro.com), down an alley around the corner from "the Ave" (as University Way is called by locals). This is a favored hangout of University of Washington students. Keep looking; you'll find it.

In Wallingford, I give up espresso so I can sip one of the wonderful gourmet hot chocolates served at **Chocolati,** 1716 N. 45th St. (✆ **206/633-7765;** www.chocolati.com). There are two other Chocolati cafes in the Greenlake neighborhood near the zoo—7810 E. Green Lake Dr. N. (✆ **206/527-5467**) and 8319 Greenwood Ave. N. (✆ **206/783-7078**).

In Fremont, try **Caffe Ladro,** 452 N. 36th St. (✆ **206/675-0854**), or the pretty little **Fremont Coffee Company,** 459 N. 36th St. (✆ **206/623-3633;** www.fremontcoffee.net), which is in a quaint little house that dates to 1904.

Bakeries, Pastry Shops & Ice Cream

DOWNTOWN If you're staying downtown in one of the city's business hotels and want a delicious treat, drop by **Belle Epicurean,** in the Fairmont Olympic Hotel, 1206 Fourth Ave. (✆ **206/262-9404;** www.belleepicurean.com), which specializes in sweet brioche buns.

PIKE PLACE MARKET The **Crumpet Shop ★,** 1503 First Ave. (✆ **206/682-1598**), specializes in its British namesake pastries, but does scones as well. It's almost a requirement that you accompany your crumpet or scone with a pot of tea. **Le Panier,** 1902 Pike Place (✆ **206/441-3669;** www.lepanier.com), is a great place to get a croissant and a latte and watch the market action. Chocolate chip cookie lovers should be sure to stop by **Cow Chips,**

111 Pike St. (✆ **206/623-3851;** www.cowchipcookies.com). If cheesecake is your vice, head to **The Confectional,** 1530 Pike Place (✆ **206/282-4422;** www.theconfectional.com), which specializes in individual cheesecakes. Just don't expect me to absolve you of your weight gain.

And when you just have to have something sweet, cold, and creamy, try the much-lauded gelato at **Bottega Italiana,** 1425 First Ave. (✆ **206/343-0200;** www.bottegaitaliana.com), or the conveniently located **Procopio,** 1501 Western Ave. (✆ **206/622-4280;** www.procopiogelati.com), which is on the Pike Street Hill Climb that links the waterfront with Pike Place Market.

BELLTOWN For some of the best baked goodies in the city, head to **Macrina ★**, 2408 First Ave. (✆ **206/448-4032;** www.macrinabakery.com), a neighborhood bakery/cafe that's a cozy place for a quick, cheap breakfast or lunch. In the morning, the smell of baking bread wafts down First Avenue and draws in many a passerby.

Tom Douglas's restaurants—Dahlia Lounge, Palace Kitchen, Etta's, Lola, Serious Pie, and Seatown—are all immensely popular, and there was such a demand for the breads and pastries served at these places that Douglas opened his own **Dahlia Bakery ★,** 2001 Fourth Ave. (✆ **206/441-4540;** www.tomdouglas.com). The croissants here are the best in Seattle—and you can even get Douglas's fabled coconut-cream pie to go.

Leave it to Seattle to take the doughnut craze and turn it into something sophisticated. **Top Pot Doughnuts,** 2124 Fifth Ave. (✆ **206/728-1966;** www.toppotdoughnuts.com), is housed in a former showroom building with big walls of glass. Books now line the walls; doughnuts fill the display cases.

PIONEER SQUARE & THE INTERNATIONAL DISTRICT The **Grand Central Bakery ★**, 214 First Ave. S. (✆ **206/622-3644;** www.grandcentralbakery.com), in Pioneer Square's Grand Central Arcade, is responsible for awakening

There's a "hole" lot of doughnuts at Top Pot.

Seattle to the pleasures of rustic European-style breads. This bakery not only turns out great bread, but also does good pastries and sandwiches.

Although the name is none too appealing, **Cow Chips,** 102A First Ave. S. (✆ **206/292-9808**), bakes Seattle's best chocolate chip cookies, which come in different sizes depending on the size of your craving.

SOUTH LAKE UNION & LAKE UNION Ever been to a biscuit bar? If you haven't, then you should be sure to stop by Chef Tom Douglas's little **Dahlia Workshop,** 401 Westlake Ave. N. (✆ **206/436-0052;** http://dahliaworkshop.com), a tiny breakfast and lunch place specializing in various biscuit sandwiches and such. The bakery here primarily produces the breads for all of Douglas's many restaurants.

Over on the east side of Lake Union, you can drool over beautiful French pastries at **Le Fournil,** 3230 Eastlake Ave. E. (✆ **206/328-6523;** www.le-fournil.com). Alternatively, check out the rustic breads at **Grand Central Bakery ★**, 1616 Eastlake Ave. E. (✆ **206/957-9505**).

SEATTLE CENTER & QUEEN ANNE My favorite Belltown bakery, **Macrina ★,** also has an outpost at 615 W. McGraw St. (✆ **206/283-5900**), which is near the top of Queen Anne Hill at the north end of the neighborhood's business district.

CAPITOL HILL If you've been on your feet at Volunteer Park for a while and need a snack, try the **North Hill Bakery,** 518 15th Ave. E. (✆ **206/325-9007;** www.northhillbakery.com), just a few blocks east of the park. There's always a good selection of baked goods in the cases. For some of the best and most unusual ice cream in Seattle, get in line at **Molly Moon's Homemade Ice Cream,** 917 E. Pine St. (✆ **206/708-7947;** www.mollymoonicecream.com). Flavors here include such untraditional ice creams as salted caramel, cardamom, rosemary-Meyer lemon, and honey lavender.

Seattle is over the moon for Molly Moon's ice cream.

It's not just a cupcake…it's a Cupcake Royale!

NORTH SEATTLE Let's say you've spent the morning or afternoon at the zoo, and you're suddenly struck with a craving for a fresh apple tart or an almond croissant. What's a person to do? Make tracks to **The Essential Baking Company Café ★**, 1604 N. 34th St. (✆ **206/545-0444;** www.essentialbaking.com), a Wallingford rustic-bread bakery and pastry shop. You can also get sandwiches here. A second Essential Baking Company Café is east of downtown in the Madison Valley neighborhood, at 2719 E. Madison St. (✆ **206/328-0078**). The above-mentioned **Molly Moon's Homemade Ice Cream** has a second location in the Wallingford neighborhood at 1622 N. 45th St. (✆ **206/547-5105**).

If you find yourself in Fremont craving some pie, head to the simply named **Pie,** 3515 Fremont Ave. N. (✆ **206/436-8590;** www.sweetandsavorypie.com), where both sweet and savory mini-pies are the specialty. If, on the other hand, you're more of a cake person, you'll want to stop by **Simply Desserts,** 3421 Fremont Ave. N. (✆ **206/633-2671;** www.simplydessertsseattle.com), where the cakes are not always so simple.

When nothing else will satisfy but a rich cupcake with buttercream frosting, stop in at Ballard's **Cupcake Royale,** 2052 NW Market St. (✆ **206/782-9557;** www.cupcakeroyale.com), which also has locations in the Capitol Hill, West Seattle, and Madrona neighborhoods. This was Seattle's very first specialty cupcake bakery. For stollen, kringles, and other classic Danish pastries, head to **Larsen's Danish Bakery,** 8000 24th Ave. NW (✆ **800/626-8631;** www.larsensbakery.com), in Ballard, Seattle's Scandinavian neighborhood.

SOUTH SEATTLE/COLUMBIA CITY Columbia City is one of Seattle's up-and-coming bohemian neighborhoods, and its commercial core has more than half a dozen restaurants, plus the **Columbia City Bakery,** 4865 Rainier Ave. S. (✆ **206/723-6023;** http://columbiacitybakery.com), which is one of the city's best bakeries. On any given morning, there might be two dozen different types of pastries in the cases.

WEST SEATTLE If you've been out on Alki Beach and are suddenly struck with a craving for a *pain au chocolate* or a slice of opera cake, don't despair. Just head to **Bakery Nouveau ★**, 4737 California Ave. SW (✆ **206/923-0534;** www.bakerynouveau.com), which many Seattleites swear is even better than the above-mentioned Columbia City Bakery. Visit them both and you can decide for yourself.

QUICK BITES

For variety, it's hard to beat the food court on the top floor of **Westlake Center,** 400 Pine St., in downtown Seattle. However, if you're a fan of Asian food, then be sure to have a quick meal from one of the vendors in the food court at **Uwajimaya,**

600 Fifth Ave. S. (✆ **206/624-6248;** www.uwajimaya.com), a huge Asian supermarket in the International District. If you're spending time at Seattle Center with the kids, you can grab a bite to eat at the food court inside **Center House,** which is the same building that houses the Children's Museum.

Market Munching

Few Seattle activities are more enjoyable than munching your way through Pike Place Market. The market has dozens of fast-food vendors, and it's nearly impossible to resist the interesting array of finger foods and quick bites. Here are some of my favorite places:

I like to start a day at the market with a bag of cinnamon mini-doughnuts from **Daily Dozen Doughnut Company** (✆ **206/467-7769**). While you stand in line waiting to order your doughnuts, (and you will wait in line), you can watch these sweet treats being made right before your eyes.

If you're planning a picnic, **DeLaurenti ★**, 1435 First Ave. (✆ **800/873-6685** or 206/622-0141; www.delaurenti.com), near the market's brass pig, is the perfect spot to get your pâté, sandwiches, and wine.

Even if you have no intention of taking a whole salmon home with you on the plane, you can sample the seafood at **City Fish Co.,** 1535 Pike Place (✆ **800/334-2669;** www.cityfish.com), which sets up a stand in front of its North Arcade fish display and sells oyster shooters and seafood cocktails. By the way, this is the oldest fishmonger in the market.

Sausage lovers should be sure to have at least one sausage sandwich at **Uli's Famous Sausage,** 1511 Pike Place (✆ **206/838-1712;** www.ulisfamoussausage.com). Pick from the long list of sausages, and have your sausage grilled up with your choice of toppings. Whether you crave a German bratwurst or a French merguez, you'll find it here.

Piroshky, Piroshky, 1908 Pike Place (✆ **206/441-6068;** www.piroshkybakery.com), lays it all out in its name. The sweet or savory Russian filled rolls

Beef and cheese, or chocolate cream piroshky...why not try both?

are the perfect finger food. In recent years, this place has become so popular that there is always a long line out the door.

At **Beecher's Handmade Cheese,** 1600 Pike Place (✆ **206/956-1964;** www.beechershandmadecheese.com), you can watch cheese being made and sample some of the products. But what brings me back here again and again is the awesome macaroni and cheese. Get some to go, and have a picnic down on the waterfront.

The Spanish Table, 1426 Western Ave. (✆ **206/682-2827;** www.spanishtable.com), is a specialty food shop on one of the lower levels of the market. You can get simple Spanish-style sandwiches, great soups, cheeses, and other light meal items, and then shop for a paella pan. This quiet corner of the market is a great place to get away from the crowds and try some food you might never have encountered before. A few doors down, you'll find the affiliated Paris Grocery.

Seattle Picnic Spots

To give focus to a tour of Pike Place Market, why not spend the morning or afternoon shopping for interesting picnic items, and then head up to the north end of the waterfront to the Olympic Sculpture Park or Myrtle Edwards Park? Or, because a picnic of foods from Pike Place Market should be as special as the food-shopping experience, consider heading a bit farther afield, perhaps to Discovery Park, Seattle's waterfront urban wilderness (take Western Ave. north along Elliott Bay to Magnolia and follow the signs). Another good place for a picnic is Volunteer Park, high atop Capitol Hill. Alternatively, you could have your picnic aboard a ferry headed to Bainbridge Island (a 30-min. trip) or to Bremerton (a 1-hr. trip).

PRACTICAL INFORMATION

While Pike Place Market is ground zero for Seattle foodies and should be your starting point if you are here to savor Seattle's flavors, it is also full of tourists. You can escape the throngs and find some excellent restaurants just north of the market in the **Belltown** neighborhood. Until a few years ago, this was Seattle's hottest restaurant neighborhood, but while there are still some good restaurants here, other neighborhoods are now generating more buzz among local foodies. The newly built South Lake Union neighborhood had the hottest restaurant scene in 2011, though Ballard's booming restaurant scene was in strong competition. Back in 2009 and 2010, Capitol Hill was where all the new restaurants were opening, and this neighborhood continues to be a great area for dining out. Capitol Hill's greatest concentration of good restaurants, is in the blocks around the corner of East Pike Street and 12th Avenue East.

If you're looking for good cheap eats, you'll find plenty of options in Pike Place Market. In fact, because the market is such a tourist attraction, it has scads of cheap places to eat; just don't expect haute cuisine at diner prices. You can, however, find a few gems, which I have listed in this chapter.

For real dining deals, though, you'll need to head to the 'hoods. Seattle is a city of self-sufficient neighborhoods, and within these urban enclaves are dozens of good, inexpensive places to eat. These are neighborhood spots that aren't usually patronized by visitors to the city. However, if you have a car and can navigate your way to outlying neighborhoods or are comfortable exploring by public bus, such neighborhoods as **Queen Anne, Madison Valley, Madison Park,**

Columbia City, and **Ballard,** are all great places to stroll around looking for just the right restaurant to fit your tastes and your budget. In the Upper Queen Anne neighborhood alone, I've counted more than a dozen restaurants within a 6-block area—and most of them have something or other to recommend them. Stroll the compact commercial blocks of one of these neighborhoods, and keep an eye out for newspaper reviews plastered in the front windows of restaurants. Pick one that the local paper liked, and you probably won't go wrong.

RESTAURANTS BY CUISINE

AMERICAN

BuiltBurger ($, p. 86)
Dick's ($, p. 89)
Elysian Fields (p. 86)
Icon Grill ★ ($$, p. 84)
Lowell's Restaurant ($, p. 82)
Lunchbox Laboratory ($, p. 94)
Maggie Bluffs Marina Grill ($, p. 91)
Portage Bay Cafe ★ ($, p. 95)
Red Mill Burgers ($, p. 103)
Sport Restaurant & Bar ($, p. 89)
Two Bells Bar & Grill ($, p. 86)

AMERICAN REGIONAL

5 Spot ★ ($, p. 90)
Matt's in the Market ★ ($$$, p. 80)
Palace Kitchen ★ ($$, p. 85)
Purple Café and Wine Bar ★ ($$, p. 79)

BAKERIES & PASTRY SHOPS

Bakery Nouveau ★ ($, p. 112)
Belle Epicurean ($, p. 109)
Columbia City Bakery ($, p. 112)
The Confectional ($, p. 110)
Cow Chips ($, p. 109 and p. 111)
Crumpet Shop ★ ($, p. 109)
Cupcake Royale/Vérité Coffee ($, p. 112)
Dahlia Bakery ★ ($, p. 110)
Dahlia Workshop ($, p. 111)
Essential Baking Company Café ★ ($, p. 112)
Grand Central Bakery ★ ($, p. 110 and p. 111)
Larsen's Danish Bakery ($, p. 112)
Le Fournil ($, p. 111)
Le Panier ($, p. 109)
Macrina ★ ($, p. 110 and p. 111)
North Hill Bakery ($, p. 111)
Pie (Fremont, $, p. 112)
Simply Desserts ($, p. 112)
Top Pot Doughnuts ($, p. 110)

CAFES, COFFEE BARS & TEA SHOPS

Ancient Grounds ★ ($, p. 107)
Bauhaus Books & Coffee ($, p. 108)
Cafe Allegro ($, p. 109)
Caffe Ladro ($, p. 107, p. 108, and p. 109)
Caffè Senso Unico ($, p. 107)
Caffè Umbria ($, p. 108)
Caffé Vita ($, p. 108)
Chocolate Box ($, p. 108)
Chocolati ($, p. 109)
Dilettante Mocha Cafe & Chocolate Martini Bar ($, p. 109)
El Diablo Coffee Co. ($, p. 108)
Espresso Vivace ★ ($, p. 108 and p. 109)
Fremont Coffee Company ($, p. 109)
Local Color ($, p. 107)
Monorail Espresso ($, p. 107)
Panama Hotel Tea & Coffee House ★ ($, p. 108)
Starbucks ($, p. 107)
Uptown Espresso ($, p. 107)
Vivace Espresso Bar at Brix ★ ($, p. 109)
Zeitgeist Art/Coffee ★ ($, p. 108)

CAJUN/CREOLE

Toulouse Petit ★ ($$, p. 89)

Key to Abbreviations: $$$$ = Very Expensive; $$$ = Expensive; $$ = Moderate; $ = Inexpensive

CHINESE

Jade Garden Restaurant ($, p. 87)

CONTINENTAL

Canlis ★★★ ($$$$, p. 90)
The Georgian ★★★ ($$$$, p. 75)

DELI

Roxy's Diner ★ ($, p. 103)

FRENCH

Boat Street Café and Kitchen ★★ ($$, p. 88)
Cafe Campagne ★★ ($$, p. 81)
Café Presse ★ ($, p. 98)
Joule ★★ ($$$, p. 101)
Le Pichet ★★ ($$, p. 81)
Luc ★★ ($$, p. 100)
Matt's in the Market ★ ($$$, p. 80)
Virginia Inn ★ ($$, p. 85)

GREEK

Lola ★★ ($$$, p. 83)

INTERNATIONAL

Baguette Box ($, p. 98)
Beach Cafe ★ ($$, p. 106)

ITALIAN

Anchovies & Olives ★★ ($$$, p. 95)
Bisato ★★ ($$$, p. 83)
Bizzarro Italian Cafe ★ ($$, p. 101)
Cascina Spinasse ★★ ($$$, p. 96)
Cuoco, ★★ ($$, p. 91)
Il Bistro ★★ ($$$, p. 80)
The Old Spaghetti Factory ($, p. 75)
Osteria La Spiga ★★ ($$$, p. 96)
The Pink Door ★ ($$, p. 81)
Salumi ★★ ($, p. 86)
Serafina ★ ($$, p. 94)
Volterra ★★ ($$$, p. 104)

JAPANESE

I Love Sushi ★ ($$, p. 94)
Maneki ★ ($$, p. 87)
Samurai Noodle ($, p. 87)
Shiro's Sushi Restaurant ★★ ($$, p. 85)

KOREAN

Joule ★★ ($$$, p. 101)

LATE-NIGHT

El Gaucho ★★ ($$$$, p. 83)
5 Spot ★ ($, p. 90)
Palace Kitchen ★ ($$, p. 85)
The Pink Door ★ ($$, p. 81)

MEDITERRANEAN

Lark ★ ($$, p. 97)
Palace Kitchen ★ ($$, p. 85)

MEXICAN

Agua Verde Cafe ★ ($, p. 100)
Cactus ★ ($$, p. 105)
El Camino ★ ($$, p. 102)
El Puerco Llorón ($, p. 82)

NEW AMERICAN

Lecōsho ★★ ($$$, p. 78)
Quinn's ★ ($$, p. 98)
Sitka & Spruce ★★ ($$$, p. 97)
Staple & Fancy Mercantile ★★ ($$$, p. 103)
Six-Seven ★★ ($$$, p. 74)
Spur Gastropub ★★ ($$$, p. 84)
Tilikum Place Café ($$, p. 89)
Tilth ★★ ($$$, p. 101)

NORTHWEST

Canlis ★★★ ($$$$, p. 90)
Dahlia Lounge ★★★ ($$$, p. 83)
Flying Fish ★★ ($$, p. 94)
The Georgian ★★★ ($$$$, p. 75)
Lark ★ ($$, p. 97)
Mistral Kitchen ★★ ($$$, p. 91)
Palisade ★★ ($$$, p. 90)
Poppy ★★★ ($$$, p. 97)
Restaurant Zoë ★★ ($$$, p. 84)
Rover's ★★★ ($$$$, p. 99)
SkyCity ★ ($$$$, p. 88)
Virginia Inn ★ ($$, p. 85)

PAN-ASIAN

Wild Ginger ★★ ($$, p. 79)

PAN-LATIN

Tango Restaurant & Lounge ★ ($$, p. 98)

PIZZA

Serious Pie ★★ ($$, p. 85)

QUICK BITES

Beecher's Handmade Cheese ($, p. 114)
Bottega Italiana ($, p. 110)
DeLaurenti ★ ($$, p. 113)
Molly Moon's Homemade Ice Cream ($, p. 111 and p. 112)
Piroshky, Piroshky ($, p. 113)
Procopio ($, p. 110)
The Spanish Table ($, p. 114)
Uli's Famous Sausage ★ ($$, p. 113)
Uwajimaya ($, p. 112)
Westlake Center food court ($, p. 112)

SEAFOOD

Alki Crab & Fish Co. ($, p. 106)
Anthony's Pier 66 and Bell Street Diner ★ ($$, p. 74)
The Brooklyn Seafood, Steak & Oyster House ★ ($$$, p. 78)
Chinook's at Salmon Bay ★ ($$, p. 104)
Elliott's Oyster House ★★ ($$, p. 75)
Etta's ★ ($$, p. 81)
Flying Fish ★★ ($$, p. 94)
Ivar's Salmon House ★ ($$, p. 100)
Pike Place Chowder ($, p. 82)
Ray's Boathouse/Ray's Cafe ★★ ($$$, p. 103)
Salty's on Alki Beach ★★ ($$$, p. 105)
The Walrus and the Carpenter ★ ($$, p. 104)

SPANISH

The Harvest Vine ★★ ($$, p. 99)

STEAK

El Gaucho ★★ ($$$$, p. 83)
Metropolitan Grill ★ ($$$, p. 78)

THAI

Chantanee Thai Restaurant ★★ ($$, p. 106)
Mae Phim Thai Restaurant ($, p. 80)
May ★ ($$, p. 102)
Thaiku ★ ($, p. 105)

TIBETAN

Ting Momo ★ ($, p. 95)

VEGETARIAN

Cafe Flora ★ ($, p. 100)
Carmelita ★★($$, p. 102)
Rover's ★★★ ($$$$, p. 99)

VIETNAMESE

Pho Than Brothers ($, p. 99)
Tamarind Tree ★★ ($$, p. 87)

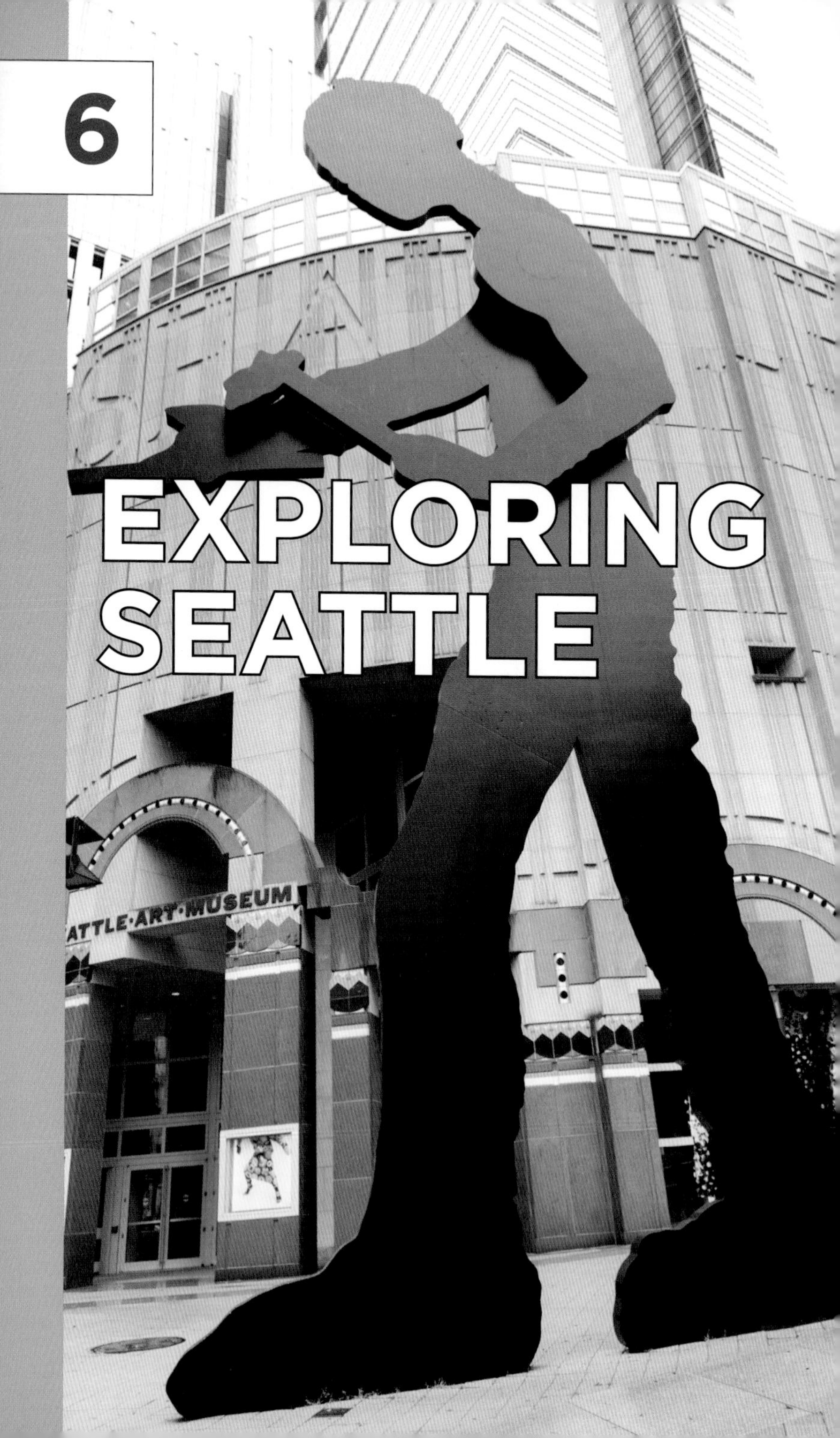

6 EXPLORING SEATTLE

I hope you've got a good pair of walking shoes and a lot of stamina (a double latte helps), because Seattle is a walking town. The city's two biggest attractions—the waterfront and Pike Place Market—are the sorts of places where you'll spend hours on your feet. When your feet are beat, you can relax on a tour boat and enjoy the views of the city from the Puget Sound, or you can take a 2-minute rest on the monorail, which links downtown with Seattle Center, home of the Space Needle. If your energy drops, don't worry; there's always an espresso cafe nearby.

And that monorail ride takes you right through the middle of Paul Allen's EMP/SFM (Experience Music Project/Science Fiction Museum), the Frank Gehry–designed rock-music and science-fiction museum that is also located in Seattle Center. Allen, who made his millions as one of the cofounders of Microsoft, has spent years changing the face of Seattle. He renovated Union Station and developed the area adjacent to Qwest Field, built for the Seattle Seahawks football team and owned by . . . you guessed it: Paul Allen. The stadium is adjacent to the Seattle Mariners' Safeco Field, which is one of the few ballparks in the country with a retractable roof. Allen has also now turned the South Lake Union neighborhood just north of downtown into a new urban village filled with high-rise condominiums, on-line retailer Amazon's headquarters, its own streetcar line, and loads of good restaurants. This redevelopment project has been the biggest thing to hit Seattle since the Space Needle first pierced the city's cloudy skies a half century ago.

OPPOSITE PAGE: **Jonathon Borofsky's *Hammering Man,* pounds out a silent beat in front of the Seattle Art Museum.** ABOVE: **The Experience Music Project/Science Fiction Museum looks as though it's ready to join the clouds above.**

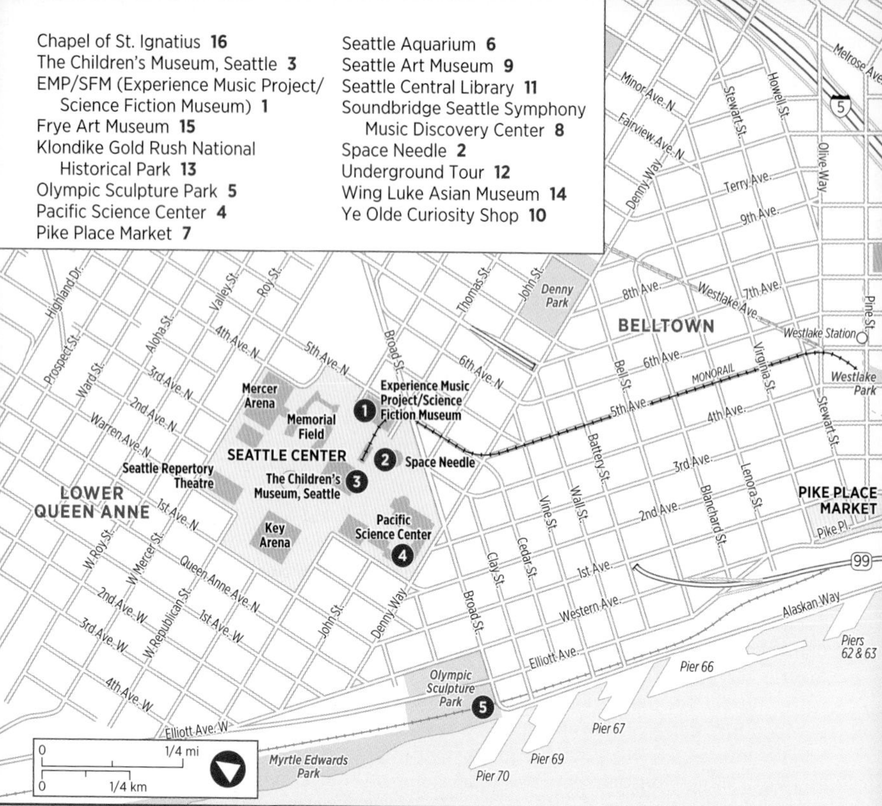

Despite Seattle's many downtown diversions, the city's natural surroundings are still its primary attraction. You can easily cover all of Seattle's museums and major sights in 2 or 3 days. Once you've seen what's to see indoors, you can begin exploring the city's outdoor life.

If you plan to spend your time in downtown Seattle, a car is a liability. However, when it comes time to explore beyond downtown, say, to the University District, Fremont, or Ballard, a car can be handy (although there are good bus connections to these neighborhoods). If you want to head farther afield—to Mount Rainier or the Olympic Peninsula—then a car is a must.

THE WATERFRONT

The waterfront is to Seattle what Fisherman's Wharf is to San Francisco, Stretching along Alaskan Way from Yesler Way, in the south, to Bay Street, Myrtle Edwards Park, and the Olympic Sculpture Park, in the north, the waterfront is Seattle's most popular and touristy destination. Tacky gift shops, candy stores selling fudge and saltwater taffy, sidewalk T-shirt vendors, overpriced restaurants, and walk-up counters serving greasy fish and chips—they're all here. Why bother fighting the jostling crowds? Well, for one thing, this is where you'll find the Seattle Aquarium and Ye Olde Curiosity Shop, which is king of the tacky gift shops and as fun as a Ripley's Believe It or Not museum. Ferries to Bainbridge Island and Bremerton, as well as several different boat tours, also operate from

the waterfront. Oh, and then there's the view, that incomparable view across Elliott Bay to the Olympic Mountains. So stay focused and stay out of the shopping arcades inside the piers (unless, of course, you really need salt-and-pepper shakers shaped like the Space Needle).

You'll find the Washington State Ferries terminal at **Pier 52,** which is at the south end of the waterfront near Pioneer Square. (A ferry ride makes for a cheap cruise.) **Pier 55** has excursion boats offering harbor cruises and trips to Tillicum Village on Blake Island. At **Pier 56,** cruise boats leave for trips through the Chittenden (Ballard) Locks to Lake Union. See "Organized Tours," later in this chapter, for details on these excursions. At **Pier 57,** you'll find the **Bay Pavilion,** which has a vintage carousel and a video arcade to keep the kids busy.

Pier 59 is home to the Seattle Aquarium (see below) and a waterfront park. If you continue up the waterfront, you'll find **Pier 66,** also called the Bell Street Pier, which has a rooftop park. **Anthony's** (p. 74), one of the best seafood restaurants on the waterfront, is also on this pier. At **Pier 67** is the **Edgewater** hotel (p. 45), a great place to take in the sunset over a drink or dinner.

Next door, at **Pier 69,** you can see the dock for the ferries that ply the waters between Seattle and Victoria, British Columbia. Just north of this pier is the **Olympic Sculpture Park** and the grassy **Myrtle Edwards Park,** which make all the schlock worth enduring, a nice finale to the waterfront. Myrtle Edwards Park has a popular paved pathway and is a great spot for a sunset stroll or a picnic.

The Olympic Sculpture park showcases/is showcased by the Seattle waterfront.

The **Olympic Sculpture Park** (see below), which covers a hillside overlooking the north end of the waterfront, is my favorite Seattle attraction, offering not only monumental sculptures, but also gardens of native plants and superb views of the Seattle skyline, Elliott Bay, and the Olympic Mountains.

Olympic Sculpture Park ★★★ Covering 9 acres of hillside, the Olympic Sculpture Park stretches from Belltown down to the waterfront at Myrtle Edwards Park. Modern and contemporary monumental sculptures are the focus of the collection, which includes works from regional, national, and international artists, including Alexander Calder, whose sculpture *Eagle* is one of the highlights of the collection. From just the right perspective, this sculpture perfectly

Saving Money on Sightseeing with CityPASS

If you're a see-it-all, do-it-all kind of person, you'll want to buy a **CityPASS** (✆ **888/330-5008** or 208/787-4300; www.citypass.com), which gets you into the Space Needle, Pacific Science Center, Experience Music Project/Science Fiction Museum (EMP/SFM), Seattle Aquarium, and either the Museum of Flight or Woodland Park Zoo, and lets you take a boat tour of the harbor with Argosy Cruises, at a savings of 50% if you visit all five attractions and do the harbor tour. The pass, good for 9 days from the date of first use, costs $59 for adults and $39 for children 4 to 12. Purchase your CityPASS at any of the participating attractions.

The **Go Seattle Card** (✆ **866/628-9029**; www.smartdestinations.com) is another interesting option for travelers who are able to plan out a daily tour route in advance. It takes careful planning to get your money's worth, but it can be done. The way it works is that you pay $50 ($33 for children 3–12) for a card that will get you into as many participating attractions as you can visit in 1 day. There are discounts for the 2-, 3-, 5-, and 7-day cards; your best bet would probably be the 3-day card.

frames the distant Space Needle. What a view! Other noteworthy works include Claes Oldenburg and Coosje van Bruggen's *Typewriter Eraser, Scale X,* Richard Serra's massive plate-steel *Wake,* and *Split,* a life-size stainless steel tree by Roxy Paine. If the sculptures aren't enough to hold your attention, turn your eyes toward the views of Elliott Bay and the distant Olympic Mountains. Down along the water, you'll also find a perfect little beach that was constructed as part of the sculpture park. This diminutive stretch of shoreline feels as wild as any beach on the Olympic Peninsula.

2901 Western Ave. ✆ **206/654-3100.** www.seattleartmuseum.org. Free admission. Park 30 min. before sunrise to 30 min. past sunset. Pavilion May to Labor Day Tues–Sun 10am–5pm; day after Labor Day to Apr Tues–Sun 10am–4pm. Pavilion closed New Year's Day, Thanksgiving, Dec 24–25, and New Year's Eve. Bus: 1, 2, 13, 15, 18, 21, or 22. Waterfront Streetcar Bus (Rte. 99): Pier 69 stop.

Seattle Aquarium ★★ ☺ The Seattle Aquarium is a fabulous introduction to the sea life of the Northwest. The **Window on Washington Waters** exhibit, a huge tank just inside the entrance, is a highlight of a visit, especially when divers feed the fish. There's also a tank that generates crashing waves, and, in the **Life on the Edge** tide-pool exhibit that focuses on life along Washington's shores, you can reach into the water to touch starfish, sea cucumbers, and anemones (kids love these tanks). The aquarium's main focus is on the water worlds of the Puget Sound region, but there are also fascinating exhibits of sea life from around the world, including a beautiful coral-reef tank. The star attractions, however, are the playful river otters and sea otters, as well as the giant octopus. From the underwater viewing dome, you get a fisheye view of life beneath the waves, and every September you can watch salmon return up a fish ladder to spawn.

Pier 59, 1483 Alaskan Way. ✆ **206/386-4300.** www.seattleaquarium.org. Admission $19 adults, $12 children 4–12, free for children 3 and under. Daily 9:30am–5pm. Bus: 10, 11, 12, 16, 18, 24, or 25, and then walk through Pike Place Market to the waterfront. Waterfront Streetcar Bus (Rte. 99): Pike St. stop.

Kids can have a hands-on experience at "Life on the Edge" at the Seattle Aquarium.

PIKE PLACE MARKET TO PIONEER SQUARE

Pike Place Market and the Pioneer Square historic district lie at opposite ends of First Avenue; midway between the two is the Seattle Art Museum.

The **Pioneer Square** area, with its historic buildings, interesting shops, museum, and Underground Tour (see "Good Times in Bad Taste," later in this chapter), is well worth a morning or afternoon of exploration. See chapter 7 for a walking tour of the area.

Klondike Gold Rush National Historical Park "At 3 o'clock this morning the steamship *Portland,* from St. Michaels for Seattle, passed up (Puget) Sound with more than a ton of gold on board and 68 passengers." When the *Seattle Post-Intelligencer* published that sentence on July 17, 1897, it started a stampede. Would-be miners heading for the Klondike gold fields in the 1890s made Seattle their outfitting center, and the prospectors helped the city to prosper. When they struck it rich up north, they headed back to Seattle, the first U.S. outpost of civilization, and unloaded their gold, making Seattle doubly rich. Although this place isn't in the Klondike (that's in Canada) and isn't really a park (it's a museum in a historic building), it's still a fascinating place, and it seems only fitting that it should be here in Seattle. (Another unit of the park is in Skagway, Alaska.) During the summer, free walking tours of the Pioneer Square neighborhood are scheduled daily.

ON THE trail OF DALE CHIHULY

Northwest glass artist Dale Chihuly, one of the founders of the Pilchuck School for art glass, north of Seattle, is recognized internationally for his fanciful, color-saturated contemporary art glass. From tabletop vessels to huge chandeliers and massive window installations, his creations in glass have a depth and richness of color treasured by collectors around the world.

His sensuous forms include vases within bowls reminiscent of Technicolor birds' eggs in giant nests. Works in his *ikebana* series, based on the traditional Japanese flower-arranging technique, are riotous conglomerations of color that twist and turn like so many cut flowers waving in the wind.

No one place in Seattle features a large collection of his work, but numerous public displays exist around the city. On the third floor of the **Washington State Convention and Trade Center,** Pike Street and Eighth Avenue, is a case with some beautifully lighted pieces. In the adjacent **Sheraton Seattle Hotel,** 1400 Sixth Ave., there is a display of art glass by Chihuly and other artists who have worked at the Pilchuck School. The **City Centre shopping arcade,** 1420 Fifth Ave., also has displays by numerous glass artists, including Chihuly. Don't miss the large wall installation that is beside this upscale shopping arcade's lounge. You'll also find two Chihuly chandeliers inside **Benaroya Hall,** Third Avenue between Union and University streets, which is the home of the Seattle Symphony. On Capitol Hill, you can see a large Chihuly chandelier in the lobby of Seattle University's **Pigott Building,** 901 12th Ave.

Many with gold fever equipped themselves in Seattle before heading off to the Klondike.

319 Second Ave. S. ✆ **206/220-4240.** www.nps.gov/klse. Free admission. Daily 9am–5pm. Closed New Year's Day, Thanksgiving, and Christmas. Bus: 3, 4, 15, 16, 18, 21, or 22. Waterfront Streetcar Bus (Rte. 99): Occidental Park stop.

Want to take home an original Chihuly as a souvenir of your visit to Seattle? Drop by the **Foster/White Gallery,** 220 Third Ave. S. (✆ **206/622-2833;** www.fosterwhite.com), in Pioneer Square.

If you're a serious fan of Chihuly's work and art glass in general, then you have to take the time for an excursion to **Tacoma,** 32 miles south of Seattle. Here you'll find the **Museum of Glass,** 1801 Dock St. (✆ **866/468-7386;** www.museumofglass.org), which is devoted to art glass in all its forms and is connected to downtown Tacoma via a pedestrian bridge designed by Chihuly. You can see more of Chihuly's work at the **Tacoma Art Museum,** 1701 Pacific Ave. (✆ **253/272-4258;** www.tacomaartmuseum.org), like the beautiful window pictured. Just up the street from here, at Tacoma's restored **Union Station,** 1717 Pacific Ave. (✆ **253/863-5173**), which is now the federal courthouse, there is a fascinating large Chihuly installation in a massive arched window. For more information on visiting Tacoma, see "Tacoma's Museums & Gardens," in chapter 10. For more information on Chihuly installations in the area, go to **www.chihuly.com/Seasites.html**.

"Rachel" is the Pike Place Market's giant piggy bank...and the departure point for tours.

Pike Place Market ★★★ Home to 100 or so farmers and fishmongers and hundreds of small specialty shops, Pike Place Market is Seattle's number one tourist destination. Add in more than 150 crafts vendors and artists and buskers who serenade the milling crowds and you have one seriously bustling marketplace. When the shuffling shoppers and sensory overload become too much, you can duck in to one of the dozens of restaurants, including some of the city's best, and take a tasty time out. At the **information booth** almost directly below the large PIKE PLACE MARKET sign, you can pick up a free map and guide.

Pike Place Market, originally a farmers market, was founded in 1907 when housewives complained that middlemen were raising the price of produce. The market allowed shoppers to buy directly from producers and save on grocery bills. For several decades, the market thrived. However, World War II deprived the market of nearly half its farmers when Japanese-Americans were moved to internment camps. With the postwar flight to the suburbs, the market was never able to recover from the war years, and by the 1960s, it was no longer the popular spot it had been. When it was announced that the site was being eyed for a major redevelopment project, a grass-roots movement arose to save the 9-acre market, and eventually, it was declared a National Historic District.

Market highlights not to be missed include *Rachel,* a giant bronze piggy bank directly below the main neon market sign and the adjacent Pike Place Fish, a fishmonger known for its "flying fish." The market's **"Gum Wall,"** in the alley down a flight of stairs from *Rachel,* is a bit of a sticky subject. No one can agree whether it is art or just a disgusting form of litter. You'll have to decide for yourself. See chapter 7 for a detailed walking tour of the best of the market.

Victor Steinbrueck Park, at the north end of the market at the intersection of Pike Place,

Don't Bug Me, Man!

If you find giant spiders more fascinating than frightening, then you should drop by Pike Place Market's unusual Seattle Bug Safari, 1501 Western Ave. (✆ 206/285-2847; www.seattlebugsafari.com), which is on the Pike Street Hill Climb and is home to more than 40 species of large and unusual insects, spiders, scorpions, centipedes, and millipedes. The zoo is open Tuesday through Saturday from 10am to 6pm and Sunday from 11am to 5pm (Mon hours vary seasonally). Admission is $8 for adults and $6 for children 4 to 12.

Virginia Street, and Western Avenue, is a popular lounging area for both the homeless and those just looking for a grassy spot in the sun. In the park, you'll see two 50-foot-tall totem poles.

See "Market Munching," in chapter 5, for a rundown of some of my favorite market food vendors. Also, if you're going to be in town in October, consider attending the annual **Feast at the Market** (✆ **206/461-6935;** www.neighborcare.org/feast), a showcase for food from market restaurants.

In summer, there are guided tours on Saturday mornings at 9am ($10 adults, $5 seniors and children). These tours leave from *Rachel,* the giant piggy bank. Advance reservations are required; call the **Friends of the Market** (✆ **206/322-2219**). We also include a walking tour of the market in our "City Strolls" chapter (starting on p. 170).

Between Pike and Pine sts., at First Ave. ✆ **206/682-7453.** www.pikeplacemarket.org. Pike Place/First Ave. businesses Mon–Sat 10am–6pm; Sun 11am–5pm. Down Under stores daily 11am–5pm. Many produce vendors open at 8am in summer; restaurant hours vary. Closed New Year's Day, Thanksgiving, and Christmas. Bus: 1–4, 10–12, 14–16, 18, 21, 22, 24, 25, 33, 36, 43, 49, 56, 57, or 70. Waterfront Streetcar Bus (Rte. 99): Pike St. Hillclimb stop.

Seattle Art Museum (SAM) ★★ This large museum verges on world-class and should not be missed. With acres of gallery space and cutting-edge exhibit designs, this is definitely not your typical, stodgy art museum. Before you step inside, you'll come face to faceless silhouette with Jonathon Borofsky's shadowy *Hammering Man,* an animated three-story steel sculpture that pounds out a silent beat in front of the museum. Inside the museum, white cars go tumbling through the air with colored lights shooting out of them in Cai Guo-Qiang's sculpture *Inopportune: Stage One.* Once you get inside the museum proper, you'll find one of the nation's premier collections of Northwest Coast Indian art and artifacts, and an equally large collection of African art. The museum is particularly strong in modern and contemporary art, but there are also good collections of European and American art ranging from ancient Mediterranean works to pieces from the medieval, Renaissance, and baroque periods. Of course, the Northwest contemporary art collection is also quite extensive. (The museum also has a smattering of Asian art, but the city's major collection of Asian art is at the affiliated **Seattle Asian Art Museum** in Volunteer Park; see p. 135.)

The Seattle Art Museum has particularly good collections of Northwest Coast Indian and African art.

1300 First Ave. ✆ **206/344-5275.** www.seattleartmuseum.org. Admission $15 adults, $12 seniors, $9 student and youths 13–17, free for children 12 and under. Free for all on 1st Thurs of each month; free for seniors on 1st Fri of each month; free for teens on 2nd Fri of each month from 5–9pm. Wed and Sat–Sun 10am–5pm; Thurs–Fri 10am–9pm. Closed New Year's Day, Thanksgiving, and Dec 24–25 (open some holiday Mon). Bus: Any downtown bus.

Soundbridge Seattle Symphony Music Discovery Center ☺ Perhaps you're an amateur musician but have always longed to conduct an orchestra, or perhaps you've never had much musical talent at all but dream of playing the cello like Yo-Yo Ma. At this fascinating little music exploration center, you can find out what it feels like to wield the baton or be first chair in the string section of the symphony. Not only do interactive exhibits allow you to play a cello, tickle the ivories, or conduct a virtual orchestra, but you can also listen to more than 500 classical recordings at the listening bar. There's an exhibit on the science of music as well.

Benaroya Hall, Second Ave. and Union St. ✆ **206/336-6600.** www.soundbridge.org. Admission $5, free for children 4 and under. Sun–Wed 10am–2pm; Tues and Fri–Sat 10am–4pm. Bus: Any downtown bus.

You can bang on the drum all day at the Soundbridge Seattle Symphony Music Discovery Center.

SEATTLE CENTER & LAKE UNION

Built in 1962 for the World's Fair, Seattle Center is today not only the site of Seattle's famous Space Needle, but also a cultural and entertainment park that doubles as the city's favorite festival grounds. Within Seattle Center's boundaries, you'll find EMP/SFM (Experience Music Project/ Science Fiction Museum), the Pacific Science Center, the Seattle Children's Museum, the Seattle Children's Theatre, Key Arena, the Marion Oliver McCaw Hall, the Intiman Theatre, the Bagley Wright Theatre, a children's amusement park, and a fountain that's a favorite summertime hangout. The "Especially for Kids" section (p. 150) lists further details on Seattle Center attractions that young travelers will enjoy. Not far away, you'll find Lake Union, with a couple of nautical attractions.

You can take some of the exhibits at the Center for Wooden Boats out for a spin.

The Center for Wooden Boats ★ Dedicated to the preservation of historic wooden boats, this unusual little museum at the south end of Lake Union is unique in that many of the exhibits (wooden boats) can be rented

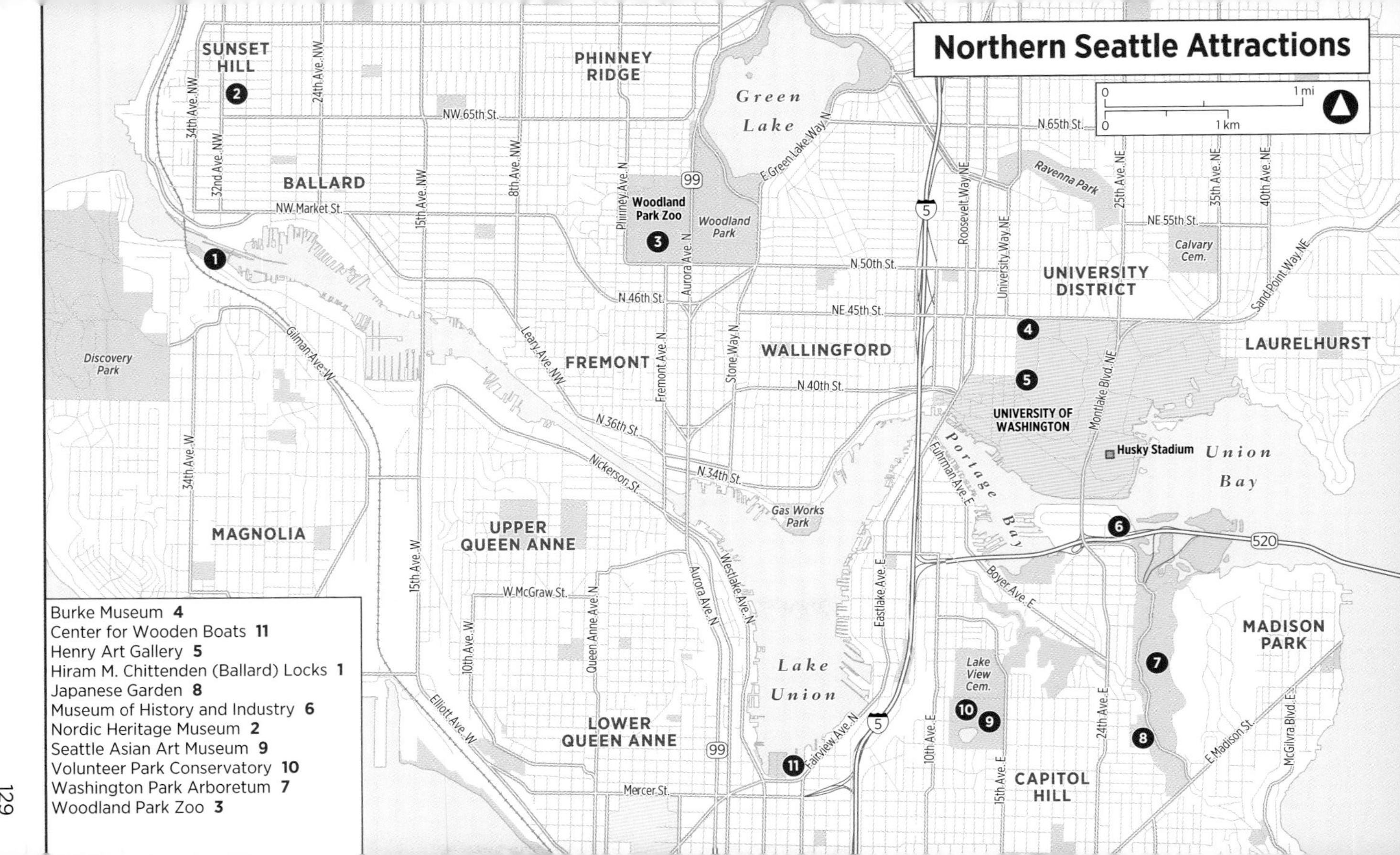

Burke Museum **4**
Center for Wooden Boats **11**
Henry Art Gallery **5**
Hiram M. Chittenden (Ballard) Locks **1**
Japanese Garden **8**
Museum of History and Industry **6**
Nordic Heritage Museum **2**
Seattle Asian Art Museum **9**
Volunteer Park Conservatory **10**
Washington Park Arboretum **7**
Woodland Park Zoo **3**

and taken out on the waters of Lake Union. Most of the center's boats are tied up to the docks surrounding the museum's floating boathouse, but some are stored on the dock itself. There are rowboats and sailboats, and rental rates range from $20 to $50 per hour (call for hours of availability). Free classic boat rides are held on Sunday at 2pm (sign up as early as 10am).

1010 Valley St. (Waterway 4, south end of Lake Union). ✆ **206/382-2628.** www.cwb.org. Free admission. May to early Sept Tues–Sun 10am–8pm; early Sept to Dec Tues–Sun 10am–6pm; Jan–Apr Tues–Sun 10am–5pm . Bus: 17, 26, 28, 30, 70–73, or 83. South Lake Union Streetcar: Lake Union Park stop.

EMP/SFM (Experience Music Project/Science Fiction Museum) ★★ The brainchild of Microsoft cofounder Paul Allen and designed by avant-garde architect Frank Gehry, who is known for pushing the envelope of architectural design, this combination rock-'n'-roll and science-fiction museum is a massive, multicolored blob at the foot of the Space Needle. Originally planned as a memorial to Seattle native Jimi Hendrix, the museum grew to encompass not only Hendrix, but also all of the Northwest rock scene (from "Louie Louie" to grunge), the general history of American popular music, and science-fiction books, movies, and TV shows.

Among the most popular exhibits here (after the Jimi Hendrix room) are the interactive rooms. In the **Sound Lab,** you can play guitars, drums, keyboards, or even DJ turntables; in **On Stage,** you can experience what it's like to be onstage performing in front of adoring fans. Another exhibit focuses on the history of guitars and includes some of the first electric guitars, which date from the early 1930s. Science-fiction exhibits tend to focus on blockbuster sci-fi movies such as *Battlestar Galactica* and *Avatar.* Give yourself plenty of time to explore this unusual museum.

Seattle Center, 325 Fifth Ave. N. ✆ **877/367-7361** or 206/770-2700. www.empsfm.org. Admission $15 adults, $12 seniors and children 5–17, free for children 4 and under. Late May to early Sept daily 10am–7pm; early Sept to late May daily 10am–5pm. Closed Thanksgiving and Christmas. Bus: 1–4, 8, 13, 15, 16, 18, 19, 24, 33, 45, 74, 81, or 82. Monorail: From Westlake Center at Pine St. and Fourth Ave.

The Science Fiction Museum exhibits props from such TV classics as "Battlestar Galactica."

Pacific Science Center ★ ☺ Although its exhibits are aimed primarily at children, the Pacific Science Center is fun for all ages. The main goal of this sprawling complex at Seattle Center is to teach kids about science and to instill a desire to study it. To that end, kids can investigate life-size robotic dinosaurs, a butterfly house and insect village (with giant robotic insects), technology exhibits where they can play virtual-reality soccer or challenge a robot to tic-tac-toe, and dozens

POLE TO pole ALL OVER SEATTLE

Totem poles are the quintessential symbol of the Northwest, and although this Native American art form actually comes from farther north, there are quite a few totem poles around Seattle. The four in **Occidental Park** at Occidental Avenue South and South Washington Street were carved by local artist Duane Pasco.

The tallest is 35-foot-tall *The Sun and Raven,* which tells the story of how Raven brought light into the world. Next to this pole is *Man Riding a Whale;* this type of totem pole was traditionally carved to help villagers during their whale hunts. The other two figures that face each other are symbols of the Bear Clan and the Welcoming Figure.

A block away, in the triangular plaza of **Pioneer Place,** you can see Seattle's most famous totem pole. It is a replacement for the plaza's original pole, which was damaged by an arsonist's fire in 1938. Seattle businessmen on a cruise to Alaska stole the original pole from a Tlingit village near Fort Tongass, Alaska, in 1899. According to local legend, after the pole caught fire in 1938, the city fathers sent a check to the tribe with a request for a new totem pole. The Tlingit response was, "Thanks for paying for the first one. Send another check for the replacement." The truth is far more prosaic: As part of a Civilian Conservation Corps program, the U.S. Forest Service paid Tlingit carver Charles Brown to create a new totem pole.

Up near Pike Place Market, at **Victor Steinbrueck Park,** which is at the intersection of Pike Place, Virginia Street, and Western Avenue, are two 50-foot-tall totem poles. To see the largest concentration of totem poles in the city, visit the **University of Washington's Burke Museum of Natural History and Culture** (see p. 136 for details, pictured). If you take the Tillicum Village tour, you'll also see totem poles outside the longhouse on **Blake Island** where the dinner and masked-dance performances are held.

of other fun hands-on exhibits addressing the biological sciences, physics, and chemistry. Throughout the year, there are special events that are guaranteed to keep your kids entertained for hours. There's a planetarium for learning about the skies (and laser shows for the fun of it), plus an IMAX theater. Be sure to check the schedule for special exhibits when you're in town.

Seattle Center, 200 Second Ave. N. ✆ **800/664-8775,** 206/443-2001, 206/443-4629 for IMAX information, or 206/443-2850 for laser-show information. www.pacificsciencecenter.org. Admission $14 adults, $12 seniors, $9 youths 6–15, $7 kids 3–5, free for children 2 and under; IMAX

Hands-on exhibits are for all ages at the Pacific Science Center.

$9–$14 adults, $8–$12 seniors, $7–$11 youths 6–15, $6–$9 kids 3–5, free for children 2 and under; laser show $5–$8.75. Various discounted combination tickets available. Summer daily 10am–6pm; other months Mon and Wed–Fri 10am–5pm, Sat–Sun 10am–6pm. Closed Thanksgiving and Christmas. Bus: 1–4, 8, 13, 15, 16, 18, 19, 24, 33, 45, 74, 81, or 82. Monorail: From Westlake Center at Pine St. and Fourth Ave.

Space Needle ★ From a distance, it looks like a flying saucer on a tripod, and when it was built for the 1962 World's Fair, the 605-foot-tall Space Needle was meant to suggest future architectural trends. Today the Space Needle is the quintessential symbol of Seattle, and at 520 feet above ground level, its observation deck provides superb views of the city and its surroundings. Displays identify more than 60 sites and activities in the Seattle area, and high-powered telescopes let you zoom in on them. You'll also find a pricey restaurant, **SkyCity** (p. 88), atop the tower. If you don't mind standing in line and paying quite a bit for an elevator ride, make this your first stop in Seattle so that you can orient yourself. (However, cheaper alternatives exist if you just want a view of the city—see "Space Needle Alternatives," below.)

The Space Needle is a striking sight, day or night.

Seattle Center, 400 Broad St. ✆ **206/905-2100.** www.spaceneedle.com. Admission $18 adults, $16 seniors, $11 children 4–12, free for children 3 and under (day-and-night tickets

SPACE NEEDLE alternatives

If you don't want to deal with the crowds at the Space Needle but still want an elevated downtown view, you have some alternatives. One is the big, black **Columbia Center** (✆ **206/386-5151**), at the corner of Fifth Avenue and Columbia Street. At 943 feet, this is the tallest building in Seattle (twice as tall as the Space Needle), with more stories (76, to be exact) than any other building west of the Mississippi.

On the 73rd floor is an observation deck with views that dwarf those from the Space Needle. Admission is only $5 for adults and $3 for seniors and children. It's open Monday through Friday from 8:30am to 4:30pm. For a view that will only cost you the price of a cup of latte, head to the Starbucks on the 40th floor of this high-rise. The view isn't quite as good as it is from the observation deck, but it comes close.

Not far from Columbia Center is the **Smith Tower,** 506 Second Ave. (✆ **206/622-4004;** www.smithtower.com). Opened in 1914, this was Seattle's first skyscraper and, for 50 years, the tallest building west of Chicago. Although the Smith Tower has only 42 stories, it still offers excellent views from its 35th-floor observation deck, which surrounds the ornate Chinese Room, a banquet hall with a carved ceiling. A lavish lobby and original manual elevators make this a fun and historic place to take in the Seattle skyline. Deck hours vary with the time of year and scheduled events in the Chinese Room; check in advance to be sure it will be open when you want to visit. Admission is $7.50 for adults, $6 for seniors and students, and $5 for children 6 to 12.

If you've ever seen a photo of the Space Needle framed by Mount Rainier and the high-rises of downtown Seattle, it was probably taken from **Kerry Viewpoint,** on Queen Anne Hill. If you want to take your own drop-dead gorgeous photo of the Seattle skyline from this elevated perspective, head north (uphill) from **Seattle Center** on the very steep Queen Anne Avenue North, and turn left on West Highland Drive. When you reach the park, you'll immediately recognize the view.

Another great panorama is from the water tower in **Volunteer Park,** on Capitol Hill at East Prospect Street and 14th Avenue East.

$24 adults, $22 seniors, $15 children 4–13). No charge if dining in the SkyCity restaurant. Mon–Thurs 10am–9:30pm; Fri–Sat 9:30am–10:30pm; Sun 9:30am–9:30pm. Bus: 1–4, 8, 13, 15, 16, 18, 19, 24, 33, 45, 74, 81, or 82. Monorail: From Westlake Center at Pine St. and Fourth Ave.

THE INTERNATIONAL DISTRICT

Seattle today boasts of its strategic location on the Pacific Rim, but its ties to Asia are nothing new. This is evident in the International District, Seattle's main Asian neighborhood, which is centered between Fifth Avenue South and 12th Avenue South (btw. S. Washington St. and S. Lane St.). Called both Chinatown and the International District (because so many Asian nationalities have made this area home), the neighborhood has been the center of the city's Asian communities for more than a century. You can learn about its history at the **Wing Luke Museum of the Asian Pacific American Experience** (or, simply, **The Wing;** see below).

Explore the role Asian culture has played in Seattle at the Wing Luke Museum.

At the corner of Maynard Avenue South and South King Street is **Hing Hay Park,** the site of an ornate and colorful pavilion given to Seattle by the city of Taipei, Taiwan. The International District also has many restaurants, import stores, and food markets, and the huge **Uwajimaya** (p. 112) is all of these rolled into one.

Wing Luke Museum of the Asian Pacific American Experience Despite much persecution in the 19th and 20th centuries, Asians, primarily Chinese and Japanese, have played an integral role in developing the Northwest, and today the connection between this region and the far side of the Pacific has opened both economic and cultural doors. Named for the first Asian-American to hold public office in the Northwest and located in the heart of Seattle's International District, this small museum has exhibits that explore the roles various Asian cultures have played in the settlement and development of the region. Other exhibits help explain Asian customs to non-Asians. If you're walking around the International District, this place will give you a better appreciation of the neighborhood.

719 S. King St. ✆ **206/623-5124.** www.wingluke.org. Admission $13 adults, $9.95 seniors and students, $8.95 children 5–12, free for children 4 and under. Free admission 1st Thurs and 3rd Sat of each month. Tues–Sun 10am–5pm (until 8pm 1st Thurs and 3rd Sat of each month). Closed New Year's Day, July 4th, Thanksgiving, Christmas Eve, and Christmas. Bus: 7, 14, or 36. Waterfront Streetcar Bus (Rte. 99) to 8th Ave. South, or any bus using the transit tunnel.

FIRST HILL (PILL HILL) & CAPITOL HILL

Seattle is justly proud of its parks, and **Volunteer Park ★★**, on Capitol Hill at 14th Avenue East and East Prospect Street (drive north on Broadway and watch for signs), is one of the most popular. Here you'll find not only acres of lawns, groves of trees, and huge old rhododendrons, but also an old water tower that provides one of the best panoramas in the city. A winding staircase leads to the top of the tower, from which you get 360-degree views. The observatory level also has an interesting exhibit about the Olmsted Brothers (the sons of Frederick Law Olmstead, the designer of New York City's Central Park) and the system of parks they designed for Seattle. To find the water tower, park near the Seattle Asian

Art Museum if you can; then walk back out of the parking lot to where the road splits. The view from directly in front of the museum, by Isamu Noguchi's *Black Sun* sculpture, isn't bad either. The doughnut-shaped sculpture makes a perfect frame for photos of the Space Needle.

Frye Art Museum ★ On First Hill, not far from downtown Seattle, this museum is primarily an exhibit space for the extensive personal art collection of Charles and Emma Frye, Seattle pioneers who began collecting art in the 1890s. The collection focuses on late-19th-century and early-20th-century representational art by European and American painters, with works by Andrew Wyeth, Thomas Hart Benton, Edward Hopper, Albert Bierstadt, and Pablo Picasso, as well as a large collection of engravings by Winslow Homer. In addition to galleries filled with works from the permanent collection, temporary exhibitions, often of more contemporary works, are held throughout the year.

704 Terry Ave. (at Cherry St.). ✆ **206/622-9250.** http://fryemuseum.org. Free admission. Tues-Wed and Fri-Sun 10am-5pm; Thurs 10am-7pm. Closed New Year's Day, July 4th, Thanksgiving, and Christmas. Bus: 3, 4, or 12.

Seattle Asian Art Museum ★ Housed in an Art Deco building in Volunteer Park, the collection at this museum places an emphasis on Chinese and Japanese art, but also includes works from Korea, Southeast Asia, South Asia, and the Himalayas. Among the museum's most notable pieces are Chinese terra-cotta funerary art, Chinese snuff bottles, and Japanese *netsuke* (belt decorations). Entire rooms are devoted to Japanese and Chinese ceramics. The central hall contains a very impressive collection of stone religious sculptures from South Asia (primarily India).

Volunteer Park, 1400 E. Prospect St. ✆ **206/654-3206.** www.seattleartmuseum.org. Admission $7 adults, $5 seniors, students, and youths 13-17, free for children 12 and under. Free to all 1st Thurs and 2nd Thurs of each month from 5-9pm; free for seniors first Fri; free for families 1st Sat. Wed and Fri-Sun 10am-5pm, Thurs 10am-9pm. Closed New Year's Day, Thanksgiving, and Dec 24-25. Bus: 10.

The walls of the Frye Art Museum are packed with classic paintings.

The gorgeous Victorian conservatory at Volunteer Park houses a large collection of plants.

Volunteer Park Conservatory ★★ This stately old Victorian conservatory, built in 1912, is one of only three on the West Coast. It is 6,200 square feet and has 3,426 panes of glass. Within the greenhouse, you'll find a large collection of tropical and desert plants, including palm trees, orchids, and cacti. There are also seasonal floral displays. Both the plants and the building are beautiful and should not be missed. It's especially rewarding to visit on a rainy day; despite the dreary weather outside, you'll get to stroll through a little bit of the tropics right here in Seattle.

Volunteer Park, 1400 E. Galer St. ✆ **206/684-4743.** www.volunteerparkconservatory.org or www.seattle.gov/parks/parkspaces/VolunteerPark/conservatory.htm. Free admission. Tues–Sun 10am–4pm. Bus: 10.

NEIGHBORHOODS IN NORTH SEATTLE

The **Fremont District,** which begins at the north end of the Fremont Bridge—near the intersection of Fremont Avenue North and North 36th Street—is one of Seattle's funkiest and most unusual neighborhoods. Even livelier, though not as eclectic or artistic, the **University District** (known as the U District) has loads of cheap restaurants and the types of shops you would associate with a college-age clientele. But the main attractions for visitors are the two excellent museums on the university campus and the nearby Museum of History & Industry, which is just across the Montlake Bridge from the U District. This latter museum, however, is scheduled to move to the south end of Lake Union some time in 2012.

The Burke Museum of Natural History and Culture ★★ At the northwest corner of the University of Washington campus, the Burke Museum features exhibits on the natural and cultural heritage of the Pacific Rim and is the Northwest's foremost museum of paleontology, archaeology, and ethnology. Permanent exhibits include **Life & Times of Washington State,** which

The Burke is the Northwest's foremost museum of paleontology, archaeology, and ethnology.

covers 500 million years of Washington history (and prehistory) with lots of fossils, including a complete mastodon. The second permanent exhibit, **Pacific Voices,** focuses on the many cultures of the Pacific Rim and their connections to Washington State. In front of the museum are several totem poles that are replicas of poles carved in the late 19th century. Because this museum is fairly large, it mounts touring shows that often make only a few other stops in the U.S., so be sure to check the exhibition schedule when you are in town.

University of Washington, 17th Ave. NE and NE 45th St. ✆ **206/543-5590** or 206/543-7907. www.burkemuseum.org. Admission $9.50 adults, $7.50 seniors, $6 children 5–18, free for children 4 and under. For $1 more, you can get admission to the nearby Henry Art Gallery. Free 1st Thurs of each month. Daily 10am–5pm (1st Thurs of each month until 8pm). Closed New Year's Day, July 4th, Thanksgiving, and Christmas. Bus: 43, 70–73.

Henry Art Gallery Expect the unexpected here—and prepare to be challenged in your concept of what constitutes art. The focus of the Henry Art Gallery, on the west side of the UW campus, is on contemporary art with retrospectives of individual artists, as well as exhibits focusing on specific themes or media. The museum has large, well-lit gallery spaces illuminated by pyramidal and cubic skylights that can be seen near the main entrance. Photography and video are both well represented, and for the most part, the exhibits are the most avant-garde in the Seattle area. The museum's permanent **Skyspace** installation, by James Turrell, who uses light to create his artwork, is worth the price of admission if you're the contemplative type. The Skyspace is a small room with an oval ceiling opening that frames the sky; at night, the outside of the glass Skyspace is illuminated by an ever-changing light show. The museum also has a cafe and a small sculpture courtyard. Parking is often available at the Central Parking Garage, at Northeast 41st Street and 15th Avenue Northeast.

University of Washington, 15th Ave. NE and NE 41st St. ✆ **206/543-2280.** www.henryart.org. Admission $10 adults, $6 seniors, free for students and children 13 and under. Free for all Thurs. Wed 11am–4pm; Thurs–Fri 11am–9pm; Sat–Sun 11am–4pm. Closed New Year's Day, July 4th, Thanksgiving, and Christmas. Bus: 43, 70–73.

Parking Tip

Parking on the University of Washington campus is expensive on weekdays and Saturday mornings, so try to visit the Burke Museum of Natural History and Culture or Henry Art Gallery on a Saturday afternoon or a Sunday, when parking is free.

Hiram M. Chittenden (Ballard) Locks ★★ For some reason, many people are intrigued by the concept of two side-by-side bodies of water on two different levels. Consequently, the Hiram M. Chittenden Locks are one of Seattle's top attractions. The two locks here link Puget Sound with the Lake Washington Ship Canal, which connects to both Lake Union and Lake Washington. Barges, commercial fishing vessels, and small private boats all use the locks. A fish ladder and fish-viewing windows here provide opportunities for salmon viewing during the summer months, and the chance to see salmon in a fish ladder is as much of a draw as the locks themselves. The locks are also the site of the **Carl S. English, Jr., Botanical Gardens,** a park filled with rare and unusual shrubs and trees. Tours of the grounds are offered March through November (call for schedule).

The locks are located a 10- to 15-minute drive north of downtown. Follow Elliott Avenue north along the waterfront from downtown Seattle; after crossing the Ballard Bridge, drive west on Northwest Market Street.

3015 NW 54th St. ✆ **206/783-7059.** Free admission. Locks daily 7am–9pm. Visitor center May–Sept daily 10am–6pm; Oct–Apr Thurs–Mon 10am–4pm. Bus: 17, 44, or 46.

Museum of History & Industry (MOHAI) ★ If the Seattle **Underground Tour's** (p. 140) vivid description of life before the 1889 fire has you curious about what the city's more respectable citizens were doing back in those days, you can find out here, where re-created storefronts provide glimpses into their lives. Located at the north end of the Washington Park Arboretum, this museum explores Seattle's history with frequently changing exhibits on more obscure aspects of the city's past. While many of the displays will be of interest only to local residents, anyone wishing to gain a better understanding of the history of the city and the Northwest may also enjoy the exhibits here. There's a Boeing mail plane

You can tour the Carl S. English, Jr., Botanical Garden when you visit the Ballard Locks.

The industries and activities that made Seattle grow are on display at MOHAI.

Ja, Seattle has a lot of Scandinavian heritage.

from the 1920s, plus an exhibit on the 1889 fire that leveled the city. MOHAI also hosts touring exhibitions that address Northwest history. Although not actually in north Seattle, this museum is just across the Montlake Bridge from the University District. ***Note:*** Some time in 2012, the museum is scheduled to relocate to Lake Union Park at the south end of Lake Union.

McCurdy Park, 2700 24th Ave. E. ✆ **206/324-1126.** www.seattlehistory.org. Admission $8 adults, $7 seniors and students, $6 youths 5–17, free for children 4 and under. Free 1st Thurs of each month. Daily 10am–5pm (until 8pm 1st Thurs of each month). Closed Thanksgiving and Christmas. Bus: 25, 43, or 48. From I-5, take Wash. 520 east (exit 168B) to the Montlake exit, go straight through the stoplight to 24th Ave. E, and turn left.

Nordic Heritage Museum ★ 🎁 Housed in a former school building, this is primarily a neighborhood museum focusing on the experiences of Scandinavian immigrants in Seattle's Ballard neighborhood. However, it also mounts exhibits of Scandinavian and Scandinavian-inspired art, and these temporary exhibits are what make the Nordic Heritage Museum worth seeking out for those who aren't of Scandinavian heritage. The "Dream of America" exhibit, on the first floor, does an excellent job of explaining why Scandinavians began immigrating to the U.S. and how they ended up in Ballard. On the third floor, each of the Nordic countries gets a display room of its own. In mid-July each year, the museum sponsors the Viking Days festival, which includes booths serving Nordic foods.

3014 NW 67th St. ✆ **206/789-5707.** www.nordicmuseum.org. Admission $6 adults, $5 seniors and college students, $4 children age 5 to 12th grade, free for children 4 and under. Tues–Sat 10am–4pm; Sun noon–4pm. Closed New Year's Day, Easter, Thanksgiving, Christmas Eve, and Christmas. Bus: 17 or 18.

Woodland Park Zoo ★ ☺ This sprawling zoo has outstanding exhibits focusing on Alaska, tropical Asia, the African savanna, and the tropical rainforest. The brown-bear enclosure, one of the zoo's best exhibits, is a realistic reproduction of an Alaskan stream and hillside. In the savanna, zebras gambol and giraffes graze near a reproduction

A giraffe has its eye on the visitors at the Woodland Park Zoo.

of an African village. An elephant forest provides plenty of space for the zoo's pachyderms, and the gorilla and orangutan habitats are also well done. A farm-animal area is a big hit with the little ones, and young kids like the **Zoomazium,** an interactive educational play area where they can see what it's like to be wild animals.

601 N. 59th St. ✆ **206/548-2500.** www.zoo.org. Admission May–Sept $18 adults, $16 seniors, $12 children 3–12, free for children 2 and under; Oct–Apr $12 adults, $9.50 seniors, $8.50 children 3–12, free for children 2 and under. May–Sept daily 9:30am–6pm; Oct–Apr daily 9:30am–4pm. Closed Christmas. Parking $5.25. Bus: 5 or 44.

GOOD TIMES IN BAD taste

If your kids (or you) love bad jokes and are fascinated by the bizarre, you won't want to miss the Underground Tour and a visit to Ye Olde Curiosity Shop. Together these two attractions should reassure you that Seattle isn't just about deep, cerebral conversations over espresso—the city has a sense of humor, too.

If you have an appreciation of off-color humor and are curious about the seamier side of Seattle history, **Bill Speidel's Underground Tour,** 608 First Ave. (✆ **206/682-4646;** www.undergroundtour.com), will likely entertain and enlighten you. The tours wander around basements in the Pioneer Square area, where you can still find the vestiges of Seattle businesses built just after the great fire of 1889. Learn the lowdown dirt on early Seattle, a town where plumbing was problematic and a person could drown in a pothole. Tours are held daily. The cost is $15 for adults, $12 for seniors and students 13 to 17 or with college ID, and $7 for children 7 to 12; children 6 and under are discouraged from participating.

Ye Olde Curiosity Shop, Pier 54, 1001 Alaskan Way (✆ **206/682-5844;** www.yeoldecuriosityshop.com), is a cross between a souvenir store and *Ripley's Believe It or Not!* It's weird! It's wacky! It's tacky! The collection of oddities was started in 1899 by Joe Standley, who developed a more-than-passing interest in strange curios. See conjoined-twin calves, a natural mummy (pictured), the Lord's Prayer on a grain of rice, a narwhal tusk, shrunken heads, a 67-pound snail, fleas in dresses—all the stuff that may have fascinated you as a kid.

The Duwamish were in Seattle when the first settlers from the East arrived.

SOUTH SEATTLE

Duwamish Longhouse & Cultural Center ★ Seattle is named for Duwamish Indian Chief Sealth, and yet, until recently, it was almost impossible for visitors to learn anything about the tribe that befriended early settlers. Although this Native American cultural center and museum is not very large and is on the edge of south Seattle's port industrial area, it is a fascinating place well worth searching out. The building is designed to resemble a modern longhouse, and in the museum, you'll find numerous Duwamish artifacts and informative displays providing the Duwamish perspective on the settlement of the area by pioneers.

4705 W. Marginal Way SW. ✆ **206/431-1582.** www.duwamishtribe.org. Free admission. Mon–Sat 10am–5pm.

The Museum of Flight ★★ ☺ This museum adjacent to Boeing Field, an active airport 15 minutes south of downtown Seattle, houses within its six-story glass-and-steel building some of history's most famous planes. The collection starts with a replica of the Wright brothers' 1903 plane and continues through to the present state of flight. Suspended in the Great Hall are more than 20 planes, including a 1935 DC-3, the first Air Force F-5 supersonic fighter, and the *Gossamer Albatross,* a human-powered airplane. The Personal Courage Wing houses 28 World War I and World War II fighter planes. You'll also see one of the famous Blackbird spy planes, which, at one time, were the world's fastest jets (you can even sit in the cockpit of one of these babies). An exhibit on the U.S. space program features an Apollo command module. The museum incorporates part of an old wooden Boeing factory building, and there are numerous Boeing planes on display.

9404 E. Marginal Way S. ✆ **206/764-5720.** www.museumofflight.org. Admission $16 adults, $14 seniors, $9 children 5–17, free for children 4 and under. Free 1st Thurs of each month 5–9pm.

The history of airplanes, past and present, is on display at the Museum of Flight.

Daily 10am–5pm (until 9pm 1st Thurs of each month). Closed Thanksgiving and Christmas. Bus: 124. Take exit 158 off I-5.

THE EASTSIDE

Bellevue Arts Museum ★ On the east side of Lake Washington a 20- to 30-minute drive from downtown Seattle, Bellevue was once just an upscale suburb but has become a city in its own right. With several large galleries that host shows and installations by regional and national artists, the Bellevue Arts Museum is one of the cultural underpinnings of this city's newfound urbanism. This museum also gives the public opportunities to interact with artists. To this end, the museum stages each July the Northwest's largest and most highly regarded art fair. During the rest of the year, it features frequent artist demonstrations. Stop by if you happen to be on the Eastside and are an art aficionado.

510 Bellevue Way NE, Bellevue. ✆ **425/519-0770.** www.bellevuearts.org. Admission $10 adults, $7 seniors and students, free for children 5 and under. Free admission for all first Fri of each month. Mon–Thurs 11am–5pm; Fri 11am–8pm; Sat–Sun noon–5pm. Closed major holidays. From Seattle, take I-90 east over Lake Washington to the Bellevue Way exit, and drive north on Bellevue Way for approx. 2 miles.

Rosalie Whyel Museum of Doll Art ★ ☺ If you're a doll collector or happen to be traveling with a child who likes dolls, this Bellevue museum should definitely be part of your Seattle itinerary. Displays include more than 1,200 dolls from around the world, including 17th-century wooden dolls, 19th-century china dolls, and the original Barbie. Throughout the year, the museum has special exhibits that focus on different types of dolls.

1116 108th Ave. NE, Bellevue. ✆ **425/455-1116.** www.dollart.com. Admission $10 adults, $9 seniors, $5 children 5–17, free for children 4 and under. Mon–Sat 10am–5pm; Sun 1–5pm. Closed major holidays. From Seattle, take Wash. 520 east over the Evergreen Point Bridge to I-405 S.; then take the NE Eighth St. westbound exit and turn right on 108th Ave. NE.

Bellevue is the site of an emerging arts scene, including its Arts Museum.

Dolls old and new reflect how children play at the Rosalie Whyel Museum.

ARCHITECTURAL GEMS

Of course, Seattle's most famous architectural landmark is the **Space Needle** (p. 132), which, when it was built for the 1962 World's Fair, was envisioned as the look of things to come. Now that the 21st century is upon us, the reality of 21st-century architecture is far stranger than was imagined. Frank Gehry's design for the building that now houses **EMP/SFM** (**Experience Music Project/ Science Fiction Museum;** p. 130) is one of the city's most bizarre buildings, but it faces stiff competition from the skewed glass-cube architecture of the **Seattle Central Library** (below).

Chapel of St. Ignatius ★ Lest you think subtlety is a concept unknown to architects commissioned to design contemporary buildings in Seattle, pay a visit to this tasteful little chapel on the campus of Seattle University, a Catholic institution. Designed by architect Steven Holl, the chapel was conceived as "seven bottles of light in a stone box," with each of those bottles reflecting an aspect of Catholic worship. The "bottles" are basically a means of channeling light into the chapel, and though the exterior seems stark and angular, on the inside, soft, multihued light suffuses the rooms. The chapel is something of an exploration of the ways natural light can illuminate a building, and the overall effect is enchanting.

Seattle University, E. Marion St. and 12th Ave. ✆ **206/296-6992.** www.seattleu.edu/chapel. Free admission. Mon–Thurs 7am–10pm; Fri 7am–7pm; Sat 8am–5pm; Sun 8am–10pm. Bus: 12.

Seattle Central Library ★ It isn't often that the library is considered one of the coolest joints in town, but Seattle's downtown library is such an architectural wonder that it is one of the city's highlights. When the building opened in 2004, its design created a rift among many locals, who either loved it or hated it.

Indeed, there wasn't much of a middle ground with this giant glass cube and its diamond-patterned steel girders and strange angles. Regardless of your reaction to Architect Rem Koolhaas's design, you can't help but notice that in a town known for its gray skies, this library abounds with natural light. Oh, and if you need to use the Internet, this place has hundreds of computer terminals, too.

1000 Fourth Ave. ✆ **206/386-4636.** www.spl.org. Free admission. Mon–Thurs 10am–8pm; Fri–Sat 10am–6pm; Sun noon–6pm. Closed major holidays. Bus: Any Fourth Ave. bus.

Seattle's Central Library is housed in a gorgeous modern building.

PARKS & PUBLIC GARDENS

Parks

Seattle's many parks are part of what make it such a livable city and an enjoyable place to visit. In the downtown area, **Myrtle Edwards Park ★**, 3130 Alaskan Way W. (✆ **206/684-4075**), at the north end of the waterfront, is an ideal spot for a sunset stroll with views of Puget Sound and the Olympic Mountains. The park includes a 1.25-mile paved pathway. At its north end, this park connects with the Port of Seattle's **Elliott Bay Park.**

Lake Union Park, at the south end of Lake Union and linked to downtown via the Seattle Streetcar, is another pleasant place for a waterfront stroll. Several

QUIT whining & START WINING

If you don't have enough time in your busy vacation schedule to head out of town to Washington's main Yakima Valley and Walla Walla wine country or to the nearby Woodinville wine region, you still can sample plenty of Washington state wines without ever leaving the Seattle city limits. Scattered all around the city there are now small urban wineries as well as tasting rooms for larger wineries.

In Pike Place Market, you can taste the wines of seven Washington wineries at **The Tasting Room,** 1924 Post Alley (✆ **206/770-9463;** http://tastingroomseattle.com). With the feel of an old wine cellar, this is my favorite urban wine-tasting spot. The Tasting Room is open Sunday through Thursday from noon to 8pm and Friday and Saturday from noon until 10 or 11pm. Here in the market, you can also sample the wines of **Patterson Cellars,** 1427 Western Ave. (✆ **206/724-0664;** www.pattersoncellars.com). In summer, this tasting room is usually open Tuesday through Sunday from noon to 8pm; other months it's open Thursday through Saturday from noon to 6pm and Sunday from noon to 5pm.

In the SoDo industrial district and the Pioneer Square neighborhood, you'll

Discovery Park is Seattle's largest, with trails, beaches, and forest.

historic boats are docked at the park, which is adjacent to the Center for Wooden Boats, and sometime in 2012, the Museum of History & Industry is scheduled to open here. This is a great spot from which to watch floatplanes take off and land.

Freeway Park, at Sixth Avenue and Seneca Street, is one of Seattle's most unusual parks. Built right on top of busy I-5, this green space is more like a series of urban plazas, with terraces, waterfalls, and cement planters creating walls of greenery. You'd never know that a roaring freeway lies beneath your feet. Unfortunately, although the park is convenient, the isolated nature of its many nooks and crannies often gives it a deserted and slightly threatening feel.

For serious communing with nature, nothing will do but 534-acre **Discovery Park ★★**, 3801 W. Government Way (✆ **206/386-4236**). Occupying a high

find the surprisingly sophisticated **Urban Enoteca,** 4130 First Ave. S (✆ **206/467-9463;** www.urbanenoteca.com). The wines from seven eastern Washington wineries can be sampled here. This tasting room is open Tuesday through Thursday from 3 to 8pm, Friday from 3 to 10pm, Saturday from noon to 10pm, and Sunday from noon to 7pm. From February through August, the wineries of **South Seattle Artisan Wineries** (www.ssaw.info), an association of area wineries, are open to the public on the second Saturday of each month from 1 to 5pm.

In Fremont, or more precisely, just across the Lake Washington Ship Canal from Fremont, you can sample a wide variety of red wines at **Almquist Family Vintners,** 198 Nickerson St. (✆ **206/859-9400;** www.almquistfamilyvintners.com). The tasting room is open Monday through Saturday from 5 to 10pm.

In Ballard, there's **Domanico Cellars,** 825 NW 49th St. (✆ **206/465-9406;** www.domanicocellars.com), a small, family winery that produces primarily Bordeaux-style red wines. The tasting room is open Wednesday and Friday from 5 to 9pm and Saturday from noon to 6pm.

bluff and sandy point jutting into Puget Sound, this is Seattle's largest and wildest park. You can easily spend a day wandering its trails and beaches. The visitor center is open Tuesday through Sunday from 8:30am to 5pm. Discovery Park is a 15-minute drive from downtown; to get here, follow the waterfront north from downtown Seattle toward the Magnolia neighborhood and watch for signs to the park. When you reach the park, follow signed trails down to the beach and out to the lighthouse at the point. Although the lighthouse is only occasionally open to the public, the views from the beach make this a good destination for an hour's walk. The beach and park's bluff-top meadows both make good picnic spots.

Little boys can play with old buoys at Jack Block Park.

Up on Capitol Hill, at East Prospect Street and 14th Avenue East, you'll find **Volunteer Park ★**, 1247 15th Ave. E. (✆ **206/684-4075**), which is surrounded by the elegant mansions of this old neighborhood. It's a popular spot for sunning and playing Frisbee,

fish GOTTA SWIM (AND CLIMB LADDERS)

It's no secret that salmon in the Puget Sound region have dwindled to dangerously low numbers. But it's still possible to witness the annual return of spawning salmon in various spots around the Sound.

In the autumn, on the waterfront, you can see returning salmon at the **Seattle Aquarium** (p. 123), which has its own fish ladder. But the best place to see salmon is at the **Hiram M. Chittenden (Ballard) Locks,** 3015 NW 54th St. (✆ **206/783-7059;** p. 138 for directions and hours). Between June and September (July–Aug are the peak months), you can view salmon through underwater observation windows as they leap up the locks' fish ladder. These locks, which are used primarily by small boats, connect Lake Union and Lake Washington with the waters of Puget Sound, and depending on the tides and lake levels, there is a difference of 6 to 26 feet on either side of the locks.

East of Seattle, in downtown Issaquah, salmon can be seen year-round at the **Issaquah Salmon Hatchery,** 125 W. Sunset Way (✆ **425/391-9094** or 425/392-1118; www.issaquahfish.org). However, it is in the fall that adult salmon can be seen returning to the hatchery. Every year on the first weekend in October, the city of Issaquah holds the **Issaquah Salmon Days Festival** to celebrate the return of the natives.

and is home to the **Seattle Asian Art Museum** (p. 135), an amphitheater, a water tower with a superb view of the city, and a **conservatory** filled with exotic plants (p. 136). With so much variety, you can easily spend half a day exploring this park.

On the east side of Seattle, along the shore of Lake Washington, you'll find not only swimming beaches but also **Seward Park ★**, 5895 Lake Washington Blvd. S. (✆ **206/684-4396**). This large park's waterfront areas may be its biggest attraction, but it also has a dense forest with trails winding through it. Keep an eye out for the bald eagles that nest here. The park is south of the I-90 floating bridge off Lake Washington Boulevard South. From downtown Seattle, follow Madison Street northeast and turn right onto Lake Washington Boulevard.

Near Alki Beach in West Seattle, **Jack Block Park,** 2130 Harbor Ave. SW (✆ **206/787-3654;** www.portseattle.org), is well worth a visit. The park, wedged between the port and Elliott Bay, has a .25-mile paved walkway that meanders along beside the water. The path eventually leads to an observation tower overlooking both the water and the port. Kids will love watching all the cool machines and boats coming and going. Now, I know I've made this park sound like it's in the middle of an industrial area, but it actually has plenty of natural shoreline. For the little ones, there's even a play area that incorporates old buoys. You'll find the park adjacent to Terminal 5 on Harbor Avenue.

North Seattle has several parks worth visiting, including the unique **Gas Works Park ★**, 2101 N. Northlake Way, at Meridian Avenue North (✆ **206/684-4075**), at the north end of Lake Union. In the middle of its green lawns looms the rusting hulk of an old industrial plant; the park's small Kite Hill is a popular kite-flying spot.

You can go fly a kite at the Gas Works.

It's a toasty evening for marshmallows at Golden Gardens Park.

Moving farther north, on Green Lake Drive North near Woodland Park Zoo, you'll find **Green Lake Park ★★**, 7201 E. Green Lake Dr. N. (✆ **206/684-4075**), a center for exercise buffs who jog, bike, and skate on its 2.8-mile paved path. It's also possible to picnic on the many grassy areas and swim in the lake (there are changing rooms and a beach with summer lifeguards).

North of the Ballard neighborhood is **Golden Gardens Park ★★**, 8498 Seaview Place NW (✆ **206/684-4075**), which, with its excellent views of the Olympic Mountains and its somewhat wild feeling, is my favorite Seattle waterfront park. It has great views, some small wetlands, and a short trail. Golden Gardens is best known as one of Seattle's best beaches, too, and even though the water here is too cold for swimming, the sandy beach is a pleasant spot for a sunset stroll. People often gather on summer evenings to build fires on the beach. To reach this park, drive north from the waterfront on Elliott Avenue, which becomes 15th Avenue West; after crossing the Ballard Bridge, turn left on Market Street and follow this road for about 2 miles (it will change names to become NW 54th St. and then Seaview Ave. NW).

Public Gardens

See also the listings for the **Volunteer Park Conservatory** (p. 136) and the **Hiram M. Chittenden (Ballard) Locks** (p. 138).

Bellevue Botanical Garden ★★ Any avid gardener should be sure to make a trip across one of Seattle's two floating bridges to the city of Bellevue and its Bellevue Botanical Garden. This 53-acre garden is one of the Northwest's most highly regarded perennial gardens. The summertime displays of flowers, in expansive mixed borders, are absolutely gorgeous. You can also see a Japanese garden, a shade border, and a water-wise garden (designed to conserve water). April through September, free guided tours are offered Saturday and Sunday at 2pm.

Bellevue Botanical Garden offers fabulous flora.

Wilburton Hill Park, 12001 Main St., Bellevue. ✆ **425/452-2750.** www.bellevuebotanical.org. Free admission. Daily dawn–dusk. Visitor center daily 9am–4pm. Take the NE Eighth St. exit east off I-405.

Japanese Garden Covering 3½ acres, the Japanese Garden is a perfect little world unto itself, with a cherry orchard (for spring color), babbling brooks, and a lake rimmed with Japanese irises and filled with colorful koi (Japanese carp). A special tea garden encloses a teahouse, where between April and October, on the fourth Saturday of the month at 1 and 2:15pm, you can attend a traditional tea ceremony ($10). Unfortunately, noise from a nearby road can be distracting. Between April and October, there are free guided tours of the gardens Saturday and Sunday at 12:30 and 2pm, additionally, between May and August, there are also tours on Tuesday and Wednesday 12:30pm.

Washington Park Arboretum, 1075 Lake Washington Blvd. E. (north of E. Madison St.). ✆ **206/684-4725.** Admission $6 adults; $4 seniors, college students, and youths 6–17; free for children 5 and under. Mid-Feb to Apr and mid-Sept to Oct Tues–Sun 10am–dusk; May to mid-Sept daily 10am–7pm; early Nov to mid-Nov Tues–Sun 10am–4pm. Closed mid-Nov to mid-Feb. Bus: 11 or 84.

Immerse yourself in the serenity of the Japanese Garden.

Kubota Garden ★ This 20-acre Japanese-style garden, in a working-class neighborhood not far from the shores of Lake Washington in South Seattle, was the life's work of garden designer Fujitaro Kubota. Today the gardens are a city park, and the mature landscaping and hilly setting make this the most impressive and enjoyable Japanese garden in the Seattle area. Kubota began work on this garden in 1927 and over the years built a necklace of ponds, a traditional stroll garden, and a mountainside garden complete with waterfalls. A tall, arched moon bridge is a highlight. The self-taught Kubota went on to design gardens at Seattle University and at the Bloedel Reserve on Bainbridge Island. Between April and October, free tours of the gardens are offered at 10am on the fourth Saturday of the month.

9817 55th Ave. S. (at Renton Ave. S). ✆ **206/684-4075** or 206/684-4584. www.kubota.org. Free admission. Daily 6am–10pm. Bus: 106. From downtown, take I-5 south to exit 158 (Pacific Hwy. S./E. Marginal Way) and turn left toward Martin Luther King Jr. Way; continue uphill on Ryan Way; turn left on 51st Ave. S., right on Renton Ave. S., and right on 55th Ave. S.

Washington Park Arboretum The acres of trees and shrubs in Washington Park Arboretum stretch from the far side of Capitol Hill all the way to the Montlake Cut (a canal connecting Lake Washington to Lake Union). Within the 230-acre arboretum are thousands of varieties of plants and quiet trails that are pleasant throughout the year but are at their most beautiful in spring, when the azaleas, cherry trees, rhododendrons, and dogwoods are all in bloom. The north end of the arboretum, a marshland that is home to ducks and herons, is popular with bird-watchers as well as kayakers and canoeists (see "Outdoor Pursuits," later in this chapter, for places to rent a canoe or kayak). A boardwalk with views across Lake Washington meanders along the waterside in this area (though noise from the adjacent freeway detracts considerably from the experience).

3501 NE 41st St. ✆ **206/543-8800.** http://depts.washington.edu/uwbg/gardens/wpa.shtml. Free admission. Daily dawn–dusk. Graham Visitors Center daily 9am–5pm. Bus: 43 or 48. Enter on Lake Washington Blvd. E. off E. Madison St.; or take Wash. 520 off I-5 north of downtown, take the Montlake Blvd. exit, and go straight through the 1st intersection.

ESPECIALLY FOR KIDS

In addition to the listings below, kids will also enjoy many of the attractions described earlier in this chapter, including the **Seattle Aquarium** (p. 123), the **Pacific Science Center** (p. 130), and the **Woodland Park Zoo** (p. 139).

Adolescent and preadolescent boys seem to unfailingly love **Ye Olde Curiosity Shop** and the **Underground Tour** (p. 140). Younger kids also love the **Museum of Flight** (p. 141). And even the surliest teenagers will think you're pretty cool for taking them to the **EMP/SFM** (**Experience Music Project/ Science Fiction Museum;** p. 130).

Kids need to burn off some energy? See "Outdoor Pursuits," later in this chapter, for descriptions of Seattle's best beaches, recreational areas, and biking; and "Spectator Sports," also later in this chapter, for details on Seattle's professional football and baseball teams.

You might also be able to catch a performance at the **Seattle Children's Theatre** (✆ **206/441-3322;** www.sct.org), in Seattle Center (see below); or at the **Northwest Puppet Center,** 9123 15th Ave. NE (✆ **206/523-2579;** www.nwpuppet.org).

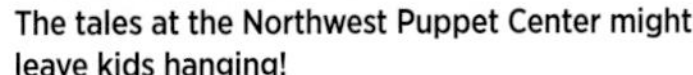

The tales at the Northwest Puppet Center might leave kids hanging!

Honk! Honk! Make way for the exhibits at the Children's Museum.

The Children's Museum, Seattle ☺ The Children's Museum is in the basement of the Center House at Seattle Center, which is partly why Seattle Center is such a great place to spend a day with the kids. The museum includes plenty of hands-on cultural exhibits, such as the **Global Village,** which allows kids to visit Ghana, the Philippines, and Japan; a child-size neighborhood; a **Discovery Bay** for toddlers; a mountain-wilderness area; and other special exhibits to keep the little ones busy learning and playing for hours.

Seattle Center, Center House, 305 Harrison St. ✆ **206/441-1768.** www.thechildrensmuseum.org. Admission $7.50 adults and children, $6.50 seniors, free for children younger than 1. Mon–Fri 10am–5pm; Sat–Sun 10am–6pm. Closed New Year's Day, Thanksgiving, and Dec 24–25. Bus: 1–4, 8, 13, 15, 16, 18, 19, 24, 33, 45, 74, 81, or 82. Monorail: From Westlake Center at the corner of Pine St. and Fourth Ave.

Seattle Center ★ ☺ If you want to keep the kids entertained all day long, head to Seattle Center. This 74-acre cultural center and amusement park stands on the northern edge of downtown at the end of the monorail line. The most visible building at the center is the **Space Needle** (p. 132), which provides an outstanding panorama of the city from its observation deck. However, of much more interest to children are the **Children's Museum** (see above) and the **Seattle Children's Theatre** (see above). This is also Seattle's main festival site, and in the summer months hardly a weekend goes by without some special event filling its grounds. On hot summer days, the **International Fountain** is a great place for kids to keep cool (bring a change of clothes). In 2012, Seattle Center will celebrate the 50th anniversary of the Seattle World's Fair.

305 Harrison St. ✆ **206/684-7200.** www.seattlecenter.com. Free admission to grounds; attractions, activities, and performances priced separately. Bus: 1–4, 8, 13, 15, 16, 18, 19, 24, 33, 45, 74, 81, or 82. Monorail: From Westlake Center at the corner of Pine St. and Fourth Ave.

ORGANIZED TOURS

For information on the **Underground Tour,** see p. 140.

Walking Tours

In addition to the walking tours mentioned here, Pike Place Market offers tours of the market itself. See the Pike Place Market listing on p. 126 for details.

If you'd like to explore downtown Seattle with a knowledgeable guide, join one of the informative walking tours offered by **See Seattle Walking Tours** (✆ **425/226-7641;** www.see-seattle.com), which visit Pike Place Market, the waterfront, and the Pioneer Square area. Tours cost $20 and usually last 6 hours. There has to be a minimum of six people signed up before these tours go out.

You can also learn a lot about local history and wander through hidden corners of the city on the 2-hour tours run by **Seattle Walking Tours** (✆ **425/885-3173;** www.seattlewalkingtours.com). These tours wind their way from the International District to Pike Place Market, taking in historic buildings, public art, and scenic vistas. Tours are $15 per person, are offered year-round by reservation, and require a minimum of three people to go out.

For an insider's glimpse of life in Seattle's Chinatown/International District, hook up with **Chinatown Discovery Tours** (✆ **206/623-5124;** www.seattlechinatowntour.com). On these walking tours, which last 1½ hours, you learn the history of this colorful and historic neighborhood. Rates (for four or more on a tour) are $18 for adults, $16 for seniors, $13 for students, and $11 for children.

Food-focused tours of Pike Place Market are offered by **Savor Seattle Food Tours** (✆ **888/987-2867;** www.savorseattletours.com), which charges $39 for a 2-hour tour and also offers a chocolate-indulgence tour; and **Seattle Food Tours** (✆ **206/725-4483;** www.seattlefoodtours.com), which charges $39 for a 2½-hour tour and also offers a tour of Belltown restaurants ($49). If you want to learn more about the famous Seattle coffee culture, go on a coffee crawl with **Seattle by Foot** (✆ **800/838-3006;** http://seattlebyfoot.com). These 2-hour tours cost $22 if you make a reservation and $26 if you just show up. This company also does an evening Seattle pub crawl.

If you're interested in architecture, be sure to check the schedule of tours offered by the **Seattle Architecture Foundation** (✆ **206/667-9184** or, 800/838-3006 for reservations; www.seattlearchitecture.org). Throughout the year, this organization offers nearly two dozen different tours that look at different aspects of Seattle history from an architectural perspective. You might join an Art Deco focused tour or one delving into buildings important in the city's musical, Chinese, or gay past. Tours begin at the SAF Gallery, 1333 Fifth Ave. and cost $15 in advance and $25 on the day of the tour. There are also many special-event tours.

Take a bite out of Seattle with a food tour.

Bus Tours

If you'd like an overview of Seattle's main tourist attractions, or if you're pressed for time, you can pack in a lot of sights on a city tour with **Gray Line of Seattle** (✆ **800/426-7532** or 206/626-5200; www.graylineseattle.com). Half-day tours cost $45 for adults, $19 for children. Many other options, including tours to Mount Rainier National Park and to the Boeing plant in Everett, are also available. Gray Line also operates a **Double-Decker Tour** in open-top buses; these city tours run from May through September and cost $35 for adults and $15 for children. Buses depart from seven stops around the city; call for details or keep an eye out for a parked double-decker bus.

To glimpse a bit more of Seattle on a guided van tour, try the "Explore Seattle City Tour" offered by **Customized Tours** (✆ **888/554-TOURS** [8687] or 206/878-3965; www.ourtoursrock.com), which charges $49 for adults and $39 for children. This tour stops at Pike Place Market, the Hiram M. Chittenden (Ballard) Locks, and Pioneer Square. The company also offers a Boeing plant tour ($59 for adults and $49 for children) and a Snoqualmie Falls and wineries tour ($83 for adults and $63 for children).

A variety of city tours and adventurous trips farther afield are offered by **EverGreen Escapes** (✆ **866/203-7603** or 206/650-5795; www.evergreenescapes.com), a company that uses biodiesel-powered vehicles. For a fun and irreverent tour of outlying Seattle neighborhoods, take the **Sub Seattle Tour,** 608 First Ave. (✆ **206/682-4646;** http://subseattletour.com), which is operated by the immensely popular Underground Tour. On the Sub Seattle Tour, you'll drive past Kurt Cobain's house and travel the route of the original Seattle gay-pride parade. Tours operate March through November, cost $30 per person, and are recommended for those 18 and older.

Boat Tours

In addition to the boat tours and cruises mentioned below, you can do your own low-budget "cruise" simply by hopping on one of the ferries operated by

Take a cruise on the ferry to Bainbridge Island.

ON THE water ON THE CHEAP

If you don't go boating a few times while you're in Seattle, you've missed the point. This city is defined by its waterways, and on sunny summer afternoons, it sometimes seems as if half the population is out on the water. However, you don't have to take an expensive dinner cruise to see Seattle from sea level. The city has lots of inexpensive options for getting out on the water. If these suggestions don't float your boat, I don't know what will.

How about an hour on Lake Union in a classic wooden boat for absolutely nothing? On Sunday afternoons, the **Center for Wooden Boats** (p. 128) offers free boat rides. Just be sure to sign up early. Just north of downtown Seattle, you can also take a very short, though free, boat ride at the **Elliott Bay Marina** at the foot of Magnolia Bluff. The boat ride crosses barely a few yards of water at the marina and drops you at a jetty with a stupendous view of Elliott Bay and the city skyline. The listing for Maggie Bluffs Marina Grill (p. 91) has details.

For $3.50, you can ride the **King County Water Taxi** (p. 306) from the Seattle waterfront to Alki Beach in West Seattle. For $7.10 you can ride a **Washington State Ferry** (p. 306) to Bainbridge Island (a 35-min. trip) or Bremerton (a 1-hr. trip). Even better, as a walk-on passenger, your return trip is free. For only $8.50 to $10 per hour, you can rent a canoe or rowboat at the University of Washington's **Waterfront Activities Center** (p. 162) and paddle around the marshes at the north end of the Washington Park Arboretum.

However, for the best free boat ride in Seattle, you will, unfortunately (or fortunately), have to stay at the metro area's most luxurious waterfront hotel. Guests at the **Woodmark Hotel, Yacht Club & Spa on Lake Washington** (p. 66) can arrange to go for a 2-hour cruise on the hotel's restored 1956 Chris-Craft speedboat.

Washington State Ferries (✆ **800/843-3779,** 888/808-7977 in Washington, or 206/464-6400; www.wsdot.wa.gov/ferries). Try the Bainbridge Island or Bremerton ferries out of Seattle for a 1½- to 2½-hour round-trip. For more information on these ferries, see p. 306.

If you don't have enough time for an overnight trip to the **San Juan Islands,** it's still possible to get a feel for these picturesque islands by riding the San Juan Islands ferry from Anacortes (75 miles north of Seattle) to Friday Harbor. If you get off in Friday Harbor, you can spend a few hours exploring this town before returning to Anacortes. Alternatively, if you have more money to spend (and even less time), boat tours of the San Juan Islands depart from the Seattle waterfront. For information on ferries and boat excursions to the San Juan Islands, see chapter 10, "Side Trips from Seattle."

If you opt for only one tour while in Seattle, the Argosy Cruises' **Tillicum Village Tour ★★**, Pier 55 (✆ **888/623-1445** or 206/622-8687; www.tillicum village.com), should be it—it's unique and truly Northwestern. The tour includes a boat excursion, a salmon dinner, and Northwest Coast Indian masked dances. The salmon is cooked over an alder-wood fire in much the same way it has been done for generations, and the traditional dances are fascinating (although more for the craftsmanship of the masks than for the dancing itself). At Blake Island State Park, across Puget Sound from Seattle, and only accessible by boat,

The ride to Tillicum Village by boat is part of the tour.

Tillicum Village was built in conjunction with the 1962 Seattle World's Fair. The "village" is actually just a large restaurant and performance hall fashioned after a traditional Northwest Coast longhouse, but with the totem poles standing vigil out front, the forest encircling the longhouse, and the waters of Puget Sound stretching into the distance, Tillicum Village is a beautiful spot. After the dinner and dances, you have a little free time to walk along the beach or stretch your legs on one of the island's trails. There are even beaches on which to relax. Tours are $80 for adults, $73 for seniors, $30 for children 5 to 12, and free for children 4 and under. They're offered daily from early June to early September, and on a more limited basis (usually weekends only) from mid-March to early June and from early September to October.

Seattle is a city surrounded by water, so while you're here, you should be sure to set sail one way or another. **Argosy Cruises ★** (✆ **888/623-1445** or 206/622-8687; www.argosycruises.com) offers the greatest variety of boat-tour options. If you're short on time, just do the 1-hour harbor cruise that departs from Pier 55 ($18–$23 adults, $15–$20 seniors, $8.50–$9.75 children 5–12) or the 2½-hour cruise from Lake Union through the Hiram M. Chittenden (Ballard) Locks to

Ducking Around Seattle

Paul Revere would have had a hard time figuring out what to tell his fellow colonists if the British had arrived by Duck. A **Duck** is a World War II amphibious vehicle that can arrive by land or by sea, and these odd-looking vehicles are now being used to provide tours of Seattle on both land and water. Duck tours take in the standard city sights, but then plunge right into Lake Union for a tour of the Portage Bay waterfront, with its many houseboats and great views. The 90-minute tours ($25 for adults and $15 for kids) leave from a parking lot across from the Space Needle. Contact **Ride the Ducks of Seattle ★**, 516 Broad St. (✆ **800/817-1116** or 206/441-3825; www.seattleducktours.net). Because these tours encourage visitors to get a little daffy, they're very popular; reservations are recommended.

Elliott Bay ($34–$40 adults, $30–$37 seniors, $12–$13 children). This latter tour departs from Pier 56 and includes a bus connection between the waterfront and Lake Union. Argosy also operates two Lake Washington cruises that will take you past Bill Gates's fabled waterfront Xanadu. The 2-hour cruise departs from the AGC Marina at the south end of Lake Union ($27–$33 adults, $23–$30 seniors, $11–$12 children), while the 1½-hour cruise departs from the city dock in downtown Kirkland on the east side of the lake ($31 adults, $27 seniors, $11 children). Of these options, I recommend the cruise through the locks; it may be the most expensive outing, but you get good views and the chance to navigate the locks. Reservations are recommended for all cruises; in rate ranges above, the higher rates are for cruises between April and September.

Want a meal with your cruise? Try one of Argosy's lunch, brunch, or dinner cruises aboard the ***Royal Argosy*** (www.argosycruises.com). Lunch and brunch cruises are $49 for adults and $20 for children 5 to 12; dinner cruises are $79 to $89 for adults and $25 for children. These cruises get my vote for best dinners afloat.

If you prefer a quieter glimpse at Seattle from the water, sail off into the sunset aboard a sleek sailboat operated by **Emerald City Charters,** Pier 54 (**✆ 206/624-3931;** www.sailingseattle.com). Between May and mid-October, this company offers 1½-hour day sails and 2½-hour sunset sails. The cruises cost $30 and $48 for adults, $25 and $44 for seniors, and $22 and $35 for children 6 to 12.

Between mid-April and mid-October, you can tour Lake Union and the Lake Washington Ship Canal aboard the ***Queen of Seattle*** (**✆ 877/783-3616** or 425/898-2701; www.queenofseattle.com), the largest steam-powered paddle wheeler west of the Mississippi. The tours include not only a narration of Seattle sights but also a live Klondike cabaret show. These tours last 2 hours and cost $32 for adults and $16 for children 5 to 12.

I also like the "Sunday Ice Cream Cruises" offered on Sunday afternoons by the M/V *Fremont Avenue.* These 45-minute cruises, operated by **Seattle Ferry Service** (**✆ 206/713-8446;** www.seattleferryservice.com), putter around Lake Union in a cute little tour boat. These tours cost $11 for adults, $10 for seniors, $7 for children 5 to 13, and $2 for children 4 and under. They even allow pets on board the boat! Ice cream is sold on board. During the summer, there are also 1-hour cruises on Fridays and Saturdays; these tours cost $15 for adults, $7 for children 5 to 13, and $2 for children 4 and under. The M/V *Fremont Avenue* departs from Lake Union Park at the south end of Lake Union (take the Seattle Streetcar to the Lake Union Park station).

Seattle Noir & Ghostly

If your tastes run to the macabre, you might be interested in the tours offered by Private Eye on Seattle Tours (✆ 206/365-3739; www.privateeyetours.com). These somewhat bizarre van tours are led by a private eye named Jake, who shares stories of interesting and unusual cases from the Emerald City. Tours are $28 per person. Another option is a tour of some haunted locales. The ghoulishly inclined might also want to take a Market Ghost Tour (✆ 206/805-0195; www.seattleghost.com) and get in touch with the souls that haunt Pike Place Market. Tours cost $15 for adults and $13 for seniors and children ages 10 to 16.

You can take an aerial tour of Seattle by plane (biplane, that is!)

Scenic Flights & Hot-Air Balloon Rides

Seattle is one of the few cities in the United States where floatplanes are a regular sight in the skies and on the lakes. If you want to see what it's like to use a lake for a runway, book a flight-seeing tour with **Seattle Seaplanes ★**, 1325 Fairview Ave. E. (✆ **800/637-5553** or 206/329-9638; www.seattleseaplanes.com), which takes off from the southeast corner of Lake Union and offers 20-minute scenic flights over the city for $88. This company also offers flights to nearby waterfront restaurants for dinner.

If you'd rather pretend you're back in the days of the Red Baron, you can go up in a vintage biplane with **Olde Thyme Aviation** (✆ **206/730-1412;** www.oldethymeaviation.com), which operates from Boeing Field. A 20-minute flight along the Seattle waterfront to the Space Needle costs $135 for two people; other flights range in price from $165 to $549 for two people. Keep in mind that these flights only operate when weather conditions are appropriate.

Seattle isn't known as a hot-air-ballooning center, but if you'd like to try floating over the Northwest landscape not far outside the city, contact **Over the Rainbow Balloon Flights** (✆ **425/861-8611;** www.letsgoballooning.com), which flies over the wineries of the Woodinville area. Flights are offered in both the morning and the afternoon and cost $165 to $215 per person.

OUTDOOR PURSUITS

See "Parks & Public Gardens" (p. 144) for a rundown of great places to play.

Beaches

Because the waters of **Puget Sound** stay chilly year-round, the saltwater beaches in the Seattle area are not really swimming beaches. They are primarily places to play in the sand, gaze across the water at the Olympic Mountains, and enjoy a picnic. However, Seattle is bordered on the east by **Lake Washington,** a large lake with numerous parks and small beaches along its shores. Even though the waters never get truly warm, the lake is still popular for swimming.

Seward Park ★, 5895 Lake Washington Blvd. S. (✆ **206/684-4396**), southeast of downtown Seattle, is a good place to hang out by the water and do a little swimming. From downtown, take Madison Street east to Lake Washington Boulevard and turn right. Although this isn't the most direct route to Seward Park, it's the most scenic. Along the way, you'll pass plenty of other small parks, including Mount Baker Beach. There is, however, one caveat: A parasite spread by geese and known as "swimmer's itch" is commonplace in the waters of Lake Washington. Consequently, you should always change out of your bathing suit and shower as soon after swimming as possible.

Alki Beach ★, across Elliott Bay from downtown Seattle, is the city's most popular beach and is the nearest approximation you'll find in the Northwest to a Southern California beach scene. The paved path that runs along this 2½-mile beach is popular with skaters, walkers, and cyclists, and the road that parallels the beach is lined with shops, restaurants, and beachy houses and apartment buildings. But the views across Puget Sound to the Olympic Mountains confirm that this is indeed the Northwest. (Despite those views, this beach lacks the greenery that makes some of the city's other beaches so much more appealing.) April through October, a water taxi operates daily between the downtown Seattle waterfront and Alki Beach. Other months, the water taxi operates Monday through Friday only. See p. 306 for details. (By the way, Alki rhymes with *sky,* not *key.*)

For a more Northwestern beach experience (which usually includes a bit of hiking or walking), head to one of the area's many waterfront parks. **Lincoln Park,** 8011 Fauntleroy Way SW (✆ **206/684-4075**), south of Alki Beach in West Seattle, has bluffs and forests backing the beach. Northwest of downtown Seattle in the Magnolia area, you'll find **Discovery Park ★★**, 3801 W. Government Way (✆ **206/386-4236**), where miles of beaches are the primary destination of most park visitors. To reach Discovery Park, follow Elliott Avenue/15th Avenue north along the waterfront from downtown Seattle; take the Dravus Street exit and turn left onto Dravus Street; take a right on 20th Avenue

There's a paved path that folks use to run, walk, or skate along Alki Beach.

West, which becomes first Gilman Avenue West and then West Government Way, which leads to the park and the park's visitor center.

Seeing the Light at Alki Point

When the first settlers arrived in the Seattle area, their ship dropped them at Alki Point. Today this point of land jutting out into Puget Sound is still important to mariners as the site of the Alki Lighthouse, 3201 Alki Ave. SW (✆ 206/217-6203). The lighthouse is open for tours from June through August on Saturday and Sunday afternoons from 1 to 4pm.

Golden Gardens Park ★★, 8498 Seaview Place NW (✆ **206/684-4075**), north of Ballard and Shilshole Bay, is my favorite Seattle beach park. Although the park isn't very large and is backed by railroad tracks, the views of the Olympic Mountains are magnificent, and on summer evenings, people build fires on the beach. Lawns and shade trees make Golden Gardens ideal for a picnic. To reach this park, take NW 54th Street west from Ballard, which is reached by following Elliott Avenue north from downtown.

Biking

Recycled Cycles, 1007 NE Boat St. (✆ **206/547-4491;** http://recycledcycles.com), rents bikes for $40 per day or $20 for a half day, and the **Montlake Bicycle Shop,** 2223 24th Ave. E. (✆ **206/329-7333;** www.montlakebike.com), rents bikes by the day for $35 to $90. Both of these shops are convenient to the **Burke-Gilman/Sammamish River Trail** ★, a 27-mile paved pathway created mostly from an old railway bed. This immensely popular path is a great place to take the family for a bike ride or to get in a long, vigorous ride without having to deal with traffic. The Burke-Gilman portion of the trail starts in the Ballard neighborhood of North Seattle, but the most convenient place to start a ride (if

Cycle along the trails at Gas Works Park.

you aren't renting a bike at Montlake Bicycle Shop) is at **Gas Works Park,** on the north shore of Lake Union. From here you can ride north and east, by way of the University of Washington, to **Kenmore Logboom Park,** at the north end of Lake Washington. Serious riders can continue on from Kenmore Logboom Park on the Sammamish River portion of the trail, which leads to **Marymoor Park,** at the north end of Lake Sammamish. Marymoor Park is the site of a velodrome (bicycle racetrack). This latter half of the trail is my favorite part; it follows the Sammamish River and passes through several pretty parks. Riding the entire trail out and back is a ride of more than 50 miles and is popular with riders in training for races. Plenty of great picnicking spots can be found along both sections of the trail.

The West Seattle bike path along **Alki Beach** is another good place to ride; it offers great views of the sound and the Olympics. If you'd like to pedal this pathway, you can rent single-speed bikes at **Alki Kayak Tours,** 1660 Harbor Ave. SW (✆ **206/953-0237;** http://kayakalki.com), which charges $10 per hour. Because this outfitter has a limited number of bikes, it's a good idea to call ahead and make a reservation. You can then take the water taxi from the downtown waterfront to West Seattle; the dock is right at the Alki Kayak Tours building.

Golf

While Seattle isn't a name that springs immediately to the minds of avid golfers, the sport inspires just as much passion here as it does across the country. Should you wish to get in a round while you're in town, Seattle has three conveniently located municipal golf courses: **Jackson Park Golf Course,** 1000 NE 135th St. (✆ **206/363-4747**); **Jefferson Park Golf Course,** 4101 Beacon Ave. S. (✆ **206/762-4513**); and **West Seattle Golf Club,** 4470 35th Ave. SW (✆ **206/935-5187**). This latter course has great views of the Seattle skyline and gets my vote as the best of the city's municipal courses. All three charge very reasonable greens fees of $33 to $37. For more information on these courses, contact **Premier Golf Centers** (✆ **206/285-2200;** http://premiergc.com).

Hiking

Within Seattle itself, there are several large nature parks laced with enough trails to allow for a few good, long walks. Among these are **Seward Park,** 5895 Lake Washington Blvd. S., southeast of downtown, and **Lincoln Park,** 8011 Fauntleroy Way SW, south of Alki Beach in West Seattle.

The city's largest natural park, and Seattleites' favorite spot for a quick dose of nature, is **Discovery Park,** 3801 W. Government Way (✆ **206/386-4236**), northwest of downtown, at the western tip of the Magnolia neighborhood. Covering more than 500 acres, this park has many miles of trails and beaches to hike—not to mention gorgeous views, forest paths, and meadows in which to laze away after a long walk. To reach Discovery Park, follow Elliott Avenue/15th Avenue north along the waterfront from downtown Seattle; take the Dravus Street exit and turn left onto Dravus Street; take a right on 20th Avenue W, which becomes first Gilman Avenue W and then W. Government Way, which leads to the park and the park's visitor center.

My favorite area hike, the trail up **Mount Si ★★**, is also the most challenging hike near Seattle. The rugged, glacier-carved peak, which is a 30- to 45-minute drive east of downtown on I-90, rises abruptly from the floor of the

The hike up (and down) Mt. Si is beautiful and challenging.

Snoqualmie Valley outside the town of North Bend and has an exhausting trail to its summit. However, the payoff is awesome views. (Take lots of water—it's an 8-mile round-trip hike.) From I-90, take exit 31 (North Bend), drive into town, turn right at the stoplight onto North Bend Way, drive through town, turn left onto Mount Si Road, and continue 2 miles to the trail head.

Farther east on I-90, at **Snoqualmie Pass** and just west of the pass, are several trail heads. Some trails lead to mountain summits, others to glacier-carved lakes, and still others past waterfalls deep in the forest. Because of their proximity to Seattle, these trails can be very crowded, and you will need a Northwest Forest Pass ($5 for a 1-day pass) to leave your car at national-forest trail heads (though not at the Mount Si trail head, which is on state land). My favorite trail in this area is the 8-mile round-trip hike to beautiful **Snow Lake,** a cool pool of subalpine waters surrounded by granite mountains. The trail head is just north of I-90 on Alpental Road (take exit 52). For more information and to purchase a Northwest Forest Pass, contact the **Snoqualmie Ranger District,** 902 SE North Bend Way (✆ **425/888-1421,** ext. 200; www.fs.fed.us/r6/mbs), in North Bend.

Jogging

The **waterfront,** from Pioneer Square north to Myrtle Edwards Park, where a paved path parallels the water, is a favorite downtown jogging route. The residential streets of **Capitol Hill,** when combined with roads and sidewalks through **Volunteer Park,** are another good choice. If you happen to be staying in the University District, you can access the 27-mile **Burke-Gilman/Sammamish River Trail** or run the ever-popular trail around **Green Lake.** Out in West Seattle, the **Alki Beach** pathway is also very popular and provides great views of the Olympics. You can access this trail via water taxi; see p. 306 for details.

Sea Kayaking, Canoeing, Rowing & Sailing

If you'd like to try your hand at **sea kayaking ★★**, head to the **Northwest Outdoor Center,** 2100 Westlake Ave. N. (✆ **800/683-0637** or 206/281-9694; www.nwoc.com), on the west side of Lake Union. Here you can rent a sea kayak for $13 to $22 per hour. You can also opt for guided tours lasting from a few hours to several days, and plenty of classes are available for those who are interested.

Moss Bay Row, Kayak, Sail & Paddle Board Center, 1001 Fairview Ave. N. (✆ **206/682-2031;** www.mossbay.net), rents sea kayaks, rowing shells, sailboats, and paddle boards at the south end of Lake Union near Chandler's Cove. Rates range from $13 per hour for a single kayak to $18 per hour for a double. Because this rental center is a little closer to downtown Seattle and can be reached on the Seattle Streetcar, it's a better choice if you are here without a car.

If you're interested in renting a wooden rowboat or sailboat, head to Lake Union and the **Center for Wooden Boats ★**, 1010 Valley St. (✆ **206/382-2628;** www.cwb.org); rates range from $20 to $50 per hour. This center can be reached from downtown on the Seattle Streetcar.

On the University of Washington campus behind Husky Stadium, you'll find the **Waterfront Activities Center** (✆ **206/543-9433;** http://depts.washington.edu/ima/IMA_wac.php), which is open to the public and rents canoes and rowboats for $8.50 to $10 per hour. With the marshes of the Washington Park Arboretum directly across a narrow channel from the boat launch, this is an ideal place for beginner canoeists to rent a boat.

In this same general area, you can rent kayaks at the **Agua Verde Cafe Paddle Club,** 1303 NE Boat St. (✆ **206/545-8570;** www.aguaverde.com), at the foot of Brooklyn Avenue on Portage Bay (the body of water between Lake

You can paddle your own canoe at the Waterfront Activities Center.

Union and Lake Washington). Kayaks can be rented from March through October and go for $15 to $20 per hour. Best of all, this place is part of the **Agua Verde Cafe** (p. 100), a great Mexican restaurant! Before or after a paddle, be sure to get an order of tacos.

At **Greenlake Boat Rentals,** 7351 E. Green Lake Dr. N. (✆ **206/527-0171;** www.greenlakeboatrentals.net), in north Seattle not far from Woodland Park Zoo, you can rent canoes, kayaks, sailboats, rowboats, pedal boats, sailboards, and stand-up paddle boards for a bit of leisurely time on the water. A paved path circles the park, which is one of the most popular in Seattle (it's a great place to join crowds of locals enjoying one of the city's nicest green spaces). Kayaks, canoes, rowboats, pedal boats, and paddle boards all rent for $15 per hour, and sailboats go for $20 per hour.

And now for something completely different. If you're not up for paddling, how about an electric boat? **The Electric Boat Company,** Westlake Landing Building, 2046 Westlake Ave. N. (✆ **206/223-7476;** www.theelectricboatco.com), rents boats that will hold your whole family (up to 10 people). The boats rent for $89 per hour (2-hr. minimum) and are a fun and safe way to cruise around Lake Union and check out the houseboats. You can even stop at one of the lakefront restaurants for a meal or drinks.

Skiing

One of the reasons Seattleites put up with long, wet winters is because they can go skiing within an hour of the city. And with many slopes set up for night skiing, it's possible to leave work and hit the slopes before dinner, ski for several hours, and be back home in time to get a good night's rest. The ski season in the Seattle area generally runs from late November to late April. Equipment can be rented

It's all downhill at Summit at Snoqualmie.

at the ski area listed below or at **R.E.I.,** 222 Yale Ave. N. (✆ **888/873-1938** or 206/223-1944; www.rei.com).

CROSS-COUNTRY SKIING In the Snoqualmie Pass area of the Cascade Range, less than 50 miles east of Seattle on I-90, the **Summit Nordic Center** (✆ **425/434-6778;** www.summitatsnoqualmie.com) offers rentals, instruction, and many miles of groomed trails. An all-day trail pass costs $18 for adults and $16 for seniors and children.

Several Sno-Parks (designated cross-country ski areas) are along I-90 at Snoqualmie Pass. Some have groomed trails; others have trails that are marked but not groomed. Be sure to get a **Sno-Park permit** ($20–$21 for a 1-day pass; $40–$41 for a season pass), which is required if you want to park at a cross-country ski area. Sno-Park permits are available at ski shops; pick one up when renting your skis.

DOWNHILL SKIING Jointly known as the **Summit at Snoqualmie** (✆ **425/434-7669** for information, or 206/236-1600 for the snow report; www.summitatsnoqualmie.com), the Alpental, Summit West, Summit Central, and Summit East ski areas are all located at Snoqualmie Pass, less than 50 miles east of Seattle off I-90. Together these four ski areas offer 1,916 acres of skiable slopes, plus rentals and lessons. Adult all-day lift tickets cost $58 for adults, $39 for seniors and children 7 to 12, and $12 for super seniors (over 70) and children 6 and under. Call for hours of operation.

Tennis

Seattle Parks and Recreation operates dozens of outdoor tennis courts all over the city. The most convenient are at **Volunteer Park,** 1247 15th Ave. E. (at E. Prospect St.).

If it happens to be raining and you have your heart set on playing tennis, indoor public courts are available at the **Amy Yee Tennis Center,** 2000 Martin Luther King Jr. Way S. (✆ **206/684-4764;** www.seattle.gov/parks/Athletics/Tennisct.htm). Rates here are $32 for singles and $40 for doubles for 1¼ hours. This center also has outdoor courts that cost $12 for 1½ hours.

SPECTATOR SPORTS

With professional football, baseball, ice hockey, soccer, and women's basketball teams, as well as the University of Washington Huskies teams, Seattle is definitely a city of sports fans. **Ticketmaster** (✆ **800/745-3000** or 866/448-7849; www.ticketmaster.com) sells tickets to almost all sporting events in the Seattle area. You'll find Ticketmaster outlets at area Fred Meyer stores.

Baseball

Seattle's most popular professional sports team is the American League's **Seattle Mariners** (✆ **206/346-4001;** www.seattlemariners.com). The team has a devoted following, so buy your tickets well in advance if you want to see a game.

The Mariners' retro-style **Safeco Field ★★** is one of the most beautiful ballparks in the country. It's also one of only a handful of stadiums with a retractable roof (which can open or close in 10–20 min.), allowing the Mariners a real grass playing field without the worry of getting rained out.

Mariners fans celebrate another strikeout at Safeco Field.

Ticket prices range from $7 (for the bleachers in advance, $8 on game day) to $65. Though you may be able to buy a single ticket on game day at the Safeco Field box office, it's tough to get two seats together. To ensure that you get good seats, order in advance at **Mariners Team Stores** (at Safeco Field, at Fourth and Stewart sts. downtown, or in the Bellevue Square shopping mall) or through **Ticketmaster** (✆ **206/622-4487;** www.ticketmaster.com). You can also sometimes find last minute or deeply discounted tickets on **StubHub.com** (www.stubhub.com/seattle-mariners-tickets) Parking is next to impossible in the immediate vicinity of Safeco Field, so plan to leave your car behind. You can get to Safeco Field on the Metro bus: 39, 41, 101, 106, 150, 177 lines.

If you'd like a behind-the-scenes look at the ballpark, you can take a **1-hour tour,** which costs $9 for adults, $8 for seniors, and $7 for kids 3 to 12. Tickets can be purchased at the Mariners Team Store at Safeco Field, at other Mariners Team Stores around the city, or through Ticketmaster. Tour times vary, and tours are not offered on days when day games are scheduled.

Basketball

The **Seattle Storm** (✆ **877/962-2849** or 206/217-9622; www.wnba.com/storm), of the Women's National Basketball Association, play in Key Arena. The Storm is anchored by fan favorites/perennial All-Stars Sue Bird and Lauren Jackson, and are consistently one of the top teams in the league's Western Conference, winning the league title in 2004 and 2010. Most ticket prices range from $18 to $62; they're available at the arena box office or through Ticketmaster (✆ 800/745-3000).

The **University of Washington Huskies** women's basketball team has also been very popular for years. For information on both the women's and the men's Huskies basketball games, call ✆ **206/543-2200** or go to www.gohuskies.com.

Storm fans cheer for their champs, like All-Star Lauren Jackson.

Football

Ever since they made it to the Super Bowl in 2006, the **Seattle Seahawks** (✆ **888/635-4295** or 206/381-7848; www.seahawks.com) have been getting much more respect in their home town than they used to get. So you may find it difficult to get your hands on tickets if you decide on the spur of the moment to attend a Seahawks game. The Seahawks play at **Qwest Field,** 800 Occidental Ave. S. (✆ **206/381-7500;** www.qwestfield.com), which is adjacent to Safeco Field. Tickets to games run from around $50 to upward of $400 and are sold through **Ticketmaster.** Regardless of how the Seahawks are doing in a particular year, games against Oakland, Denver, and a couple of other teams usually sell out as soon as tickets go on sale in July or August. You may also be able to pick up last minute tickets at prices ranging from close to face value to far above it, depending on the game, at **StubHub.com** (www.stubhub.com/seattle-seahawks-tickets). Traffic and parking in the vicinity of Qwest Field is a nightmare on game days, so take the bus if you can. If you want a behind-the-scenes look at Qwest Field, you can take a tour of the stadium. Tours operate daily at 12:30

A Seahawks fan shows pride in the team (and artistic merit).

Rabid fans cheer the Washington Huskies on the gridiron.

and 2:30pm between June and August, and only on Friday and Saturday in other months (note that there are no tours on game days or when other events are scheduled). Tours cost $7 for adults and $5 for seniors and children 4 to 12. During pre-season, fans can attend some training camp practices at the Virginia Mason Athletic Center in Renton, about 30 minutes south of Seattle. Visit the team website for information/admission fees.

Not surprisingly, the **University of Washington Huskies** (✆ **206/543-2200;** www.gohuskies.com), who play in Husky Stadium on the university campus, have a loyal following. Big games (Oregon or Washington State) sell out as soon as tickets go on sale in the summer. Other games can sell out in advance, but obstructed-view tickets are usually available on game day. Ticket prices range from $38 to $80 for reserved seats, and from $32 to $80 for general admission.

Horse Racing

The state-of-the-art **Emerald Downs,** 2300 Emerald Downs Dr., Auburn (✆ **888/931-8400** or 253/288-7000; www.emeralddowns.com), is south of Seattle, off Wash. 167 (reached from I-405 at the south end of Lake Washington). To get to the racetrack, take the 15th Street Northwest exit. Admission is $7. The season runs from early April to late September.

The Marathon

The **Seattle Marathon** (✆ **206/729-3660;** www.seattlemarathon.org), which attracts more than 13,000 participants, takes place the Sunday after Thanksgiving. The race starts and ends at Seattle Center and crosses the I-90 floating bridge to Mercer Island.

Runners traverse the city in the annual Seattle Marathon.

Soccer

If you're a soccer fan, you can catch Major League Soccer's **Seattle Sounders FC** (✆ **877/657-4625** or 206/682-2800; www.soundersfc.com) at Qwest Field. The season runs February through March, and tickets, which sell for $28 to $98, are available through Ticketmaster (✆ **800/745-3000**). The team's owners include the ubiquitous Paul Allen and comedian Drew Carey. The team is quite popular: since its start in 2009, they've sold out every league game, and won the league's Open Cup in 2009 and '10.

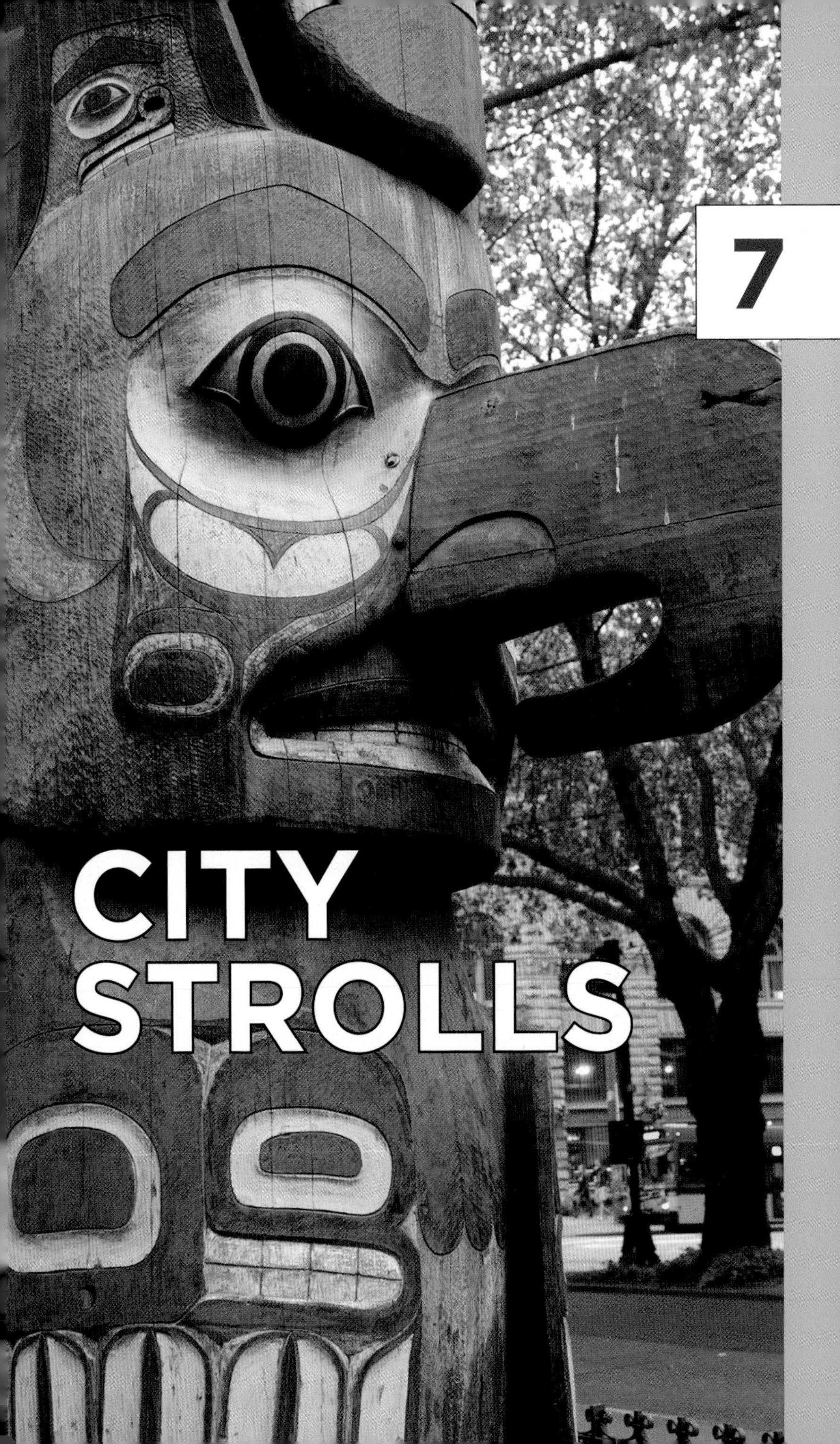

7

CITY STROLLS

Downtown Seattle is compact and easily explored on foot (if you don't mind hills), and among visitors to the city, the most popular stroll is along the waterfront, from Pioneer Square to Pike Place Market. Everything along the waterfront is right there to be seen, so you don't really need me to outline the specifics. Instead, I've focused on spots that can be a little confusing, the sorts of places where you might overlook some of the gems.

Although you can easily enjoy Pike Place Market simply by getting lost in the market maze for several hours, you might want to consult the first walking tour I've outlined below just so you don't miss any of the highlights.

Some people make the mistake of dismissing the Pioneer Square area as a neighborhood of street people, but it is much more than that. To help you get the most out of downtown Seattle's only historic neighborhood, my second walking tour takes in interesting shops, art galleries, and historic buildings.

The third walking tour will take you through the Fremont District. Home to counterculture types, Fremont is a quirky area filled with tongue-in-cheek art and unusual shops.

WALKING TOUR 1: PIKE PLACE MARKET

START:	**At the corner of Pike Street and First Avenue.**
FINISH:	**At the corner of Pike Street and First Avenue.**
TIME:	**Approximately 4 hours, including shopping and dining.**
BEST TIMES:	**Weekends, when crafts vendors set up along Pike Place.**
WORST TIMES:	**Weekends, when the market is extremely crowded.**

Despite the crowds of visitors and locals, Pike Place Market, a sprawling complex of historic buildings and open-air vendors' stalls, remains Seattle's most fascinating attraction. You'll find aisles lined with fresh produce, cut flowers, and seafood, as well as unusual little shops tucked away in the hidden corners of this multilevel maze. Street performers also perform here, adding another level of fun to a meander through the market. Because Pike Place Market is so large, it is easy to overlook some of the more interesting businesses and its many quirky works of public art. The following walking tour is meant to lead you through the market, past the many places you wouldn't want to miss. For more information on the market, see p. 126.

Start your tour at the corner of Pike Street and First Avenue at the:

1 Pike Place Market Information Kiosk

This cubicle is one of the most important buildings in the market. Here you can pick up a copy of the market newspaper, which has a map of the market.

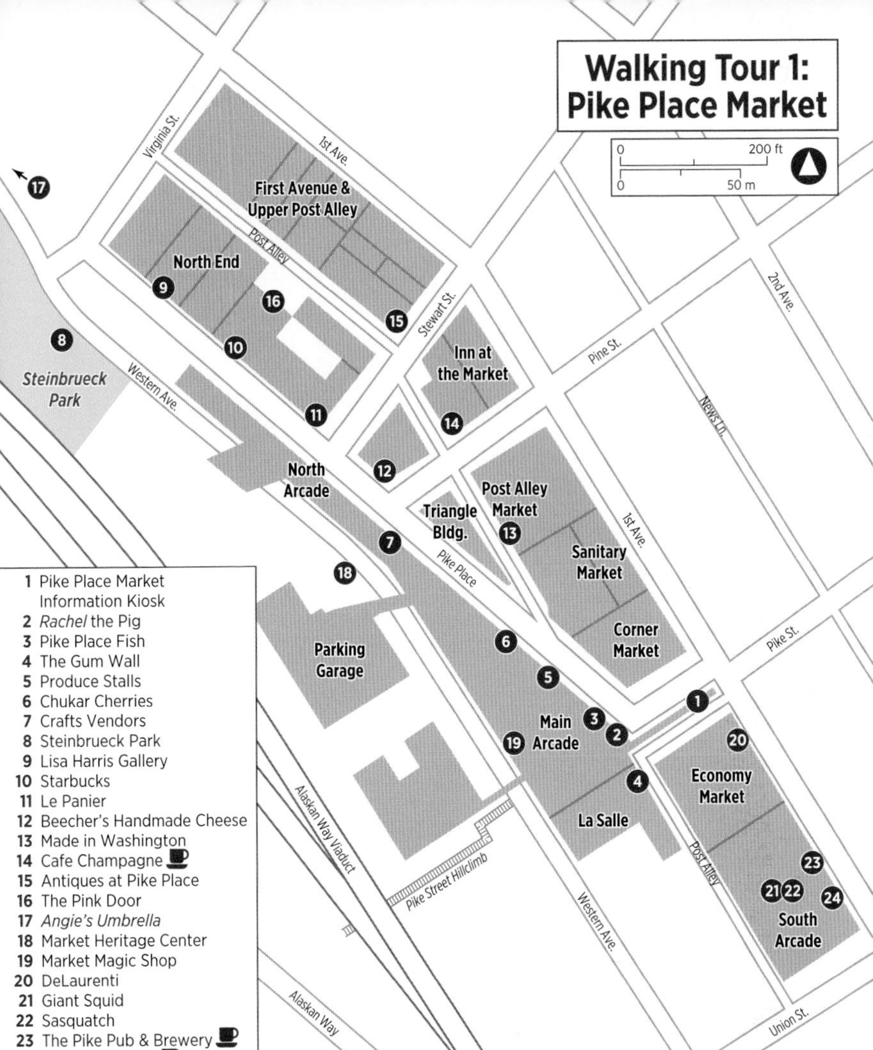

Directly behind the information kiosk rises the famous Pike Place Market neon sign and clock. Just below this sign, you'll find:

2 Rachel the Pig

This life-size bronze statue of a pig is the unofficial Pike Place Market mascot and also doubles as the market piggy bank. Every year people deposit thousands of dollars into *Rachel*. Hardly any visitor to the market goes home without a shot of some friend or family member sitting on the pig.

It's sometimes difficult to spot *Rachel* because of the crowds that gather here to watch the flying fish at:

Watch out for flying fish when you tour Pike Place Market!

3 Pike Place Fish

The antics of the fishmongers at Pike Place Fish are legendary. No, they don't actually sell flying fish, but if you decide to buy, say, a whole salmon, your fish will go flying through the air (amid much shouting and gesticulating) from the front of the stall to the back, where someone will steak it or fillet it for you and even pack it on dry ice so that you can take it home with you on the plane.

On the far side of *Rachel* from Pike Place Fish, you'll find a flight of stairs leading down to cobblestone Lower Post Alley. Walk 50 feet down this alley to:

4 The Gum Wall

The brick wall along one side of the alley has been covered with thousands of wads of ABC (Already Been Chewed) gum. The wall started out simply, with a few bits of colorful gum wads, but has grown more and more creative (and disgusting) over the years. Is it art or a revolting form of littering? You decide.

You can leave your own sticky mark on the gum wall.

Walk back up the stairs, and at the top, to the right of Pike Place Fish, begin the market's main:

5 Produce Stalls

In summer, look for fresh cherries, berries, peaches, and melons; in the fall, it's Washington state apples. Stalls full of colorful cut flowers also line this section of the market.

As you wander through this crowded section of the market, keep an eye out for:

6 Chukar Cherries

This Washington State candy company, at 1529B Pike Place (✆ **206/623-8043**), specializes in chocolate-covered dried cherries. Samples are always available.

A little farther along, you'll come to the North Arcade, where you'll find lots of:

7 Crafts Vendors

This is a good place to shop for handmade souvenirs. These craftspeople know their clientele, so most of the work here is small enough to fit in a suitcase.

On weekends, you can find more crafts vendors along this side of the street just past the end of the covered market stalls. Across Western Avenue from the last of these outdoor crafts stalls is:

8 Steinbrueck Park

Although this small, grassy park is favored by the homeless, it is also home to a pair of impressive totem poles and offers a superb view of Elliott Bay. Watch for the comings and goings of the giant car ferries that link Seattle to Bainbridge Island and Bremerton, on the far side of Puget Sound.

Ask for a free sample of the chocolate-covered fruit at Chukar Cherries!

Get a unique, handmade gift from the crafty vendors.

From the park, walk back across Western Avenue and Pike Place and head toward your starting point. You'll now be on the opposite side of Pike Place from the produce stalls. This stretch of the market has lots of great prepared-food stalls, so be sure to do a little grazing. If you've become convinced that Pike Place Market is strictly for tourists, climb the stairs to the:

9 Lisa Harris Gallery

This art gallery, at 1922 Pike Place (✆ **206/443-3315**), always seems to have interesting contemporary artwork, largely by Northwestern artists.

A little way up the street, you'll find what was once the only:

10 Starbucks

That's right, years ago this narrow space, at 1912 Pike Place (✆ **206/448-8762**), was the only Starbucks in the world. Unlike today's Starbucks, this espresso bar has no tables or chairs; it's strictly a grab-it-and-go spot. Because you've already been on your feet for a while and still have a lot of the market to see, you may want to stop in and order a Grande Mocha to see you through the rest of your walking tour. Also be sure to notice how different the mermaid here looks compared to today's official logo. By the way, this was not the first Starbucks; it had been in a previous location before moving to the market.

How about a little something tasty to go with that mocha?

11 Le Panier

Located at 1902 Pike Place (✆ **206/441-3669**), this French-style bakery has good croissants and other pastries to accompany your espresso. They also have fresh bread to go with anything you might buy at the next stop.

Continue along Pike Place in the same direction, and on the next block you'll see:

12 Beecher's Handmade Cheese

Here, at 1600 Pike Place (✆ **206/956-1964**), you can watch cheese being made and taste samples. This place also does a yummy macaroni and cheese.

Continue along Pike Place for another block, passing several more prepared-food stalls, and then turn left into Post Alley. This narrow lane cuts through several blocks of the market, and many shops and restaurants open onto it. For Seattle souvenirs, it's hard to beat:

13 Made in Washington

Shortly after you start up the narrow lane, you'll come to this store, at 1530 Post Alley (✆ **206/467-0788**). It carries smoked salmon, prepared foods, crafts, books, and plenty of other inexpensive stuff from here in Washington.

14 Take a Break

Pike Place Market is full of surprises, not the least of which are the many excellent restaurants hidden away in quiet corners of the complex. One of my very favorites is **Cafe Campagne,** 1600 Post Alley (✆ **206/728-2233**), a little French cafe serving delicious lunches. The atmosphere is *très* French.

Continue up the alley, and at Stewart Street, on the north side of the street, you'll see:

15 Antiques at Pike Place

This large antiques mall, at 92 Stewart St. (✆ **206/441-9643**), has more than 80 dealers. The stalls are packed full of interesting collectibles.

Back on Post Alley, watch for:

16 The Pink Door

This restaurant, at 1919 Post Alley (✆ **206/443-3241**), is one of the market's most famous dinner spots. No sign marks it out front, just the pink door. A flight of stairs leads down to an Italian restaurant and cabaret/bar. The deck is *the* place to eat on summer evenings.

From Post Alley, descend to Pike Place via the staircase to the left of the Pink Door. These stairs lead down to a building with a shady courtyard. After walking through the building, turn right and go 2 blocks to the corner of Western Avenue and Lenora Street where you'll find:

17 Angie's Umbrella

This giant steel-and-aluminum umbrella sculpture seems to have gone the way of so many Seattle umbrellas. It seems to have been blown inside out by the wind. The umbrella also acts as a weather vane, so you won't need a weatherman to know which way the wind blows. The answer, my friend, is blowing in the wind.

Walk back the way you came and continue downhill on Western Avenue to the:

18 Market Heritage Center

At 1533 Western Ave., in this open-air exhibit on the history of Pike Place Market, you can learn all about the various incarnations of the market since its inception. If you'd like to do a guided walking tour similar to this one, you can contact **Friends of the Market** (✆ **206/322-2219**).

Continue down Western Avenue, and in a couple of blocks, you'll come to the Pike Street Hill Climb, a network of stairways that connect the waterfront with Pike Place Market. If you head up the stairs, you'll find the market's Down Under area, which consists of long hallways lined with small shops. My favorite shop in the Down Under is the:

19 Market Magic Shop

Located on the Down Under's fourth level, the **Market Magic Shop** (✆ **206/624-4271**) sells all kinds of tricks and paraphernalia for magicians. Kids love this shop, as do aspiring magicians. Across the hall from this shop are some unusual coin-operated window displays of giant shoes. Don't miss them!

For all your magic needs...head to the Market Magic Shop.

If you leave the Down Under by way of the market stairs that are an extension of the Pike Street Hill Climb, you will find yourself back in the vicinity of Rachel the pig and Pike Place Fish. From here, make your way through the crowd of people waiting to see the fish fly and head into the Economy Building. In the walkway leading toward First Avenue, you'll find:

See the spectentacle...er, spectacular giant squid.

20 DeLaurenti

This Italian grocery, at 1435 First Ave. (✆ **206/622-0141**), has a great deli case full of Italian cheeses and meats. It also sells imported pastas and has a good selection of wines and beers. Samples of various olive oils are often available.

If you exit DeLaurenti through the door in the wine shop area, you'll be in an atrium, from the ceiling of which hangs a:

21 Giant Squid

This life-size copper sculpture was created by a local artist. Although you won't see any squid this size in the nearby Seattle Aquarium (on the waterfront), you can see a live giant octopus there.

22 Sasquatch

Beneath the giant squid, you'll come face to face with a life-size wooden sculpture of the Northwest's legendary and elusive Sasquatch, aka "Bigfoot."

23–24 Winding Down

From Sasquatch and the giant squid, head down the hall to **The Pike Pub & Brewery,** 1415 First Ave. (✆ **206/622-6044**), where you can enjoy a cool microbrewed beer. Alternatively, you can head outside to First Avenue, where you can get a creamy gelato at **Bottega Italiana,** 1425 First Ave. (✆ **206/343-0200**).

WALKING TOUR 2: PIONEER SQUARE AREA

START: **Pioneer Place at the corner of Yesler Way and First Avenue.**
FINISH: **DRY Soda tasting room, First Avenue South.**
TIME: **Approximately 5 hours, including shopping, dining, and museum stops.**

BEST TIMES:	**Weekdays, when the neighborhood and the Underground Tour are not so crowded.**
WORST TIMES:	**Weekends, when the area is very crowded, and Mondays, when galleries are closed.**

In the late 19th century, Pioneer Square was the heart of downtown Seattle, so when a fire raged through these blocks in 1889, the city was devastated. Residents and merchants quickly began rebuilding and set about to remedy many of the infrastructure problems that had faced Seattle before the fire. The rebuilding outpaced the city's plans to raise the level of city streets, and by the time streets were raised, many of the Pioneer Square area's buildings had already been constructed. Consequently, the street level of today was originally the second story for many of the neighborhood's buildings. You can learn all about this area's history on one of the tours operated by the **Underground Tour** (p. 140).

Today this small section of the city is all that remains of old Seattle, and because one architect, Elmer Fisher, was responsible for the design of many of the buildings constructed after the fire, the neighborhood has a distinctly uniform architectural style.

While wandering these streets, don't bother looking for a specific site called Pioneer Square; you won't find it. The name actually applies to the whole neighborhood, not a plaza surrounded by four streets, as you would surmise. Do keep your eye out for interesting manhole covers, many of which were cast with maps of Seattle or Northwest Coast Indian designs. Also be aware that this neighborhood, the original Skid Row, still has several missions and homeless shelters—consequently, expect to see a lot of street people in the area.

To get the most out of downtown Seattle's only historic neighborhood, I've outlined a walking tour that takes in shops, art galleries, and historic buildings.

Start your tour of this historic neighborhood at the corner of Yesler Way and First Avenue on:

1 Pioneer Place

The triangular plaza at the heart of Pioneer Square is the site of both a bust of Chief Sealth and a Tlingit totem pole. For information on the history of this totem pole, see "Pole to Pole," in chapter 6. Also on this plaza is a 1905 cast-iron pergola that was reconstructed after a truck crashed into it back in 2001.

Facing the square are several historic buildings, including the gabled Lowman Building and three buildings noteworthy for their terra-cotta facades. In one of these buildings, at 608 First Ave., you'll find the ticket counter for:

The manhole covers around Pioneer Place are artfully designed.

2 The Underground Tour

This tour takes a look at the Pioneer Square area from beneath the sidewalks. The tour (✆ **206/682-4646**) is a great introduction to the history of the area (if you don't mind off-color jokes) and actually spends quite a bit of time aboveground, duplicating much of the walking tour outlined here.

Running along the south side of Pioneer Place is:

3 Yesler Way

This was the original Skid Row. In Seattle's early years, logs were skidded down this road to a lumber mill on the waterfront, and the road came to be known as Skid Road. These days, Yesler Way is trying hard to live down its reputation, but because of the number of missions in this neighborhood, a lot of street people are still in the area (and they'll most certainly be asking you for change as you wander the streets).

4 Take a Break

If you skipped the Underground Tour, then cross Yesler Way to the **Starbucks** at Yesler and First Avenue, where you can pick up a latte to help fuel you through this walking tour. Right next door to Starbucks is **Cow Chips,** 102A First Ave. S. (✆ **206/292-9808**), where you can get one of the best (though messiest) chocolate chip cookies you'll ever eat.

With cookie and coffee in hand, glance up Yesler Way, past a triangular parking deck (a monstrosity that prompted the movement to preserve the rest of this neighborhood), and you will see:

Refuel with a cowchip (cookie) as you walk around Pioneer Place.

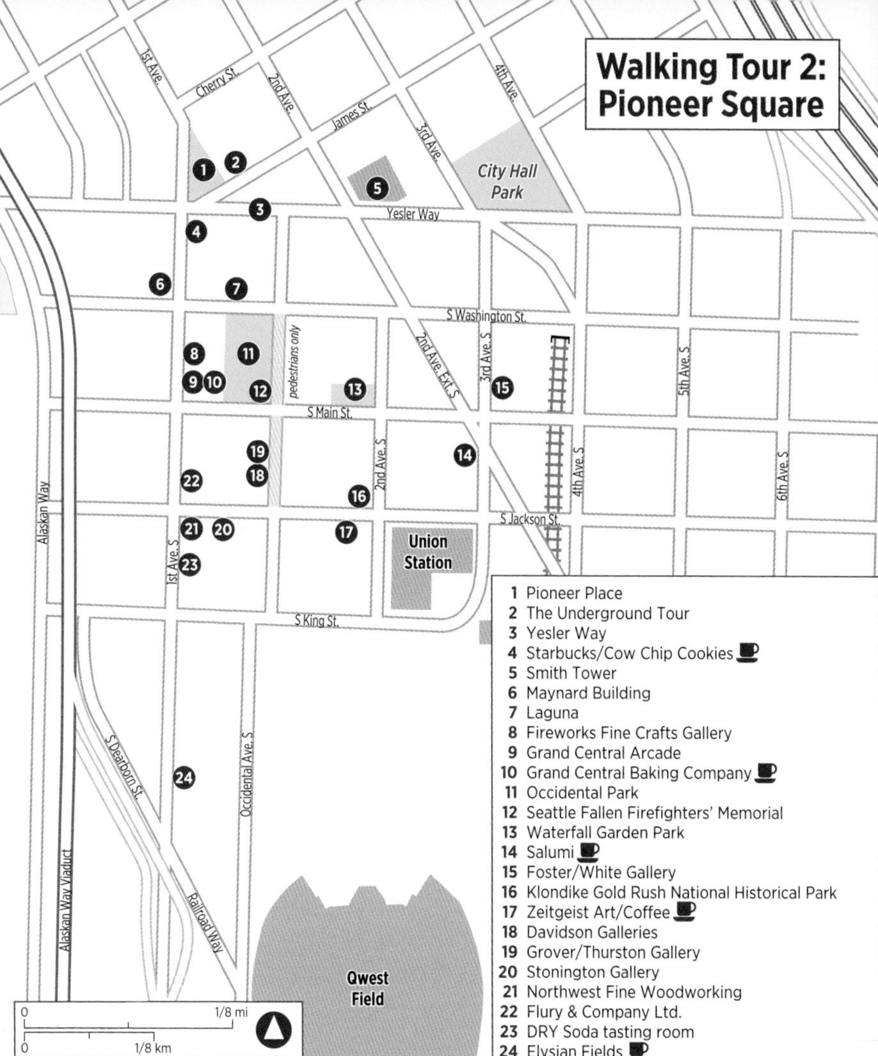

5 Smith Tower

This building, at 506 Second Ave. (✆ **206/622-4004**), was the tallest building west of the Mississippi when it was completed in 1914. The observation floor, near the top of this early skyscraper, is open to the public and provides a very different perspective of Seattle than does the Space Needle. The ornate lobby and elevator doors are also worth checking out.

Now walk back down to First Avenue and turn left, away from Pioneer Place. At the next corner, Washington Street, look across First Avenue and admire the:

Potter around for awhile at Laguna for the perfect gift.

The ivy-covered walls of Grand Central Arcade contain all kinds of interesting shops to explore.

6 Maynard Building

This ornate building, which was named for Seattle founding father David "Doc" Maynard, was the site of Seattle's first bank.

Heading up Washington Street away from the water for half a block will bring you to:

7 Laguna Vintage American Pottery Shop

This vintage pottery shop, at 116 S. Washington St. (✆ **206/682-6162**), specializes in mid-20th-century pottery, primarily from California. Fiesta, Bauer, and Weller are all well represented.

From here, head back to First Avenue and turn left. On this block, you'll find:

8 Fireworks Fine Crafts Gallery

This gallery, at 210 First Ave. S. (✆ **206/682-9697**), sells colorful and unusual crafts by Northwest artisans.

Next, at 214 First Ave. S., you'll come to the:

9 Grand Central Arcade

Inside this small, European-style shopping arcade, with its brick walls and wine-cellar-like basement, are several interesting shops and studios.

10 Take a Break

In the arcade, you'll also find the **Grand Central Bakery** (✆ **206/622-3644**), plus some tables and even a fireplace, which together make this a great place to stop for a pastry to nibble on while you walk.

Leaving Grand Central Arcade through the door opposite where you entered will bring you to:

11 Occidental Park

On this shady, cobblestone plaza stand four totem poles carved by Northwest artist Duane Pasco. The tallest is the 35-foot-high *The Sun and Raven,* which tells the story of how Raven brought light into the world. Next to this pole is *Man Riding a Whale.* This type of totem pole was traditionally carved to help villagers during their whale hunts. The other two figures that face each other are symbols of the Bear Clan and the Welcoming Figure.

Have a seat and watch the waterfall for awhile.

This shady park serves as a gathering spot for homeless people, so you may not want to linger. However, before leaving the park, be sure to notice the grouping of bronze statues, the:

12 Seattle Fallen Firefighters' Memorial

This memorial is a tribute to four firefighters who died in a 1995 warehouse fire in Chinatown.

The statues are adjacent to South Main Street, and if you walk up this street to the corner of Second Avenue, you will come to:

13 Waterfall Garden Park

The roaring waterfall here looks as if it were transported straight from the Cascade Range. The park is built on the site of the original United Parcel Service (UPS) offices and makes a wonderful place for a rest or a picnic lunch.

Continue up Main Street to the corner of Third Avenue South.

14 Take a Break

For the perfect picnic repast, stand in line for a sandwich of house-cured salami from **Salumi,** 309 Third Ave. S (✆ **206/621-8772**). This hole in the wall, owned by celebrity chef Mario Batali's father, is legendary for its superb cured meats. Arrive early or late to avoid the longest line. With sandwich in hand, head back to Waterfall Garden Park.

Across from Salumi, at 220 Third Ave. S., you'll find another of my favorite Seattle galleries, the:

15 Foster/White Gallery

This gallery (✆ **206/622-2833**), one of the largest in the West, is best known for its art glass. It's the Seattle gallery for famed glass artist Dale Chihuly and always has several of his works on display.

You'll find fine art at the Foster/White Gallery.

Now walk south on Third Avenue South to South Jackson Street and turn right. Continue to the corner of Second Avenue South, where, at 319 Second Ave. S., you'll find the:

16 Klondike Gold Rush National Historical Park

Not really a park, this small museum (✆ **206/220-4240**) is dedicated to the history of the 1897–98 Klondike gold rush, which helped Seattle grow from an obscure town into a booming metropolis.

17 Take a Break

If it's time for another latte, cross South Jackson Street to **Zeitgeist Art/Coffee,** 171 S. Jackson St. (✆ **206/583-0497**), which serves good coffee in a sort of vintage bookstore setting.

One block west is Occidental Mall, where you'll find a couple of art galleries, including:

18 Davidson Galleries

You never know what to expect when you walk through the front door here at 313 Occidental Ave. S. (✆ **206/624-7684**). The gallery sells everything from 16th-century prints to contemporary prints and drawings by Northwest artists.

19 Grover/Thurston Gallery

Colorful, cartoonish, whimsical art—often with an edginess to it—is frequently featured at this gallery at 309 Occidental Ave. S. (✆ **206/223-0816**), just down from Davidson Galleries. Lots of abstract art also makes it onto the walls here.

Around the corner from these two galleries, at 119 S. Jackson St., you'll find the:

20 Stonington Gallery

This gallery (✆ **206/405-4040**) is one of Seattle's top showcases for contemporary Native American art and crafts. It displays a good selection of Northwest Coast Indian masks, woodcarvings, prints, and jewelry.

Continue to the corner of First Avenue, where you'll find:

Taste the unusual flavors at DRY Soda's tasting room.

21 Northwest Fine Woodworking

This large store, at 101 S. Jackson St. (✆ **206/625-0542**), sells exquisite handcrafted wooden furniture, as well as some smaller pieces. It's definitely worth a visit.

Cross South Jackson Street, and on the opposite corner, you'll find:

22 Flury & Company Ltd.

This gallery, at 322 First Ave. S. (✆ **206/587-0260**), specializes in prints by famed early-20th-century Seattle photographer Edward S. Curtis, who is known for his portraits of Native Americans. There's also an excellent selection of antique Native American artifacts.

Go back across South Jackson Street and walk along First Avenue South. In the middle of the block, you'll come to the:

23 DRY Soda tasting room

Maybe you've been to a winery's tasting room, but I bet you've never been to a soda tasting room. Then again, **DRY Soda,** 410 First Ave. S. (✆ **888/379-7632** or 206/652-2345; www.drysoda.com), doesn't make your average soda, and they feel that they should let people taste them first before they buy. Flavors include cucumber, rhubarb, lavender, lemongrass, blood orange, vanilla bean, and juniper berry. The tasting room is usually open Monday through Saturday from noon to 5pm.

24 Winding Down

If, after tasting DRY Soda's unusual beverages, you find yourself craving something a little stronger and more traditional, continue south one more block to **Elysian Fields,** 542 First Ave. S. (✆ **206/382-4498**), which is one of my favorite Seattle brewpubs.

WALKING TOUR 3: FUN, FUNKY FREMONT

START: **South end of Fremont Bridge, near Ponti restaurant.**
FINISH: **North end of Fremont Bridge.**
TIME: **Approximately 2 hours, not including time spent dining.**
BEST TIMES: **Sunday, during the Fremont Sunday Market.**
WORST TIMES: **Early morning or evening, when shops are closed.**

The Fremont District definitely marches to the beat of a different drummer. Styling itself "The Republic of Fremont" and the center of the universe, this small, tight-knit community is the most eclectic neighborhood in the city. It has taken as its motto *De Libertas Quirkas,* which, roughly translated, means "free to be peculiar." Fremont residents have focused on art as a way to draw the community together, and in so doing, they've created a corner of the city where silliness reigns. At this crossroads business district, you find unusual outdoor art, the Fremont Sunday Market (a European-style flea market), several vintage-clothing and furniture stores, a couple of pubs, and many other unexpected and unusual shops, galleries, and cafes. During the summer, outdoor movies are shown on Saturday nights, and in June there's the wacky Solstice Parade, a countercultural promenade of giant puppets, wizards, fairies, naked bicyclists, and hippies of all ages.

Start your tour by finding a parking spot around the corner from Ponti restaurant, at the south end of the:

1 Fremont Bridge

This is one of the busiest drawbridges in the United States and spans the Lake Washington Ship Canal.

As you approach the north side of the bridge, glance up; in the window of the bridge-tender's tower (on the west side of the bridge), you'll see:

2 Rapunzel

This is a neon sculpture of the famous fairy-tale maiden with the prodigious mane. Her neon tresses cascade down the wall of the tower.

As you land in the Republic of Fremont, you will see, at the end of the bridge on the opposite side of the street from *Rapunzel,* Seattle's most beloved public artwork:

3 Waiting for the Interurban

This sculpture features several people waiting for the trolley that

Let down your hair to tour the Republic of Fremont.

no longer runs between Fremont and downtown Seattle. The statues are frequently dressed up by local residents, with costumes changing regularly.

Cross to the far side of 34th Street and walk east along this street, past some of Fremont's interesting shops, to the:

4 History House of Greater Seattle

This neighborhood museum of history, at 790 N. 34th St. (✆ **206/675-8875**), is complete with interactive exhibits and a beautiful artistic fence out front.

Turn left at History House and head uphill underneath the Aurora Bridge, which towers high above. At the top of the hill, you will see, lurking in the shadows beneath the bridge, the:

5 Fremont Troll

This massive monster is in the process of crushing a real Volkswagen Beetle. No need to run in fear, though, as a wizard seems to have cast a powerful spell that has turned the troll to cement.

Turn left at the troll and walk a block down North 36th Street; then turn left on Fremont Avenue North, and continue another block to the corner of Fremont Avenue North and North 35th Street, where, a few doors from the corner, is:

There really is a troll under the bridge in Fremont.

6 Frank and Dunya

This shop, at 3418 Fremont Ave. N. (✆ **206/547-6760**), sells colorful household decor, including switch plates, cups and saucers, mirrors, jewelry, art, rustic furniture, and little shrines. It's all very playful.

And a little farther on is:

7 Dusty Strings

This basement music shop, at 3406 Fremont Ave. N. (✆ **206/634-1662**), specializes in acoustic music and instruments. Need a new ukulele, autoharp, or hammered dulcimer? You'll have plenty of choices here; in fact, the shop manufactures harps and hammered dulcimers.

Go back up to the corner and cross Fremont Avenue North to the traffic island, where you'll find both the center of the universe and Fremont's:

8 Directional Marker

This old-fashioned signpost has arrows that point to such important locations as the center of the universe (straight down), the *Fremont Troll, Rapunzel,* the Louvre, and the North Pole.

For all your dulcimer needs, head to Dusty Strings.

9 Take a Break

For a sinfully rich slice of cake, cross Fremont Avenue to **Simply Desserts,** 3421 Fremont Ave. N. (✆ **206/633-2671**), a tiny cake shop on the corner across from Frank and Dunya.

From the directional marker, continue west (away from the intersection) on Fremont Place, and in 1 block (at the corner of N. 36th St.) you'll come across a larger-than-life statue of:

10 Lenin

This 20-foot-tall statue in no way reflects the attitudes of the many very capitalistic merchants in the neighborhood.

After communing with Comrade Lenin, cross North 36th Street, where you'll find:

11 Bitters Co.

This import shop, at 513 N. 36th St. (✆ **206/632-0886**), has some of the coolest ethnic arts and crafts you'll see. This is a great place to pick up gifts.

From here, walk a block down Evanston Avenue to:

12 Les Amis

This boutique, at 3420 Evanston Ave. N. (✆ **206/632-2877**), is done up to look like a little potting shed; it stocks fun and trendy women's fashions from European and American designers.

Right outside this shop is the launching pad for the:

13 Fremont Rocket

Although there is speculation that this rocket was used by the aliens who founded Fremont, the truth is far stranger. You can read the history of the rocket on the accompanying map board. (If you haven't already figured it out, the locals don't want you getting lost in their neighborhood, so they've put up maps all over to help you find your way from one famous locale to the next.)

The Fremont Rocket is, well, not ready to blast off.

From here, head down North 35th Street for 1 long block, and then turn left on Phinney Avenue North, where you'll find:

14 Theo Chocolate

This chocolate factory, at 3400 Phinney Ave. N. (✆ **206/632-5100**), specializes in organic, fair-trade chocolate and makes

Stop at Theo's for some chocolatey goodness.

These boots are made for walking...tours of Fremont.

some delicious and often unusually flavored confections. Tours of the factory are available daily. Call ahead for the times and schedule your walk around the neighborhood so that you end up here in time for a tour (be sure to make a reservation first).

From Theo, continue 1 block down to the foot of Phinney Avenue, where you'll find:

15 Fremont's Dinosaurs

Don't worry, no velociraptors here—just a pair of friendly topiary *Apatosauruses* (sort of like brontosaurs) donated to the neighborhood by the Pacific Science Center.

If it happens to be Sunday, you'll see crowds of people and vendors' stalls stretching back toward the Fremont Bridge from the dinosaur park. This is the:

16 Fremont Sunday Market

You never know what you might find at this European-style flea market—perhaps some locally made kilts or a rack of vintage Hawaiian shirts. If you've still got energy, fortify yourself at the market and continue your stroll.

From the market, walk down to the water where you will find the:

17 Burke-Gilman Trail

This section of the popular walking, biking, and skating trail follows the north bank of the Lake Washington Ship Canal. You might see a big commercial fishing boat or a rowing team in the canal as you walk along.

Head east on the paved path, and in 15 minutes or so you will reach:

18 Gas Works Park

This park on the shore of Lake Union represents one of the city's biggest recycling projects. The grassy lawns are built around the rusted remains of an industrial plant that once turned coal into gas. Today the park is a popular picnic and kite-flying spot, and from atop the park's "Kite Hill" there is a stupendous view of the Seattle skyline on the far side of Lake Union.

8

SEATTLE SHOPPING

Nordstrom, Eddie Bauer, R.E.I—these names are familiar to shoppers all across the country. They're also the names of stores that got their start here in Seattle. Throw in such regional favorites as Pendleton, Nike, and Filson, and you'll find that Seattle is a great place to shop, especially if you're in the market for recreational and outdoor gear and clothing.

As Washington's largest city, Seattle is also home to all the national retail chains you would expect to find in a major metro area, including Banana Republic, Old Navy, Levi Strauss, Ann Taylor, Coach, St. John, Louis Vuitton, Tiffany & Co., and Barneys New York. If you forgot to pick up that dress in Chicago or those running shoes in New York, have no fear—you can find them here.

Seattle does, however, have one last bastion of local merchandising: **Pike Place Market.** Whether shopping is your passion or just an occasional indulgence, you shouldn't miss this historic market, which is one of Seattle's top attractions. Once the city's main produce market (and quite a few produce stalls remain), this sprawling collection of buildings is today filled with hundreds of unusual shops, including **Seattle's Market Magic,** for magicians and aspiring magicians (**© 206/624-4271;** www.marketmagicshop.com); **Tenzing Momo,** which sells essential oils, incense, herbs, and the like (**© 206/623-9837;** www.tenzingmomo.com); and **Left Bank Books,** a bookstore for anarchists and their kin (**© 206/622-0195;** www.leftbankbooks.com). See also the listing for **Pike Place Market** on p. 126.

After tasting the bounties of the Northwest, it's hard to go back to Safeway, Sanka, and Chicken of the Sea. Sure, you can get wine, coffee, and seafood where you live, but do a little food shopping in Seattle, and you'll be tapping the

PREVIOUS PAGE: **You'll find a treasure trove of cool items to buy in Seattle, from major hometown brands to handmade objects.** ABOVE: **Tenzing Momo is one of the unique shops in Pike Place Market.**

source. Washington State wines, coffee from the original Starbucks, and fish that fly—these are just a few of the culinary treats that await you here.

THE SHOPPING SCENE

Although Seattle is a city of neighborhoods, many of which have great little shops, the heart and soul of the Seattle shopping scene is the corner of **Pine Street and Fifth Avenue.** Within 2 blocks of this intersection are two major department stores (**Nordstrom** and **Macy's**) and two upscale urban shopping malls (**Westlake Center** and **Pacific Place**). A sky bridge between Nordstrom and Pacific Place makes shopping that much easier. Fanning out east and south from this intersection are blocks of upscale stores that have started to look more and more familiar as small, local shops have been replaced by national and international boutiques and megastores. Here in this neighborhood, you can now find Ann Taylor, Banana Republic, Barneys New York, Coach, Gap, and Niketown. Among these, a few local independents remain.

Within this downtown shopping district, you also find the loosely affiliated shops of **Rainier Square** (www.rainier-square.com). Although not actually a shopping mall, Rainier Square, which is bordered by University and Union streets and Fourth and Sixth avenues, is packed with great upscale shops and boutiques, including Brooks Brothers, Gucci, Louis Vuitton, Northwest Pendleton, and St. John.

Pike Place Market is the city's main tourist shopping district. The market is a fascinating warren of cubbyholes that pass for shops and it has dozens of T-shirt and souvenir shops, as well as import shops and stores appealing to teenagers and 20-somethings. While produce isn't usually something you stock up on during a vacation, several market shops sell ethnic cooking supplies that are less perishable than a dozen oysters or a king salmon. You may not find anything here you really need, but it's fun to look.

Just west of and downhill from Pike Place Market is the Seattle **waterfront,** site of many more gift and souvenir shops. This is the city's tackiest and most touristy neighborhood—save your money for somewhere else.

Have fun window-shopping on the streets of Capitol Hill.

South of downtown, in the historic **Pioneer Square** area, you'll find numerous art galleries, some of which specialize in Native American art. This neighborhood has several antiques stores but is also home to a dozen or more bars (and attracts a lot of homeless people). It's fun to explore by day, but it's strictly for young partiers by night.

As the center of both the gay community and the city's youth culture, **Capitol Hill** has the most eclectic selection of shops in Seattle. Beads, imports,

CDs, vintage clothing, politically correct merchandise, and gay-oriented goods fill the shops along Broadway. The Pike-Pine District, a pair of streets connecting downtown with Capitol Hill, is my favorite shopping neighborhood in this area. Lots of small, independently owned shops offer a satisfying variety of gifts and other goods.

Pick up a stunning accessory in Wallingford.

The **Wallingford** neighborhood, just north of Lake Union, is anchored by an old school building that has been converted into a shopping arcade full of boutiques selling interesting crafts, fashions, and gifts. This area seems to be most popular with young moms and their kids.

The **Fremont** neighborhood, a couple of miles west of Wallingford, has an assortment of shops. The neighborhood clings to its fun, funky, countercultural roots despite its ongoing gentrification. There are still some retro clothing stores here, as well as import stores, craft galleries, and a few clothing boutiques.

To the west of Fremont, you'll find **Ballard,** a former Scandinavian neighborhood that is currently one of my favorite shopping districts in Seattle. Tree-shaded Ballard Avenue Northwest is lined with historic brick buildings, most of which are now home to great little shops operated by highly creative individuals. You never know what you'll find in these shops, which is why it's so fun to shop here.

The **University District,** also in North Seattle, has everything necessary to support a student population—and also goes upscale at the University Village shopping center.

There are a lot of great little shops in Ballard.

SHOPPING A TO Z

Antiques & Collectibles

If antiques are your passion, don't miss the opportunity to spend a day browsing the many antiques stores in the historic farm town of **Snohomish,** roughly 30 miles north of Seattle. The town has hundreds of antiques dealers and is without a doubt the antiques capital of Washington state.

Chidori Asian Antiques This little Pioneer Square shop is jampacked with exotic antiques from China, Japan, Korea, India, and Southeast Asia. Chidori has been in business for more than 25 years and always has lots of fascinating pieces for sale. 108 S. Jackson St. ✆ **206/343-7736.** www.chidoriantiques.com.

Crane Gallery Chinese, Japanese, and Korean antiquities are the focus of this Lower Queen Anne shop, which prides itself on selling only the best pieces. Imperial Chinese porcelains, bronze statues of Buddhist deities, rosewood furniture, Japanese ceramics, *netsukes,* snuff bottles, and Chinese archaeological artifacts are just some of the quality antiques found here. A selection of Southeast Asian and Indian objects is also available. 104 W. Roy St. ✆ **206/298-9425.** www.cranegallery.com.

Curtis Steiner ★ 🎁 This unusual shop is a little hard to categorize, but it's so cool, you just have to see it. Designed to resemble a Victorian-era mercantile, the store is a work of art, and, in fact, owner Curtis Steiner has had art installations at the Seattle Art Museum. Throughout this triangular space in a Ballard historic building, you'll find artistic displays of small antiques and curios. 5349 Ballard Ave. NW. ✆ **206/297-7116.** www.curtissteiner.com.

Cuttysark Nautical Antiques Seattle, with its maritime history, seems like a great place to search for nautical antiques, and this is the best place in town to look for old binnacles, telescopes, quadrants, sextants, and octants. 320 First Ave. S. ✆ **206/262-1265.** www.cuttyantiques.com.

Honeychurch Antiques ★ For high-quality Asian antiques, including Japanese woodblock prints, textiles, furniture, and ivory and woodcarvings, few Seattle antiques stores can approach Honeychurch Antiques. Regular special exhibits give this shop the feel of a tiny museum. The store's annex, called **Glenn Richards,** 964 Denny Way (✆ **206/287-1877;** www.glennrichards.com), specializes in "entry-level" antiques. 411 Westlake Ave. N. ✆ **206/622-1225.** www.honeychurch.com.

Jean Williams Antiques ★ If your taste in antiques runs to 18th- and 19th-century country French, English, or Biedermeier furniture, this Belltown antiques dealer may have something for your collection. 3025 First Ave. ✆ **206/622-1110.** www.jeanwilliamsantiques.com.

Laguna ★ Twentieth-century art pottery is the specialty of this Pioneer Square shop. With pieces from such midcentury pottery factories as Fiesta, Roseville, Bauer, Weller, and Franciscan, the shelves here are a riot of colors. It's true eye candy for collectors of vintage pottery and a great place to look for dinnerware and vintage tiles. 116 S. Washington St. ✆ **206/682-6162.** www.lagunapottery.com.

Michael Maslan Vintage Photographs, Postcards & Ephemera This store, across the street from the Seattle Art Museum, is crammed full of vintage travel posters, ethnographic photos, and thousands of postcards. With a focus on social, industrial, and historical images, Michael Maslan's philosophy is to collect (and sell) just about anything "written, printed, or painted" that's old or interesting. 109 University St. ✆ **206/587-0187.**

ANTIQUES MALLS & FLEA MARKETS

Antiques at Pike Place Located in the Pike Place Market area, this antiques and collectibles mall is one of the finest in Seattle. There are more than 80 dealers, and much of what's available here is fairly small, which means you might be able to fit your find into a suitcase. 92 Stewart St. ✆ **206/441-9643.** www.antiquesatpikeplace.com.

Fremont Sunday Street Market ★★ Crafts, imports, antiques, and collectibles combine in a sort of European-style flea market that is Seattle's second-favorite public market (after Pike Place Market). This street market is fun and funky, just like this whole neighborhood. N. 34th St. (1 block west of the Fremont Bridge). ✆ **206/781-6776.** www.fremontmarket.com.

Seattle Antiques Market Down in a big, dark warehouse space under the Alaskan Way Viaduct, you can shop for old Japanese fishing floats, Victorian furniture, old pocket knives, whatever. This place reminds me of the big antiques stores my parents used to drag me to as a child, and I almost always find something here that I just have to have. The store is just a few doors south of the Pike Street Hill Climb. 1400 Alaskan Way. ✆ **206/623-6115.** www.seattleantiquesmarket.com.

Art Galleries

The **Pioneer Square** area is Seattle's main gallery district, and anyone interested in art should be sure to wander south of Yesler Way. ***Note:*** Some galleries are closed on Monday.

GENERAL ART GALLERIES

Davidson Galleries ★ In the heart of the Pioneer Square neighborhood, this gallery focuses on both contemporary prints by American and European artists and antique prints, some of which date from the 1500s. The gallery also features contemporary paintings and sculptures, with an emphasis on Northwest artists. 313 Occidental Ave. S. ✆ **206/624-7684.** www.davidsongalleries.com.

Greg Kucera Gallery Established in 1983, this space in the Pioneer Square area serves as one of Seattle's most reliably cutting-edge galleries. The shows here often address political or social issues, or movements within the art world. 212 Third Ave. S. ✆ **206/624-0770.** www.gregkucera.com.

Grover/Thurston Gallery This Pioneer Square gallery features works by numerous Northwest artists, including Fay Jones, whose colorful, playful works have long graced public spaces around Seattle. Works on display often tend toward bright colors and almost cartoonish imagery. Fun and worth a visit. 309 Occidental Ave. S. ✆ **206/223-0816.** www.groverthurston.com.

Lisa Harris Gallery ★ Landscapes and figurative works, by both expressionist and realist Northwest and West Coast artists, are specialties of this gallery, which is located on the second floor of a building in Pike Place Market. 1922 Pike Place. ✆ **206/443-3315.** www.lisaharrisgallery.com.

Patricia Rovzar Gallery Bold, colorful, often whimsical art can be seen at this gallery adjacent to the Seattle Art Museum. Look for the dreamy Northwest landscapes of Z.Z. Wei and the circus-inspired surrealist works of Tyson Grumm. 1225 Second Ave. ✆ **800/889-4278** or **206/223-0273**. www.rovzargallery.com.

ART GLASS

Canlis Glass If you've seen the glass bamboo sculptures at Seattle's Hotel 1000 and Boka Kitchen restaurant, you've seen the work of this gallery's co-owner, Jean-Pierre Canlis. Large, abstract glass forms predominate, many inspired by ocean waves. 3131 Western Ave., Ste. 329. ✆ **206/282-4428.** www.canlisglass.com.

Foster/White Gallery ★★ If you are enamored of art glass, be sure to stop by this gallery, which represents Dale Chihuly and always has works by this master glass artist. Foster/White also represents top-notch Northwest artists in the disciplines of painting, ceramics, and sculpture. 220 Third Ave. S. ✆ **206/622-2833.** www.fosterwhite.com.

Glasshouse Studio In the Pioneer Square area and founded in 1972, Glasshouse claims to be the oldest glass-blowing studio in the Northwest. In the studio, you can watch handblown art glass being made; then, in the gallery, you can check out the works of numerous local glass artists. 311 Occidental Ave. S. ✆ **206/682-9939.** www.glasshouse-studio.com.

Seattle Glassblowing Studio With a gallery out front and glass-blowing studio in back, this is another great place to get a feel for the Seattle art-glass scene. The gallery/shop has lots of small glass-art pieces that you can take home in your luggage (or have shipped). 2227 Fifth Ave. ✆ **206/448-2181.** www.seattleglassblowing.com.

Traver Gallery ★★ This is one of the nation's top art-glass galleries and showcases the work of dozens of glass artists. The pieces displayed are on the cutting edge of glass art, so to speak, and illustrate the broad spectrum of contemporary work by artists in this medium. The gallery is on the second floor. 110 Union St. ✆ **206/587-6501.** www.travergallery.com.

Vetri ★ Affiliated with the prestigious Traver Gallery, Vetri showcases innovative work primarily from emerging glass artists and local area studios, but it also sells pieces by artists from other countries. It's all high-quality and riotously colorful. Prices are relatively affordable. 1404 First Ave. ✆ **206/667-9608.** www.vetriglass.com.

NATIVE AMERICAN ART

Ancient Grounds ★ This eclectic downtown antiques shop and natural-history gallery sells not only quality Northwest Coast Indian masks but also Japanese masks, rare mineral specimens, and a wide variety of other rare and unusual pieces from all over the world. An espresso bar is on the premises. 1220 First Ave. ✆ **206/749-0747.**

Flury & Company Ltd. ★ This Pioneer Square gallery specializes in prints by famed Seattle photographer Edward S. Curtis, known for his late-19th- and early-20th-century portraits of Native Americans. The gallery also has an excellent selection of antique Native American art and artifacts. 322 First Ave. S. ✆ **206/587-0260.** www.fluryco.com.

The Legacy Ltd. ★★ In business since 1933, this is Seattle's oldest and finest gallery of contemporary and historic Northwest Coast Indian and Alaskan Eskimo art and artifacts. You'll find a large selection of masks, boxes, bowls, baskets, ivory artifacts, jewelry, prints, and books for the serious collector. 1003 First Ave. ✆ **800/729-1562** or 206/624-6350. www.thelegacyltd.com.

Steinbrueck Native Gallery With art and crafts by both emerging and established Native American artists, this gallery near Pike Place Market is a good place to shop for deals. 2030 Western Ave. ✆ **206/441-3821.** www.steinbruecknativegallery.com.

Stonington Gallery This is another of Seattle's top galleries specializing in contemporary Native American arts and crafts. It offers a good selection of Northwest Coast Indian masks, totem poles, mixed-media pieces, prints, carvings, and Northwest Coast–style jewelry. 119 S. Jackson St. ✆ **866/405-4485** or 206/405-4040. www.stoningtongallery.com.

Books

In addition to the stores listed below, you'll find more than a half-dozen **Barnes & Noble** locations in the metro area, including one downtown in the Pacific Place shopping center at 600 Pine St. (✆ **206/264-0156**).

Elliott Bay Book Company ★★ This Capitol Hill bookstore is a huge destination bookstore well worth searching out for its excellent selection of titles on Seattle and the Northwest. There's also a cafe operated by Tamara Murphy, one of my favorite Seattle chefs. 1521 10th Ave. ✆ **800/962-5311** or 206/624-6600. www.elliottbaybook.com.

Flora & Fauna Books ★ Gardeners, bird-watchers, and other naturephiles should search out this fascinating little specialty bookstore near the entrance to Discovery Park in the Magnolia neighborhood. You'll find shelves packed with books that'll have you wishing you were in your garden or out in the woods identifying birds and flowers. 3212 W. Government Way. ✆ **206/623-4727.** www.ffbooks.net.

Metsker Maps of Seattle If you're already thinking about your next vacation and want to peruse some travel guidebooks, or if you simply need a good map of Seattle, drop by this maps-filled shop in Pike Place Market. 1511 First Ave. ✆ **800/727-4430** or 206/623-8747. www.metskers.com.

Peter Miller Looking for a picture book of Frank Gehry's architectural follies? How about a retrospective on the work of Alvar Aalto? You'll find these and loads of other beautiful and educational books on architecture and design at this specialty bookstore on the edge of Belltown. 1930 First Ave. ✆ **206/441-4114.** www.petermiller.com.

Seattle Mystery Bookshop If whodunits are your passion, don't miss an opportunity to peruse the shelves of this specialty bookstore in the Pioneer Square area. You'll find all your favorite mystery authors, lots of signed copies, and regularly scheduled book signings. 117 Cherry St. ✆ **206/587-5737.** www.seattlemystery.com.

Wessel & Lieberman Booksellers Offering new, used, rare, and out-of-print books, Wessel & Lieberman is a good place to look for hard-to-find books on the Northwest, art, architecture, and poetry. The shop often has art exhibits and displays on the book arts. 208 First Ave. S. ✆ **888/383-3631** or 206/682-3545. www.wlbooks.com.

Coffee & Tea

All over the city, on almost every corner, you'll find espresso bars, cafes, and coffeehouses. And even though you can get coffee back home, you might want to stock up on whatever local coffee turns out to be your favorite. If you're a latte junkie, you can even make a pilgrimage to the shop that started it all: the Pike Place Market Starbucks, listed below, that was once the only Starbucks in the world.

MarketSpice In business in Pike Place Market since 1911, this shop sells all kinds of spices and spice mixes, but its best known for its flavorful cinnamon-orange tea. There are usually samples to be had in the shop, and one sip is usually enough to get anyone hooked. 85A Pike Place. ✆ **206/622-6340.**

Seattle Best Tea Co. ★ 🎁 Ever wondered what $150-a-pound Chinese tea tastes like? At this International District tea shop, you can find out. You'll discover not only dozens of different teas here, but also tables where you can sit down, sample the varieties, and experience the traditional Chinese tea ceremony. 506 S. King St. ✆ **206/749-9855.**

Starbucks Seattle is well known as a city of coffeeholics, and Starbucks is the main reason. This company has coffeehouses all over town (and all over the world), but this was once the only Starbucks. Although you won't find any tables or chairs here, Starbucks fans shouldn't miss an opportunity to get their coffee at the source. Pike Place Market, 1912 Pike Place. ✆ **206/448-8762.** www.starbucks.com.

Vital Tea Leaf Down at the south end of Pike Place Market, across from the entrance to the luxurious Four Seasons Hotel Seattle, you'll almost always find people sitting at a long counter sipping tea from exotic-looking teapots. This is Vital Tea Leaf, a great place to sample and purchase teas you've never tried before. There are also lots of Chinese teapots and teacups for sale. 1401 First Ave. ✆ **206/262-1628.** www.vitaltealeaf.net. Also at 2003 Western Ave., Ste. 109 (✆ **206/441-7476**).

Crafts

The Northwest is a magnet for skilled craftspeople, and shops all around town sell a wide range of high-quality and imaginative pieces. At **Pike Place Market** (p. 205), you can see what area craftspeople are creating and meet the artisans themselves.

Fireworks Fine Crafts Gallery Playful, outrageous, bizarre, beautiful—these are just some of the adjectives that can be used to describe the eclectic collection of Northwest crafts on sale at this Pioneer Square gallery. Cosmic clocks, wildly creative jewelry, artistic picture frames, and creative works of Judaica are among the fine and unusual items found here. 210 First Ave. S. ✆ **206/682-9697.** www.fireworksgallery.net. Also at Westlake Center, 400 Pine St. (✆ **206/682-6462**); University Village, 2617 NE Village St. (✆ **206/527-2858**); and Bellevue Square, 196 Bellevue Sq., Bellevue (✆ **425/688-0933**).

Frank and Dunya Located in Fremont, this store epitomizes the fun-and-funky Fremont aesthetic. The art, jewelry, and crafts tend toward the colorful and the humorous, and just about everything is made by Northwest artists and artisans. 3418 Fremont Ave. N. ✆ **206/547-6760.** www.frankanddunya.com.

Northwest Craft Center ★ 🎁 This large gallery at Seattle Center is the city's premier ceramics showcase. In the main gallery, you'll find art ceramics that push the envelope of what can be made from clay. There's also a gift shop selling less expensive pieces. Seattle Center, 305 Harrison St. ✆ **206/728-1555.** www.northwestcraftcenter.com.

Northwest Fine Woodworking ★★ This store has some of the most amazing woodworking you'll ever see. Be sure to stroll through here while you're in the Pioneer Square area, even if you aren't in the market for a one-of-a-kind piece of furniture. The warm hues of the exotic woods are soothing, and the designs are beautiful. Furniture, boxes, sculpture, vases, bowls, and much more are created by nearly 20 Northwest artisans. 101 S. Jackson St. ✆ **206/625-0542.** www.nwfinewoodworking.com.

Gorgeous, unique furniture is on sale at Northwest Fine Woodworking.

Department Stores

Macy's ★ Seattle's "other" department store, formerly the Bon Marché, which was established in 1890, is every bit as well stocked as the neighboring Nordstrom. With such competition nearby, this large department store tries hard to keep its customers happy. 1601 Third Ave. ✆ **206/506-6000.** www.macys.com.

Nordstrom ★★★ Known for personal service, Nordstrom is among the premier department stores in the United States. The company originated in Seattle (opening its first store in 1901), and its customers are devotedly loyal. This is a state-of-the-art store, with all sorts of little boutiques, cafes, and other features to make your shopping excursion an experience.

Whether it's your first visit or your fiftieth, the knowledgeable staff will help you in any way they can. Prices may be a bit higher than those at other department stores, but for your money, you get the best service available. The store is packed with shoppers during the semiannual sales for women and kids in May and November, the semiannual sales for men in mid-June and late December, and the anniversary sale in July. You'll also find Nordstrom stores at area shopping malls. 500 Pine St. ✆ **206/628-2111.** http://shop.nordstrom.com.

Discount Shopping

Nordstrom Rack This is the Nordstrom overflow shop, where you'll find three floors of discontinued lines as well as overstock, all at greatly reduced prices. Women's fashions make up the bulk of the merchandise, but there is also a floor full of men's clothes and shoes, plus plenty of kids' clothes. 1601 Second Ave. ✆ **206/448-8522.** http://shop.nordstrom.com/c/nordstrom-rack. Also at 3920 124th St. SE, Bellevue (✆ **425/746-7200**); and 19500 Alderwood Mall Pkwy., Lynnwood (✆ **425/774-6569**).

Fashion

In addition to the stores listed below, you'll find quite a few familiar names in downtown Seattle, including Ann Taylor, Banana Republic, Barneys New York, Eddie Bauer, and Gap.

ACCESSORIES

Byrnie Utz Hats ★ Boasting the largest selection of hats in the Northwest, this cramped hat-wearer's heaven looks as if it hasn't changed in 50 years; in fact, it's been in the same location since 1934. There are Borsalino Panama hats, Kangol caps, and, of course, plenty of Stetsons. 310 Union St. ✆ **206/623-0233.**

CHILDREN'S CLOTHING

Flora and Henri Timeless, precious, classy, classic. All these words apply to the beautiful children's clothes at this shop in the Pike-Pine section of Capitol Hill. You'll find the shop just a few uphill blocks from downtown Seattle's convention center. 919 E. Pine St. ✆ **206/325-5520.** www.florahenri.com.

Boston Street Baby This Pike Place Market kids' store stocks fun play clothes as well as dressier fashions. You'll see lots of locally made 100% cotton clothing. Prices are moderate to expensive, but there are usually plenty of great deals on the sale racks. 1902 Post Alley. ✆ **206/634-0580.**

MEN'S CLOTHING

Utilikilts If you're man enough to wear a kilt, then you've come to the right town. Seattle has been home to this unique clothing manufacturer since 2000, and the canvas kilts have become a local phenomenon. This store is in the heart of the Pioneer Square neighborhood. 620 First Ave. ✆ **206/282-4226.** www.utilikilts.com.

MEN'S & WOMEN'S CLOTHING

Eddie Bauer Eddie Bauer got his start here in Seattle back in 1920, and today the chain that bears his name is one of the country's foremost purveyors of outdoor fashions—although these days, outdoor fashion is looking quite a bit more urban. Pacific Place, 600 Pine St. ✆ **206/622-2766.** www.eddiebauer.com.

Ex Officio ★ If you've already started planning your next trip, be sure to stop by this travel-clothing store up toward the north end of Belltown. It's an outlet for the Seattle-based Ex Officio and is packed full of lightweight, easy-care clothes designed for world travelers. 114 Vine St. ✆ **206/283-4746.** www.exofficio.com.

Kuhlman From classic to cutting edge, this Belltown boutique has it all. However, regardless of the cut, the clothes are impeccably made and generally not to be found in other shops in the area. They even offer custom tailoring here. 2419 First Ave. ✆ **206/441-1999.** www.kuhlmanseattle.com.

Northwest Museum Store ★★ For Northwesterners, and for many other people across the nation, Pendleton is and always will be *the* name in classic wool items. This store features tartan plaids and American Indian–pattern separates, accessories, shawls, and blankets. 1313 Fourth Ave. ✆ **800/593-6773** or 206/682-4430. www.indianblanket.com.

SimoSilk Silk scarves, silk camisoles, men's silk shirts, silk long underwear, even silk sheets and duvet covers—it's all about silk at this shop, which has locations in both Pioneer Square and Pike Place Market. 118 First Ave. S. ✆ **800/700-4393** or 206/521-8816. www.simosilk.com. Also at 1411 First Ave., Ste. 108.

WOMEN'S CLOTHING

Alhambra World Style Alhambra stocks a very eclectic collection of women's clothing and jewelry. There are purses from France, shoes from Italy, and fashions from Turkey and the U.S. These add up to a unique European look that's a little more refined than what you find at Baby & Co. (see below). 101 Pine St. ✆ **206/621-9571.** www.alhambranet.com.

Baby & Co. ★★ Claiming to have stores in Seattle and on Mars, Baby & Co. stocks fashions that can be trendy, outrageous, or out of this world. The designs are strictly French, so you aren't likely to find these fashions in too many other places in the U.S. Whether you're into earth tones or bright colors, you'll likely find something you can't live without. 1936 First Ave. ✆ **206/448-4077.** www.babyandco.us.

betty lin This boutique is packed with deeply discounted designer fashions and shoes for both women and men. You'll save up to 75% on such names as Prada, Balenciaga, Gucci, Miu Miu, and Christian Dior. The catch is that the racks are filled with last season's designs. 608 Second Ave. ✆ **206/442-6888.** www.shopbettylin.com.

Endless Knot ★ If you've ever had a thing for funky fashions from Asia, you'll be amazed at how tasteful and upscale such styles can be. The racks of this Belltown boutique are lined with drapey natural-fiber fashions in bold colors—plus, there are lots of accessories to accompany the clothes. 2300 First Ave. ✆ **206/448-0355.**

Les Amis In the Fremont neighborhood, in a funky old wooden building, this little boutique is designed to look a bit like an old cottage or potting shed. The fashions and accessories are fresh and fun and come mostly from France and Italy. 3420 Evanston Ave. N. ✆ **206/632-2877.** www.lesamis-inc.com.

Margaret O'Leary Classic and classy, the sweaters at this Belltown boutique are hand-knit from cashmere, silk, cotton, and merino wool. Prices are high, but the designs are meant to stand the test of time. There are also lots of other separates to go with the knitted sweaters. 2025 First Ave. ✆ **206/441-6691.** www.margaretoleary.com.

Pirrko This store lends a bit of Scandinavian aesthetic to Pike Place Market. There are imported Finnish fashions, accessories, jewelry, and home decor, plus lots of Marimekko fabrics. 1407 First Ave. ✆ **206/223-1112.**

Ragazzi's Flying Shuttle ★★ Fashion becomes art and art becomes fashion at this chic boutique-cum-gallery in the Pioneer Square area. Hand-woven fabrics and hand-painted silks are the specialties, but of course, such sophisticated fashions require equally unique body decorations in the form of exquisite jewelry creations. Designers and artists from the Northwest and the rest of the nation find an outlet for their creativity at the Flying Shuttle. 607 First Ave. ✆ **206/343-9762.** www.ragazzisflyingshuttle.com.

Sandylew With the motto "Having fun getting dressed," you can be sure the clothes here will be far from conservative. Expect bright colors and occasionally wacky fashions. There are also plenty of accessories to complete that fun new outfit. 1408 First Ave. ✆ **206/903-0303.** www.sandylew.com.

Food

Chocolate Box Ahhh! If only all boxes of chocolate were this big and full of so much chocolate. Chocoholics will be in heaven when they step through the doors of this temple of chocolate half a block from Pike Place Market. The shop and cafe are dedicated to all things chocolate. 108 Pine St. ✆ **888/861-6188** or **206/443-3900**. www.sschocolatebox.com.

Chocolopolis I admit it; I am a chocoholic. As luck would have it, in Seattle I never have to go very far for my next truffle and neither will you. If you happen to be exploring the pretty upper Queen Anne shopping district, don't miss this shop, which boasts of having more than 200 chocolate bars from 20 countries. 1527 Queen Anne Ave. N. ✆ **206/282-0776.** www.chocolopolis.com.

Chukar Cherries ★ Washington is one of the nation's premier cherry-growing regions, and here at the Pike Place Market, you can sample all kinds of candy-coated dried cherries. These little confections are positively addictive. Pike Place Market, Main Arcade, 1529-B Pike Place. ✆ **800/624-9544** or 206/623-8043. www.chukar.com.

DeLaurenti Specialty Food & Wine ★ I love wandering the aisles of this specialty food market, adjacent to the main entrance of Pike Place Market. The emphasis is on Italian cooking ingredients, but you'll find lots of other interesting items as well. There are great cheeses and cured meats, a wine shop, and a cafe. 1435 First Ave. ✆ **800/873-6685** or 206/622-0141. www.delaurenti.com.

Fran's Chocolates That Fran's Welsh smoked-salt caramels are a favorite of President Obama should give you an idea that this downtown chocolatier is worth a visit. While caramels are the specialty, there are lots of other delicious chocolates, including unusual chocolate-dipped figs. 1325 First Ave. ✆ **800/422-3726** or **206/682-0168**. www.franschocolates.com. Also at University Village, 2626 NE University Village St. (✆ **206/528-9969**) and 10036 Main St., Bellevue (✆ **425/453-1698**).

La Buona Tavola ★★ Truffle oils are the specialty of this little Pike Place Market shop. In addition to the bottles of olive oil infused with white or black truffles, there's an astonishingly fragrant truffle cream. Yum! Pike Place Market, 1524 Pike Place. ✆ **206/292-5555.** www.trufflecafe.com.

Paris Grocery ★ 🎁 What the adjacent Spanish Table is to the flavors of the Iberian Peninsula, this little market is to French cuisine. Here you'll find everything you could ever need for a perfect French picnic. There are pâtés and cheeses, French wines, crackers, jams, candies, and much more. 1418 Western Ave. ✆ **206/682-0679.** www.parisgroceryseattle.com.

The Spanish Table ★ Cases full of imported meats and cheeses are on display here, as are all manner of other Spanish ingredients, and if you've decided your life's goal is to prepare the ultimate paella, this store will set you on the path to perfection. Paella pans, and everything you could ever want for cooking Spanish cuisine, fill this Pike Place Market shop. 1426 Western Ave. ✆ **206/682-2827.** www.spanishtable.com.

Theo Chocolate ★★ Although there's lots of good chocolate to be had in Seattle, Theo is the first roaster of fair-trade cocoa beans. At its Fremont factory, you can sample chocolates, tour the factory, and, of course, buy yummy chocolate confections. Tours, which cost $6 per person, are offered daily, and reservations are recommended. 3400 Phinney Ave. N. ✆ **206/632-5100.** www.theochocolate.com.

World Spice Merchants You probably will never before have seen as many different spices as are on display at this Pike Place Market shop. The shop sells more than 100 spices from around the world, so if you are into ethnic cooking and want to take home some interesting spices, peruse the shelves here. Sample jars let you sniff before you buy. 1509 Western Ave. ✆ **206/682-7274.** www.worldspice.com.

Check out the regionally-inspired art at Millstream.

Gifts/Souvenirs

Pike Place Market (p. 205) is Seattle souvenirs central, with stiff competition from the Seattle Center and Pioneer Square areas.

Bitters Co. ★ This hole-in-the-wall shop in Fremont sums up the neighborhood's design aesthetic. The shop is full of fun and funky imports from Asia, Latin America, and Africa. Even if you're a big fan of ethnic imports, you'll find things here that you've never seen before. Lots of reclaimed materials go into Bitters Co. housewares. 513 N. 36th St. ✆ **206/632-0886.** www.bittersco.com.

Lucca Great Finds ★ 🎁 Designed to resemble Parisian gift salons of the 1920s and 1930s, this little Ballard shop is an absolute joy to explore. You never know what might turn up amid the vintage classics and chic contemporary items. Perhaps you're in need of some mounted insects for your curiosity cabinet, or maybe you just need some French toothpaste. Whatever you seek, you'll find it here. 5332 Ballard Ave. NW. ✆ **206/782-7337.**

Made in Washington Whether it's salmon, wine, or Northwest crafts, you'll find a varied selection of Washington State products in this shop. This is an excellent place to pick up gifts for all those friends and family members who didn't get to come to Seattle with you. Pike Place Market, 1530 Post Alley (at Pine St.). ✆ **206/467-0788.** www.madeinwashington.com. Also at Westlake Center, 400 Pine St. (✆ **206/623-9753**).

Millstream If you want to take home a bit of the woodsy Northwest, drop by this Pioneer Square store and check out the regional and Native American art. You don't even have to live in a log cabin for this stuff to look good. There are also plenty of Seattle-themed souvenirs. 112 First Ave. S. ✆ **206/623-1960.** www.millstreamseattle.com.

Pelindaba Lavender If you're as crazy about lavender as I am, be sure to stop in this large store in the Westlake Center shopping mall. You'll find all manner

Lovely lavender is the theme at Pelindaba.

of lavender products from lotions to teas, and all in beautiful packages. This shop is affiliated with a lavender farm on San Juan Island. Westlake Center, 400 Pine St. ✆ **206/623-3236.** www.pelindaba.com.

Watson Kennedy Fine Living This little gift shop, in the courtyard of the Inn at the Market, has a light and airy sort of French-country feel. The emphasis is on fine soaps, candles, and small gifts. Owner Ted Kennedy Watson has such an eye for gifts and interior decor that he was called on to help out with Bill and Melinda Gates's wedding. Displays are beautiful. 86 Pine St. ✆ **206/443-6281.** www.watsonkennedy.com.

Ye Olde Curiosity Shop ☺ If you can elbow your way into this waterfront institution, you'll find nearly every inch of space, horizontal and vertical, covered with souvenirs and crafts, both tacky and tasteful (but mostly tacky). Surrounding this merchandise are shrunken heads, a mummy, preserved conjoined-twin calves, and many other oddities that have made this one of the most visited shops in Seattle. See also "Good Times in Bad Taste" on p. 140. Pier 54, 1001 Alaskan Way. ✆ **206/682-5844.** www.yeoldecuriosityshop.com.

Housewares, Home Furnishings & Garden Accessories

Kasala Boldly styled contemporary furnishings are this store's main business. While you probably don't want to ship a couch home, they do have lots of easily packed accent pieces (vases, candlesticks, picture frames) that are just as wildly modern as the furniture. 1505 Western Ave. ✆ **800/527-2521** or 206/623-7795. www.kasala.com. Also in Bellevue at 1018 116th Ave. NE, Ste. 110 (✆ **866/527-2522** or 425/453-2823).

Kobo ★★ 🎁 Japanophiles won't want to miss this unusual little Capitol Hill shop and gallery, located in one of the most interesting old buildings in the neighborhood. There are all manner of very tasteful decorative items inspired by the Japanese artistic aesthetic. A second, and larger, Kobo can be found at 602 S. Jackson St. (✆ **206/381-3000**), in Chinatown/International District. 814 E. Roy St. ✆ **206/726-0704.** www.koboseattle.com.

Sur La Table Gourmet cooks should be sure to visit Pike Place Market's Sur La Table, where every imaginable kitchen utensil is available. There are a dozen different kinds of whisks, an equal number of muffin tins, and all manner of cake-decorating tools, tableware, napkins, cookbooks—simply everything a cook could need. By the way, this is the original Sur La Table. 84 Pine St. ✆ **206/448-2244.** www.surlatable.com.

Jewelry

Unique artist-crafted jewelry can be found at **Ragazzi's Flying Shuttle** (p. 200). And Fremont's **Frank and Dunya** (p. 197).

Facèré Jewelry Art Gallery ★ At this tiny shop inside the City Centre shopping gallery, rings, earring, necklaces, and brooches are miniature works of art made from a fascinating range of materials. If you're searching for something unique with which to adorn your body, don't miss this shop. City Centre, 1420 Fifth Ave., Ste. 108. ✆ **206/624-6768.** www.facerejewelryart.com.

Fox's Gem Shop Seattle's premier jeweler, Fox's has been around for a century now and always has plenty of a girl's best friends. Colorless or fancy colored diamonds available here are of the finest cut. 1341 Fifth Ave. ✆ **800/733-2528** or 206/623-2528. www.foxsgemshop.com.

Goldmine Design ★ 🎁 At this hole-in-the-wall jewelry shop/jeweler's workshop in Pike Place Market, owner Cindi Hansen works with clients to design one-of-a-kind pieces of jewelry, including hand-cast story rings. Plan a new ring in advance, and you can even help cast the ring yourself. 1405 First Ave. ✆ **206/622-3333.** www.goldminedesignjewelers.com.

TWIST ★ While this shop does have some fun, colorful, and uniquely creative housewares, it is really more of a jewelry store. The display cases are filled with beautiful and unusual artist-created jewelry. You'll find everything from classic elegance to colorful kitsch. Pacific Place, 600 Pine St. ✆ **206/315-8080.** www.twistonline.com.

Malls/Shopping Centers

Bellevue Square ★ Over in Bellevue, on the east side of Lake Washington, is one of the area's largest shopping malls. Its 200-plus stores include Nordstrom, Banana Republic, Eddie Bauer, Coach, and Made in Washington. Bellevue Way and NE Eighth St., Bellevue. ✆ **425/454-8096.** www.bellevuesquare.com.

The Bravern ★★ Also in Bellevue, this luxury shopping mall is home to such high-end retailers as Neiman Marcus, Hermès, Jimmy Choo, Salvatore Ferragamo, and Louis Vuitton. NE Eighth St. and 110th Ave., Bellevue. ✆ **425/456-8795.** www.thebravern.com.

Pacific Place ★ This downtown mall, adjacent to Nordstrom, contains five levels of upscale shop-o-tainment, including Tiffany & Co., bebe, Barneys New York, Coach, seven restaurants, and a multiplex movie theater. A huge skylight fills the interior space with much-appreciated natural light, and an adjoining garage means you usually have a place to park. 600 Pine St. ✆ **877/883-2400** or 206/405-2655. www.pacificplaceseattle.com.

Westlake Center In the heart of Seattle's main shopping district, this upscale, urban shopping mall has more than 80 specialty stores, including Godiva Chocolatier, Fireworks (a great contemporary crafts shop), and Made in Washington, along with an extensive food court. The mall is also the southern terminus for the monorail to Seattle Center. 400 Pine St. ✆ **206/467-1600.** www.westlakecenter.com.

Markets

Melrose Market ★ Of course the massive Pike Place Market is an absolute must on a visit to Seattle, but if you want to see where in-the-know local foodies do their shopping, head across I-5 from downtown to this fascinating little market. With the converted old warehouse space, you'll find a butcher shop, cheese shop, wine shop, flower shop, and great little rustic kitchenwares shop. You might not buy anything here, but it sure is worth a peek. 1501-1535 Melrose Ave. http://melrosemarketseattle.com.

Pike Place Market ★★★ Pike Place Market is one of Seattle's most famous landmarks and tourist attractions. Besides produce vendors, fishmongers, and butchers, it shelters artists, craftspeople, and performers. Hundreds of shops and dozens of restaurants (including some of Seattle's best) are tucked away in nooks and crannies on the numerous levels of the market. With so much to see and do, a trip to Pike Place Market can easily become an all-day affair. See also the listing on p. 126. Pike St. and First Ave. ✆ **206/682-7453.** www.pikeplacemarket.org.

Uwajimaya ★★ Typically, your local neighborhood supermarket probably has a section of Chinese cooking ingredients that's about 10 feet long, with half that space taken up by various brands of soy sauce. Now imagine your local supermarket with nothing but Asian foods, housewares, produce, and toys. That's Uwajimaya, Seattle's Asian supermarket in the heart of the International District. A big food court here serves all kinds of Asian food. 600 Fifth Ave. S. ✆ **206/624-6248.** www.uwajimaya.com.

Music & Musical Instruments

Dusty Strings This basement shop in the Fremont neighborhood specializes in hammered dulcimers, ukuleles, harps, and guitars. They also manufacture their own harps and dulcimers. 3406 Fremont Ave. N. ✆ **866/634-1662** or **206/634-1662**. www.dustystrings.com.

Singles Going Steady Right in the heart of Belltown, which was the heart of the Seattle grunge scene, this indie record store is one of the best places in town to search out oldies but goodies from Seattle's glory days. Of course, you'll also find the latest in punk, heavy metal, hip-hop, and other alt-rock genres. 2219 Second Ave. ✆ **206/441-7396.**

Perfume

Parfumerie Nasreen ★★ Just inside the lobby of the luxurious Alexis Hotel, this perfume shop is packed with thousands of bottles of perfume from all over the world. You'll find some of the world's most expensive scents. 1005 First Ave. ✆ **888/286-1825** or 206/623-9109. www.parfumerienasreen.com.

Recreational Gear

Columbia Sportswear Okay, so this company is from Portland not Seattle, but it makes such great outdoor clothing that it is well worth a visit, especially if you won't be visiting the original flagship store in Portland. The store, which is 2 blocks from Pike Place Market, was built using "green" construction techniques and is certified by Leadership in Energy and Environmental Design (LEED). 290 Pine St. ✆ **206/443-7639.** www.columbia.com.

Filson ★★ This Seattle company has been outfitting people headed outdoors ever since the Alaskan gold rush at the end of the 1890s. You won't find any high-tech fabrics here—just good old-fashioned wool, and plenty of it. Filson's clothes are meant to last a lifetime (and have the prices to prove it), so if you demand only the best, even when it comes to outdoor gear, be sure to check out this local institution. 1555 Fourth Ave. S. ✆ **866/860-8906** or 206/622-3147. www.filson.com.

KAVU ★ Rock jocks and rafters, rejoice: Now you can get your favorite rugged outdoor clothes at half-price. KAVU is a Seattle-based clothing manufacturer with a tiny outlet store on a shady street in the Ballard neighborhood. Its durable outdoor clothing is great not just for rafters and rock climbers, but for everyone. 5419 Ballard Ave. NW. ✆ **206/783-0060.** www.kavu.com.

R.E.I ★★★ Recreational Equipment, Inc. (R.E.I) is the nation's largest co-op selling outdoor gear, and the company's impressive flagship is a cross between a high-tech warehouse and a mountain lodge. This massive store sells almost anything you could ever need for pursuing your favorite outdoor sport. It also has a 65-foot climbing pinnacle. With all this under one roof, who needs to go outside? 222 Yale Ave. N. ✆ **888/873-1938** or 206/223-1944. www.rei.com.

Salmon

If you think that the fish at Pike Place Market looks great but that you could never get it home on the plane, think again. Any of the seafood vendors in Pike Place Market will pack your fresh salmon or Dungeness crab in an airline-approved container that will keep it fresh for up to 48 hours. Alternatively, you can buy vacuum-packed smoked salmon that will keep for years without refrigeration.

Pike Place Fish ★ Located behind *Rachel,* Pike Place Market's life-size bronze pig, this fishmonger is just about the busiest spot in the market most days. What pulls in the crowds are the antics of the workers here. Order a big silvery salmon, and you'll have employees shouting out your order and throwing the fish over the counter. These "flying fish" are a major Seattle attraction, so just step right up and pick your salmon. Pike Place Market, 86 Pike Place. ✆ **800/542-7732** or 206/682-7181. www.pikeplacefish.com.

Trident Seafoods Store If the sight of all the salmon swimming through the fish ladder at the Chittenden Locks has you craving some smoked salmon, just head 2 blocks east from the locks to the retail outlet of this big mail-order smoked-salmon store. They've got all kinds of smoked fish that you can have for a picnic or to bring home with you. 2821 NW Market St. ✆ **800/872-5666** or 206/781-7260. www.tridentseafoods.com.

Totem Smokehouse ★ Northwest Coast Indians used alder-wood smoke to preserve fish, and the tradition is carried on today with smoked salmon, one of the Northwest's delicacies. This store sells vacuum-packed smoked salmon that will keep without refrigeration for several years. Pike Place Market, 1906 Pike Place. ✆ **800/972-5666** or 206/443-1710. www.totemsmokehouse.com.

Toys

Archie McPhee ★★ ☺ You may already be familiar with this temple of the absurd through its mail-order catalog or website. Now imagine the fun of wandering through aisles full of goofy gags and all that other wacky stuff. Give yourself plenty of time and take a friend. Archie's place is in the Wallingford neighborhood. 1300 N. 45th St. ✆ **206/297-0240.** www.archiemcpheeseattle.com.

Magic Mouse Toys ★ ☺ Adults and children alike have a hard time pulling themselves away from this, the wackiest toy store in downtown Seattle. It's conveniently located in Pioneer Square and has a good selection of European toys. 603 First Ave. ✆ **206/682-8097.**

Seattle's Market Magic ★★ This little Pike Place Market shop is a must for aspiring magicians. You'll find all kinds of great tricks and all the tools of the

Calling all kids: Archie McPhee is where you'll find great toys and novelties.

trade. There are also juggling supplies and cool posters. Pike Place Market, 1501 Pike Place, No. 427. ✆ **206/624-4271.** www.marketmagicshop.com.

Not A Number Cards & Gifts This shop in the Wallingford neighborhood of north Seattle is packed full of all kinds of wacky toys and gifts and appeals primarily to adults. I love this place, and whenever I take friends by, they always leave with bags in hand and smiles on their faces. 1907½ N. 45th St. ✆ **206/784-0965.** www.notanumbergifts.com.

Wine

Because the relatively dry summers, with warm days and cool nights, provide an ideal climate for growing grapes, Washington has become one of the nation's foremost wine-producing states. After you've sampled some Washington vintages, you might want to take a few bottles home.

Pike & Western Wine Shop ★★ Visit this shop for an excellent selection of Washington and Oregon wines, as well as bottles from California, Italy, and France. The extremely knowledgeable staff will be happy to send you home with the very best wine available in Seattle. Free tastings are held Friday afternoons between 3 and 6pm. Pike Place Market, 1934 Pike Place. ✆ **206/441-1307.** www.pikeandwestern.com.

Portalis Wine Shop + Wine Bar This dark little wine shop and wine bar is worth searching out not only for its wide selection of wines from around the world, but also because it is in the heart of the historic Ballard neighborhood, on a shady, tree-lined street. 5205 Ballard Ave. NW. ✆ **206/783-2007.** www.portaliswines.com.

Soul Wine The South Lake Union neighborhood is currently Seattle's boomtown neighborhood, and this wine shop, affiliated with Pike Place Market's Pike & Western Wine Shop is where to look for wines from Washington and around the world. At the shop's little wine bar, there are daily tastings ($5–$10). 401-B Westlake Ave. N. ✆ **206/436-2350.** www.soulwineseattle.com.

SEATTLE AFTER DARK

9

Seattleites may spend much of their free time enjoying the city's natural surroundings, but that doesn't mean they overlook the more cultured evening pursuits. In fact, the winter weather that keeps people indoors, combined with a longtime desire to be the cultural mecca of the Northwest, has fueled a surprisingly active and diverse nightlife scene. Music lovers will find a plethora of classical, jazz, and rock offerings. The Seattle Opera is ranked one of the top companies in the country, and its stagings of Wagner's *Ring* series have achieved near-legendary status. The Seattle Symphony also receives frequent accolades. Likewise, the Seattle Repertory Theatre has won Tony awards for its productions, and a thriving fringe theater scene keeps the city's lovers of avant-garde theater contentedly discoursing in cafes and bars about the latest hysterical or thought-provoking performances.

Much of Seattle's evening entertainment scene is clustered in the **Seattle Center** and **Pioneer Square** areas. The former hosts theater, opera, and classical-music performances; the latter is a bar-and-nightclub district. Other concentrations of nightclubs can be found in **Belltown,** where crowds of the young and hip flock to the neighborhood's many trendy clubs, and in **Capitol Hill,** with its ultracool gay scene. **Ballard,** formerly a Scandinavian neighborhood in North Seattle, attracts a primarily middle-class, not-too-hip, not-too-old crowd, including lots of college students and techies. It's not the hipster Belltown scene, it's not the PBR-swilling blues scene of Pioneer Square, and it's not the sleek gay scene of Capitol Hill. It's just a comfortable neighborhood nightlife scene.

While winter is a time to enjoy the performing arts, summer brings an array of outdoor festivals. These take place during daylight hours as much as they do after dark; information on all these festivals and performance series is in this chapter.

To find out what's going on when you're in town, pick up a free copy of ***Seattle Weekly*** (www.seattleweekly.com), Seattle's arts-and-entertainment newspaper. You'll find it in bookstores, convenience stores, grocery stores, newsstands, and newspaper boxes around downtown and other neighborhoods. On Friday the ***Seattle Times*** includes a section called "NW Ticket," a guide to the week's arts-and-entertainment offerings.

THE PERFORMING ARTS

The Seattle Symphony performs downtown in Benaroya Hall, but the main venues for the performing arts in Seattle are primarily clustered at **Seattle Center,**

OPPOSITE PAGE: **Teatro ZinZanni is one of Seattle's favorite nights out: guests enjoy a cabaret, circus acts, and fine food in a *spiegeltent*.**

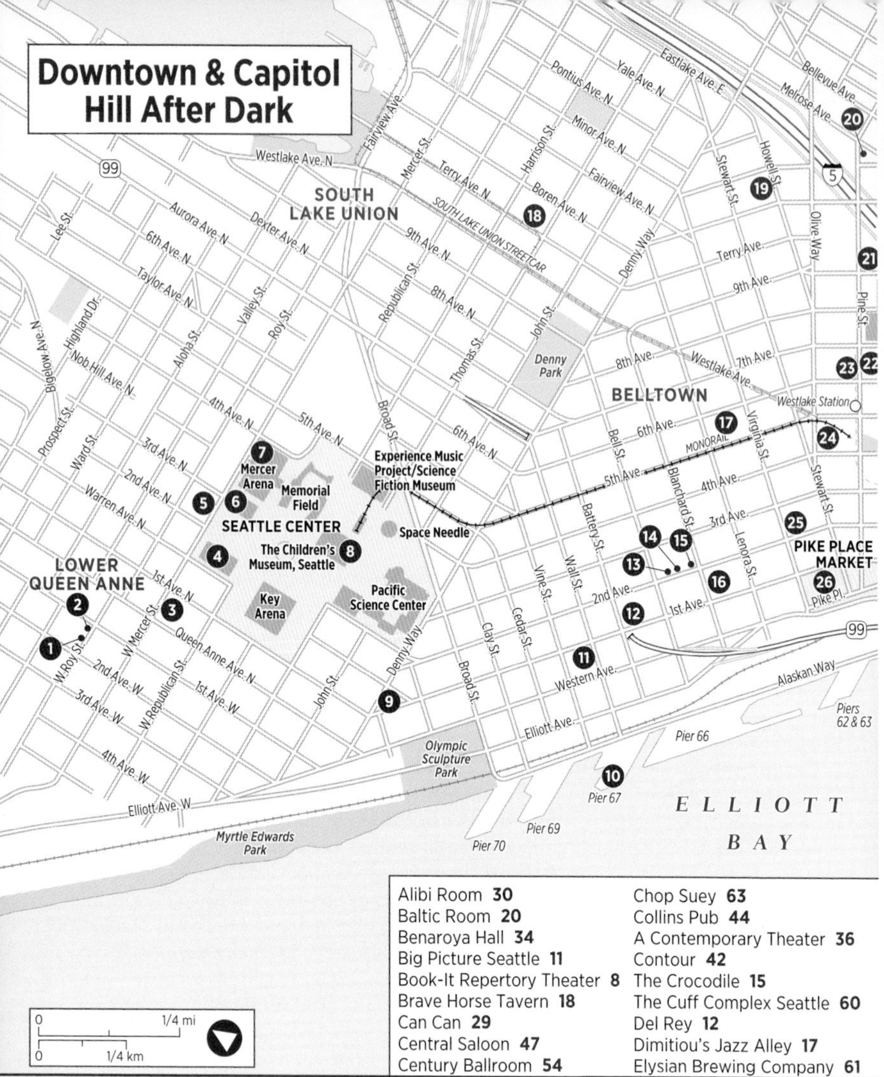

the special-events complex built for the 1962 World's Fair. Here, in the shadow of the Space Needle, are McCaw Hall, Bagley Wright Theatre, Center House Theatre, and Seattle Children's Theatre.

Opera & Classical Music

The **Seattle Opera ★** (✆ **800/426-1619** or 206/389-7676; www.seattleopera.org), which performs at Seattle Center's McCaw Hall, 321 Mercer St., is considered one of the finest opera companies in the country and is *the* Wagnerian opera company in the United States. The stagings of Wagner's four-opera *The Ring of the Nibelungen* are breathtaking spectacles that draw crowds from around the country. However, Wagner's magnum opus is staged only every 4 years. In

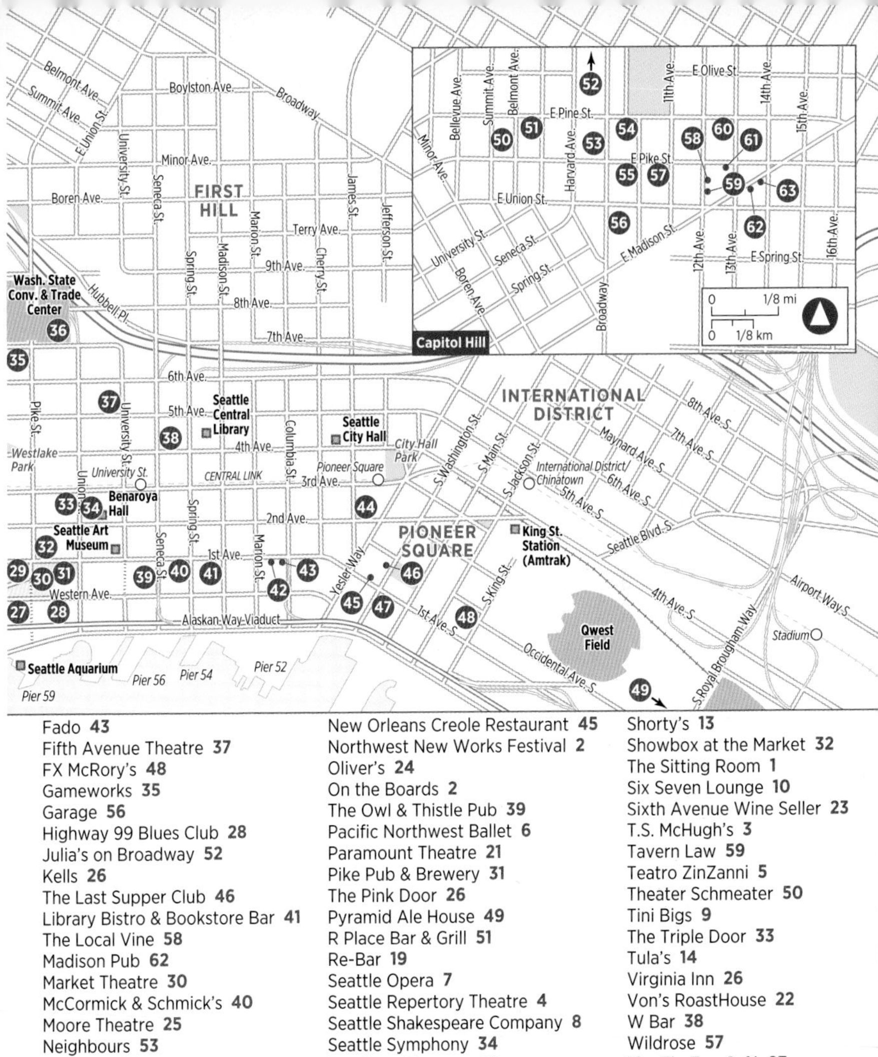

Fado **43**
Fifth Avenue Theatre **37**
FX McRory's **48**
Gameworks **35**
Garage **56**
Highway 99 Blues Club **28**
Julia's on Broadway **52**
Kells **26**
The Last Supper Club **46**
Library Bistro & Bookstore Bar **41**
The Local Vine **58**
Madison Pub **62**
Market Theatre **30**
McCormick & Schmick's **40**
Moore Theatre **25**
Neighbours **53**
Neumos **55**
New Orleans Creole Restaurant **45**
Northwest New Works Festival **2**
Oliver's **24**
On the Boards **2**
The Owl & Thistle Pub **39**
Pacific Northwest Ballet **6**
Paramount Theatre **21**
Pike Pub & Brewery **31**
The Pink Door **26**
Pyramid Ale House **49**
R Place Bar & Grill **51**
Re-Bar **19**
Seattle Opera **7**
Seattle Repertory Theatre **4**
Seattle Shakespeare Company **8**
Seattle Symphony **34**
See Sound Lounge **16**
Shorty's **13**
Showbox at the Market **32**
The Sitting Room **1**
Six Seven Lounge **10**
Sixth Avenue Wine Seller **23**
T.S. McHugh's **3**
Tavern Law **59**
Teatro ZinZanni **5**
Theater Schmeater **50**
Tini Bigs **9**
The Triple Door **33**
Tula's **14**
Virginia Inn **26**
Von's RoastHouse **22**
W Bar **38**
Wildrose **57**
The Zig Zag Café **27**

addition to such classical operas as *Tristan und Isolde* and *The Magic Flute,* the regular season usually includes a more contemporary production. Ticket prices range from around $25 to more than $198.

The multifaceted **Seattle Symphony** (✆ **866/833-4747** or 206/215-4747; www.seattlesymphony.org), which performs at the acoustically superb Benaroya Hall, offers an amazingly diverse season that runs year around. With several different series, there is a little something for every type of classical-music fan, including evenings of classical, light classical, and pops music, plus afternoon concerts, children's concerts, guest artists, and more. Ticket prices range from $15 to $107.

Theater

MAINSTREAM/REGIONAL THEATERS

The **Seattle Repertory Theatre ★** (✆ **877/900-9285** or 206/443-2222; www.seattlerep.org), which performs at the Bagley Wright and Leo K. theaters at Seattle Center, 155 Mercer St., is Seattle's top professional theater, and one of the most important regional theaters in the U.S. They stage the most consistently entertaining productions in the city. The Rep's season runs from September to May, with seven or more plays staged in the two theaters. Productions range from classics to world premieres. Tickets go for $15 to $54. When available, rush tickets are distributed a half-hour before showtime for $22.

Mike Daisey's "The Agony and the Ecstasy of Steve Jobs" at Seattle Rep.

A Contemporary Theater (ACT), Kreielsheimer Place, 700 Union St. (✆ **206/292-7676;** www.acttheatre.org), performing in the historic Eagles Building theater adjacent to the Washington State Convention and Trade Center, offers slightly more adventurous productions than the other major theater companies in Seattle, though it's not nearly as avant-garde as some of the smaller companies. ACT also puts on Seattle's annual staging of *A Christmas Carol*. The season runs from March to December. Ticket prices usually range from $15 to $65.

Although the **Seattle Shakespeare Company ★,** Center House Theatre, Seattle Center, 305 Harrison St. (✆ **206/733-8222;** www.seattleshakes.org), is neither very large nor very well known even in Seattle, it has been staging productions of the Bard's plays for more than 20 years. The season, which runs from October to May, includes three plays by Shakespeare plus a couple of other productions. Tickets run $15 to $40.

INDEPENDENT THEATERS

The city's more avant-garde/fringe performance companies frequently grab their share of the limelight with daring, outrageous, and thought-provoking productions. **Book-It Repertory Theatre,** Center House Theatre, Seattle Center, 305 Harrison St. (✆ **206/216-0833;** www.book-it.org), specializes in adapting literary works for the stage and also stages works by local playwrights. Most performances are held at Seattle Center.

The **Seattle Public Theater at the Bathhouse,** 7312 W. Green Lake Dr. N. (✆ **206/524-1300;** www.seattlepublictheater.org), stages a range of comedies and dramas at the old Green Lake bathhouse. The location right on the lake makes this a great place to catch some live theater. Capitol Hill's **Theater Schmeater,** 1500 Summit Ave. (✆ **206/324-5801;** www.schmeater.org), produces lots of weird and sometimes wonderful comedy, including ever-popular

Northern Seattle After Dark
BalMar 1
Big Time Brewery & Alehouse 11
Brouwer's Café 7
Fremont Outdoor Cinema 7
Fu Kun Wu @ Thaiku 2
Hale's Ales Brewery & Pub 6
Nectar Lounge 8
Old Town Alehouse 3
Portalis 5
Seattle Public Theater at the Bathhouse 10
Tractor Tavern 4
UW World Series 12
Woodland Park Zoo 9
0
1 mi
0
1 km
GREEN LAKE
PHINNEY RIDGE
BALLARD
WALLINGFORD
FREMONT
UNIVERSITY DISTRICT
MAGNOLIA
UPPER QUEEN ANNE
Green Lake
Green Lake Park
Woodland Park
Woodland Park Zoo
Ballard Locks
Burke Museum
UNIVERSITY OF WASHINGTON
Husky Stadium
Museum of History and Industry
Calvary Cem.
Gas Works Park
Mount Pleasant Cem.
David Rodgers Park
Portage Bay
Lake Union
NW 75th St.
NW 65th St.
N 65th St.
NW Market St.
N 50th St.
N 46th St.
NE 45th St.
N 40th St.
N 36th St.
N 34th St.
34th Ave. NW
32nd Ave. NW
24th Ave. NW
15th Ave. NW
8th Ave. NW
Greenwood Ave. N
Phinney Ave. N
Fremont Ave. N
Aurora Ave. N
Stone Way N
Winona Ave. N
Roosevelt Way NE
11th Ave. NE
12th Ave. NE
University Way NE
25th Ave. NE
Montlake Blvd. NE
Leary Ave. NW
W Nickerson St.
Nickerson St.
Gilman Ave. W
W Dravus St.
34th Ave. W
15th Ave. W
W McGraw St.
Westlake Ave. N
Eastlake Ave. E
Fuhrman Ave. E
Boyer Ave. E
99
5
520

live late-night stagings of episodes from *The Twilight Zone* and an annual summertime outdoor performance in Volunteer Park.

Catch some live theater at the Bathhouse.

Dance

Although it has a well-regarded ballet company and a theater dedicated to contemporary dance and performance art, Seattle is not nearly as devoted to dance as it is to theater and classical music. That said, hardly a week goes by without some sort of dance performance being staged somewhere in the city. Touring companies of all types, the University of Washington Dance Department faculty and student performances, the UW World Series (see below), and the NW New Works Festival (see below) all bring plenty of creative movement to the stages of Seattle. Check *Seattle Weekly* or the *Seattle Times* for a performance calendar.

The **Pacific Northwest Ballet** (**© 206/441-2424;** www.pnb.org), is Seattle's premier dance company. During the season, which runs from September to June, the company presents a wide range of classics, new works, and (the company's specialty) pieces choreographed by George Balanchine. This company's performance of *The Nutcracker,* with sets and costumes by children's book author Maurice Sendak, is the highlight of every season. The Pacific Northwest Ballet performs at Seattle Center's McCaw Hall, 301 Mercer St. Ticket prices range from $27 to $165.

Much more adventurous choreography is the domain of **On the Boards,** Behnke Center for Contemporary Performance, 100 W. Roy St. (**© 206/217-9888;** www.ontheboards.org), which, although it stages a wide variety of performance art, is best known as Seattle's premier modern-dance venue. In addition to dance performances by Northwest artists, there are a variety of productions every year by internationally known performance artists. Tickets go for $20 to $25.

Major Performance Halls

With ticket prices for shows and concerts so high these days, it pays to be choosy about what you see, but sometimes the venue is just as important. Benaroya Hall, the Seattle Symphony's downtown home, has such excellent acoustics that a performance here is worth attending simply for the sake of hearing how a good symphony hall should sound. Seattle also has two restored historic theaters (see below) that are as much a part of a performance as what happens on stage.

Benaroya Hall (**© 206/215-4747;** www.seattlesymphony.org/benaroya), on Third Avenue between Union and University streets in downtown Seattle, is the home of the Seattle Symphony. This state-of-the-art performance hall houses two concert halls—the main hall and a smaller recital hall. It's home to the Watjen concert organ, a magnificent pipe organ, as well as a Starbucks, a cafe, a symphony store, and a pair of Dale Chihuly chandeliers. Amenities aside, the main hall's excellent acoustics are the big attraction.

The **5th Avenue Theatre,** 1308 Fifth Ave. (✆ **888/584-4849** or 206/625-1900; www.5thavenue.org), which first opened its doors in 1926 as a vaudeville house, is a loose re-creation of the imperial throne room in Beijing's Forbidden City. Don't miss an opportunity to attend a performance here. Touring Broadway shows are the theater's mainstay; ticket prices usually range from $35 to $108.

The 5th Avenue Theatre has been in business since the days of vaudeville.

The Paramount Theatre, 911 Pine St. (✆ **206/682-1414;** www.stgpresents.org), one of Seattle's few historic theaters, has been restored to its original beauty and today shines with all the brilliance it had when it first opened in 1928. New lighting and sound systems have brought the theater up to contemporary standards. The theater hosts everything from rock concerts to Broadway musicals.

Affiliated with the Paramount Theatre, the **Moore Theatre,** 1932 Second Ave. (✆ **206/682-1414;** www.stgpresents.org), in Belltown, gets lots of national rock acts that aren't likely to draw quite as many people as bands that play at the Paramount.

Performing Arts Series

When Seattle's own resident performing-arts companies aren't taking to the dozens of stages around the city, various touring companies from around the world are. If you're a fan of Broadway shows, check the calendars at the Paramount Theatre and the 5th Avenue Theatre, both of which regularly serve as Seattle stops for touring shows.

The **UW World Series** (✆ **800/859-5342** or 206/543-4880; http://uwworldseries.org), held at Meany Hall on the University of Washington campus, is actually several different series that include chamber music, classical piano, dance, and world music and theater. Together these four series keep the Meany Hall stage busy between October and May. Special events are also scheduled. Tickets go for $30 to $46. The box office is at 3901 University Way NE, which is off campus.

Seattle loves the theater, including fringe works. Avant-garde performances are the specialty of the **NW New Works Festival** (✆ **206/217-9888;** www.ontheboards.org), an annual barrage of contemporary dance and performance art staged each spring by On the Boards, a performing-arts association that sponsors music, theater, and dance performances.

City Hall Turns Concert Hall

A few times a month year-round, Seattle's City Hall, 600 Fourth Ave. (✆ 206/684-7171; www.seattle.gov/arts), stages free lunchtime performances from noon to 1:30pm.

The NW New Works Festival features contemporary dance and performance art.

Summer is a time of outdoor festivals and performance series in Seattle, and if you're in town during the sunny months, you'll have a wide variety of alfresco performances from which to choose. The city's biggest summer music festivals are the **Northwest Folklife Festival,** over Memorial Day weekend, and **Bumbershoot,** over Labor Day weekend. See "Seattle Calendar of Events" (p. 22) for details.

At **Woodland Park Zoo** (✆ **206/548-2500;** www.zoo.org/zootunes), the **Zootunes** concert series brings in more big-name performers from the world of jazz, easy listening, blues, and rock. Tickets go for $19 to $35; bear in mind that they usually sell out almost as soon as they go on sale in early May.

North of Seattle, in Woodinville, **Chateau Ste. Michelle Summer Concert Series ★,** 14111 NE 145th St. (✆ **800/745-3000** or 425/415-3300; www.ste-michelle.com), is the area's most enjoyable outdoor summer concert series. It's held at the Chateau Ste. Michelle's amphitheater, which is surrounded by beautiful estatelike grounds. This is Washington's largest winery, so plenty of wine is available. The lineup is calculated to appeal to the 30- to 50-something crowd (past performers have included Bruce Hornsby, Lyle Lovett, Madeleine Peyroux, and Harry Connick, Jr.). Ticket prices usually range from $35 to $95, with a few shows priced a bit higher. See "The Woodinville Wine Country," in chapter 10, for more about Woodinville and Chateau Ste. Michelle.

At the summertime **Concerts at Marymoor,** 6046 W. Lake Sammamish Pkwy. NE (✆ **800/745-3000;** www.concertsatmarymoor.com), at Marymoor Park, 20 to 30 minutes east of Seattle at the north end of Lake Sammamish, you can expect the likes of Alison Krauss and UB40. Tickets for most shows are between $30 and $70, although prices sometimes go higher.

The **White River Amphitheatre,** 40601 Auburn Enumclaw Rd., Auburn (✆ **360/825-6200;** www.whiteriverconcerts.com), is the Seattle area's top amphitheater and pulls in big-name rock bands. Ticket prices can be anywhere from $29 to around $125, with the lowest prices being space on the lawn. The amphitheater is on the Muckleshoot Indian Reservation, 35 miles southeast of Seattle.

Then, of course, there's Seattle's perennially popular **Shakespeare in the Park** festival, which is staged in July and August in a dozen parks around the Seattle metro area. **GreenStage** (✆ **206/748-1551;** www.greenstage.org) usually produces two Shakespeare plays per summer and has free performances three to four times a week.

From mid-June to early September, the **Out to Lunch Concert Series** (http://downtownseattleevents.com/otl) stages 1½-hour lunchtime concerts at half a dozen or more parks around downtown Seattle. Musical styles range from rock to folk to jazz to gospel to Celtic.

THE CLUB & MUSIC SCENE

Whether you want to hear a live band, hang out in a dive bar, or dance, **Pioneer Square** is a good place to start. Keep in mind that this neighborhood tends to attract a very rowdy crowd (lots of frat boys) and can be pretty rough late at night.

Belltown, north of Pike Place Market, is a more sophisticated and trendy place to club-hop. Clubs here are way more style-conscious than those in Pioneer Square and tend to attract 20- and 30-something hipsters.

Seattle's other main nightlife district is the former Scandinavian neighborhood of **Ballard,** where you'll find more than a half-dozen nightlife establishments, including taverns, bars, and live-music clubs.

Capitol Hill, a few blocks uphill from downtown Seattle, is the city's main gay nightlife neighborhood, with much of the action centered on the corner of East Madison Street and 15th Avenue East.

Seattle rocks out at the Summer Concerts at Chateau Ste. Michelle.

The music is diverse and the crowd sophisticated at The Triple Door.

Rock, Folk, Reggae & World Beat

DOWNTOWN

The Triple Door ★★ Popular music for adults? What a concept! This swanky nightclub is a total novelty in the Seattle club world. It isn't geared toward the 20-something crowd. The music is diverse—from jazz to world beat to flamenco to Maria Muldaur, the Tubes, and Ottmar Liebert. You'll find the club in the basement below the ever-popular Wild Ginger restaurant, across the street from Benaroya Hall. 216 Union St. ✆ **206/838-4333.** www.thetripledoor.net. Cover $15–$35 (occasionally more for special shows).

BELLTOWN, PIKE PLACE MARKET & ENVIRONS

The Crocodile Back in the days when grunge music was sweeping the nation, this was one of Seattle's top live-music venues. After closing down for a while, it has come back again and is as popular as ever, with alternative rock dominating the schedule. 2200 Second Ave. (at Blanchard St.). ✆ **206/441-7416.** http://thecrocodile.com. Cover $8–$20.

Showbox at the Market Across the street from Pike Place Market, this large club books a wide variety of local and name rock acts. Definitely *the* downtown rock venue for performers with a national following. There's a second club, **Showbox SoDo,** at 1700 First Ave. S. 1426 First Ave. ✆ **206/628-3151.** www.showboxonline.com. Cover $15–$25 (occasionally higher).

PIONEER SQUARE

Central Saloon Established in 1892, the Central is the oldest saloon in Seattle. As a local institution, it's a must-stop during a night out in Pioneer Square, although you should have an appreciation of dive bars before stepping through the doors here. You might catch sounds ranging from funk to punk. 207 First Ave. S. ✆ **206/622-0209.** www.centralsaloon.com. Cover $5–$10.

CAPITOL HILL

Chop Suey Looking like a cross between a down-market Chinese restaurant and a Bruce Lee shrine, this kitschy Capitol Hill club books a very eclectic mix of music. Hip-hop and various alt-rock styles predominate, and the crowd is young with a mix of straights and gays. 1325 E. Madison St. ✆ **206/324-8005.** www.chopsuey.com. Cover $5–$20.

Neumos Located in a space that has housed numerous clubs over the years, Neumos is currently Seattle's leading club for indie rock bands that haven't yet developed a big enough following to play the Showbox. 925 E. Pike St. ✆ **206/709-9467.** www.neumos.com. Cover $8–$25.

FREMONT & BALLARD

Nectar Lounge This little warehouselike space is just the sort of nightclub you'd expect to find in Fremont. Appealing primarily to the area's neo-hippie types, Nectar puts on an eclectic array of world-beat, reggae, hip-hop, and indie rock shows, both live and DJs. There's a nice patio out front for warm summer nights. 412 N. 36th St. ✆ **206/632-2020.** www.nectarlounge.com. Cover none–$20.

Tractor For an ever-eclectic schedule of music for people whose tastes go beyond the latest rapper, the Tractor is the place to be. You can catch almost anything from alt-country to Celtic to folk to Hawaiian slack-key guitar to singer-songwriters to square dancing to zydeco. Sound like your kind of place? 5213 Ballard Ave. NW. ✆ **206/789-3599.** www.tractortavern.com. Cover $5–$25.

Jazz & Blues

Dimitriou's Jazz Alley ★★ Cool and sophisticated, this Belltown establishment is reminiscent of a New York jazz club and has been around for more than 30 years. As Seattle's premier jazz venue (and one of the top jazz clubs on the West Coast), it books only the best performers, including many name acts. 2033 Sixth Ave. ✆ **206/441-9729.** www.jazzalley.com. Cover usually $21–$45.

Highway 99 Blues Club In the basement of an old brick building beneath the waterfront's Alaskan Way Viaduct, this club not far from Pike Place Market is Seattle's quintessential blues joint. You can hear the best of local blues bands, as well as touring national acts. 1414 Alaskan Way. ✆ **206/382-2171.** www.highwayninetynine.com. Cover $5–$15.

New Orleans Creole Restaurant If you like your food and your jazz hot, check out the New Orleans in Pioneer Square. Throughout the week, there's Cajun, Dixieland, R&B, jazz, and blues. 114 First Ave. S. ✆ **206/622-2563.** www.neworleanscreolerestaurant.com. Cover none–$12.

You'll hear the real thing (as in jazz) at Tula's.

Tula's ★ This is the real thing: a jazz club that's a popular jazz musicians' after-hours hangout, and a good place to catch up-and-coming performers. American and Mediterranean food is served. 2214 Second Ave. ✆ **206/443-4221.** www.tulas.com. Cover $5–$15.

Comedy, Cabaret & Dinner Theater

Can Can Right at the entrance to Pike Place Market, you'll find this Moulin Rouge–inspired cabaret, which stages neo-burlesque shows, Django Reinhardt–style jazz performances, and other forms of obscure and imaginative retro entertainment. Yes, the ladies in petticoats really do kick up their heels here! 94 Pike St. ✆ **206/652-0832.** www.thecancan.com. Cover none–$40.

Le Faux Show Several nights a week, Julia's on Broadway restaurant, in the heart of Capitol Hill's Broadway commercial strip, lets its hair down and offers a show designed to appeal to the area's gay population (aka drag show…). Currently, there is a female celebrity impersonators show on Friday and Saturday nights, called "Le Faux Show." 300 Broadway E. ✆ **206/860-1818.** www.lefauxshow.com. Cover $20–$55.

Market Theater Competitive improv comedy at this small back-alley theater in Pike Place Market pits two teams against each other. Suggestions from the audience inspire sketches that can sometimes be hilarious but that just as often fall flat. The young, rowdy crowd never seems to mind one way or the other. 1428 Post Alley. ✆ **206/587-2414.** www.unexpectedproductions.org. Cover $7–$15.

The Pink Door ★★ Better known as Pike Place Market's unmarked restaurant, the Pink Door has a hopping after-work bar scene that tends to attract a

TEATRO zinzanni: WHO NEEDS CIRQUE DU SOLEIL?

Visiting Seattle without seeing this show would be like going to Las Vegas without seeing Cirque du Soleil. According to **Teatro ZinZanni ★,** 222 Mercer St. (✆ **206/802-0015;** http://dreams.zinzanni.org), a European-style cabaret of the highest order, circus acts aimed at the upper crust should be accompanied by gourmet cuisine.

Staged in an authentic Belgian *spiegeltent* (mirror tent), this evening of comedy, dance, theater, and fine food (catered by celeb-chef Tom Douglas) features clowns, acrobats, illusionists, and cabaret singers—more entertainment packed into one night than you'll find anywhere else in Seattle. Tickets are $106 Sunday and Wednesday through Friday, and $126 on Saturday (premium seating $126–$141 Sun and Wed–Fri, and $141–$161 Sat). There are also children's shows, brunch shows, and late-night cabaret shows.

Ooh la la! It's Le Faux Show at Julia's.

30-something crowd. It also doubles as a cabaret featuring Seattle's most eclectic lineup of performers, including trapeze artists, accordionists, burlesque dancers, and the like. Lots of fun and not to be missed. 1919 Post Alley. ✆ **206/443-3241.** www.thepinkdoor.net. Sun–Fri no cover; Sat $15.

Dance Clubs

The Baltic Room This swanky Capitol Hill hangout for the beautiful people stages a wide range of contemporary dance music (mostly DJs) encompassing everything from electronica to hip-hop and *bhangra* (contemporary Indian disco). 1207 Pine St. ✆ **206/625-4444.** www.thebalticroom.net. Cover none–$15.

Century Ballroom With a beautiful wooden dance floor, this is *the* place in Seattle for a night out if you're into swing, salsa, or tango. Every week there are a couple of nights of swing and a couple of nights of salsa dancing, complete with lessons early in the evening. Tuesday nights are currently tango nights. The crowd here is very diverse, with patrons of all ages. 915 E. Pine St. ✆ **206/324-7263.** www.centuryballroom.com. Cover $5–$15 (sometimes higher for special shows).

Contour A few blocks up First Avenue from Pioneer Square, this modern dance club attracts a more diverse crowd than most other Pioneer Square clubs. The music ranges from deep house to trance to drum and bass, and the partying on Friday and Saturday goes on until 6am the next day. 807 First Ave. ✆ **206/447-7704.** www.clubcontour.com. Cover none–$10.

You can swing it at the Century Ballroom.

The Last Supper Club Way more stylin' than your average Pioneer Square juke joint, this place may look small from the street, but it actually has three levels of bars and dance floors. DJs and live bands keep the beats pounding several nights a week. 124 S. Washington St. ✆ **206/748-9975.** www.lastsupperclub.com. Cover none–$10 (some higher for special shows).

See Sound Lounge With walls of colored lights and a front wall that swings open to let in the summer air, this retro-mod club, on one of the prettiest streets in Belltown, is among the neighborhood's hottest nightclubs. The nightly drink specials are also a big attraction. The cool scene here is a required stop during a night out in trendy Belltown. 115 Blanchard St. ✆ **206/374-3733.** www.seesoundlounge.com. Cover none–$10.

THE BAR SCENE

Bars

THE WATERFRONT

Six Seven ★ If you got any closer to the water than this bar, you'd have wet feet. Located inside downtown Seattle's only waterfront hotel, this bar boasts what just might be the best bar view in the city. Watch the ferries come and go, or see the sun set over Puget Sound and the Olympics. The Edgewater, Pier 67, 2411 Alaskan Way. ✆ **206/269-4575.** www.edgewaterhotel.com.

DOWNTOWN

Library Bistro & Bookstore Bar Just off the lobby of the posh Alexis Hotel, this cozy little bar is—surprise—filled with books. There are plenty of interesting magazines on hand as well, so if you want to sip a single malt but don't want to deal with crowds and noise, this is a great option. Very classy. 92 Madison St. ✆ **206/624-3646.** www.librarybistro.com.

McCormick & Schmick's The mahogany paneling and sparkling cut glass lend this restaurant bar a touch of class, but otherwise the place could have been the inspiration for *Cheers*. Very popular as an after-work watering hole of Seattle moneymakers, McCormick & Schmick's is best known for its excellent and inexpensive happy-hour snacks. 1103 First Ave. ✆ **206/623-5500.** www.mccormickandschmicks.com.

Oliver's Lounge★ Maybe you've been to one too many places that claim to make the best martini and you're feeling dubious. But here at Oliver's, they've repeatedly put their martinis to the test and come out on top. The atmosphere is classy and the happy-hour appetizers are good, but in the end, only you can decide whether or not these martinis are the best in Seattle. Mayflower Park Hotel, 405 Olive Way. ✆ **206/623-8700.** www.mayflowerpark.com.

Sixth Avenue Wine Seller Up on the third floor of the Pacific Place shopping center, you'll find a well-stocked little wine shop that also has a small bar in the back room. Some nights there's even live piano music. 600 Pine St. ✆ **206/621-2669.**

Von's RoastHouse Although best known for its $3.50 house martinis that are basically gin with a spritz of vermouth from a spray bottle, this popular downtown bar also boasts the largest selection of spirits in Seattle. 619 Pine St. ✆ **206/621-8667.** www.vonsroasthouse.com.

W Bar ★ Beautiful decor, beautiful people, flavorful cocktails. What more could you ask for, especially if black on black is your favorite fashion statement? The bar here at the W Seattle hotel really is the prettiest bar in the downtown business district. 1112 Fourth Ave. ✆ **206/264-6000.** www.whotels.com/seattle.

You can buy your wine, and drink it too at Sixth Avenue Wine Seller.

SOUTH LAKE UNION

Brave Horse Tavern Local celeb-chef Tom Douglas has branched out beyond restaurants to give the trendy South Lake Union neighborhood a throwback tavern that feels inside like a cross between an Appalachian moonshiner's shack and a garage turned man cave. There are dart boards and shuffleboard tables, plus house-made pretzels and lots of local beers on tap. 310 Terry Ave. N. ✆ **206/971-0717.** http://bravehorsetavern.com.

BELLTOWN

Del Rey Sexy, sophisticated, and small, this Belltown bar seems to be where everyone wants to start the evening, so it can be hard to get in or get a drink ordered once you do get in. On the other hand, if you're here to make the scene, be sure to put Del Rey on the schedule. There's good bar food, and on Friday and Saturday nights, there are DJs. 2332 First Ave. ✆ **206/770-3228.** www.delreyseattle.com.

Shorty's Are you a pinball wizard? Want to find out what all the fuss was about back in the days before video games? Either way, check out this retro pinball-parlor bar in Belltown. It's tiny and funky, but you'll be surrounded by likeminded aficionados of the silver balls. And don't forget to have a hot dog with your beer. 2222 Second Ave. ✆ **206/441-5449.** www.shortydog.com.

PIKE PLACE MARKET

Alibi Room If you've been on your feet all day in Pike Place Market and have had it with the crowds of people, duck down the alley under the market clock and slip through the door of this hideaway. The back-alley setting gives this place an atmospheric speakeasy feel. Popular with artists and other creative types. 85 Pike St., No. 410. ✆ **206/623-3180.** www.seattlealibi.com.

The Tasting Room ★★ Located in Pike Place Market, this cozy wine bar has the feel of a wine cellar and is cooperatively operated by several small Washington State wineries. You can taste the wines of Camaraderie Cellars, Harlequin Wine Cellars, Latitude 46° N Winery, Mountain Dome, Naches Heights Vineyards, Wilridge Winery, and Wineglass Cellars, or buy wine by the glass or bottle. Light snacks are also available. 1924 Post Alley. ✆ **206/770-9463.** www.winesofwashington.com.

Virginia Inn This bistro/bar on the edge of the Pike Place Market neighborhood has been around since 1903 and is a great place to soak a bit of historic Seattle character without having to hang out in one of the rowdy Pioneer Square watering holes. Quite surprising for a bar, the Virginia Inn serves decent, inexpensive French food! 1937 First Ave. ✆ **206/728-1937.** http://virginiainnseattle.com.

The Zig Zag Café ★★ You'll have to look hard to find this hidden Pike Place Market bar. It's on one of the landings of the Pike Street Hill Climb, which is the staircase that links the market with the waterfront. Perfectly crafted cocktails, both classic and contemporary, are the specialty here and are so well made that the bar has garnered national recognition. 1501 Western Ave. ✆ **206/625-1146.** http://zigzagseattle.com.

PIONEER SQUARE

F.X. McRory's Right across the street from the Seattle Seahawks' Qwest Field, and not far from Safeco Field, this bar attracts well-heeled sports fans (with the occasional Mariners and Seahawks player thrown in for good measure). You'll find the city's (and perhaps the country's) largest selection of bourbons here. There's also an oyster bar and good food. 419 Occidental Ave. S. ✆ **206/623-4800.** www.fxmcrorys.com.

CAPITOL HILL

The Local Vine Atop Capitol Hill away from the tourists and the panhandlers, you'll find one of the prettiest and most sophisticated wine bars in the city. With its curved wooden ceiling, the Local Vine is a very pretty space, perfect for sipping a Washington wine. It also has free Wi-Fi, in case you want to check your e-mail while you drink your wine. 1410 12th Ave. ✆ **206/257-5653.** www.thelocalvine.com.

Tavern Law With the feel of a lawyer's library and a secret upstairs speakeasy, this Capitol Hill bar celebrates historic cocktails. The sophisticated setting and great location in the middle of the neighborhood's restaurant district makes this a great place for a drink before or after dinner. 1406 12th Ave. ✆ **206/322-9734.** www.tavernlaw.com.

QUEEN ANNE

The Sitting Room With a casual, Euro-bistro vibe, this tucked-away cocktail bar in the Lower Queen Anne neighborhood is the perfect spot for a drink before or after a show at On the Boards next door. It's a fun find for anyone exploring this part of town. 108 W. Roy St. ✆ **206/285-2830.** www.the-sitting-room.com.

Tini Bigs On the border between Lower Queen Anne and Belltown, this bar led the revival of the martini as the cocktail of choice in Seattle. The martinis on the menu feature such an array of ingredients that it's hard to consider most of them to even be martinis. Nevertheless, the drinks are good and the location is convenient to Seattle Center and the Space Needle. 100 Denny Way. ✆ **206/284-0931.** www.tinibigs.com.

BALLARD

BalMar The name makes it sound like some Miami-inspired tropical Deco place, but that's far from reality. The brick-walled neighborhood bar/restaurant takes its name from the fact that it's at the corner of Ballard and Market streets. It's classy yet casual, and it's one of the most upscale drinking establishments in Ballard. 5449 Ballard Ave. NW. ✆ **206/297-0500.** www.thebalmar.com.

Fu Kun Wu @ Thaiku ★  You'll find this unforgettable bar at the back of Ballard's Thaiku, which is one of my favorite Thai restaurants in Seattle. Designed to look like an old Chinese apothecary and filled with Asian woodcarvings and artifacts, Fu Kun Wu specializes in various herb-infused cocktails. There's live jazz on Wednesday and Thursday nights. 5410 Ballard Ave. NW. ✆ **206/706-7807.** www.fukunwu.com.

Portalis In a dark cellarlike space in an old brick building on a shady back street in Ballard, you'll find one of Seattle's best wine bars. This is a great place to hang out and have a glass of wine—and because this is also a wine shop, you can search the racks for your favorite Washington vintages, too. 5205 Ballard Ave. NW. ✆ **206/783-2007.** www.portaliswines.com.

At Fu Kun Wu, you can imbibe in an old Chinese apothecary (or a reasonable facsimile).

Brewpubs

Big Time Brewery & Alehouse Big Time, Seattle's oldest brewpub, is in the University District and is done up to look like an old tavern, complete with a 100-year-old back bar and a wooden refrigerator. The pub serves as many as 12 of its own brews at any given time, and some of these are pretty unusual. 4133 University Way NE. ✆ **206/545-4509.** www.bigtimebrewery.com.

Elysian Brewing Company ★ This large Capitol Hill brewpub has an industrial feel that sums up the Northwest concept of "local brewpub." The stouts and strong ales are especially good, and the brewers' creativity here just can't be beat. Hands down, Elysian is the best brewpub in Seattle. Other Elysian pubs are at 542 First Ave. S. (✆ **206/382-4498**), and 2106 N. 55th St. (✆ **206/547-5929**). 1221 E. Pike St. ✆ **206/860-1920.** www.elysianbrewing.com.

Hale's Ales Brewery & Pub Located about a mile west of the Fremont Bridge, toward Ballard, this big, lively brewpub produces some of Seattle's favorite beers. In business for more than 25 years, Hale's has long enjoyed a loyal following. This is a good place to stop after a visit to Chittenden Locks to see migrating salmon. 4301 Leary Way NW. ✆ **206/706-1544.** www.halesbrewery.com.

Get Your Game On

Seattle is a computer nerd's town, and downtown's massive GameWorks, 1511 Seventh Ave. (✆ 206/521-0952; www.gameworks.com), is where the geeks go gaming. This place has more than 175 video games and simulators, plus a full bar.

Things are hopping at Elysian Brewing Company.

The Pike Pub & Brewery In an open, central space inside Pike Place Market, this brewpub makes excellent stout and pale ale but is best known for its Kilt Lifter Scottish ale. This is a great place to get off your feet after a long day in the market. 1415 First Ave. ✆ **206/622-6044.** www.pikebrewing.com.

Pyramid Alehouse This pub, south of Pioneer Square in a big old warehouse, is part of the brewery that makes the Northwest's popular Pyramid beers. It's a favorite spot for dinner and drinks before or after baseball games at Safeco Field and football games at Qwest Field. There's good pub food, too. 1201 First Ave. S. ✆ **206/682-3377.** www.pyramidbrew.com.

Irish Pubs

Fadó This Irish pub is part of a national chain but has the feel of an independent pub. Lots of antiques, old signs, and a dark, cozy feel make it a very comfortable place for a pint. There's live Irish music on Saturday nights and Sunday afternoons, a weekly pub quiz, and, of course, you can watch soccer and rugby matches on the telly. 801 First Ave. ✆ **206/264-2700.** www.fadoirishpub.com.

Kells ★ At one time, the space now occupied by this pub was the embalming room of a mortuary.

Bowled Over in Seattle

A hip bowling alley? Why not? Up on Capitol Hill, you can do a little bowling, shoot some pool, and take in the hipster scene at Garage, 1130 Broadway Ave. (✆ 206/322-2296; www.garagebilliards.com). When the weather gets warm, the garage doors roll up to let in the fresh air. Definitely not your small-town bowling alley.

Knock some pins over (and have a drink) at Garage on Capitol Hill.

These days the scene is much livelier and has the feel of a casual Dublin pub. Kells pulls a good pint of Guinness, serves traditional Irish meals, and features live Irish music 7 nights a week. Pike Place Market, 1916 Post Alley. ✆ **206/728-1916.** www.kellsirish.com. Cover none–$5.

Owl & Thistle Pub Right around the corner from Fadó is this equally authentic-feeling pub. The Post Alley entrance gives this place the ambience of a back-street Dublin pub. There's live music most nights, with the house band playing Irish music most weekends. 808 Post Alley. ✆ **206/621-7777.** www.owlnthistle.com. Cover none–$5.

T. S. McHugh's In the Lower Queen Anne neighborhood adjacent to Seattle Center and many of Seattle's mainstream theaters, T. S. McHugh's has a very authentic feel. It's a good place to relax after an afternoon spent exploring Seattle Center. 21 Mercer St. ✆ **206/282-1910.**www.tsmchughs.com.

Other Pubs

Brouwer's Cafe ★ Beer geeks (and I count myself among this tribe) swarm to this friendly, modern Fremont pub for its huge selection of Belgian beers. Of the 64 beers on tap and more than 300 bottled beers, a preponderance of them are Belgian. Of course, you can also get Belgian food to accompany your beer. 400 N. 35th St. ✆ **206/267-2437.** www.brouwerscafe.blogspot.com.

Collins Pub If you're looking for someplace in the Pioneer Square area where you can sip a beer without having your nostrils assaulted by the stench of stale beer and industrial cleaners, you don't have a lot of options, which is why the Collins Pub is the only place I'll drink beer in the neighborhood. There's a good selection of regional microbrews and decent food, too. 526 Second Ave. ✆ **206/623-1016.** www.thecollinspub.com.

Old Town Alehouse This old-fashioned pub on shady Ballard Avenue feels like the sort of place dock workers would have frequented a century ago. The beer list focuses on small Washington breweries and also includes a respectable assortment of Belgian beers. 5233 Ballard Ave. NW. ✆ **206/782-8323.** www.oldtownalehouse.com.

THE GAY & LESBIAN SCENE

Capitol Hill is Seattle's main gay neighborhood; consequently, it has the city's greatest concentration of gay and lesbian bars and clubs. Look for the readily available ***Seattle Gay News*** (✆ **206/324-4297;** www.sgn.org), in which many of the city's gay bars and nightclubs advertise.

Bars

Madison Pub This low-key darts-and-pool sports pub on Capitol Hill is popular with guys who have outgrown or just aren't into cruising. So if you just want to hang out with local gay men and aren't out to pick up someone, this is a good choice. 1315 E. Madison St. ✆ **206/325-6537.** www.madisonpub.com.

Wildrose This bar claims to be the oldest lesbian bar on the West Coast and is a popular hangout for the Capitol Hill lesbian community. That said, it is notoriously unfriendly if you are not a regular. In spring and summer, there is an outdoor seating area. Pool tournaments and karaoke are mainstays here. 1021 E. Pike St. ✆ **206/324-9210.** www.thewildrosebar.com. Cover none–$5.

Dance Clubs

The Cuff Complex Seattle A virtual multiplex of gay entertainment, this place has three separate bars. There's a quiet bar, a dance club, and a patio for those rain-free nights. It's primarily a leather-and-Levis crowd, but you're still welcome even if you forgot to pack your leather pants. 1533 13th Ave. ✆ **206/323-1525.** www.cuffcomplex.com. Cover none–$5.

Where the girls are: at Wildrose on Capitol Hill.

Neighbours This has been the favorite dance club of Capitol Hill's gay community for years. As at other clubs, different nights of the week feature different styles of music. You'll find this club's entrance down the alley. 1509 Broadway. ✆ **206/324-5358.** www.neighboursnightclub.com. Cover none–$10.

Re-Bar Every night there's a different theme, with the DJs spinning everything from funk to punk. This club isn't exclusively gay, but it's still a gay-Seattle favorite. 1114 Howell St. ✆ **206/233-9873.** www.rebarseattle.com. Cover none–$15.

R Place Bar & Grill With three floors of entertainment, including a video bar on the ground floor, pool tables and video games on the second floor, and a dance floor up on the top level, you hardly need to go anywhere else for a night on the town. 619 E. Pine St. ✆ **206/322-8828.** www.rplaceseattle.com. Cover none–$7.

Only in Seattle . . .

While Seattle has plenty to offer in the way of performing arts, some of the city's best after-dark offerings have nothing to do with music or theater. There's no better way to start the evening (that is, if the day has been sunny or only partly cloudy) than to catch the sunset from the waterfront. The Bell Street Pier and Myrtle Edwards Park are two of the best vantages for taking in nature's light show. Keep in mind that sunset can come as late as 10pm in the middle of summer.

Want the best view of the city lights? Put off your elevator ride to the top of the Space Needle until after dark. Or you can hop a ferry and sail off into the night.

MOVIES

Summertime in the Fremont neighborhood always means **Fremont Almost Free Outdoor Cinema** (http://fremontoutdoormovies.com), a series that features modern classics, B movies (sometimes with live overdubbing by a local improv comedy company), and indie shorts. Films are screened on Saturday nights in the parking lot at North 35th Street and Phinney Avenue North. The parking lot opens at 7:30pm, and there is a $5 suggested donation.

Want to sip a martini while you watch the latest indie film hit? Find out what's playing at Belltown's **Big Picture Seattle,** 2505 First Ave. (✆ **206/256-0566;** www.thebigpicture.net). This little basement theater below **El Gaucho** steakhouse (p. 83) is the coolest little theater in the city and a favorite of fans of indie films.

10 SIDE TRIPS FROM SEATTLE

After you've explored Seattle for a few days, you'll want to head out of town on a day trip or two. Within a few hours of the city, you can find yourself hiking in a national park, cruising up a fjord-like arm of Puget Sound, exploring the San Juan Islands, strolling the streets of a Victorian seaport, or tasting wine at some of Washington's top wineries. With the exception of the San Juan Islands and the Olympic Peninsula, the excursions listed below are all fairly easy day trips that will give you glimpses of the Northwest outside the Emerald City.

For more in-depth coverage of the areas surrounding Seattle, pick up a copy of ***Frommer's Washington State*** (John Wiley & Sons, Inc.). For a map of the region you'll be exploring in this chapter, see the inside front cover.

THE SAN JUAN ISLANDS

In late afternoon on a clear summer day, the sun slants low, suffusing the scene with a golden light. The fresh salt breeze and the low rumble of the ferry's engine lull you into a dream state. All around you, rising from a shimmering sea, are emerald-green islands, the tops of glacier-carved mountains inundated with water at the end of the last ice age. A bald eagle swoops from its perch on a twisted madrona tree. Off the port bow, you spot several fat harbor seals lounging on a rocky islet. As the engine slows, you glide toward a narrow dock with a simple sign above it that reads ORCAS ISLAND. With a sigh of contentment, you step out onto the San Juan Islands and into a slower pace of life.

There's something magical about traveling to the San Juans. Some people say it's the light, some say it's the sea air, some say it's the weather (temperatures are always moderate, and rainfall is roughly half what it is in Seattle). Whatever the answer, the San Juans have become the favorite getaway of urban Washingtonians, and if you make time to visit these idyllic islands, I think you, too, will fall under their spell.

There is, however, one caveat: The San Juans are *not* undiscovered. In summer, if you're driving a car, you may encounter waits of several hours to get on the ferries (although there is talk of implementing a reservation system). One solution is to leave your car on the mainland and come over either on foot or by bicycle. If you choose to come over on foot, you can then rent a car, moped, or bike; take the San Juan island shuttle bus; or use taxis to get around. Then again, you can just stay in one place and relax.

Along with crowded ferries come hotels, inns, and campgrounds booked up months in advance, and restaurants that can't seat you unless you have a reservation. If it's summer, you likely won't find a place to stay if you don't have a reservation.

OPPOSITE PAGE: **Marymere Falls are just one of the amazing sights you'll see in Olympia National Park.**

In other seasons, it's a different story. Spring and fall are often clear, and in spring the islands' gardens and hedgerows of wild roses burst into bloom, making this one of the nicest times of year to visit. Perhaps best of all, room rates in spring and fall are much lower than they are in summer.

No one seems to be able to agree on how many islands there actually are in the San Juans; there may be fewer than 200 or almost 800. The lower number represents those islands large enough to have been named, while the larger number includes all the islands, rocks, and reefs that poke above the water at low tide. Of all these islands, only four (San Juan, Orcas, Lopez, and Shaw) are serviced by the Washington State Ferries, and of these only three (San Juan, Orcas, and Lopez) have anything in the way of tourist accommodations.

Visitor Information

For information on all the islands, contact the **San Juan Islands Visitors Bureau,** P.O. Box 1330, Friday Harbor, WA 98250 (✆ **888/468-3701** or 360/378-9551; www.visitsanjuans.com). For specific information on San Juan, contact the **San Juan Island Chamber of Commerce,** 135 Spring St. (P.O. Box 98), Friday Harbor, WA 98250 (✆ **360/378-5240;** www.sanjuanisland.org). For Orcas, contact the **Orcas Island Chamber of Commerce,** 65 N. Beach Rd. (P.O. Box 252), Eastsound, WA 98245 (✆ **360/376-2273;** http://orcasislandchamber.com). And for Lopez, contact the **Lopez Island Chamber of Commerce,** 6 Old Post Rd. (P.O. Box 102), Lopez Island, WA 98261 (✆ **877/433-2789** or 360/468-4664; www.lopezisland.com). Also check out www.thesanjuans.com.

Getting There

If it's summer and you'd like to visit the San Juans without a car, I recommend booking passage through **Victoria Clipper** (see below), which operates excursion boats from the Seattle waterfront. If you're traveling by car, you'll need to drive north from Seattle to Anacortes and head out to the islands via **Washington State Ferries** (✆ **800/843-3779,** 888/808-7977 in Washington, or 206/464-6400; www.wsdot.wa.gov/ferries). Boats run between Anacortes, four of the San Juan Islands (Lopez, Shaw, Orcas, and San Juan), and Sidney, British Columbia (on Vancouver Island near Victoria).

The round-trip fare for a vehicle and driver from Anacortes to Lopez is $28 to $38; to Shaw or Orcas, $34 to $45; to San Juan, $40 to $54; and to Sidney, $45 to $56. The higher fares reflect a summer surcharge.

The fare for passengers from Anacortes to any of the islands is $12 ($17 between Anacortes and Sidney). The fare for a vehicle and driver on all westbound interisland ferries is $19 to $24; walk-on passengers and passengers in cars ride free. Except for service from Sidney, fares are not collected on eastbound ferries, nor are walk-on passengers charged for interisland ferry service. If you plan to explore the islands by car, you'll save some money by starting your tour on San Juan Island and making your way back east through the islands.

During the summer, you may have to wait several hours to get on a ferry, so arrive early. If you plan to leave your car on the mainland any time between May 1 and September 30, you'll pay $10 to park it overnight at the Anacortes ferry terminal ($25 for 3 days, $40 for 1 week). The rest of the year, parking rates are mostly half the summer rates.

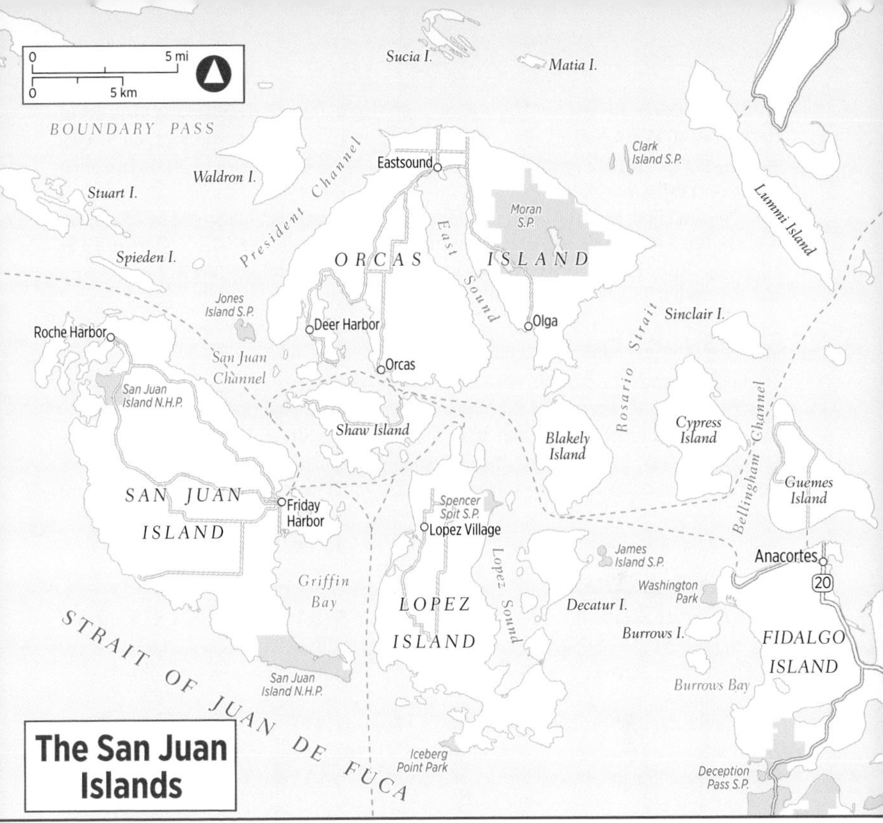

Note: To cross into Canada and return to the United States by ferry, you will need a passport, passport card, trusted-traveler program card, or an enhanced driver's license. If you are a foreign citizen but a permanent resident of the United States, be sure to carry your passport and your A.R.R. card (green card) or permanent-resident card. Foreign citizens who are only visiting the United States must carry a passport and, if they need one, a visa when traveling to or from Canada. U.S. children 15 and under traveling to or from Canada with both parents must have a birth certificate or passport; a child traveling with only one parent should have both a birth certificate and a notarized letter from the other parent giving permission for the child to travel out of the country.

From late May to late September, **Victoria Clipper** (✆ **800/888-2535,** 206/448-5000, or 250/382-8100; www.clippervacations.com) operates excursion boats between Seattle and Friday Harbor on San Juan Island. There are also boats that go to Victoria. The round-trip fare to Friday Harbor is $80 to $120 ($40–$60 for children 11 and under), depending on the time of year. Discounted 1-day advance-purchase round-trip tickets are available, and if you book in advance, children travel for free.

If you're short on time, you can fly to the San Juans. **Kenmore Air** (✆ **866/435-9524** or 425/486-1257; www.kenmoreair.com) offers floatplane flights that take off from either Lake Union or the north end of Lake Washington. Round-trip fares to the San Juans are between $232 and $282. Flights go to

Friday Harbor and Roche Harbor on San Juan Island; Rosario Resort, Deer Harbor, and West Sound on Orcas Island; and the Lopez Islander on Lopez Island. This company also operates flights out of Boeing Field, which is just south of downtown Seattle.

You can also get from Sea-Tac Airport or downtown Seattle to the San Juan Islands ferry terminal in Anacortes on the **Airporter Shuttle** (**© 866/235-5247** or 360/380-8800; www.airporter.com), which charges $33 one-way and $61 round-trip. Expect to also pay a fuel surcharge.

San Juan Island

Although neither the largest nor the prettiest of the archipelago, San Juan is the most populous and touristy of the San Juan Islands. **Friday Harbor,** where the ferry docks, is the county seat for San Juan County and is the only real town on all the islands. As such, it is home to numerous shops, restaurants, motels, and bed-and-breakfasts that cater to tourists. It's also where you'll find the grocery and hardware stores that provide the necessities of island life. With its large, well-protected marina, it's one of the most popular places in the islands for boaters to drop anchor.

GETTING AROUND

Car rentals are available on San Juan Island from **M&W Auto Sales & Rentals,** 725 Spring St. (**© 800/323-6037** or 360/378-2886; www.sanjuanauto.com), which charges between $50 and $80 per day during the summer ($40–$60 in other months).

Cars can also be rented from **Susie's Mopeds,** 125 Nichols St. (**© 800/532-0087** or 360/378-5244; www.susiesmopeds.com), which is 1 block from the top of the ferry lanes in Friday Harbor. Susie's charges $32 per hour and $96 per day for a car and also rents scooters and mopeds ($30–$60 per hour or $65–$130 per day). Mopeds are also available at the north end of the island at Roche Harbor.

For a cab, call **Bob's Taxi & Tours** (**© 360/378-6777;** http://bobs-taxi.com) or **Friday Harbor Taxi** (**© 360/298-4434;** http://fridayharbortaxi.com).

During the summer, **San Juan Transit** (**© 800/887-8387** or 360/378-8887; www.sanjuantransit.com) operates a San Juan Island shuttle bus that can be boarded at the ferry terminal. It operates frequently throughout the day, stopping at all the island's major attractions, which makes it a great way to get around for those traveling without a car. Day passes are $15 for adults and $5 for children 5 to 12. Two-day passes ($25 for adults and $10 for children), one-way tickets ($5 adults, $2 children), and round-trip tickets ($10 adults, $3 children) are also available. Children 4 and under ride free.

EXPLORING THE ISLAND

If you arrive by car, you'll first want to find a parking space, which can be difficult in the summer. Once on foot, take a stroll around **Friday Harbor** to admire the simple wood-frame shop buildings, constructed in the early 20th century. At that time, Friday Harbor was a busy little harbor sometimes referred to as the southernmost port in Alaska. Schooners and steamships hauled the island's fruit, livestock, and lime (for cement) off to more populous markets. Today such pursuits have all ceased, but reminders of the island's rural roots linger on, and these memories now fuel San Juan's new breadwinner: tourism.

Throughout Friday Harbor, there are numerous art galleries and interesting shops. At **Waterworks Gallery,** 315 Argyle Ave. (**© 360/378-3060;** www.waterworksgallery.com), you'll find fine art and contemporary crafts by local and regional artists. **Arctic Raven Gallery,** S. 130 First St. (✆ **888/378-3222** or 360/378-3433; www.arcticravengallery.com), specializes in contemporary Native American arts and crafts. Also here in town, you can visit the little **Island Museum of Art,** 285 Spring St. (✆ **360/370-5050;** www.sjima.org), which is affiliated with the Westcott Bay Sculpture Park. The museum, which highlights local and regional artists, is open Wednesday through Sunday from 11am to 5pm. Admission is by donation.

The tasting room at **Island Wine Company,** 2 Cannery Landing (✆ **800/248-9463** or 360/378-3229; www.sanjuancellars.com), sells a wide variety of Washington wines and is the only place you can buy wine from the shop's own San Juan Cellars. You'll find the wine shop on the immediate left as you leave the ferry. Here in Friday Harbor, you'll also find a tasting room for **San Juan Vineyards,** 65 Spring St. (✆ **360/378-9463;** www.sanjuanvineyards.com), which in summer is open daily from 11am to 6pm.

If you walk over to the other side of the ferry landing and then out on the pier that serves as the dock for passenger ferries, you can take a peek at the **Spring Street Landing Aquarium,** a modest tank full of local denizens of the deep. The tank is in a building at the end of the pier. Also keep an eye out for wildlife here; I once saw an otter swimming around by this pier.

Continuing along the waterfront toward the marina, you'll come to **Fairweather Park,** where you'll find artist Susan Point's traditional Northwest Coast Indian house-post sculpture, which is similar to a totem pole. The sculpture represents the human-animal relationship and the marine ecosystem. Here in the park, you'll also find some covered picnic tables.

Whale-watching is one of the most popular summer activities in the San Juans, and no one should visit the islands at this time of year without going out to see the area's orca whales. Before you head out, stop by the **Whale Museum★★,**

Explore the world of orcas at the Whale Museum.

62 First St. N. (✆ **360/378-4710;** www.whale-museum.org), where you can see whale skeletons and models of whales, and learn all about the area's pods of orcas (also known as killer whales). The museum is open daily from 10am to 5pm; admission is $6 for adults, $5 for seniors, and $3 for students and children 5 to 18. The museum is closed Thanksgiving, Christmas, and New Year's Day.

If you're interested in learning more about island history, stop by the **San Juan Historical Museum,** 405 Price St. (✆ **360/378-3949;** www.sjmuseum.org), which is housed in an 1894 farmhouse and also includes several other historic buildings on its grounds. May to September, the museum is open Wednesday through Saturday from 10am to 4pm and Sunday from 1 to 4pm; April and October, the museum is open Saturday from 1 to 4pm. Open by appointment in other months. Admission is $5 for adults, $4 for seniors, $3 for children 6 to 18, and free for children 5 and under.

Most of the island's main attractions can be seen on a long loop drive around the perimeter of San Juan Island. Start the drive by following Roche Harbor signs north out of Friday Harbor (take Spring St. to Second St. to Tucker Ave.).

ALL ABOUT orcas

Orcas, which can grow to 30 feet long and weigh almost 9,000 pounds, are also known as killer whales and were once much maligned as the wolves of the deep. However, these highly intelligent marine mammals are actually the largest members of the porpoise family. While orcas can be found in every ocean, one of their highest concentrations is in the waters stretching north from Puget Sound along the coast of British Columbia. Consequently, this has become one of the most studied and most publicized orca populations in the world.

Orcas are among the most family-oriented creatures on earth, and related whales often live together their entire lives, sometimes with three generations present at the same time (orcas have a life span of up to 80 years, with females commonly living 20 to 30 years longer than males). Family groups frequently band together with other closely related groups into extended families known as pods. A community of orcas consists of several pods, and in this region the community numbers around 100 individuals. There are three distinct populations of orcas living in the waters off Vancouver Island, British Columbia. They are referred to as the northern and southern resident communities and the transient community. It's the southern resident community that whale-watchers in the San Juan Islands are most likely to encounter.

As predators, orcas do live up to the name "killer whale" and have been known to attack whales much larger than themselves. Some orcas off the coast of Argentina even swim up onto the shore, beaching themselves to attack resting sea lions, and then thrash and twist their way back into the water. But not all orcas feed on other marine mammals. Of the three communities frequenting the waters near Vancouver Island, only the transients feed on mammals. The two resident communities feed primarily on salmon, which are abundant in these waters, especially off the west side of San Juan Island during the summer.

In about 3 miles, you'll come to **San Juan Vineyards ★**, 3136 Roche Harbor Rd. (✆ **360/378-9463;** www.sanjuanvineyards.com), which makes wines both from grapes grown off the island and from its own estate-grown Siegerrebe and Madeleine Angevine grapes. The tasting room is housed in an old schoolhouse built in 1896. It's open daily from 11am to 5pm in summer (call for hours in other months).

A little farther north is **Roche Harbor,** once the site of large limestone quarries that supplied lime to much of the West Coast. Some of the quarries' old structures are still visible, but amid the abandoned quarry sites stands the historic **Hotel de Haro,** a simple whitewashed wooden building with verandas across its two floors. Stop to admire the old-fashioned marina and colorful gardens, and have a drink or a meal on the deck of the hotel's lounge. In an old pasture on the edge of the resort property, you'll find the **IMA Sculpture Park** at Roche Harbor (✆ **360/370-5050;** www.sjima.org), which includes more than 100 works of art set in grassy fields and along the shores of a small pond. Admission to the sculpture park is a suggested $5 donation. Back in the woods near the resort is an unusual **mausoleum,** which was erected by the founder of the quarries and the Hotel de Haro.

South of Roche Harbor, on West Valley Road, you'll come to the **English Camp** unit of **San Juan Island National Historical Park ★** (✆ **360/378-2240;** www.nps.gov/sajh). This park commemorates the San Juan Island Pig War, one of North America's most unusual and least remembered confrontations. Way back in 1859, San Juan Island nearly became the site of a battle between the British and the Americans. The two countries had not yet agreed upon the border between the United States and Canada when a British pig on San Juan Island

The English Camp dates from the days when the U.S. was still defining its borders.

decided to have dinner in an American garden. Not taking too kindly to this, the owner of the garden shot the pig. The Brits, instead of welcoming this succulent addition to their evening's repast, demanded redress. In less time than it takes to smoke a ham, both sides were calling in reinforcements. Luckily, this pigheadedness was defused, and a more serious confrontation was avoided.

The English Camp unit of the historical park is set on picturesque Garrison Bay, and with its huge old shade trees, wide lawns, and white wooden buildings, it's the epitome of British civility. There's even a formal garden surrounded by a white picket fence. You can look inside the reconstructed buildings and imagine the days when this was one of the most far-flung corners of the British Empire. If you're full of energy, hike the 1.25-mile trail to the top of 650-foot **Mount Young** for a beautiful panorama of the island. An easier 1-mile hike hugs the shoreline out to the end of **Bell Point.** The grounds are open daily from dawn to 11pm, and the visitor center is open from early June through early September daily from 9am to 5pm. Throughout the summer, various living-history programs are held here on weekends.

South of English Camp, watch for the Mitchell Bay Road turnoff. This connects to the Westside Road, which leads down the island's west coast. Along this road, you'll find **San Juan County Park,** a great spot for a picnic. A little farther south is **Lime Kiln Point State Park ★★**, 1567 Westside Rd. (✆ **360/902-8844;** www.parks.wa.gov), the country's first whale-watching park and a great place to spot these gentle giants in summer. This latter park is open daily from 8am to dusk. Flanking the state park are Deadman Bay Nature Preserve and Lime Kiln Nature Preserve, two properties acquired for public use by the San Juan County Land Bank. Together the state park and the two preserves have more than 3 miles of hiking trails, making this the best hiking area on the island.

As Westside Road moves inland, it becomes Bailer Hill Road. As you cross the island, watch for the picture-perfect **Shepherd's Croft,** 2575 Bailer Hill Rd. (✆ **360/378-6372**), a sheep farm set behind a white picket fence. A small store here sells sheepskins, yarn, baby sweaters, and a variety of other products. Tours of the farm can be arranged. From here, take a left onto Wold Road, and you will come to **Pelindaba Lavender Farms,** 33 Hawthorne Lane (✆ **866/819-1911;** www.pelindabalavender.com). The farm has roughly 20 acres of lavender plants, including a cutting field where visitors can cut their own lavender stems. May through October, the farm's gift shop is open daily from 9:30am to 5:30pm; it's closed the rest of the year. The gift shop is packed with lavender-scented products, as is **Pelindaba Lavender Friday Harbor,** Friday Harbor Center shopping plaza, 150 First St., in downtown Friday Harbor. This shop is open Wednesday to Sunday from 9:30am to 5pm. The farm holds its San Juan Island Lavender Festival every year in mid-July.

At the far south end of the island is the wind-swept promontory on which **American Camp** stood during the Pig War. Here you'll find two reconstructed buildings and a visitor center (early June to Sept daily 8:30am–5pm; Oct to early June Wed–Sun 8:30am–4:30pm); before American Camp was built here, this was the site of a Hudson's Bay Company farm. The meadows sweeping down to the sea were once grazed by sheep and cattle, but today you'll see only rabbits browsing amid the high grasses and wildflowers (and the occasional red fox stalking the rabbits). Hiking trails here lead along the bluffs and down to the sea. My favorites are the **Mount Finlayson Trail,** which leads to the top of a grassy hill, and the **Lagoon Trail,** which passes through a dark forest of Douglas fir to

Watching the sun set over Roche Harbor is the perfect way to end a day.

Jackle's Lagoon, a great spot for bird-watching. Keep your eyes peeled for bald eagles, which are relatively plentiful around here. If you'd just like to picnic at a pleasant and secluded beach, head to the park's **Fourth of July Beach.**

Continuing past American Camp will bring you to Cattle Point, site of a lighthouse and the **Cattle Point Interpretive Area,** one of the best picnic spots on the island. In the 1920s, the Interpretive Area served as a Navy Radio Compass Station that helped ships navigate the nearby waters. Today there are rock outcrops, two tiny beaches, great views of Lopez Island, interpretive signs, and a few picnic tables. Cattle Point is also a good destination for a bike ride from Friday Harbor.

SPORTS & OUTDOOR PURSUITS

BICYCLING ★ Winding country roads are ideal for leisurely trips. You can rent a bike in Friday Harbor from **Island Bicycles,** 380 Argyle Ave. (✆ **360/378-4941;** www.islandbicycles.com), which charges $9.50 to $19 per hour (2-hr. minimum) or $38 to $76 per day.

HIKING In addition to the hiking trails at English Camp and American Camp, and adjacent to Lime Kiln Point State Park, you'll find a network of almost 20 miles of trails just outside Roche Harbor, on the north end of the island. You can find out more about all the island trails at the website of the **San Juan Island Trails Committee** (www.sanjuanislandtrails.org), which also has printable trail maps. The trails near Roche Harbor link up with trails in the English Camp unit of San Juan Island National Historical Park.

SEA KAYAKING ★★ If you're staying up at the north end of the island, you can take a kayak tour out of Roche Harbor with **San Juan Outfitters** (✆ **866/810-1483** or 360/378-1962; www.sanjuanoutfitters.com). This company operates 3-hour ($75), 5-hour ($89), and multiday ($379–$979) tours, and also does family-oriented trips that stick to calm waters. **Crystal Seas Kayaking** (✆ **877/732-7877** or 360/378-4223; www.crystalseas.com) also does everything from 3-hour tours ($79) and sunset tours ($79) to all-day tours ($99) and multiday trips. Three- and 4-day trips are offered by **San Juan Kayak Expeditions** (✆ **360/378-4436;** www.sanjuankayak.com), which charges $520 and $620, respectively, for its outings. You can also rent unusual pedal kayaks ($25 to $40 per hour) and electric boats ($75 to $80 per hour) in Friday Harbor from **Friday Harbor Marine Center,** 4 Front St. (✆ **360/378-6202;** www.sjimarine.com).

Thar She Blows!

While summer visitors to San Juan have a plethora of ways to go whale-watching, as far as I'm concerned, the best way to search for orcas is from a sea kayak, and the best kayaking company for such an outing is Outdoor Odysseys (✆ 800/647-4621, 360/378-3533 in summer, or 206/361-0717 in winter; www.outdoorodysseys.com), which has been operating in the San Juans for 25 years. This company's trips start from San Juan County Park and head out through the local orca pods' favorite feeding grounds near Lime Kiln Point State Park. In the summer, you stand a good chance of seeing orcas, and any time of year, you're likely to see harbor seals and bald eagles. Day tours, offered late May through October, cost $96 and include lunch.

WHALE-WATCHING ★★ When it's time to spot some whales, you have three choices. You can take a whale-watching cruise, go out in a sea kayak, or head over to **Lime Kiln Point State Park ★★**, where a short trail leads down to a rocky coastline from which orca whales, minke whales, Dall's porpoises, and sea lions can sometimes be seen. The best months to see orcas are June through September, but it's possible to see them throughout the year.

In the summer, 3- to 4-hour whale-watching cruises from Friday Harbor are offered by **San Juan Safaris** (✆ **800/450-6858** or 360/378-1323; www.sanjuansafaris.com), which charges $75 for adults and $49 for children 12 and under. Similar cruises are offered by **San Juan Excursions** (✆ **800/809-4253** or 360/378-6636; www.watchwhales.com), which also operates out of Friday Harbor. Cruises are $79 for adults and $52 for children 2 to 12. Up at the north end of the island, contact **San Juan Outfitters** (see above), which operates out of Roche Harbor and charges $75 for adults and $49 for children 2 to 12.

For a speedier and more personalized whale-watching excursion, book a tour with **Maya's Westside Charters** (✆ **360/378-7996;** www.mayaswhalewatch.biz), which operates one of the fastest whale-watching boats in the islands and usually takes out no more than six people at a time. A 3-hour tour costs $75.

WHERE TO STAY

Friday Harbor House ★★ With its contemporary yet distinctly Northwest architecture, this luxurious little boutique hotel brings urban sophistication to Friday Harbor. From the hotel's bluff-top location, you have excellent views of the ferry landing, the Friday Harbor marina, and, in the distance, Orcas Island. Guest rooms have gas fireplaces and oversize whirlpool tubs, making this place a great choice for a romantic getaway. In some rooms, you can relax in your tub and gaze at both the view out the window and the fire in the fireplace. Many units have small balconies. Rooms and suites here are some of the best in the San Juan Islands, and if you enjoy contemporary styling, you'll love this place.

130 West St. (P.O. Box 1385), Friday Harbor, WA 98250. www.fridayharborhouse.com. ✆ **866/722-7356** or 360/378-8455. Fax 360/378-8453. 23 units. Memorial Day weekend to Sept $215–$325 double, $360 suite; Oct to Memorial Day weekend $145–$215 double, $280 suite. Lower midweek rates in winter. Rates include continental breakfast. Children 15 and under stay free in parent's room. AE, DC, DISC, MC, V. Pets accepted ($50 fee). **Amenities:** Restaurant, lounge; concierge; spa treatment room. *In room:* A/C, TV, fridge, hair dryer, MP3 docking station, free Wi-Fi.

Juniper Lane Guest House ★ This cedar-shingled house, with its colorful trim, sits on the outskirts of Friday Harbor and has views of pastures just over the back fence. Constructed primarily from salvaged wood, this eco-friendly guesthouse is a labor of love for owner Juniper Maas, who patterned her lodging after places she's visited in her world travels. The interior is a bold blend of burnished wood and bright colors, with eclectic artwork on display throughout. Some guest rooms have shared bathrooms, while others have private bathrooms. My personal favorite is the Regal room, with its claw-foot tub. Although breakfast is not included in the rates, guests have use of the kitchen. Young travelers, and the young at heart, should like this place as much as I do.

1312 Beaverton Valley Rd., Friday Harbor, WA 98250. www.juniperlaneguesthouse.com. ✆ **888/397-2597** or 360/378-7761. 6 units. $65–$85 double with shared bathroom; $89–$135 double with private bathroom; $100–$185 family room; $150–$199 cabin. Children 7 and under allowed only in cabin. MC, V. *In room:* Hair dryer, no phone, free Wi-Fi.

Olympic Lights Bed & Breakfast ★★ At San Juan's dry southwestern tip, the Olympic Lights is a Victorian farmhouse surrounded by wind-swept meadows, and if it weren't for the sight of Puget Sound out the window, you could easily mistake the setting for the prairies of the Midwest. There are colorful flower gardens, an old barn, even some hens to lay the eggs for your breakfast. The ocean breezes, nearby beach, and friendliness of innkeepers Christian and Lea Andrade lend a special feel to this American classic. My favorite room here is the Ra Room, which is named for the Egyptian sun god and features a big bay window. The view is enough to soothe the most stressed-out soul.

146 Starlight Way, Friday Harbor, WA 98250. www.olympiclights.com. ✆ **888/211-6195** or 360/378-3186. Fax 360/378-2097. 4 units. Mid-May to mid-Oct $155–$165 double; mid-Oct to mid-May $105 double. Rates include full breakfast. 2-night minimum July–Sept. No credit cards. *In room:* Hair dryer, no phone.

Roche Harbor ★★ ☺ At the north end of San Juan, Roche Harbor is steeped in island history and makes a fascinating getaway. The centerpiece of this resort is the historic Hotel de Haro, which was built in 1886 and overlooks the resort's marina and a gorgeous formal garden. Because the old hotel has not been renovated in recent years, its rooms are the most basic here. To fully appreciate Roche Harbor's setting, you should stay in a suite (the Quarryman Hall suites are among the finest rooms on the island), a Company Town cottage, or one of the carriage houses or cottages on the green. The condominiums, although dated, are good bets for families. The waterfront dining room has a view of the marina, and the deck makes a great spot for a sunset cocktail. In addition to the amenities listed below, there are moped rentals, whale-watching cruises, and sea-kayak tours.

248 Reuben Memorial Dr. (P.O. Box 4001), Roche Harbor, WA 98250. www.rocheharbor.com. ✆ **800/451-8910** or 360/378-2155. Fax 360/378-6809. 78 units, 16 with shared bathroom. Summer $109 double with shared bathroom, $249–$449 suite, $269–$379 condo, $319–$799 cottage or town house; other months $79 double with shared bathroom, $149–$259 suite, $179–$279 condo, $179–$599 cottage or town house. Children stay free in parents' room.AE, MC, V. **Amenities:** 3 restaurants, lounge; outdoor pool; full-service spa; 2 tennis courts. *In room:* Hair dryer.

WHERE TO EAT

In addition to the restaurants listed below, Friday Harbor has several other places where you can get a quick, simple meal. About a block from the top of the ferry lanes is **The Market Chef,** 225 A St. (✆ **360/378-4546**), a combination espresso bar and gourmet take-out restaurant that also bakes outrageously good chocolate chip cookies. This place is open Monday through Friday from 10am to 4pm. If you're staying someplace with a kitchen and want fresh seafood for dinner, stop by **Friday Harbor Seafood** (✆ **360/378-5779**), on the main dock in the Friday Harbor marina. This seafood market also sells smoked fish (including succulent smoked oysters), which makes great picnic fare. For breakfast pastries, check out **Café Demeter,** 80 Nichols St. (✆ **360/370-5443**), in downtown Friday Harbor. If you're craving pizza or want some bread for a picnic, search out **Bakery San Juan,** 775 Mullis St. (✆ **360/378-5810;** www.bakerysanjuan.com), which is in an industrial park near the Friday Harbor airport. For good espresso, head to **Roy's Drive-Thru Espresso,** 25 Nichols St. (✆ **360/378-8822**).

If you're near the north end of the island at lunchtime or cocktail hour, you've got a couple of good options at the Roche Harbor resort. For cocktails overlooking the marina, don't miss the **Madrona Bar and Grill** (✆ **360/378-5757;** www.rocheharbor.com), which, of course, is popular with the boating crowd. The Madrona is famous among boaters for its Fluffy Duck cocktail, which is made with vodka, rum, orange juice, and cream. The Madrona's deck is the perfect place from which to watch the striking of the colors ceremony. For breakfast, lunch, or a light dinner, head to the **Lime Kiln Cafe** (✆ **360/378-5757;** www.rocheharbor.com), on the dock at Roche Harbor. This lively little cafe serves good chowder and fish and chips. Big windows let you gaze out at the boats in the marina. If you're an early riser, you can also drop by for a hearty breakfast or some fresh cinnamon-and-sugar donuts.

Backdoor Kitchen ★ INTERNATIONAL This is the sort of gem that travelers dream of

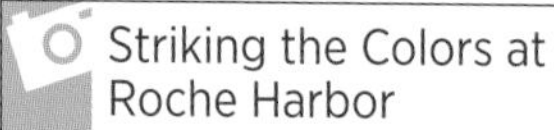

Striking the Colors at Roche Harbor

As the summer sun sets over the San Juans, strains of the "Colonel Bogey March" drift over the boats docked at the Roche Harbor marina. The music signals the nightly lowering of the four flags that fly over the marina. With plenty of pomp and circumstance, Roche Harbor employees lower the flags of Washington State, the United States, Canada, and Great Britain. Appropriate music accompanies the lowering of each flag, and a cannon is fired as the U.S. flag is lowered. There's no better way to end a summer day on San Juan Island.

discovering. Hidden at the back of a warehouse-like building in Friday Harbor, the Backdoor Kitchen is a back-alley find serving some of the best food in the islands. The clientele seems to be primarily locals, many of whom come to sip creative cocktails and hang out in the restaurant's little bar. The menu ranges all over the globe for inspiration and changes seasonally. I've had a delicious and unusual spiced-duck cake as an appetizer here, and there are also well-prepared salads and seafood dishes from which to choose. Entrees are as diverse as pan-seared scallops with ginger-sake beurre blanc, and a classic Mediterranean lamb sirloin. Don't miss this place.

400B A St. ✆ **360/378-9540.** www.backdoorkitchen.com. Reservations recommended. Main courses $24–$34. MC, V. Summer Wed–Mon 5–9 or 9:30pm; other months Wed–Sat 5–8:30 or 9pm.

Coho Restaurant ★★ NORTHWEST Coho, in a little Craftsman bungalow a block from the ferry lanes, serves the best food in Friday Harbor. Small and sophisticated, this restaurant features a short menu that changes with the season. The hazelnut-encrusted lavender chicken I once had here ranked right up there with some of the best chicken I've ever had. The owners, Anna Maria de Freitas and David Pass, also own the nearby Tucker House and Harrison House B&Bs. Coho gets much of its produce locally and participates in the Island's Certified Local Program. Be sure to ask about off-season specials.

120 Nichols St. ✆ **360/378-6330.** www.cohorestaurant.com. Reservations recommended. Main courses $25–$30. AE, DISC, MC, V. Mid-June–Sept Mon–Sat 5–9pm; call for days and hours in other months.

Duck Soup Inn ★★ NORTHWEST/INTERNATIONAL This restaurant, 4½ miles north of Friday Harbor, perfectly sums up the San Juan Islands experience. It's rustic and casual, set in tranquil rural surroundings beside a small pond, and yet it serves superb multicourse dinners. Inside the quintessentially Northwest building, you'll find lots of exposed wood and a fieldstone fireplace. The menu changes frequently, depending on the availability of fresh produce, but it's always very creative (Chef Gretchen Allison has a penchant for the flavors of Asia and the Mediterranean). On the menu, you'll often find duck of some sort, perhaps duck leg confit or grilled duck breast with cherry sauce. Just keep in mind that it is way too easy to fill up on the delicious fresh-baked bread.

50 Duck Soup Lane. ✆ **360/378-4878.** www.ducksoupinn.com. Reservations highly recommended. Main courses $17–$35. MC, V. July to mid-Sept Tues–Sun 5–10pm; call for days and hours in other months. Closed Nov–Mar.

McMillin's Dining Room ★ AMERICAN Located in the 1886 home of John McMillin, the founder of Roche Harbor, this waterfront restaurant at the north end of the island is absolutely timeless. The menu emphasizes local ingredients as much as possible. In season, you can have local spot prawns served a number of different ways or Orcas Island's Judd Cove oysters on the half shell. Lamb on the menu comes from here in the islands, and the crab and salmon are caught by local fishermen. If you aren't a fan of seafood, rest assured there are plenty of steaks, as well as prime rib, on the menu. If possible, schedule your dinner to take in the striking the colors ceremony (see "Striking the Colors at Roche Harbor," above), which takes place at sunset on summer evenings.

248 Reuben Memorial Dr. ✆ **360/378-5757.** www.rocheharbor.com. Reservations recommended. Main courses $18–$38; 3-course dinner $38. AE, MC, V. Apr–Oct daily 5–10pm; Nov–Mar Thurs–Mon 5–10pm.

SAN JUAN ISLANDS: DID YOU know?

- With 375 miles of saltwater shoreline, San Juan County, which encompasses the San Juan Islands, has more shoreline than any other county in the United States.
- Channels between the San Juan Islands range from 600 to 1,000 feet deep.
- Water temperatures off the San Juan Islands range from 45°F (7°C) in winter to 52°F (11°C) in summer.
- Lt. Henry Martyn Robert, author of *Robert's Rules of Order,* was stationed on San Juan Island during the Pig War.
- Puget Sound's first ferry went into operation on January 1, 1889, and car ferries were added in 1915. The first ferry cost 5¢.

The Place Restaurant & Bar ★ NORTHWEST Just to the right as you get off the ferry, and housed in a small wooden building that was once part of a U.S. Coast Guard station, the Place is the island's finest waterfront restaurant. The menu changes regularly and emphasizes local and regional sustainable fish and shellfish. The baked oysters with hazelnut-garlic butter, available both as appetizer and an entree, is one of my favorite dishes here and is prepared with Judd Cove oysters from Orcas Island. If you're not a fan of seafood, The Place is still a good choice. Try the lamb chops or the filet mignon. No matter what you order, I recommend starting your meal with the mushroom sauté, which has been featured in *Bon Appétit* magazine.

1 Spring St. ✆ **360/378-8707.** www.theplacesanjuan.com. Reservations recommended. Main courses $24–$36. DISC, MC, V. Fri–Tues 5–8:30pm.

Orcas Island

Shaped like a horseshoe and named for an 18th-century Mexican viceroy (not for the area's orca whales, as is commonly assumed), Orcas Island has long been a popular summer vacation spot and is the most beautiful of the San Juan Islands. Orcas is a favorite of nature lovers, who come to enjoy the views of green rolling pastures, forested mountains, and fjordlike bays.

GETTING AROUND

For car rentals on Orcas Island, contact **M&W Auto Sales & Rentals** (✆ **800/323-6037** or 360/376-5266; www.sanjuanauto.com), which charges $60 from late May through September and $50 in other months.

From late June to early September, the **Orcas Island Shuttle** (✆ **360/376-7433;** www.orcasislandshuttle.com) can transport you around Orcas Island. The fare is $6 per person between any two points on the island or $12 for a day pass (children 6–12 are half price). This same company also provides rental cars.

EXPLORING THE ISLAND

Eastsound, the largest town on the island, has several interesting shops and good restaurants. Other villages on Orcas include Deer Harbor, West Sound, and Olga.

Under Sail in the San Juans

The waters surrounding the San Juan Islands are ideal for exploring by boat, and one of my favorite ways to see the San Juans is from the deck of a sailboat. A good option is Emerald Isle Sailing Charters (✆ 866/714-6611 or 360/376-3472; www.emeraldislesailing.com), which offers 6-hour day sails, as well as overnight and multiday sailboat charters. On a sail through the islands, you're likely to see orcas, harbor seals, harbor porpoises, and plenty of bald eagles. A 6-hour tour is $135 per person. Tours lasting 3 to 7 days are also offered.

To learn more about Orcas Island, stop by Eastsound's interesting **Orcas Island Historical Museum,** 181 N. Beach Rd. (✆ **360/376-4849;** www.orcasmuseum.org), which is housed in a collection of six interconnected historic buildings that were moved to the center of Eastsound from locations around the island. Late May through late September, the museum is open Wednesday through Sunday from 11am to 4pm (if funding allows, open Mon also); other months it is open Saturday from 10am to 3pm (also open Sun on holiday weekends). Admission is $5 for adults, $4 for seniors, $3 for students, and children 12 and under are free.

In Eastsound, be sure to stop in at **Darvill's Bookstore,** 296 Main St. (✆ **360/376-2135;** www.darvillsbookstore.com), which specializes in Northwest fiction, history, and guidebooks. Chocoholics won't want to miss **Kathryn Taylor Chocolates,** 109 N. Beach Rd. (✆ **360/376-1030;** www.ktchocolates.com), where you can get hand-dipped chocolates made with local fruits and nuts. If you're a gardener, don't miss the fascinating **Smith & Speed Mercantile,** 294 A St. (✆ **360/376-1006;** www.smithandspeed.com), which sells homestead supplies and tools. You've never seen so many different spades and garden forks in one place.

Several interesting pottery shops are located around the island. A few miles west of Eastsound off Enchanted Forest Road is **Orcas Island Pottery,** 338 Old Pottery Rd. (✆ **360/376-2813;** www.orcasislandpottery.com), the oldest pottery studio in the Northwest. Between Eastsound and Orcas, on Horseshoe Highway, is **Crow Valley Pottery,** 2274 Orcas Rd. (✆ **877/512-8184** or 360/376-4260; www.crowvalley.com), housed in an 1866 log cabin. There's also a second Crow Valley Pottery shop in Eastsound at 296 Main St. And on the east side of the island in the community of Olga, you'll find **Orcas Island Artworks,** 11 Point Lawrence Rd. (✆ **360/376-4408;** www.orcasartworks.com), which is full of beautiful works by island artists. Just a couple of blocks from this gallery, you'll find the much smaller **Olga Pottery,** 6928 Olga Rd. (✆ **360/376-4648;** www.olgapottery.com), which showcases the work of potter Jerry Weatherman.

SPORTS, OUTDOOR PURSUITS & TOURS

Moran State Park ★★ (✆ **360/902-8844;** www.parks.wa.gov) covers 5,252 acres of the island. This is the largest park in the San Juans and the main destination for most island visitors. If the weather is clear, you'll enjoy great views from the summit of Mount Constitution, which rises 2,409 feet above Puget Sound. Also within the park are five lakes, 33 miles of hiking trails, and an environmental learning center. Popular park activities include fishing, hiking, boating, mountain biking, and camping (for campsite reservations, contact **Washington**

The views over Puget Sound from Mount Constitution are worth the hike.

State Parks at ✆ **888/226-7688;** www.parks.wa.gov/reservations). The park is off Horseshoe Highway, approximately 13 miles from the ferry landing.

BIKING ★ Although Orcas is considered the most challenging of the San Juan Islands for biking, plenty of cyclists pedal the island's roads. **Dolphin Bay Bicycles** (✆ **360/376-4157** or 360/317-6734; www.rockisland.com/~dolphin), located just to the right as you get off the ferry, has long been my favorite place in the islands to rent a bike. It's so close to the ferry dock that you can come to Orcas without a car, walk up the street to the shop, and hop on a bike. From here you can explore Orcas Island or take a free ferry to Lopez Island or Shaw Island. Bikes rent for $30 per day, $70 for 3 days, and $100 per week.

If you're already on the island and staying up near Eastsound, try **Wildlife Cycles,** 350 N. Beach Rd., Eastsound (✆ **360/376-4708;** www.wildlifecycles.com), where bikes rent for $30 to $45 per day.

HIKING Moran State Park ★★, with its 33 miles of trails, is the best known and most popular place on Orcas to hike. The park offers hikes ranging from short, easy strolls alongside lakes to

Winging It on Orcas

While the view from the top of Mount Constitution, in Moran State Park, is pretty impressive, you can get an even more memorable view of Orcas and the rest of the San Juan Islands from the cockpit of a Travel Air biplane operated by Magic Air Tours (✆ 800/376-1929 or 360/376-2733; www.magicair.com). Plane rides for one person cost $249, and rides for two people cost $299. Flights are offered April through October and occasionally in other months.

You get the best view of the Orcas Island coast (and some exercise) in a sea kayak.

strenuous, all-day outings. However, the very best hiking on the island is in the 1,576-acre **Turtleback Mountain Preserve** (✆ **360/378-4402;** www.sjclandbank.org/turtle_back.html), which is on the west side of the island. A trail runs north and south through the preserve, and the hike up from the southern trail head is the best hike in the entire Puget Sound region. In 1 hour's strenuous uphill walking, you'll climb nearly 1,000 feet and reach a rocky knoll from which you can look east to the pastures and hedgerows of Crow Valley, and west across West Sound to dozens of islands scattered across shimmering waters. In the distance rise the Olympic Mountains and the hazy blue ridges of Canada's Vancouver Island. Come in June and you'll likely see wildflowers on Turtleback Mountain's open slopes. To reach the southern trail head, drive 1¼ miles west from the community of West Sound on Deer Harbor Road and turn right on Wild Rose Lane. The parking area is about 300 feet up this gravel road.

Another good hiking spot can be found south of the community of Olga, on the east arm of the island, where you'll find a .5-mile trail through **Obstruction Pass State Park ★★**. This trail leads to a quiet little cove that has a few walk-in/paddle-in campsites. The park is at the end of Trailhead Road, which is off Obstruction Pass Road.

You can learn about the natural history and plant life of the islands on guided hikes offered by **Gnats Nature Hikes** (✆ **360/376-6629;** www.orcasislandhikes.com). Half-day hikes ($30) head out on the trails of Moran State Park.

SEA KAYAKING ★★ The best way to see the Orcas Island coast is by sea kayak. My favorite local kayaking company is **Shearwater Adventures** (✆ **360/376-4699;** www.shearwaterkayaks.com), which offers guided

3-hour tours ($69). These tours go out from several locations around the island, but I think those departing from Deer Harbor are the most scenic. There are also all-day tours ($159) around Sucia Island, which is off Orcas's north shore.

If you're on the island without a car, it's possible to go out from right at the ferry landing with **Orcas Outdoors** (✆ **360/376-4611**; www.orcasoutdoors.com), which offers guided sea-kayak tours lasting from 1 to 3 hours ($30–$60). Multiday tours can also be arranged.

Two-hour paddle tours ($30) are offered morning and evening by the owners of **The Cabin on Spring Bay** (✆ **360/376-5531**; www.springbayinn.com), which is on the east side of the island near the village of Olga. These trips are in an area where bald eagles nest in summer.

WHALE-WATCHING ★★★ If you want to see some of the orca whales for which the San Juans are famous, you can take a whale-watching excursion with **Deer Harbor Charters** (✆ **800/544-5758** or 360/376-5989; www.deerharborcharters.com), which operates out of both Deer Harbor and Rosario Resort and charges $59 to $72 for adults and $39 to $45 for children; or with **Orcas Island Eclipse Charters** (✆ **360/376-6566**; www.orcasislandwhales.com), which operates out of the Orcas Island ferry dock and charges $72 for adults and $45 for children.

WHERE TO STAY

Inn at Ship Bay ★★ Set on a high bluff just outside the village of Eastsound, this inn boasts a tranquil setting and very comfortable rooms. There are pillow-top king beds, and most rooms have gas Franklin stoves. Together these features make it easy to spend way too much of your visit just cozying up in the rooms here. If you sit back in the Adirondack chairs on your balcony and gaze out over the water, you may never leave. Although guest rooms are in modern buildings that have been designed to look old, the inn's centerpiece is an 1869 home that serves as the restaurant.

326 Olga Rd., Orcas Island, WA 98245. www.innatshipbay.com. ✆ **877/276-7296** or 360/376-5886. 11 units. Summer $175–$195 double, $275–$295 suite; fall–spring lower rates. Rates include continental breakfast in summer. Additional guest/child in room $25 plus tax.MC, V. **Amenities:** Restaurant, lounge. *In room:* TV/DVD, fridge, hair dryer, free Wi-Fi.

The Inn on Orcas Island ★★★ Looking as if it were transplanted directly from Cape Cod or Martha's Vineyard, this inn blends traditional styling with contemporary lines to create a classically inspired beauty. Situated on a meadow overlooking a small bay just off Deer Harbor, this elegant inn has luxurious rooms in the main house plus a cottage and a more casually decorated carriage house with its own kitchen. Some rooms have balconies; suites have jetted tubs. All accommodations feature water views, impeccable decor, and the plushest beds in the San Juans. Innkeepers Jeremy Trumble and John Gibbs once owned a frame shop and spent years collecting and framing all the art that now hangs in the inn. A sunroom in the main house is a wonderful place to while away the morning. Breakfasts are lavish affairs that will leave you full until dinner.

114 Channel Rd. (P.O. Box 309), Deer Harbor, WA 98243. www.theinnonorcasisland.com. ✆ **888/886-1661** or 360/376-5227. Fax 360/376-5228. 8 units. July–Aug $205 double, $235–$305 suite, cottage, or carriage house; June and Sept $185 double, $215–$285 suite, cottage, or

carriage house; Oct–May $145 double, $185–$245 suite, cottage, or carriage house. Rates include full breakfast. 2-night minimum May–Oct, holidays, and all weekends. AE, MC, V. No children 15 or under. **Amenities:** Bikes. *In room:* Fridge, hair dryer, free Wi-Fi.

Turtleback Farm Inn ★★ Nowhere on Orcas will you find a more pastoral setting than this bright-green restored farmhouse overlooking 80 acres of farmland at the foot of Turtleback Mountain. Simply furnished with antiques, the guest rooms range from cozy to spacious, and each has its own special view. My favorite unit in the main house is the Meadow View Room, which has a private deck and a claw-foot tub. The four rooms in the Orchard House are among the biggest and most luxurious on the island (with gas fireplaces, claw-foot tubs, balconies, wood floors, and fridges). Days start with a big farm breakfast served at valley-view tables that are set with bone china, silver, and linen—or, if you're staying in the Orchard House, with a breakfast delivered to your room. Finish your day with a sherry by the fire.

1981 Crow Valley Rd., Eastsound, WA 98245. www.turtlebackinn.com. ✆ **800/376-4914** or 360/376-4914. Fax 360/376-5329. 11 units. Main house Memorial Day weekend to Sept $115–$195 double; Orchard House June–Sept $260 double; lower rates other months. Rates include full breakfast. 2-night minimum June–Sept, weekends, and holidays. Children 5 and under stay free in parent's room in Orchard House. DISC, MC, V. Pets accepted. Children 8 and over welcome in farmhouse. **Amenities:** Concierge; access to nearby health club. *In room:* CD player, free Wi-Fi.

WHERE TO EAT

Housed in a little cottage in Eastsound, **The Kitchen,** 249 Prune Alley (✆ **360/376-6958;** www.thekitchenorcas.com), is my favorite spot on the island for healthy, light meals. This place isn't strictly vegetarian, but it does lots of great Asian-inspired wraps and rice-and-noodle dishes. In summer, the Kitchen is open Monday through Saturday from 11am to 7pm; hours are shorter in other months. If you just need some wine for a picnic, head to the **Wine Shop at Country Corners,** 837 Crescent Beach Dr. (✆ **360/376-6907**), which is behind the gas station just east of Eastsound. When you need something sweet, grab a cookie at **Teezer's Cookies,** North Beach Road and A Street (✆ **360/376-2913;** www.teezerscookies.com), or, if it's hot, some gelato across the street at **Enzo's,** 365 North Beach Rd. (✆ **360/376-3732**), which also serves sandwiches, crepes, and espresso. For a sunset cocktail, it's hard to beat the view from the **Madrona Bar and Grill,** 310 Main St. (✆ **360/376-7171**).

You really shouldn't leave the island without having a picnic somewhere. My favorite spots include Eastsound Waterfront Park (right on the water in the village of Eastsound), Deer Harbor Waterfront Park (just before the marina in the village of Deer Harbor), and, if you don't mind a 30-minute uphill hike to your picnic spot, Turtleback Mountain Preserve.

Allium ★★ NEW AMERICAN Both chef/owner Lisa Nakamura and the pastry chef here at Allium cooked at Woodinville's celebrated Herbfarm restaurant before moving to Orcas to take over this second-story Eastsound restaurant space. The menu is driven by fresh, seasonal flavors and incorporates a wide range of local and regional ingredients. You might even get to start your meal with clam chowder that's made with saffron grown in nearby Sequim, on the Olympic Peninsula. The daily gnocchi, drizzled with white truffle oil, is always a good bet, and caramelized scallops with braised fennel and foie gras butter was a huge hit at a recent meal. This is the perfect spot for a sunset dinner. The beautiful view down the sound is a big part of what makes this place special, and if the weather is pleasant, the deck is the place to be.

310 Main St., Eastsound. ✆ **360/376-4904.** www.alliumonorcas.com. Reservations highly recommended. Main courses $21–$38. AE, MC, V. Thurs–Fri 5–8pm; Sat–Sun 10am–2pm and 5–8pm; Mon 5–8pm (longer hours in summer).

Cafe Olga ★ INTERNATIONAL Housed in an old strawberry-packing plant that dates from the days when these islands were known for their fruit, Cafe Olga is a good spot for reasonably priced breakfasts and lunches. Everything is homemade, using fresh local produce whenever possible. The scalibut cakes, made with scallops and halibut and served with Thai dipping sauce, are a local favorite. The blackberry pie is a special treat, especially when accompanied by Lopez Island Creamery ice cream. This building also houses Orcas Island Artworks, a gallery representing more than 40 Orcas Island artists.

11 Point Lawrence Rd., Olga. ✆ **360/376-5098.** Main courses $12–$20. MC, V. Late May or early June to mid-Sept daily 8am–4pm; shorter hours other months. Closed Jan to mid-Feb.

Inn at Ship Bay ★★ NORTHWEST About midway between Eastsound and the turnoff for Rosario Resort, you'll spot the Inn at Ship Bay, a cluster of farmhouse-style buildings set behind an old orchard in a field high above the water. Chef Geddes Martin, who worked at Rosario for many years, runs the kitchen here and relies heavily on fresh local seafood. There are always local oysters and mussels, and these are usually quite good, but it's the restaurant's scallops that are a local favorite. Have these with one of the excellent salads (and maybe a starter of oysters on the half shell) for the perfect dinner. Try to get a table near a window so you can enjoy the views of the water.

326 Olga Rd., Orcas Island. ✆ **877/276-7296** or 360/376-5886. www.innatshipbay.com. Reservations recommended. Main courses $20–$30. MC, V. Tues–Sat 5:30–9 or 9:30pm. Closed late Nov to mid-Feb.

Rose's ★★ NEW AMERICAN This is one of my favorite island eateries. With its Tuscan-influenced decor, big patio, and stone pizza oven, Rose's is both a casual and a stylish place for lunch. The menu features creative sandwiches, flavorful soups, designer pizzas, and a few more substantial entree specials. Be sure to save room for one of the great desserts they make. The restaurant also has an associated gourmet-food shop where you can pick up imported cheeses, baked goods, wine, and other foodstuffs.

382 Prune Alley, Eastsound. ✆ **360/376-4292.** Reservations accepted only for parties of 6 or more. Main dishes $9–$20. MC, V. Mon–Sat 10am–4pm. Closed Jan.

Lopez Island

Of the three islands with accommodations, Lopez is the least developed, and although it is less spectacular than Orcas or San Juan, it is flatter, which makes it popular with bicyclists who tend to prefer easy grades to stunning panoramas. Lopez maintains more of its agricultural roots than either Orcas or San Juan, and likewise has fewer activities for tourists. If you just want to get away from it all and hole up with a good book for a few days, this may be the place for you.

EXPLORING THE ISLAND

Lopez Village is the closest this island has to a town, and it's where you'll find almost all the island's restaurants and shops. Be sure to check out the **Chimera Gallery,** Lopez Village Plaza, Lopez Road (✆ **360/468-3265;** www.chimeragallery.com), which is full of art by Lopez Island artists.

At the **Lopez Island Historical Museum,** Weeks Road (✆ **360/468-2049;** www.lopezmuseum.org), in Lopez Village, you can learn about the island's history and pick up a map of its historic buildings. The museum is open May through September, Wednesday to Sunday from noon to 4pm.

Lopez Island Vineyards ★ (✆ **360/468-3644;** www.lopezislandvineyards.com), was the first winery to make wine from grapes grown here in the San Juans. Both its Siegerrebe and Madeleine Angevine are from local grapes, and its organic fruit wines are made with local fruit. Lopez Island Vineyards also makes wines from grapes grown in the Yakima Valley. The winery has a tasting room in Lopez Village, at 265 Lopez Rd.; in July and August, the tasting room is open Tuesday to Sunday from noon to 5pm; in May, June, and September, it's open on Friday to Sunday from noon to 5pm; and March to April and October through mid-December, it's open on Saturday from noon to 5pm.

SPORTS & OUTDOOR PURSUITS

Seven county parks, one state park, and numerous preserves provide plenty of access to the woods and water on Lopez Island. The first park off the ferry is **Odlin County Park** (✆ **360/378-8420;** www.sanjuanco.com/parks/lopez.aspx), which has a long beach, picnic tables, and a campground. Athletic fields make this more a community sports center than a natural area.

A more natural setting for a short, easy hike is **Upright Channel State Park,** on Military Road (about a mile north of Lopez Village in the northwest corner of the island). Right in Lopez Village, you can walk out into the marshes at the 22-acre **Weeks Wetland** unit of the **Fisherman Bay Preserves** (✆ **260/378-4402;** www.sjclandbank.org/lopez.html). The trail through the wetlands begins on Weeks Point Way just behind the little shopping complex that houses Holly B's Bakery. There are a few interpretive plaques along the trail.

On the east side of the island, you'll find **Spencer Spit State Park** ★ (✆ **360/902-8844;** www.parks.wa.gov), which has a campground. Here the forest meets the sea on a rocky beach that looks across a narrow channel to Frost Island. You can hike the trails through the forest or explore the beach.

South of Lopez Village on Bay Shore Road is the small **Otis Perkins County Park,** which is between Fisherman Bay and the open water. It has one of the longest beaches on the island. Continuing to the end of this road (it turns to gravel) will bring you to **The Spit,** a unit of the **Fisherman Bay Preserves.** The preserve is at the end of the spit that forms the mouth of Fisherman Bay. This preserve has trails and access to

The Lopez Wave

Lopez Islanders are particularly friendly—they wave to everyone they pass on the road. This usually isn't a big, wide sweep of a beauty-queen wave, but more often than not just finger or two raised from steering wheel. The custom has come to be known as the "Lopez Wave," and to fit in and feel like a local, you should be sure to wave back.

the beach along the sandy spit. It's one of the prettiest and most serene spots on the island; don't miss it.

Down at the south end of Lopez, you'll find the tiny **Shark Reef Sanctuary ★★**, where a short trail leads through the forest to a rocky stretch of coast that is among the prettiest on any of the ferry-accessible islands. Small offshore islands create strong currents that swirl past the rocks here. Seals and the occasional whale can be seen just offshore as well. It's a great spot for a picnic. To reach this natural area, drive south from Lopez Village on Fisherman Bay Road, turn right on Airport Road, and then turn left onto Shark Reef Road.

Also down toward the south end of the island, you'll find the **Watmough Bay Preserve ★★** (✆ **260/378-4402;** www.sjclandbank.org/lopez.html), which protects a beautiful little cove that is a well-guarded local secret. The cove has a 100-yard-long gravel beach and is bordered on one side by cliffs and on the other by forest. The beach is a short, easy walk on a wide path. To reach the trail head parking area, drive Fisherman Bay Road south from Lopez Village, turn right on Center Road and right again on Mud Bay Road, and follow this road through twists and turns to a right onto Aleck Bay Road. When this latter road makes a 90-degree curve to the right, go straight onto a gravel road and quickly fork left onto Watmough Head Road for ¾ mile to a left into the signed Watmough Bay Preserve.

BICYCLING ★★ Because of its size, lack of traffic, numerous parks, and relatively flat terrain, Lopez is a favorite of cyclists. You can rent bikes for $7 to $45 an hour or $30 to $70 a day from **Lopez Bicycle Works,** 2847 Fisherman Bay Rd. (✆ **360/468-2847;** www.lopezbicycleworks.com), at the marina on Fisherman Bay Road south of Lopez Village.

Lopez Island offers such pristine treasuers as Watmough Bay.

SEA KAYAKING ★★ To explore the island's coastline by kayak, contact **Cascadia Kayak Tours,** 135 Lopez Rd. (✆ **360/468-3008;** www.cascadiakayakandbike.com), which offers trips of varying lengths along some of the most picturesque stretches of the Lopez coastline. A half-day trip costs $69, full-day trips are $90, and sunset paddles are $49. Alternatively, May through September, you can rent a kayak from **Lopez Island Sea Kayak** (✆ **360/468-2847;** www.lopezkayaks.com), at the marina on Fisherman Bay Road. Single kayaks rent for $15 to $25 per hour, $30 to $50 per half-day. Double kayaks rent for $25 to $35 per hour, $50 to $70 per half-day.

WHERE TO STAY

Edenwild Inn ★ This modern Victorian country inn, located right in Lopez Village, is a good choice if you've come here to bike or want to use your car as little as possible. Within a block of the inn are all of the island's best restaurants and cafes. Most of the guest rooms are quite large, and most have views of the water. All rooms have interesting antique furnishings, and several have fireplaces. In summer, colorful gardens surround the inn, and guests can breakfast on a large brick patio. The front veranda, overlooking distant Fisherman Bay, is a great place to relax in the afternoon.

132 Lopez Rd. (P.O. Box 271), Lopez Island, WA 98261. www.edenwildinn.com. ✆ **800/606-0662** or 360/468-3238. 8 units. $170–$195 double. Rates include full breakfast. MC, V. No children 11 or under. **Amenities:** Bikes. *In room:* Fridge, hair dryer, no phone, free Wi-Fi.

Lopez Farm Cottages and Tent Camping ★★ Set on 30 acres of pastures, old orchards, and forest between the ferry landing and Lopez Village, these modern cottages are tucked into a grove of cedar trees on the edge of a 2-acre meadow. From the outside, the board-and-batten cottages look like old farm buildings, but inside you'll find a combination of Eddie Bauer and Scandinavian design. There are kitchenettes, plush beds with lots of pillows, and, in the bathrooms of four of the cottages, showers with double shower heads. If showering together isn't romantic enough for you, a hot tub is tucked down a garden path. Also on the property is a deluxe tents-only campground.

555 Fisherman Bay Rd. (P.O. Box 610), Lopez Island, WA 98261. www.lopezfarmcottages.com. ✆ **800/440-3556.** 5 units. July–Aug $180–$215 double; June and Sept $170–$205 double; Oct–May $135–$170 double. Tent sites $45–$85 double. Cottage rates include continental breakfast. DISC, MC, V. No children 13 and under. **Amenities:** Jacuzzi. *In room:* Hair dryer, kitchenette.

MacKaye Harbor Inn ★ This former sea captain's home at the south end of the island was built in 1927 and was the first home on the island to have electric lights. Since that time, this old house has gone through many incarnations and today is a very comfortable B&B with a mix of classic country styling and plenty of creature comforts. The big white farmhouse is set on a pretty little stretch of flat beach, and with kayaks for rent and the calm water of MacKaye Harbor right across the road, this is a good place to give sea kayaking a try. Bikes are also available for guests, and the innkeepers can direct you to good hikes in the area.

949 MacKaye Harbor Rd., Lopez Island, WA 98261. www.mackayeharborinn.com. ✆ **888/314-6140** or 360/468-2253. Fax 360/468-2393. 5 units. July–Aug $175–$235 double; May–June and Sept $155–$215 double; Oct–Apr $135–$165 double. 2-night minimum weekends and holidays. Rates include breakfast. MC, V. No children 10 and under. **Amenities:** Bikes; concierge; watersports equipment/boat rentals. *In room:* CD player, hair dryer, free Wi-Fi.

WHERE TO EAT

When it's time for espresso, head to Lopez Village and drop by **Isabel's Espresso,** 308 Lopez Rd. (✆ **360/468-4114**), a local hangout in the Village House Building on the corner of Lopez Road North, Lopez Road South, and Old Post Road. Across the street, you'll find divinely decadent pastries and other baked goods at **Holly B's Bakery,** Lopez Plaza, Lopez Road South (✆ **360/468-2133;** www.hollybsbakery.com). Note that this bakery is closed from late November to early April.

For fresh-squeezed juices and healthy, light meals, try **Vortex Juice Bar & Café,** 135A Lopez Road (✆ **360/468-4740;** www.vortexjuicebarandcafe.com), in Lopez Village in the Old Homestead. Next door to the juice bar, you can shop for natural foods at **Blossom Grocery,** 135 Lopez Rd. (✆ **360/468-2204;** www.blossomgrocery.com).

Turn up Village Road North, and you'll find **Vita's Wildly Delicious,** 77 Village Rd. (✆ **360/468-4268;** www.vitaswildlydelicious.com), which sells wines and tasty gourmet take-out food from a colorfully painted Victorian house. In summer, this place is open Monday through Friday from 10am to 5pm and Saturday from 10am to 3pm. A little farther along this same street is the **Lopez Island Old-Fashioned Soda Fountain,** 157 Village Rd. (✆ **360/468-4511;** www.lopezislandpharmacy.com), in the Lopez Island Pharmacy.

For local produce (and handicrafts), check out the **Lopez Farmers Market,** which is held on summer Saturday mornings in a park on Village Road across from Vita's and the soda fountain. Down at the south end of the island, you can get snacks and prepared deli sandwiches **Islandale Store,** 3024 Mud Bay Rd. (✆ **360/468-2315**).

Bay Cafe ★★ INTERNATIONAL/NORTHWEST Housed in a classic old waterfront commercial building with a deck that overlooks Fisherman Bay, this cafe serves some of the best food in the state. This is the sort of place where diners animatedly discuss what that other flavor is in the *mole* sauce on the pork tenderloin, and where people walk through the door and exclaim, "I want whatever it is that smells so good." The menu is short and eclectic and emphasizes local ingredients as much as possible, so expect lots of local seafood, islands-raised lamb, and produce from nearby farms. Come with a hearty appetite; the desserts are absolutely to die for. For the quintessential Lopez dinner, accompany your meal with a bottle of wine from Lopez Island Vineyards.

Village Center, 9 Old Post Rd., Ste. C, Lopez Village. ✆ **360/468-3700.** www.bay-cafe.com. Reservations highly recommended. Main courses $14–$26. AE, DISC, MC, V. Summer daily 5:30–8 or 8:30pm; other months Wed–Sun 5:30–8pm.

PORT TOWNSEND: A RESTORED VICTORIAN SEAPORT

Named by English explorer Capt. George Vancouver in 1792, Port Townsend did not attract its first settlers until 1851. However, by the 1880s, the town had become an important shipping port and was expected to grow into one of the most important cities on the West Coast. Port Townsend felt that it was the logical end of the line for the transcontinental railroad that was pushing westward in the 1880s, and based on the certainty of a railroad connection, real estate speculation and development boomed. Merchants and investors erected mercantile palaces along Water Street and elaborate Victorian homes on the bluff above the wharf district. However, the railroad never arrived; Tacoma got the rails, and Port Townsend got the shaft.

With its importance as a shipping port usurped, Port Townsend slipped into quiet obscurity. Progress passed it by, and its elegant homes and commercial buildings were left to slowly fade away. However, in 1976 the waterfront district and bluff-top residential neighborhood were declared a National Historic District, and the town began a slow revival. Today the streets of Port Townsend are once again crowded with people. The waterfront district is filled with boutiques, galleries, and other interesting shops, and several of the Victorian homes atop the bluff have become bed-and-breakfast inns.

Essentials

VISITOR INFORMATION Contact the **Port Townsend Chamber of Commerce Visitor Information Center,** 440 12th St., Port Townsend, WA 98368 (✆ **888/365-6978** or 360/385-2722; www.ptguide.com).

GETTING THERE Port Townsend is on Wash. 20, off U.S. 101 in the northeast corner of the Olympic Peninsula. The Hood Canal Bridge, which connects the Kitsap Peninsula with the Olympic Peninsula and is on the route from Seattle to Port Townsend, sometimes closes due to high winds; if you want to be certain that it's open, call ✆ **511.**

Washington State Ferries (✆ **800/843-3779,** 888/808-7977 in Washington, or 206/464-6400; www.wsdot.wa.gov/ferries) operates a ferry between Port Townsend and Coupeville (on Whidbey Island). The crossing takes 30 minutes and costs $9.35 to $12 for a vehicle and driver, $2.75 per passenger (discounted fares for seniors and youths). This is one of the few ferry routes for which reservations are taken.

From May through October, passenger-boat service between Port Townsend and Friday Harbor (in the San Juan Islands) is offered by **Puget Sound Express** (✆ **360/385-5288;** www.pugetsoundexpress.com), which will also carry bicycles and sea kayaks. One-way fares are $56 for adults and $43 for children; round-trip fares are $89 for adults and $49 for children.

GETTING AROUND Because parking spaces in downtown Port Townsend are hard to come by on weekends and anytime in summer, **Jefferson Transit** (✆ **800/371-0497** or 360/385-4777; www.jeffersontransit.com), the local public bus service, operates a shuttle into downtown Port Townsend from a park-and-ride lot on the south side of town. Jefferson Transit also operates other buses around Port Townsend. The fare is $1.50.

FESTIVALS As a tourist town, Port Townsend schedules quite a few festivals throughout the year. The end of July brings the **Centrum's Jazz Port Townsend** (✆ **360/385-3102;** www.centrum.org). The **Wooden Boat Festival** ★ (✆ **360/385-3628;** www.woodenboat.org), the largest of its kind in the United States, is on the first weekend after Labor Day. During the **Kinetic Sculpture Race** (www.ptkineticrace.org), held the first weekend in October, outrageous human-powered vehicles race on land, on water, and through a mud bog. In September, there's the **Port Townsend Film Festival** (✆ **360/379-1333;** www.ptfilmfest.com). The **Olympic Music**

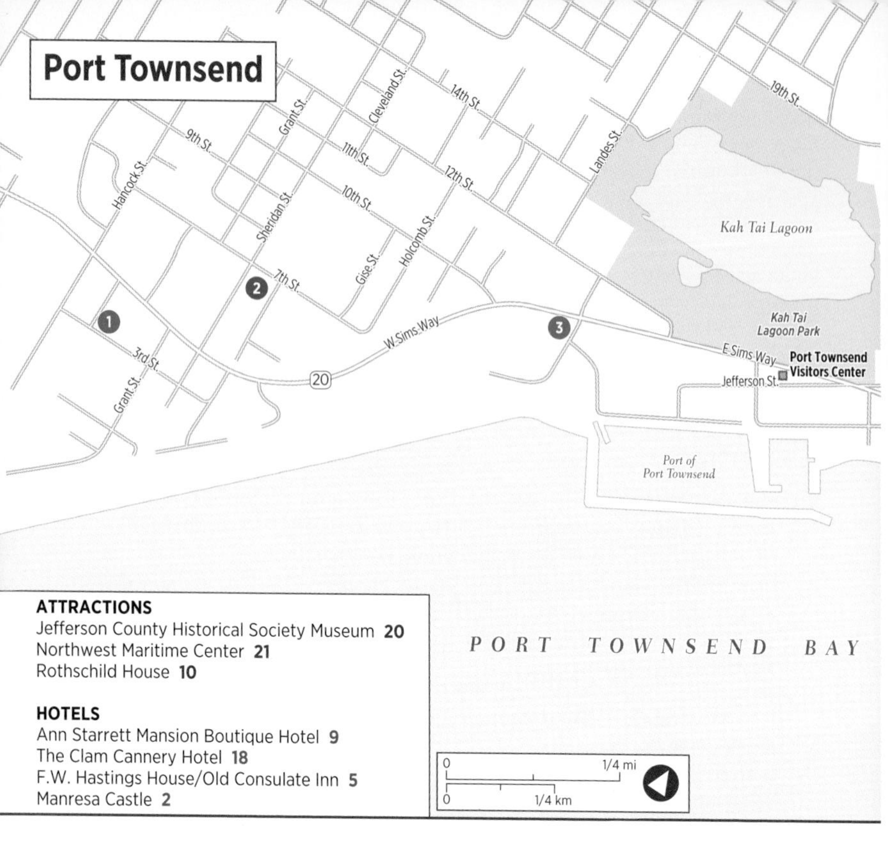

Festival (**✆ 360/732-4800;** www.olympicmusicfestival.org), held nearby in an old barn near the town of Quilcene, is the area's most important music festival. This series of weekend concerts takes place between late June and early September.

Exploring the Town

With its abundance of restored Victorian homes and commercial buildings, Port Townsend's most popular activity is simply walking or driving through the historic districts. The town is divided into the waterfront commercial district and the residential uptown area. This latter neighborhood is atop a bluff that rises precipitously only 2 blocks from the water. Uptown Port Townsend developed in part so that proper Victorian ladies would not have to associate with the riffraff that frequented the waterfront. At the **Port Townsend Visitor Information Center** (p. 255), you can pick up a guide that lists the town's many historic homes and commercial buildings.

Water Street is the town's main commercial district. It is lined for several blocks with restored 100-year-old brick buildings, many of which have ornate facades. Within these buildings are dozens of interesting shops and boutiques, several restaurants, and a handful of hotels and inns. To gain a different perspective on Port Townsend, walk out on **Union Wharf,** at the foot of Taylor Street. At the north end of the waterfront, you'll find Point Hudson Marina, which has

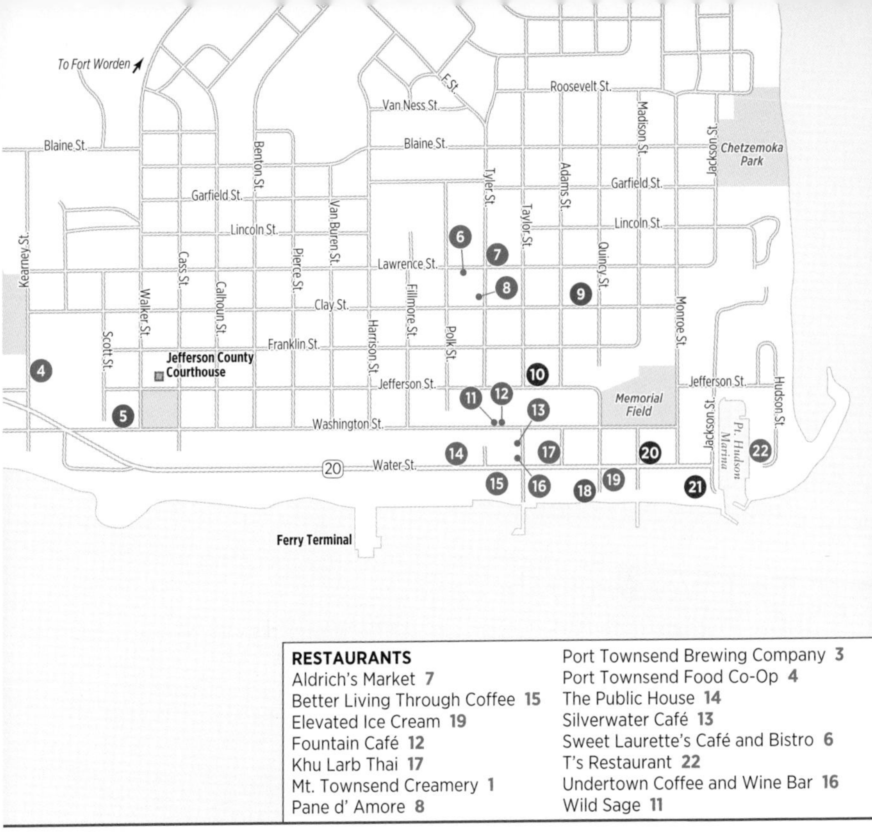

a great view across the sound to Mount Baker and the North Cascades. Here at the marina, you can look around the **Northwest Maritime Center,** 431 Water St. (✆ **360/385-3628;** www.nwmaritime.org), a facility dedicated to wooden boats and preserving Port Townsend's maritime history.

Make one of your first stops in town the **Jefferson County Historical Society Museum,** 540 Water St. (✆ **360/385-1003;** www.jchsmuseum.org), where you can learn about the history of the area. Among the collections here are regional Native American artifacts and antiques from the Victorian era. The museum is open daily from 11am to 4pm. Admission is $4 for adults and $1 for children 3 to 12. June through September, the museum sponsors guided history walks on Saturday and Sunday at 2pm. These tours cost $10 for adults and $5 for children 3 to 12.

The town's noted Victorian homes are in uptown Port Townsend, atop the bluff that rises behind the waterfront's commercial buildings. This is where you'll find stately homes, views, and the city's favorite park. To reach the uptown area, either drive up Washington Street (1 block over from Water St.) or walk up the stairs at the end of Taylor Street, which start behind the Haller Fountain.

At the top of the stairs, you'll see both an 1890 bell tower, which once summoned volunteer firemen, and the **Rothschild House,** at Taylor and Franklin streets (✆ **360/385-1003;** www.jchsmuseum.org). Built in 1868, this Greek Revival house is one of the oldest buildings in town and displays a sober architecture compared to other area homes. The gardens contain a wide variety of roses, peonies, and lilacs. It's open May through September daily from 11am to 4pm. Admission is $4 for adults and $1 for children 3 to 12.

Also here in the uptown neighborhood, at the corner of Garfield and Jackson streets, is **Chetzemoka Park,** established in 1904 and named for a local S'Klallam Indian chief. The park is perched on a bluff overlooking Admiralty Inlet and has access to a pleasant little beach. However, most visitors head straight for the rose garden, arbor, and waterfall garden.

Shopping is just about the most popular activity in Port Townsend's old town, and of the many stores in the historic district, several stand out. **Earthenworks Gallery,** 702 Water St. (✆ **360/385-0328;** www.earthenworksgallery.com), showcases colorful ceramics, glass, jewelry, and other American-made crafts. **Ancestral Spirits Gallery,** 701 Water St. (✆ **360/385-0078;** www.ancestral spirits.com), is a large space with a great selection of Northwest Native American prints, masks, and carvings. The **William's Gallery,** 914 Water St. (✆ **360/385-3630;** www.williams-gallery.com), is another good place to see works by regional artists.

Fort Worden State Park

Fort Worden State Park (✆ **360/344-4400;** www.parks.wa.gov), once a military installation that guarded the mouth of Puget Sound, is north of the historic district and can be reached by turning onto Kearney Street at the south end of town, or onto Monroe Street at the north end of town, and following the signs. Built at the turn of the 20th century, the fort is now a 360-acre state park where a wide array of attractions and activities ensure that it's busy for much of the year. Many of the fort's old wooden buildings have been restored and put to new use.

At the **Commanding Officer's Quarters** (✆ **360/385-1003;** www.jchsmuseum.org/coq.html), you can see what life was like for a Victorian-era officer and his family. The home has been fully restored and is filled with period antiques. May through September, it's open daily from noon to 5pm (closed other months). Admission is $4 for adults and $1 for children 3 to 12. Within the park, you'll also find the **Coast Artillery Museum** (✆ **360/385-0373**), which is open daily from 11am to 4pm (July–Aug 10am–5pm Sat). Admission is $3 for adults and $1 for children 6 to 12.

Here at the park, you can also learn about life below the waters of Puget Sound at the **Port Townsend Marine Science Center,** 532 Battery Way (✆ **800/566-3932** or 360/385-

Explore the area's sea life at the Marine Science Center.

5582; www.ptmsc.org). The center has great tide-pool touch tanks filled with crabs, starfish, anemones, and other marine life. A fascinating exhibit on the area's terrestrial natural history includes fossils from around the peninsula. Don't miss the exhibit on the glaciers that once covered this region. Mid-June through Labor Day, the center is open Wednesday through Monday from 11am to 5pm; fall through spring hours are Friday through Sunday from noon to 4pm. Between November and March, only the natural history exhibit is open, and in January the center is closed. Admission is $5 for adults and $3 for youths 6 to 17; discounted admissions in winter.

For many people, however, the main reason to visit the park is to hang out on the beach or at one of the picnic areas. Scuba divers also frequent Fort Worden, which has an underwater park just offshore. In spring, the Rhododendron Garden puts on a colorful floral display. Throughout the year, there is a wide variety of concerts and other performances at the **Centrum** (✆ **360/385-3102;** www.centrum.org). Also on the premises are campgrounds, a restaurant, and restored officers' quarters that can be rented as vacation homes.

Port Townsend from the Water

If you'd like to explore this area from the water, you've got several options. Three-hour sailboat tours ($65) are offered by **Brisa Charters** (✆ **877/412-7472** or 360/385-2309; www.brisacharters.com). Several times a year, the **Port Townsend Marine Science Center** (✆ **800/566-3932** or 360/385-5582; www.ptmsc.org) operates boat tours ($55) to nearby Protection Island, a wildlife refuge that is home to puffins, rhinoceros auklets, and other nesting seabirds. One trip a year is done on a 101-foot historic schooner ($80).

From early March to early September, whale-watching cruises ($64–$95 for adults, $49–$65 for children 2–10) are offered by **Puget Sound Express,** Point Hudson Marina, 227 Jackson St. (✆ **360/385-5288;** www.pugetsoundexpress.com), which also operates passenger-ferry service to Friday Harbor. The less expensive tours are in March and April and go out in search of gray whales. The more expensive tours are summertime orca-whale tours.

You can rent sea kayaks in downtown Port Townsend from **PT Outdoors,** 1017B Water St. (✆ **360/379-3608;** www.ptoutdoors.com), which charges between $20 and $40 for a 1-hour rental. This company also offers guided kayak tours ($60–$80). At the nearby **Port Ludlow Marina** (✆ **877/344-6725;** www.portludlowresort.com), south of Port Townsend, you can rent sea kayaks ($15–$20 per hour) and motorboats ($35–$75 per hour).

Area Wineries & Cideries

While you're visiting the area, you might want to check out some of the wineries and cideries south of town. **Sorensen Cellars,** 274 S. Otto St. (✆ **360/379-6416;** www.sorensencellars.com), is open March through May and September through November, Friday through Sunday from noon to 5pm; June through August, it's open daily noon to 5pm. To find this winery, turn east off Wash. 20 onto Frederick Street and then south on Otto Street.

Fair Winds Winery, 1984 Hastings Ave. W. (✆ **360/385-6899;** www.fairwindswinery.com), is one of the only wineries in the state producing Aligoté, a French-style white wine and has also received awards for its port-style dessert wine. Memorial Day to Labor Day, the winery is open daily from noon to 5pm;

other months it's open Friday to Sunday from noon to 5pm. To get here, drive south from Port Townsend on Wash. 20, turn west on Jacob Miller Road, and continue 2 miles to Hastings Avenue.

Cideries open on a regular basis include **Finnriver Farm,** 62 Barn Swallow Rd. (off Country Meadow Road), Chimacum (✆ **360/732-6822;** www.finnriver.com), which currently makes two types of dry hard cider as well as perry (pear cider), fruit wines, and fortified apple wine as well. To find Finnriver, drive south from Port Townsend to Chimacum and continue south about 2¾ miles on Center Road. May to September, they're open Thursday to Monday from noon to 5pm, and October through April, they're open Friday to Sunday from noon to 5pm. A few miles away, you can sample semisweet and sweet hard ciders at **Eaglemount Wine & Cider,** 2350 Eaglemount Rd. (✆ **360/732-4084;** www.eaglemountwinery.com). To reach this cidery, drive south from Chimacum on Center Road and turn right on Eaglemount Road. Eaglemount is open Friday to Sunday (and holidays) from noon to 6pm.

Where to Stay

Ann Starrett Mansion Boutique Hotel ★ Built in 1889 for $6,000 as a wedding present for Ann Starrett, this Victorian jewel box is by far the most elegant and ornate historic hotel in Port Townsend. The rose-and-teal-green mansion is a museum of the Victorian era: A three-story turret towers over the front door, and every room is exquisitely furnished with period antiques. Note that although this hotel seems as though it would be a bed-and-breakfast inn, it does not serve breakfast. However, you'll find plenty of good breakfast places in the area.

744 Clay St., Port Townsend, WA 98368. www.starrettmansion.com. ✆ **800/321-0644.** 11 units. $85–$225 double. Children 17 and under stay free in parent's room. AE, MC, V. **Amenities:** Concierge. *In room:* No phone, free Wi-Fi.

The Clam Cannery Hotel ★★ Housed within this brick clam cannery from 1885 are the most luxurious and upscale nightly rentals in Port Townsend. However, there is little besides the beautiful doors of this unusual old industrial building to suggest that there might be luxurious guest suites inside. The suites are all very spacious and have lots of interesting details, including kitchen cabinets made with wood salvaged from the old cannery and cement countertops that incorporate pieces of clam shells left over from when the cannery was active. To top it all off, the hotel is built on a pier over the water, so you just can't get much closer to the water than this.

111 Quincy St., Port Townsend, WA 98368. www.clamcannery.com. ✆ **360/385-4315.** 5 units. $345–$495 suite. Rates include continental breakfast. DISC, MC, V. Children stay free in parents' room. Pets accepted (no fee). **Amenities:** Bikes; concierge; access to nearby health club; spa services. *In room:* TV, CD player, hair dryer, kitchen, MP3 docking station, free Wi-Fi.

Old Consulate Inn ★★ The Old Consulate Inn is another example of the Victorian excess so wonderfully appealing today. The attention to detail and quality craftsmanship, both in the construction and the restoration of this elegant mansion, are evident wherever you look. Despite its heritage, however, the Old Consulate avoids being a museum; it's a comfortable yet elegant place to stay. If you're here for a special occasion, consider splurging on one of the turret rooms. Of the other units, my favorite is the Parkside. For entertainment you'll find a grand piano, a billiards table, and a VCR, as well as stunning views out most of the windows. A multicourse breakfast is meant to be lingered over, so don't make any early morning appointments. Afternoon tea and home-baked treats are served when you arrive.

313 Walker St., Port Townsend, WA 98368. www.oldconsulate.com ✆ **800/300-6753** or 360/385-6753. Fax 360/385-2097. 8 units. June–Oct $110–$210 double; Nov–May $99–$189 double. Rates include full breakfast. MC, V. Children 14 and over welcome ($30 per child to stay in parents' room). **Amenities:** Free Wi-Fi. *In room:* Hair dryer, no phone.

Manresa Castle ★ Built in 1892 by the first mayor of Port Townsend, this reproduction of a medieval castle later became a Jesuit retreat and school. Today traditional elegance pervades Manresa Castle, and of all the hotels and B&Bs in Port Townsend, this place offers the most historic elegance for the money. The guest rooms have a genuine vintage appeal that manages to avoid the contrived feeling that so often sneaks into the room decor of B&Bs. The tower suite is my favorite room in the hotel and is worth a splurge; in this huge room, you get sweeping views from a circular seating area. An elegant lounge and dining room further add to the "grand hotel" feel of this unusual accommodation. Oh, and by the way, the hotel is haunted.

Seventh and Sheridan sts. (P.O. Box 564), Port Townsend, WA 98368. www.manresacastle.com. ✆ **800/732-1281** or 360/385-5750. 40 units. $109–$119 double; $169–$229 suite. $10 additional per extra person. Rates include continental breakfast. DISC, MC, V. **Amenities:** Restaurant, lounge. *In room:* TV, free Wi-Fi.

Where to Eat

When I need coffee, I like to head to **Better Living Through Coffee,** 100 Tyler St. (✆ **360/385-3388;** www.bltcoffee.com), which is right on the water and serves organic coffee with non-homogenized milk. Alternatively, on cold, dark days, the wine-cellar-like underground vaults of **Undertown Coffee and Wine Bar,** 211 Taylor St. (✆ **360/385-1410;** www.theundertown.com), are hard to beat for old Port Townsend atmosphere. If you're a tea drinker, check out **Wild Sage,** 924 Washington St. (✆ **360/379-1222;** www.wildsageteas.com). One place on nearly everyone's itinerary is **Elevated Ice Cream,** 627 Water St. (✆ **360/385-1156;** www.elevatedicecream.com), which scoops up the best ice cream in town. For pastries, head to uptown Port Townsend and **Sweet Laurette's Cafe and Bistro,** 1029 Lawrence St. (✆ **360/385-4886;** www.sweetlaurette.com), which has a patisserie that makes the best pastries in Port Townsend.

If you're heading out to Fort Worden State Park for a picnic, you can pick up supplies at **Aldrich's Market,** 940 Lawrence St. (✆ **360/385-0500;** www.aldrichs.com), a wonderful little upscale market in the uptown neighborhood. Across the street from Aldrich's, you can stock up on artisan bread at **Pane d'Amore,** 617 Tyler St. (✆ **360/385-1199;** www.panedamore.com), and south of downtown, at **Mt. Townsend Creamery,** 338 Sherman St. (✆ **360/379-0895;** www.mttownsendcreamery.com), which is just off West Sims Way (Wash. 20), you can pick up some local cheese to put on your bread. Also south of downtown, you can stop by the **Port Townsend Food Co-Op,** 414 Kearney St. (✆ **360/385-2883;** www.foodcoop.coop), which is at the turn-off for Fort Worden. If you happen to be in town on a Saturday between April and mid-December, be sure to stop by the **Port Townsend Farmers Market** (✆ **360/379-9098;** www.ptfarmersmarket.org), held on the corner of Lawrence and Tyler streets. The market is open from 9am to 2pm. June through September, at the corner of Polk and Lawrence streets, there is also a Wednesday farmers market from 3 to 6pm.

If you're looking for someplace interesting to have a drink, check out the **Port Townsend Brewing Company,** 330 10th St. (✆ **360/385-9967;** www.porttownsendbrewing.com), which has a tasting room and beer garden south of downtown in the Port Townsend Boat Haven marina. For good beer and pub food, check out **The Public House Grill,** 1038 Water St. (✆ **360/385-9708;** www.thepublichouse.com), which has the feel of a 19th-century tavern.

Fountain Cafe ★ INTERNATIONAL Housed in a narrow clapboard building, this funky little place has long been a favorite of Port Townsend locals and counterculture types on a tight budget. Eclectic furnishings decorate the dining room, which has a handful of tables and a few stools at the counter. The menu changes seasonally, but you can rest assured that the simple fare will be utterly fresh and that the offerings will include plenty of shellfish and pasta. The Greek pasta is a mainstay that's hard to beat, and the clam chowder is excellent. The wide range of flavors here assures that everyone will find something to his or her liking.

920 Washington St. ✆ **360/385-1364.** Reservations accepted only for parties of 5 or more. Main courses $10–$15 lunch, $16–$30 dinner. MC, V. Daily 11:30am–3pm and 5–9pm (Fri–Sat until 9:30pm).

Khu Larb Thai ★ THAI Located half a block off busy Water Street, Khu Larb seems a world removed from Port Townsend's sometimes-overdone Victorian decor. Thai easy-listening music plays on the stereo, while the pungent fragrance of Thai spices wafts through the dining room. One taste of any dish on the menu, and you'll be convinced that this is great Thai food. The *tom kha gai,* a sour-and-spicy soup with a coconut-milk base, is particularly memorable. The curry dishes made with mussels are also good bets.

225 Adams St. ✆ **360/385-5023.** www.khularbthai.com. Reservations accepted only for parties of 6 or more. Main courses $10–$15. AE, MC, V. Sun–Mon and Wed–Thurs 11am–9pm, Fri–Sat 11am–10pm.

Silverwater Cafe ★ NORTHWEST Port Townsend is equal parts history, hippies, and artists, and this restaurant, in business for more than 20 years, sums up that aesthetic. Works by local artists, lots of plants, and New Age music on the stereo set the tone for this casual restaurant in a historic downtown building. While the menu focuses on Northwest dishes, it also includes preparations from around the world. You can start your meal with an artichoke-and-parmesan pâté and then move on to ahi tuna with lavender pepper, prawns with cilantro-ginger-lime butter, or pappardelle pasta with buffalo Bolognese sauce. There are always plenty of vegetarian options as well.

237 Taylor St. ✆ **360/385-6448.** www.silverwatercafe.com. Reservations recommended. Main courses $9–$16 lunch, $13–$25 dinner. MC, V. Mon–Thurs 11:30am–2:30pm and 5–9pm; Fri–Sat 11:30am–9:30pm; Sun 10:30am–9pm. Bar stays open later.

T's Restaurant ★★ ITALIAN Port Townsend is Washington's quintessential boaters' town, and no other restaurant better captures the town's historical, nautical character. Housed in a historic building in the Point Hudson Marina at the north end of downtown, this romantic, low-key place has long been my favorite restaurant in town. The menu usually features plenty of daily specials, and local shellfish are menu mainstays. It is hard to resist a starter of steamed local manila clams or herby pan-fried oysters. Scallops and wild salmon make frequent appearances. You'll also find a wide variety of interesting pasta dishes from which to choose, but the rigatoni Gorgonzola is my favorite.

141 Hudson St. ✆ **360/385-0700.** www.ts-restaurant.com. Reservations recommended. Main courses $10–$19 lunch, $12–$28 dinner. AE, MC, V. Wed–Mon 11am–3pm and 5–9pm.

SEQUIM: LAVENDER FIELDS FOREVER

If the economy and the exchange rate have combined to keep you from that long-dreamed-of vacation in Provence, then perhaps you need to spend a day in sunny Sequim. In the rain shadow of the Olympic Mountains, Sequim (pronounced *Skwim*) is the state's driest region west of the Cascade Range—and, consequently, it is an almost perfect place to grow lavender plants. Every summer, beginning in mid-June and extending through July, parts of Sequim take on the look of Provence. Lavender fields paint the landscape with billowy rows of purple, and visitors descend on Sequim to immerse themselves in it. Throughout the area, there are "U-pick" farms where you can cut your own lavender, shops selling lavender products, and, of course, an annual lavender festival.

The lack of rainfall and the temperate climate have also made Sequim a very popular retirement community. Sodden Northwesterners have taken to retiring here in droves. While the rains descend on the rest of the region, the fortunate few who call Sequim home bask in their own personal microclimate of sunshine and warmth.

Before lavender and retirement homes lured people to the area, there were the crabs. To the north of Sequim lies the Dungeness Spit, a 6-mile-long sand spit that is the longest such spit in the United States. This sand spit lends its name to the Dungeness crab, the most popular crab in the Northwest. Dungeness crab is as much a staple of Washington waters as the blue crab is in the Chesapeake Bay region.

Essentials

VISITOR INFORMATION For information, contact the **Sequim-Dungeness Valley Chamber of Commerce,** 1192 E. Washington St. (P.O. Box 907), Sequim, WA 98382 (✆ **800/737-8462** or 360/683-6197; www.cityofsequim.com).

GETTING THERE From Seattle, take the Bainbridge Island ferry; once on the west side of Puget Sound, follow Wash. 305 to Wash. 3 to Wash. 104 to U.S. 101. Sequim and the Dungeness Valley lie to the north of U.S. 101, between Port Townsend and Port Angeles. It's about an hour's drive from Bainbridge Island to Sequim.

Lavender, Wine & Wildlife

Sequim has become well known around the Northwest for its many lavender farms, which paint the landscape with their colorful blooms every summer from late June through August. Sequim's climate is ideal for growing lavender, and

Sequim is where you'll find fields of lavender.

you'll likely pass numerous large fields of this fragrant Mediterranean plant as you tour the area.

To find your way around the area's lavender farms, stop by the Sequim-Dungeness Valley Chamber of Commerce visitor center (see above) or contact the **Sequim Lavender Farmers Association** (**✆ 360/452-6300;** www.sequimlavenderfarms.org). In mid-July, when the lavender gardens are in full bloom, the town observes the season with its **Sequim Lavender Festival** (**✆ 360/670-8150** or 360/582-1907; www.lavenderfestival.com) and **Sequim Lavender Farm Faire** (**✆ 360/452-6300;** www.sequimlavenderfarms.org), which includes both a Lavender Farm Tour and Lavender in the Park (at Carrie Blake Park, which is at the east end of Sequim just off U.S. 101).

If you'd like to wander through fragrant fields of lavender, you've got plenty of options. **Purple Haze Lavender Farm,** 180 Bell Bottom Rd. (**✆ 888/852-6560** or 360/683-1714; www.purplehazelavender.com), an organic "U-pick" farm east of downtown Sequim off West Sequim Bay Road, is one of my favorites. June through Labor Day, the farm is open daily from 10am to 5pm (call for spring and fall hours). The farm has a seasonal gift shop in a small barn as well as the year-round **Purple Haze Lavender Downtown Store,** 127 W. Washington St., in downtown Sequim. This latter shop is open Monday to Friday from 9am to 5pm, Saturday from 10am to 5pm, and Sunday from noon to 4pm. North of here, don't miss **Graysmarsh Farm,** 6187 Woodcock Rd. (**✆ 800/683-4367** or 360/683-0624; www.graysmarsh.com), which has both beautiful lavender fields and "U-pick" berry fields, where, in season, you can pick strawberries, raspberries, blueberries, and loganberries.

Up near the Dungeness Spit, a very pretty organic lavender farm, **Jardin du Soleil,** 3932 Sequim-Dungeness Way (**✆ 877/527-3461** or 360/582-1185; www.jardindusoleil.com), surrounds an old farmhouse and its Victorian gardens. From April to September, the farm is open daily from 10am to 5pm; in October,

November, December, February, and March, it's open Friday to Monday from 10am to 4pm.

Off to the southwest of Sequim is **Lost Mountain Lavender,** 1541 Taylor Cutoff Rd. (✆ **888/507-7481** or 360/681-2782; www.lostmountainlavender.com). This farm is open daily from 10am to 6pm in June, July, and August; September through May, it's open Thursday through Monday from 10am to 5pm.

If you're interested in tasting some locally produced wine, you can also stop at **Olympic Cellars,** 255410 U.S. 101 (✆ **360/452-0160;** http://olympiccellars.com), which is housed in a large barn on the west side of Sequim. April through October, the tasting room is open daily from 11am to 6pm; November to March, it's open daily 11am to 5pm.

If you've got the kids with you, Sequim's **Olympic Game Farm ★**, 1423 Ward Rd. (✆ **800/778-4295** or 360/683-4295; www.olygamefarm.com), is a must. You'll get up close and personal with bison, Kodiak bears, zebras, wolves, elk, deer, and many other species of wild animals. When the farm was created back in the 1970s, many of the animals had starred in Walt Disney nature films. Today, however, the animals here are no longer screen stars. There are drive-through and walking tours as well as a petting farm. The farm is open daily from 9am; admission is $11 to $14 for adults, $10 to $13 for seniors and children 6 to 14, and free for children 5 and under.

The biggest local attraction is Dungeness Spit, which is protected as the **Dungeness National Wildlife Refuge ★★** (✆ **360/457-8451;** www.fws.gov/washingtonmaritime/dungeness/index.html). Within the refuge, there's a .5-mile trail to a bluff-top overlook, but the best reason to visit is to hike the spit, which leads for more than 5 miles to the historic New Dungeness Lighthouse. Along the way, you're likely to see numerous species of birds as well as harbor seals. There's a fee of $3 per family to visit the spit.

Hike the spit at the Dungeness National Wildlife Refuge.

Near the base of the Dungeness Spit, you'll also find the **Dungeness Recreation Area,** 554 Voice of America Rd. (✆ **360/683-5847;** www.clallam.net/CountyParks/html/parks_dungeness.htm), which has a campground, picnic area, and trail leading out to the spit. If you're not up for a 10-mile round-trip hike to the lighthouse, **Dungeness Kayaking,** 5021 Sequim-Dungeness Way (✆ **360/681-4190;** www.dungenesskayaking.com), charges $100 per person for a 4-hour kayak tour to the lighthouse.

Where to Stay

Dungeness Bay Cottages ★ This pretty little collection of cottages is set on a bluff overlooking the Strait of Juan de Fuca and is located across the street from the waters of Dungeness Bay. Great views and economical accommodations make this an outstanding getaway. Most units actually have views of both the water and the Olympic Mountains. My favorite is the large San Juan Suite, which has a fireplace. The summer sunsets here simply cannot be beat.

140 Marine Dr., Sequim, WA 98382. www.dungenessbay.com. ✆ **888/683-3013** or 360/683-3013. 6 units. Apr 16–Oct 14 $120–$180 double; Oct 15–Apr 15 $100–$155 double. Non-infant children $15 per night extra in parents' room. 2- to 3-night minimum. DISC, MC, V. *In room:* TV/DVD, hair dryer, kitchen, MP3 docking station, free Wi-Fi.

Juan de Fuca Cottages ★ Right across the street from the water and surrounded by wide green lawns, these well-tended cottages have excellent views. While most face the water, the best views are actually from the one cottage that faces the Olympic Mountains to the south; this cabin has skylights and a long wall of windows. Other units have skylights as well, and all have whirlpool tubs and kitchenettes. The cottages also have their own private beach, and kayaks can be rented here. Each cottage sleeps at least four people. Massages can be arranged.

182 Marine Dr., Sequim, WA 98382. www.juandefuca.com. ✆ **866/683-4433** or 360/683-4433. 11 units. July–Sept $165–$260 double; Oct–June $99–$230 double. 2-night minimum July–Aug. Children 1 and under stay free in parent's room, $20 additional per night for older children DISC, MC, V. Pets accepted ($20 per night). **Amenities:** Concierge; sauna; watersports equipment/boat rentals. *In room:* TV/VCR/DVD, CD player, hair dryer, kitchen, free Wi-Fi.

Where to Eat

For the best breakfast in Sequim, head to **The Oak Table Cafe,** 292 W. Bell St. (✆ **360/683-2179;** www.oaktablecafe.com). If you're in need of a light lunch, don't miss **Lippert's** ★, 134 S. Second St. (✆ **360/683-6727;** www.lippertsrestaurant.com), which is in a historic church building a block off Sequim's main street. For a retro diner experience, try **Hiway 101 Diner,** 392 W. Washington St. (✆ **360/683-3388**). My brother's family won't let him drive through Sequim without stopping here for burgers and milkshakes.

For a caffeine fix, head to **The Buzz,** 128 N. Sequim Ave. (✆ **360/683-2503;** www.thebuzzbeedazzled.com), which is just

K-E-L-K Radio

Sequim is home to a herd of around 100 Roosevelt elk, which have a habit of wandering back and forth across U.S. 101. To reduce the number of automobile-elk collisions, several members of the herd have had radio collars put on them. When these elk approach the highway, the signals emitted by their collars trigger yellow ELK CROSSING warning lights to start flashing.

north of Washington Street in downtown Sequim. Pick up tasty picnic fare at **Sunny Farms Country Store,** 261461 U.S. 101 (✆ **360/683-8003;** www.sunnyfarms.com), on the west side of Sequim. If you need a pastry or artisan bread for a picnic, stop by **Bell Street Bakery,** 173 W. Bell St. (✆ **360/681-6262;** www.bellstreetbakery.com).

Alder Wood Bistro ★ NEW AMERICAN With a menu that changes seasonally and incorporates lots of local, organic, and sustainably produced ingredients, the casual little Alder Wood Bistro is a local's favorite here in Sequim. The wood-fired oven turns out great pizzas as well as various other dishes. At lunch don't miss the savory tart, which is made with a delicious butter crust; at dinner you'll find the likes of polenta lasagna, duck-confit pizza, and bacon-wrapped meatloaf. Lunch or dinner, you might want to get a side of the truffled French fries. For dessert? Try the apple pie warmed in the wood oven.

139 W. Alder St. ✆ **360/683-4321.** www.alderwoodbistro.com. Reservations recommended. Main courses $7–$18 lunch, $7–$26 dinner. AE, DISC, MC, V. Tues–Sat 11am–3pm and 5–9pm.

The 3 Crabs SEAFOOD The 3 Crabs is an Olympic Peninsula institution—folks drive from miles around to enjoy the fresh seafood and sunset views at this friendly waterfront restaurant overlooking the Strait of Juan de Fuca and the New Dungeness Lighthouse. For more than 50 years, this place has been serving up Dungeness crabs in a wide variety of styles: You can order your crabs as a cocktail, in a sandwich, cracked, or as crab Louie salad. Clams and oysters also come from the local waters and are equally good. There's great bird-watching here, too, especially in winter.

11 Three Crabs Rd. ✆ 360/683-4264. www.the3crabs.com. Reservations recommended. Main courses $9–$26. MC, V. Summer daily noon–8 or 9pm; shorter hours other months.

OLYMPIC NATIONAL PARK & ENVIRONS

Snow-capped peaks, rainforests, miles and miles of deserted beaches—Olympic National Park has all this and more. Preserving more than 900,000 acres of wilderness, this national park, because of its amazing diversity, is recognized as one of the world's most important wild ecosystems. The park is unique in the contiguous United States for its temperate rainforests, which are found in the west-facing valleys of the Hoh, Queets, Bogachiel, Clearwater, and Quinault rivers. In these valleys, rainfall can exceed 150 inches per year, trees (such as Sitka spruce, western red cedar, Douglas fir, and western hemlock) can grow more than 300 feet tall, and mosses enshroud the limbs of big-leaf maples.

Within a few miles of the park's rainforests, the Olympic Mountains rise to the 7,965-foot peak of Mount Olympus and an alpine zone where no trees grow at all. Together elevation and heavy snowfall (the rain of lower elevations is replaced by snow at higher elevations) combine to form dozens of glaciers. It is these glaciers that have carved the Olympic Mountains into the jagged peaks that mesmerize visitors and beckon hikers and climbers. Rugged and spectacular sections of the coast have also been preserved as part of the national park, and the offshore waters are designated the Olympic Coast National Marine Sanctuary.

With fewer than a dozen roads, none of which leads more than a few miles into the park, Olympic National Park is, for the most part, inaccessible to the

Rialto Beach features the famous "Hole in the Wall."

casual visitor. Only two roads penetrate the high country, and only one of these is paved. Likewise, only two paved roads lead into the park's famed rainforests. Although a long stretch of beach within the national park is paralleled by U.S. 101, the park's most spectacular beaches can be reached only on foot.

The park may be inaccessible to cars, but it is a wonderland for hikers and backpackers. Its rugged beaches, rainforest valleys, alpine meadows, and mountaintop glaciers offer an amazing variety of hiking and backpacking opportunities. For alpine hikes, there are the trail heads at Hurricane Ridge and Deer Park. To experience the rainforest in all its drippy glory, you can take to the trails of the Bogachiel, Hoh, Queets, and Quinault valleys. Of these rainforest trails, the Hoh Valley has the most accessible (and consequently most popular) trails, including the trail head for a multiday backpack trip to the summit of Mount Olympus. Favorite coastal hikes include the stretch of coast between La Push and Oil City, and from Rialto Beach north to Lake Ozette and onward to Shi Shi Beach.

Visitor Information

For more information on the national park, contact **Olympic National Park,** 600 E. Park Ave., Port Angeles, WA 98362 (✆ **360/565-3130** or 360/565-3131 for road and weather conditions; www.nps.gov/olym). For information on Port Angeles and the rest of the northern Olympic Peninsula, contact the **Olympic Peninsula Visitor Bureau,** 338 W. First St., Ste. 104 (P.O. Box 670), Port Angeles, WA 98362 (✆ **800/942-4042** or 360/452-8552; www.olympic peninsula.org), or the **Port Angeles Regional Chamber of Commerce Visitor Center,** 121 E. Railroad Ave., Port Angeles, WA 98362 (✆ **360/452-2363;** www.portangeles.org).

Getting There

U.S. 101 circles Olympic National Park, with main park entrances south of Port Angeles, at Lake Crescent, and at the Hoh River south of Forks. To reach the Olympic Peninsula from Seattle, take the Bainbridge Island ferry, and then follow Wash. 305 to Wash. 3 to Wash. 104 to U.S. 101. Allow 3 hours to get to Hurricane Ridge (on the north side of the park).

Kenmore Air Express (✆ **866/435-9524;** www.kenmoreair.com) flies between Seattle's Boeing Field and Port Angeles's William Fairchild International Airport (with a free shuttle from Seattle-Tacoma International Airport to Boeing Field). Rental cars are available in Port Angeles from **Budget** (✆ **800/527-0700;** www.budget.com).

Exploring the Park's North Side

The northern portions of Olympic National Park are both the most accessible and most popular. It is here, south of Port Angeles, that two roads lead into the national park's high country. Of the two areas reached by these roads, Hurricane Ridge is the more accessible. Deer Park, the other road-accessed high-country destination, is at the end of a harrowing gravel road and is little visited. West of Port Angeles within the national park's lowlands lie two large lakes, Lake Crescent and Lake Ozette, that attract boaters and anglers. Also in this region are two hot springs—the developed Sol Duc Resort and the natural Olympic Hot Springs.

Outside the park boundaries, along the northern coast of the peninsula, are several campgrounds, a beautiful stretch of coastline that is popular with kayakers, and a couple of small sportfishing ports, Sekiu and Neah Bay, that are also popular with scuba divers. Neah Bay, which is on the Makah Indian Reservation, is also the site of one of the most interesting little museums in the state. This reservation encompasses Cape Flattery, which is the northwesternmost point in the contiguous United States.

Port Angeles, primarily a lumber-shipping port, is the largest town on the north Olympic Peninsula and serves as a base for people exploring the national park and as a port for ferries crossing the Strait of Juan de Fuca to Victoria, British Columbia. Here you'll find the region's greatest concentration of lodgings and restaurants.

Port Angeles is also home to the national-park headquarters and the **Olympic National Park Visitor Center,** 3002 Mount Angeles Rd. (✆ **360/565-3130;** www.nps.gov/olym), on the south edge of town. In addition to offering lots of information, maps, and books about the park, the center has exhibits on the park's flora and fauna. It's open daily throughout the year, with hours varying with the seasons.

HURRICANE RIDGE

From the main visitor center, continue another 17 miles up Mount Angeles Road to Hurricane Ridge, which on clear days offers the most breathtaking views in the park. In summer, the surrounding subalpine meadows are carpeted with wildflowers, and you're likely to see deer grazing on wildflowers and marmots lazing on rocks. (Marmots are large members of the squirrel family; if you get too close to one, it's likely to let out an ear-piercing whistle.)

Several trails lead into the park from here, and several day hikes are possible. The 3-mile **Hurricane Hill Trail** and the 1-mile **Meadow Loop Trail**

You can hike up Mount Storm King near Lake Crescent.

are the most scenic. Stop by the **Hurricane Ridge Visitor Center** to see its exhibits on plants and wildlife; this is a good place to learn about the fragile nature of this beautiful alpine landscape.

In winter, Hurricane Ridge is a popular cross-country skiing area and also has two rope tows and a Poma lift for downhill skiing. However, because the ski area is so small and the conditions so unpredictable, it is used almost exclusively by local families. For more information, contact the **Hurricane Ridge Ski and Snowboard Area** (✆ **360/457-2879** or 360/565-3131 for road conditions; www.hurricaneridge.com).

LAKE CRESCENT

West of Port Angeles on U.S. 101 lies 624-foot-deep Lake Crescent, a sapphire-blue body of water that is one of the most beautiful lakes in the state. The glacier-carved lake is surrounded by steep forested mountains that give it the feel of a fjord. Near the east end of the lake, you'll find the 1-mile trail to 90-foot-high Marymere Falls and the Storm King Ranger Station (✆ 360/928-3380), which is usually open in the summer (and in other seasons when a ranger is in the station). From the Marymere Falls Trail, you can hike the steep 1.7 miles up Mount Storm King to a viewpoint overlooking Lake Crescent (climbing above the viewpoint is not recommended).

SOL DUC HOT SPRINGS

Continuing west from Lake Crescent, watch for the turnoff to **Sol Duc Hot Springs** (✆ **888/896-3818;** www.olympicnationalparks.com). For 14 miles, the road follows the Soleduck River, passing the picturesque Salmon Cascades along the way. In the fall, you can often see salmon leaping up these falls. However, the cascades are beautiful any time of year. Sol Duc Hot Springs were, for centuries, considered healing waters by local Native Americans, and after white settlers

Relax your aching muscles at Sol Duc Hot Springs.

arrived in the area, the springs became a popular resort. In addition to the hot swimming pool and soaking tubs, you'll find cabins, a campground, a restaurant, and a snack bar. The springs are open daily from late March to late October; admission is $12 for adults, $9 for seniors and children 4 to 12. A 4.5-mile loop trail leads from the hot springs to **Sol Duc Falls,** which are among the most photographed falls in the park. Alternatively, you can drive to the end of the Sol Duc Road and make this an easy 1.5-mile hike. Along this same road, you can hike the .5-mile **Ancient Groves Nature Trail.** Note that Sol Duc Road is one of the roads on which you have to pay an Olympic National Park entry fee.

Rainforests & Wild Beaches: Exploring Olympic National Park West

The western regions of Olympic National Park can be roughly divided into two sections—the rugged coastal strip and the famous rainforest valleys. Of course, these are the rainiest areas within the park, and many a visitor has cut short a

TWILIGHT TIME IN forks

If the names Bella and Edward mean anything to you, then you or your children must be fans of the *Twilight* teen vampire novels. Set on the Olympic Peninsula, the young-adult romance novels feature real locales in Forks and Port Angeles, and promoting *Twilight* has become big business on the peninsula.

In Port Angeles, you can dine at **Bella Italia** (p. 276), where characters Bella and Edward went on their first date; you can even order the same thing they ordered. As luck would have it, Bella Italia also happens to be one of my favorite restaurants on the peninsula.

In Forks, outside the **Forks Chamber of Commerce** (see above), you'll find an old red pickup truck just like the one Bella drives in the books. Inside the visitor center, you can pick up a map of the town's *Twilight* locations. Among the places you'll want to visit are Forks High School, where Bella and Edward go to school; Forks Hospital, where Dr. Cullen works (look for his reserved parking space); and Forks Police Station, where Police Chief Charlie Swan works. You can also visit the Thriftway where Bella did her shopping, and Forks Outfitters, where she worked. More settings from the book can be found west of Forks in the Native American community of La Push. In Forks, the **Miller Tree Inn** has been designated the official Cullen house. There are also vampire-themed *Twilight* rooms at the **Dew Drop Inn Motel,** 100 Fern Hill Rd. (✆ **888/433-9376** or 360/374-4055; www.dewdropinnmotel.com) and at the **Pacific Inn Motel,** 352 S. Forks Ave. (✆ **800/235-7344** or 360/374-9400; www.pacificinnmotel.com). Of course, shops around town are full of *Twilight* and vampire souvenirs. **Olympic Cellars winery** (discussed earlier in this chapter) in Port Angeles even makes a Sparkling Twilight wine. If you want to be sure you see it all, book a tour with **Dazzled by Twilight Tour Company,** 11 N. Forks Ave. (✆ **360/374-8687;** www.dazzledbytwilight.com), which is affiliated with the Dazzled by Twilight gift shop.

vacation here because of rain. Well, what do you expect? It is, after all, a *rainforest.* Come prepared to get wet.

The coastal strip can be divided into three segments. North of La Push, which is on the Quileute Indian Reservation, the 20 miles of shoreline from Rialto Beach to Cape Alava are accessible only on foot. The northern end of this stretch of coast is accessed from Lake Ozette off Wash. 112 in the northwest corner of the peninsula. South of La Push, the park's coastline stretches for 17 miles from Third Beach to the Hoh River mouth and is also accessible only on foot. The third segment of Olympic Park coastline begins at Ruby Beach, just south of both the Hoh River mouth and Hoh Indian Reservation, and stretches south to South Beach. This stretch of coastline is paralleled by U.S. 101.

Inland of these coastal areas lie the four rainforest valleys of the Bogachiel, Hoh, Queets, and Quinault rivers. Of these valleys, only the Hoh and Quinault are penetrated by roads, and it is in the Hoh Valley that the rainforests are the primary attraction.

Forks is the largest community in the northwest corner of the Olympic Peninsula and is on U.S. 101, which continues south along the west side of the peninsula to the town of Hoquiam. For more information on the Forks area, contact the **Forks Chamber of Commerce,** 1411 S. Forks Ave. (P.O. Box 1249), Forks, WA 98331 (✆ **800/443-6757** or 360/374-2531; www.forkswa.com). West of Forks lie miles of pristine beaches and a narrow strip of forest (called the Olympic Coastal Strip) that are part of the national park, but are not connected to the inland mountainous section. The first place where you can actually drive right to the Pacific Ocean is just west of Forks. At the end of a spur road, you come to the Quileute Indian Reservation and the community of **La Push.** Right in town, there's a beach at the mouth of the Quillayute River; however, before you reach La Push, you'll see signs for **Third Beach ★★** and **Second Beach ★★**, which are two of the prettiest beaches on the peninsula. Third Beach is a 1½-mile walk, and Second Beach is just over a half-mile from the trail head. **Rialto Beach ★★**, just north of La Push, is another beautiful and rugged beach; it's reached from a turnoff east of La Push. From here you can backpack north for 24 miles to Cape Alava; this is also a very popular spot for shorter day hikes. One mile up the beach is a spot called **Hole in the Wall,** where ceaseless wave action has bored a large tunnel through solid rock. On any of these beaches, keep an eye out for bald eagles, seals, and sea lions.

HOH RIVER VALLEY

Roughly 8 miles south of Forks is the turnoff for the Hoh River Valley. It's 17 miles up this side road to the **Hoh Rain Forest Visitor Center** (✆ **360/374-6925**), campground, and trail heads. This valley receives an average of 140 inches of rain per year—and sometimes as much as 200 inches—making it the wettest region in the continental United States. At the visitor center, you can learn all about the natural forces that cause this tremendous rainfall.

To see the effect of so much rain on the landscape, walk the .8-mile **Hall of Mosses Trail,** where the trees (primarily Sitka spruce, western red cedar, and western hemlock) tower 200 feet tall. Here you'll also see big-leaf maple trees with limbs draped in thick carpets of mosses. If you're up for a longer walk, try the **Spruce Nature Trail.** If you've come with a backpack, there's no better way to see the park and its habitats than by hiking the **Hoh River Trail,** which is 17 miles long and leads to Glacier Meadows and Blue Glacier, on the flanks of Mount Olympus. A herd of elk live in the Hoh Valley and can sometimes be seen along these trails.

Continuing south on U.S. 101, but before crossing the Hoh River, you'll come to a secondary road (Oil City Rd.) that heads west from the Hoh Oxbow campground. From the end of the road, it's a hike of less than a mile to a rocky beach at the **mouth of the Hoh River.** You're likely to see sea lions or harbor seals feeding just offshore here, and to the north are several haystack rocks that are nesting sites for numerous seabirds. Primitive camping is permitted on this beach, and from here backpackers can continue hiking for 17 miles north along a pristine wilderness of rugged headlands and secluded beaches.

RUBY BEACH, KALALOCH & QUEETS

U.S. 101 finally reaches the coast at **Ruby Beach.** This beach gets its name from its pink sand, which is composed of tiny grains of garnet. With its colorful sands, tide pools, sea stacks, and driftwood logs, Ruby Beach is the prettiest of the beaches along this stretch of coast.

For another 17 miles or so south of Ruby Beach, the highway parallels the wave-swept coastline. Along this stretch of highway are turnoffs for four beaches that have only numbers for names. The Beach 6 overlook is a good place to look for whales and sea lions, and also to see the effects of erosion on this coast (the trail that used to lead down to the beach has been washed away). At low tide, the northern beaches offer lots of tide pools to explore. Near the south end of this stretch of road, you'll find **Kalaloch Lodge,** (p. 275) which has a gas station.

QUINAULT LAKE

From Kalaloch you'll drive through a long stretch of clear-cuts and tree farms, mostly on the Quinault Indian Reservation, to scenic **Quinault Lake.** Surrounded by forested mountains, this deep lake is the site of the rustic Lake Quinault Lodge and offers boating and freshwater fishing opportunities, as well as more rainforests to explore on a couple of short trails (a total of about 10 miles of trails are on the south side of the lake). On the north shore of the lake, you'll find one of the world's largest western red cedar trees. This is a good area in which to spot Roosevelt elk.

Where to Stay

In addition to the lodgings listed here, there are numerous campgrounds in or near Olympic National Park. For general information on all of the national park's campgrounds, contact **Olympic National Park** (✆ **360/565-3130**). Make reservations at the national park's Kalaloch Campground, the only facility that accepts reservations, by contacting the **National Recreation Reservation Service** (✆ **877/444-6777** or 518/885-3639; www.recreation.gov).

EAST OF PORT ANGELES

Domaine Madeleine ★★ Seven miles east of Port Angeles, this contemporary B&B is set on 5 wooded acres and has a very secluded feel. Big windows take in the views, while inside you'll find lots of Asian antiques and other interesting touches. Combine this with the waterfront setting and you have a fabulous hideaway. The guest rooms are in several different buildings surrounded by colorful gardens. All rooms have fireplaces as well as views of the Strait of Juan de Fuca and the mountains beyond. Some have whirlpool tubs; some have kitchens or air-conditioning. For added privacy, there is a separate cottage.

146 Wildflower Lane, Port Angeles, WA 98362. www.domainemadeleine.com. ✆ **888/811-8376** or 360/457-4174. 5 units. $140–$310 double. Rates for rooms in main house include full breakfast. 2-night minimum mid-Apr to mid-Oct, holidays, and weekends throughout the year. AE, DISC, MC, V. No children 11 or under. **Amenities:** Access to nearby health club. *In room:* TV/VCR/DVD, hair dryer, free Wi-Fi.

WEST OF PORT ANGELES

Beyond Port Angeles, accommodations are few and far between, and those places worth recommending tend to be very popular. Try to have room reservations before heading west from Port Angeles.

Lake Crescent Lodge ★ Built in 1916, this historic lodge, 20 miles west of Port Angeles on the south shore of picturesque Lake Crescent, is the lodging of choice for national-park visitors wishing to stay on the north side of the park. Wood paneling, hardwood floors, a stone fireplace, and a sunroom make the lobby a popular spot for just sitting and relaxing. The guest rooms in the main lodge building have the most historic character but have shared bathrooms; other rooms are mostly aging motel-style rooms that lack the character of the lodge rooms. The best accommodations are the Roosevelt cabins, which have fireplaces. However, a couple of the Singer cabins (nos. 20 and 21) do have great views. All but the main lodge rooms have views of the lake or the mountains. From mid-October to early May, the lodge is closed, but the Roosevelt cabins are still available.

416 Lake Crescent Rd., Port Angeles, WA 98363. www.olympicnationalparks.com. ✆ **888/732-7127** or 360/928-3211. 52 units, 5 with shared bathroom. $105 double without bathroom; $159–$169 double with bathroom; $189–$239 cottage. Children 12 and under stay free in parent's room. AE, DC, DISC, MC, V. Pets accepted in cottages ($25 fee). **Amenities:** Restaurant, lounge; watersports equipment/boat rentals; free Wi-Fi. *In room:* No phone.

Sol Duc Hot Springs Resort ☺ The Sol Duc Hot Springs have for decades been a popular family vacation spot, with campers, day-trippers, and resort guests spending their days soaking and playing in the mineral hot-spring pools. The grounds of the resort are grassy and open, and the forest is kept just at arm's reach. Unfortunately, the cabins have little character and are basically free-standing motel rooms. Don't come expecting a classic mountain cabin experience. There's a **restaurant,** as well as a poolside deli, coffee shop, and grocery store. Three hot-spring-fed soaking pools and a large swimming pool are the focal point and are open to the public for a small fee. Massage services are available.

12076 Sol Duc Hot Springs Rd. (P.O. Box 2169), Port Angeles, WA 98363. www.olympicnationalparks.com. ✆ **866/476-5382.** Fax 360/327-3593. 33 units. $157–$189 cabin; $320 suite. Children 5 and under stay free in parent's room, children over 5 $25 a night. AE, DC, DISC, MC, V. Closed late Oct to early Mar. Pets accepted ($25 per night). **Amenities:** 2 restaurants; outdoor pool and 3 hot-spring-fed soaking pools. *In room:* Hair dryer, no phone.

IN THE FORKS AREA

The town of Forks has several inexpensive motels and is a good place to look for cheap lodgings if you happen to be out this way without a reservation P. 272).

ALONG THE PARK'S WEST SIDE, SOUTH OF FORKS

Kalaloch Lodge ★★ These are the national park's only oceanfront accommodations, comprising a rustic, cedar-shingled lodge and a cluster of cabins perched on a grassy bluff above the thundering Pacific Ocean. Wide sand beaches stretch north and south from the lodge, and huge driftwood logs are scattered at the base of the bluff like so many twigs. The rooms in the old lodge are the least expensive, and the oceanview bluff cabins the most in-demand. The log cabins behind the bluff cabins don't have the knockout views. For modern comforts, the Sea Crest House has motel-like rooms. The **dining room** serves three meals a day, and there's a casual coffee bar as well. The lodge also has a general store and a gas station. Because this place is popular throughout the year, you should make reservations well in advance.

157151 U.S. 101, Forks, WA 98331. www.olympicnationalparks.com. ✆ **866/525-2562.** Fax 360/962-3391. 64 units. Late May to mid-Oct $179–$199 double, $309 suite, $219–$319 bluff cabin, $189–$209 log cabin; lower rates other months. Children 12 and under stay free in parent's room; over 12, $15 plus tax.. AE, DC, DISC, MC, V. Pets accepted in cabins ($25 fee). **Amenities:** Restaurant, lounge. *In room:* Hair dryer, no phone.

Lake Quinault Lodge ★★ On the shore of Lake Quinault in the southwest corner of the park, this imposing grande dame of the Olympic Peninsula wears an ageless tranquillity. Huge old firs and cedars shade the historic lodge, and Adirondack chairs on the deck command a view of the lawn. The accommodations include small rooms in the historic main lodge, modern rooms with TVs and small balconies, and rooms with fireplaces. These latter rooms were renovated a few years ago, as were many of the Lakeside rooms. The annex rooms are the least attractive, but they do have large bathtubs. The **dining room** has the most creative menu this side of the peninsula. For diversion, the lodge offers lawn games, boat rentals, and rainforest tours.

345 S. Shore Rd., Quinault, WA 98575. www.olympicnationalparks.com. ✆ **800/562-6672** or 360/288-2900. Fax 360/288-2901. 91 units. Mid-June to late Sept and winter holidays $169–$219 double, $319 suite; late Sept to mid-June $109–$179 double, $209 suite. Children 12 and under stay free in parent's room. AE, DC, DISC, MC, V. Pets accepted ($25 fee). **Amenities:** Restaurant, lounge; children's programs; indoor pool; sauna; seasonal watersports equipment/boat rentals; free Wi-Fi. *In room:* Hair dryer, no phone.

Where to Eat

IN PORT ANGELES

For great espresso and the best pastries on the peninsula, don't miss downtown's **Itty Bitty Buzz,** 110 E. First St. (✆ **360/565-8080;** www.thebuzzbeedazzled.com), which is affiliated with the Buzz in Sequim. If you're thinking of having a picnic, you might want to pick up some smoked salmon at **Sunrise Meats,** 1325 E. First St. (✆ **800/953-3211** or 360/457-3211; www.sunrisemeats.com).

Bella Italia ★ ITALIAN This downtown Port Angeles restaurant is only a couple of blocks from the terminal for ferries to and from Victoria, which makes it very convenient for many travelers. Dinners start with a basket of delicious bread accompanied by a garlic-and-herb dipping sauce. Local seafood makes it onto the menu in the form of smoked-salmon fettuccine, steamed mussels and clams, crab cakes, and other dishes, and these are among your best choices on the menu. There are also some interesting individual pizzas and a good selection of wines, as well as a wine bar, an espresso bar, and plenty of excellent Italian desserts. Oh, and for all you *Twilight* fans, this is where Bella and Edward had their first date.

118 E. First St. ✆ **360/457-5442.** www.bellaitaliapa.com. Reservations recommended. Main courses $9–$32. AE, DC, DISC, MC, V. Sun–Thurs 4–9pm; Fri–Sat 4–10pm.

WEST OF PORT ANGELES

Outside of Port Angeles, the restaurant choices become exceedingly slim. Your best options are the dining rooms at a couple of the area's more popular lodges. **Lake Crescent Lodge** (see above), on the shore of Lake Crescent, is open from early May to mid-October. Continuing west you'll find food at the dining room of **Sol Duc Hot Springs Resort,** open late March through late October.

If you've worked up an appetite hiking or just need some fortification to get you out to the far side of the Olympic Peninsula, you can tuck into a logger's breakfast, a 1-pound burger, or just a good slice of pie at the **Hungry Bear Cafe,** U.S. 101 at milepost 206, Beaver (✆ **360/327-3225;** www.hungrybearcafemotel.com), which is just east of the turnoff for Neah Bay. Way out in the peninsula's northwest corner, at Lake Ozette, you can get breakfast, lunch, and espresso at **The Lost Resort,** 208660 Hoko-Ozette Rd. (✆ **800/950-2899** or 360/963-2899; www.lostresort.net).

Although there are a handful of restaurants in Forks, none are really worth recommending. However, if you just want a burger, stop by **Sully's Drive-In,** 220 N. Forks Ave. (✆ **360/374-5075**), a classic burger joint popular with local high-school students. *Twilight* fans can get a Bella Burger here. About halfway between Forks and La Push, you can get a good burger at **Three Rivers Resort,** 7765 La Push Rd. (✆ **360/374-5300;** www.forks-web.com/threerivers), which also plays up *Twilight* with its Werewolf Burger and a sign marking the treaty boundary separating vampires from werewolves. South of Forks, your best bets are the dining rooms at **Kalaloch Lodge** (p. 275) and **Lake Quinault Lodge** (p. 275). If you happen to be hungry up the Hoh River, don't miss the juicy burgers at the **Hard Rain Cafe,** 5763 Upper Hoh Rd. (✆ **360/374-9288;** www.hardraincafe.com).

MOUNT RAINIER

Weather forecasting for Seattleites is a simple matter: Either the Mountain is out and the weather is good, or it isn't (out or good). "The Mountain" is, of course, Mount Rainier, the 14,410-foot-tall dormant volcano that looms over Seattle on clear days; and though it looks as if it's on the edge of town, it's actually 90 miles southeast of the city.

The mountain and more than 200,000 acres surrounding it are part of **Mount Rainier National Park,** which was established in 1899 as the fifth U.S. national park. From downtown Seattle, the preferred route to the mountain is via I-5 south to exit 142A. Then take Wash. 18 east to Wash. 164 to Enumclaw, continuing east on Wash. 410, which will take you to the northeast corner of the park. The route is well marked. Allow yourself 2½ hours to reach the park's Sunrise area. ***Note:*** This is a summer-only routing; during the winter, Sunrise is closed by snow, as are the roads to Ohanapecosh and from Ohanapecosh to Paradise. From October to late June you can visit the Paradise area of the park via the southwest (Nisqually) entrance to the park.

Exploring the Park

It's advisable to leave as early in the day as possible, especially if you're heading to the mountain on a summer weekend. Traffic along the route and crowds at the park can be daunting.

Before you go, get information by contacting **Mount Rainier National Park,** 55210 238th Ave. E., Ashford, WA 98304 (✆ **360/569-2211, ext. 3314;**

Take a hike from Sunrise toward Mt. Rainier.

www.nps.gov/mora). Keep in mind that during the winter, only the Longmire and Paradise areas of the park are open. Park entrances other than the Nisqually entrance are closed by snow throughout the winter.

The entry fee to Mount Rainier National Park is $15 per motor vehicle.

Follow signs for **Sunrise,** which, at 6,400 feet in elevation, is the highest spot in the park accessible by car. A beautiful old log lodge here serves as the visitor center. From here you can see not only Mount Rainier, seemingly at arm's length, but also Mount Baker and Mount Adams. During July and August, the alpine meadows here are ablaze with wildflowers. Some of the park's most scenic trails begin at Sunrise. Because this area is usually less crowded than Paradise, it is my favorite spot for an alpine hike. For maps and information on area trails, stop by the **Sunrise Visitor Center** (✆ **360/663-2425**).

Drive back down from Sunrise to Wash. 410 and continue south to Cayuse Pass, where you can make a short detour east to scenic Chinook Pass. From Cayuse Pass, continue south on Wash. 123 to the **Ohanapecosh Visitor Center** (✆ **360/569-6046**), where you can walk through a forest of old-growth trees, some more than 1,000 years old. This visitor center is usually open from late May to early October. From here, follow signs west to Paradise. On the way to Paradise, be sure to stop at the aptly named **Reflection Lakes** for the best photo op in the park.

Paradise (elevation 5,400 ft.), an aptly named mountainside aerie, affords a breathtaking close-up view of Mount Rainier. However, Paradise is the park's most popular destination, so expect crowds. As at Sunrise, July and August bring spectacular displays of wildflowers, which makes this another great place for day hikes. With only a short walk from the **Henry M. Jackson Memorial Visitor Center at Paradise** (✆ **360/569-6036**), you can view Nisqually Glacier. Many miles of other trails lead out from Paradise, looping through meadows and up onto snowfields above the timberline. It's not unusual to find plenty of snow at Paradise as late as July. In 1972, the area set a world record for snowfall in 1 year: 93½ feet! This record held until the 1998–99 winter season, when 94 feet of snow fell on Mount Baker, which is north of Mount Rainier.

Continuing west and downhill from Paradise will bring you to Longmire, site of the National Park Inn and the **Longmire Museum** (✆ **360/569-2211,** ext. 3314), which has exhibits on the park's natural and human history. You'll also find a hiker information center that issues backcountry permits. In winter, when this is one of the only areas of the park open to vehicles, a ski-touring center in Longmire rents cross-country skis and snowshoes.

At both Paradise and Sunrise, hikers can choose from a good variety of outings, from short, flat nature walks to moderately difficult loops to long, steep, out-and-back hikes.

If you don't have a car but still want to visit Mount Rainier National Park, book a tour through **Tours Northwest** (✆ **888/293-1404** or 206/768-1234; www.seattlecitytours.com), which charges $109 for adults and $79 for children 3 to 12 for a 10-hour tour starting in Seattle. These tours, which operate between late April and early November, spend most of the day in transit, but you get to see the mountain up close and can do a couple of hours of hiking at Paradise.

Where to Stay

In addition to the two lodges listed below, there are several campgrounds within the national park. Two of these—Cougar Rock and Ohanapecosh—take reservations, which should be made several months in advance for summer weekends. To make reservations, contact the **National Recreation Reservation Service** (✆ **877/444-6777** or 518/885-3639; www.recreation.gov).

National Park Inn ★ Located in Longmire, in the southwest corner of the park, this rustic lodge opened in 1920 and is set in the dense forests that blanket the lower slopes of Mount Rainier. The inn's front veranda has a good view of the mountain, and it is here that guests gather at sunset on clear days. The lounge, with its river-rock fireplace, is the perfect place to relax on a winter's night. Guest rooms vary in size and contain rustic furnishings but are definitely not the most memorable part of a stay here. The inn's restaurant manages to have something for everyone. The National Park Inn is popular in winter with cross-country skiers and snowshoers, and equipment can be rented at the gift shop inside the National Park Inn.

Mount Rainier National Park, Longmire, WA 98397. www.mtrainierguestservices.com. ✆ **360/569-2275.** Fax 360/569-2770. 25 units, 7 with shared bathroom. $116 double with shared bathroom; $155–$231 double with private bathroom. Children 1 and under stay free in parent's room. Older children $18.. AE, DC, DISC, MC, V. **Amenities:** Restaurant. *In room:* Hair dryer, no phone.

Paradise Inn ★★ Built in 1916 high on the flanks of Mount Rainier in an area aptly known as Paradise, this rustic lodge should be your first choice of accommodations in the park (book early). Cedar-shake siding, huge exposed beams, cathedral ceilings, and a gigantic stone fireplace make this the quintessential mountain retreat. Offering breathtaking views of the mountain, the inn is also the starting point for miles of trails that in summer wander through flower-filled meadows. Guest rooms vary in size.

Mount Rainier National Park, Paradise, WA 98398. www.mtrainierguestservices.com. ✆ **360/569-2275.** Fax 360/569-2770. 121 units, 33 with shared bathroom. $109 double with shared bathroom; $160–$264 double with private bathroom; $268 suite. Children 1 and under stay free in parent's room. AE, DC, DISC, MC, V. Free parking. Closed early Oct to mid-May. **Amenities:** 2 restaurants. *In room:* No phone.

Where to Eat

Within the park, your first choice for meals should be the dining room at the **Paradise Inn** (above). There's also a dining room in Longmire at the National Park Inn. For quick meals, there are snack bars at the Henry M. Jackson Memorial Visitor Center, at Paradise Inn, and at Sunrise Lodge. In Ashford the **Copper Creek Restaurant,** 35707 Wash. 706 E. (✆ **360/569-2326;** www.coppercreekinn.com), makes good berry pies; breakfast and espresso are served at **Whittaker's Bunkhouse Cafe,** 30205 Wash. 706 E. (✆ **360/569-2439;** www.whittakersbunkhouse.com). In summer, you can get pizza, burgers, and beer at **BaseCamp Grill,** 30027 Wash. 706 E. (✆ **360/569-2727;** www.basecampgrill.com), next door to Whittaker's. If you're heading up to the mountain from Seattle, be sure to stop in Eatonville at **Truly Scrumptious Bakery & Cafe,** 212 Washington Ave. (✆ **360/832-2233;** www.trulyscrumptiousbakery.com), where you can get a slice of pie, some bread for a picnic, or a sandwich to go.

Alexander's ★ AMERICAN Alexander's, which is also a popular B&B, is the best place to dine outside the Nisqually entrance to the park. Fresh trout from the inn's pond is the dinner of choice, but you'll also find salmon, lamb chops, steaks, pork loin, and pastas on the menu. Whatever you order, save room for the wild blackberry pie.

37515 Wash. 706 E., Ashford. ✆ **360/569-2300.** www.alexanderscountryinn.com. Reservations recommended. Main courses $9–$24. DISC, MC, V. Summer Mon–Thurs 11:30am–3pm and 4–9pm, Fri–Sun 11:30am–3pm and 4–9pm; shorter hours other months.

FERRY EXCURSIONS FROM SEATTLE

Among Seattle's most popular excursions are ferry trips across Puget Sound to Bainbridge Island (Seattle's quintessential bedroom community) and Bremerton (home of the Puget Sound Naval Shipyard). If your interests run to shopping, small towns, wineries, parks, and gardens, you'll want to head over to Bainbridge Island. If, on the other hand, you're more interested in naval history and antiques and collectibles, visit Bremerton. It's also possible to link these two excursions by taking one ferry out and the other ferry back. It's not a long drive between Bainbridge Island and Bremerton (less than 1 hr.), but if you stop often to enjoy the sights, you can certainly have a long day's outing.

Bainbridge Island & Poulsbo

Start the trip by taking the Bainbridge Island ferry from the Colman Dock ferry terminal at Pier 52 on the Seattle waterfront. For a current sailing schedule, contact **Washington State Ferries** (✆ **800/843-3779,** 888/808-7977 in Washington, or 206/464-6400; www.wsdot.wa.gov/ferries). Onboard you can see the Seattle skyline and, on a clear day, Mount Rainier to the southeast and the Olympic Mountains to the west. One-way fares for the 35-minute crossing from Seattle to Bainbridge Island are $12 ($15 May to second Sat in Oct) for a car and driver, $7.10 for adult car passengers or walk-ons, $3.55 for seniors, and $5.70 for children 5 to 18. Car passengers and walk-ons pay fares only on westbound ferries.

Just up the hill from the Bainbridge Island ferry terminal is the island's main shopping district, where you'll find lots of interesting shops and restaurants. A stroll around town will give you a good idea of what island life is all about and will probably leave you wondering how you, too, can live here. Start a tour of town by dropping by **Blackbird Bakery,** 210 Winslow Way E. (✆ **206/780-1322**), for a pastry and a coffee. If it's a hot day, you can get some of the Puget Sound region's best ice cream at **Mora Ice Creamery,** 139 Madrone Lane (✆ **206/855-8822;** moraicecream.com), which is just off Winslow Way East in the middle of the shopping district. Here, amid the many interesting shops and boutiques, you'll also find the tasting room of **Eleven Winery,** 287 Winslow Way E. (✆ **206/780-0905;** www.elevenwinery.com), which makes a wide range of wines, including a couple of different port-style wines. The tasting room is open daily in summer and Thursday through Sunday in other months; call for hours. For information on other Bainbridge Island wineries, check the **Bainbridge Wineries** website (www.bainbridgewineries.com).

If you'd like to do a little paddling in a sea kayak or canoe, turn left as you get off the ferry and head to **Back of Beyond Explorations,** 181 Winslow Way (✆ **206/842-9229;** www.tothebackofbeyond.com), which rents boats at Waterfront Park. Sea kayaks and canoes rent for $15 to $20 per hour depending on the type of boat. Some unusual swan boats (patterned after those in Boston) can be rented for $15 per half-hour. Want to get out on the water without expending any energy? Rent an electric boat from **Eagle Harbor Electric Boat Rentals** (✆ **206/949-2661;** www.theeagleharborinn.com), which operates out of the Harbor Marina at the corner of Madison Avenue and Parfitt Way SW. Boats hold up to 10 people and rent for $79 to $89 per hour, with a 2-hour minimum.

You can also pedal your way around Bainbridge Island by renting a bike from **Classic Cycle,** 740 Winslow Way NE. (✆ **206/842-9191;** www.classiccycleus.com), which rents bikes at the ferry dock bike barn during the summer. Bike rentals start at $25 for 2 hours. Outside of the summer months, go to the shop to rent bikes.

You can also wander along the town's Waterfront Trail, which for part of its short length is a boardwalk that skirts a marina. This trail will lead you to the **Pegasus Coffee House** (see below), which is my favorite lunch spot in town. A little farther on the Waterfront Trail will bring you to the **Harbour Public House,** 231 Parfitt Way SW (✆ **206/842-0969;** www.harbourpub.com), a tavern with a nice view of the marina.

To learn more about Bainbridge Island history, stop in at the **Bainbridge Island Historical Museum,** 215 Ericksen Ave. NE (✆ **206/842-2773;** www.bainbridgehistory.org). This little museum, housed partly in a little red 1908 schoolhouse, is open Wednesday through Monday from 1 to 4pm (in summer, from 10am on Sat). Admission is $4 for adults and $3 for students and seniors (children 4 and under are free). If you have the family along, you may also want to spend some time at the new green-built **Kids Discovery Museum (KiDiMu),** 301 Ravine Lane (✆ **206/855-4650;** www.kidimu.org), which is open Tuesday through Saturday from 10am to 4pm and Sunday from noon to

4pm. Admission is $5 for adults and children and $4 for seniors. Between mid-April and late October, on Saturdays from 9am to 1pm, the **Bainbridge Island Farmers' Market** (✆ **206/855-1500;** www.bainbridgefarmers market.com) sets up in the center of town at City Hall Park.

Down at the south end of the island is **Fort Ward State Park,** 2241 Pleasant Beach (✆ **360/902-8844**), on the quiet shore of Rich Passage. The park offers picnicking, good bird-watching, and a 2-mile hiking trail.

Stroll amid the fauna of the Bloedel Reserve.

Garden enthusiasts will want to make a reservation to visit the **Bloedel Reserve ★★**, 7571 NE Dolphin Dr.(✆ **206/842-7631;** www.bloedelreserve.org), 6 miles north of the ferry terminal off Wash. 305 (turn right on Agate Point Rd.). The expansive and elegant grounds are the ideal place for a quiet stroll amid plants from around the world. Admission is $13 for adults, $9 for seniors, and $5 for college students and children 13 to 18. June through August, the gardens are open Tuesday through Saturday from 10am to 7pm and Sunday from 10am to 4pm; other months the gardens are open Tuesday through Sunday from 10am to 4pm. Nearby, at the northern tip of the island, you'll find **Fay Bainbridge State Park,** 15446 Sunrise Dr. (✆ **360/902-8844**), which offers camping and great views across the sound to the Seattle skyline.

After crossing the Agate Pass Bridge to the mainland of the Kitsap Peninsula, take your first right, and at the gas station on the edge of the village of **Suquamish,** turn left to reach the grave of Chief Sealth, for whom Seattle was named. Nearby is **Old Man House Park,** which preserves the site of a large Native American longhouse. The Old Man House itself is long gone, but you'll find an informative sign and a small park with picnic tables. To find this park, go back to the gas station and go straight across the main road.

From Suquamish, head back to Wash. 305, continue a little farther west, and watch for signs to the **Suquamish Museum,** 15838 Sandy Hook Rd. (✆ **360/394-8496;** www.suquamish.org/museum.aspx), on the Port Madison Indian Reservation. The museum houses a compelling history of Puget Sound's native people, with lots of historic photos and quotes from tribal elders about growing up in the area. From May through September, the museum is open daily from 10am to 5pm; October through April, it's open Thursday to Sunday from 11am to 5pm. Admission is $4 for adults, $3 for seniors, and $2 for children 12 and under. A new museum is currently under construction and may be open by the time you visit, so be sure to call first for directions.

Continuing north on Wash. 305, you'll come to the small town of **Poulsbo,** which overlooks fjordlike Liberty Bay. Settled in the late 1880s by Scandinavians, Poulsbo was primarily a fishing, logging, and farming town until it decided to play up its Scandinavian heritage. Today shops in the Scandinavian-inspired downtown sell all manner of Viking and Scandinavian souvenirs, but there are also restaurants, art galleries, fashion boutiques, and other interesting stores. Throughout the year, numerous Scandinavian-themed celebrations are held. For more information, contact the **Greater Poulsbo Chamber of Commerce,** 19351 Eighth Ave., Ste. 108 (P.O. Box 1063), Poulsbo, WA 98370 (© **877/768-5726** or 360/779-4848; www.poulsbochamber.com).

Between downtown and the waterfront, you'll find Liberty Bay Park, at one end of which is the **Poulsbo Marine Science Center,** 18743 Front St. NE (© **360/598-4460;** www.poulsbomsc.org), which has aquariums full of local sea life. The center is open Thursday through Sunday from 11am to 4pm, and admission is free. If you'd like to get out on the waters of Liberty Bay, rent a boat from **Northwest Boat Rentals & Adventures,** 18779 Front St., Ste. 108 (© **360/265-8300;** www.northwestboatrentals.com), which rents sailboats, speedboats, canoes, and electric boats.

If you have a sweet tooth, don't miss **Sluys Poulsbo Bakery ★,** 18924 Front St. NE (© **360/697-2253**), which bakes mounds of Scandinavian-inspired goodies (very sweet), as well as stick-to-your-ribs breads. When you need a cup of espresso, head to the **Poulsbohemian Coffeehouse,** 19003 Front St. (© **360/779-9199;** www.poulsbohemian.com), which has an excellent view of Liberty Bay from atop the bluff on the edge of downtown.

If you have time and enjoy visiting historic towns, continue north from Poulsbo on Wash. 3 to **Port Gamble** (www.portgamble.com), which looks like a New England village dropped down in the middle of the Northwest woods. This community was established in 1853 as a company town for the Pope and Talbot lumber mill. Along the town's shady streets are Victorian homes that were restored by Pope and Talbot. Stop by the **Port Gamble General Store and Cafe,** 32400 Rainier Ave. (© **360/297-7636;** http://portgamblegeneralstore.com), a classic general store that is home to the **Of Sea and Shore Museum** (www.ofseaandshore.com). This little museum houses an exhibit of seashells from around the world and is open daily from 9am to 5pm; admission is free. Around the back of the building that houses the general store, you'll find the **Port Gamble Historic Museum** (© **360/297-8078**), a collection of local memorabilia. Admission is $4 for adults and $3 for seniors and students (free for children 6 and under). From May through October, the museum is open daily from 9:30am to 5pm; the rest of the year, it's open Friday through Sunday, and major holiday Mondays, from noon to 5pm.

If you're interested in seeing Port Gamble from the water, you can rent a sea kayak from **Olympic Outdoor Center,** 32379 Rainier Ave. (© **800/592-5983** or 360/297-4659; www.olympicoutdoorcenter.com), which charges $15 to $22 per hour or $65 to $90 by the day. This shop also rents kayaks on the waterfront in Poulsbo.

WHERE TO EAT

Mor Mor Bistro and Bar ★★ NORTHWEST You'll find downtown Poulsbo's best and most upscale restaurant partially hidden by a big magnolia tree. The space is sophisticated and unpretentious, a description that fits the food as well.

The menu changes daily, but you can bet there will be simple comfort foods such as fish and chips, as well as the likes of grilled wild salmon and pumpkin pappardelle pasta with sage cream, almonds, and chanterelle mushrooms. The raviolis are usually good bets as well. If you aren't worried about putting on pounds, try snacking on the garlic-and-parmesan fries with aioli (they also come with the fish and chips).

18820 Front St., Poulsbo. ✆ **360/697-3449.** www.mormorbistro.com. Reservations recommended. Main courses $8–$16 lunch, $10–$24 dinner. AE, DISC, MC, V. Mon–Sat 11am–9pm; Sun 10am–3pm.

Pegasus Coffee House ★ NEW AMERICAN In business for more than 30 years, Pegasus is the island's best lunch spot, with delicious salads and sandwiches. Keep an eye out for sandwiches made with locally-made Salumi salami. There are always good specials, too. Locals also pack this place for its wonderful breakfasts, which makes it a great first stop on the island. More substantial meals are available on weekend nights when the coffee house stays open late and has live music. You'll find Pegasus near the marina at the bottom of Madison Avenue.

131 Parfitt Way SW., Bainbridge Island. ✆ **206/842-6725.** www.pegasuscoffeehouse.com. Main dishes $8–$10. AE, MC, V. Sun–Thurs 7am–6pm; Fri–Sat 7am–10pm.

Bremerton & Its Naval History

If you are interested in big ships and naval history, ride the ferry from Seattle to Bremerton (see above for information on Washington State Ferries). Bremerton is home to the Puget Sound Naval Shipyard, and there are always plenty of Navy ships in the harbor. Over the years, mothballed U.S. Navy ships have included the aircraft carriers USS *Nimitz* and USS *Midway* and the battleships USS *Missouri* and USS *New Jersey.* Along the town's waterfront, several attractions are linked by the Bremerton Boardwalk, which provides a pleasant place to stroll along the waters of Sinclair Inlet. In this area, you'll also find a couple of pretty little parks with unusual fountains. **Harborside Fountain Park,** beside the ferry dock, has fountains reminiscent of the conning towers of submarines. A block away, at Pacific Avenue and Second Street, you'll find the **Puget Sound Naval Shipyard Memorial Plaza,** with fountains and interpretive displays about the shipyard.

To learn more about Naval history, visit the **USS *Turner Joy* Museum Ship,** 300 Washington Beach Ave. (✆ **360/792-2457;** www.ussturnerjoy.org), a mothballed destroyer that is open to the public as a memorial to those who served in the U.S. Navy and who helped build the Navy's ships. You'll find the ship about 150 yards east of the Washington State Ferries terminal. From March through October, the ship is open daily from 10am to 5pm; November through February, it's open Wednesday through Sunday from 10am to 4pm. Admission is $12 for adults, $10 for seniors, and $7 for children 5 to 12.

Nearby is the **Puget Sound Navy Museum,** 251 First St. (✆ **360/479-7447;** www.history.navy.mil/museums/psnm/psnm.htm), an official U.S. Navy museum that showcases naval history and the historic contributions of the Puget Sound Naval Shipyard. The museum is open Monday through Saturday from 10am to 4pm and Sunday from 1 to 4pm (closed on Tues Oct–Apr). Admission is free.

Heading north from Bremerton on Wash. 3, you'll soon see signs for the **Naval Undersea Museum,** 1 Garnett Way. (✆ **360/396-4148;** www.history.

Explore the *Turner Joy*...once a U.S. Navy destroyer, now a museum.

navy.mil/museums/keyport/index1.htm), 3 miles east of Wash. 3 on Wash. 308 near the town of Keyport. The museum examines all aspects of undersea exploration, with interactive exhibits, models, and displays that include a deep-sea exploration-and-research craft, a Japanese kamikaze torpedo, and a deep-sea rescue vehicle. The museum is open daily from 10am to 4pm (closed on Tues Oct–May); admission is free. The reason this museum is here: The **Bangor Navy Base,** home port for a fleet of Trident nuclear submarines, is nearby. The base is on Hood Canal, a long, narrow arm of Puget Sound.

Bremerton isn't just about naval history; it's also home to the **Aurora Valentinetti Puppet Museum,** 257 Fourth St. (✆ **360/373-2992;** www.ectandpuppets.com), which has a large collection of puppets and marionettes and is sure to be a hit with your younger children. The museum is open Wednesday to Saturday from 11am to 4pm. Admission is by donation. Also in Bremerton, the **Kitsap County Historical Society Museum,** 280 Fourth St. (✆ **360/479-6226;** www.kitsaphistory.org), is housed in a 1940s-era streamline-modern bank building. The interesting architecture of the building is reason enough for a visit. The museum is open Tuesday through Saturday from 10am to 4pm (in summer, also open Sunday from noon to 4pm). Admission is $2 for adults and $1 for children 7 to 17.

Two of the last remaining "mosquito-fleet" foot ferries still operate between Bremerton and **Port Orchard.** If you park your car on the waterfront in Bremerton, you can step aboard the little passenger-only ferry and cross the bay to Port Orchard. In this little waterfront town, you'll find several antiques malls that can provide hours of interesting browsing. The second ferry crosses from Bremerton to a dock in the Annapolis neighborhood, just east of Port Orchard. For more information, contact **Kitsap Transit** (✆ **800/501-RIDE [7433]** or 360/373-2877; www.kitsaptransit.com/Footferry.html). The one-way fare is $2.

WHERE TO EAT

Anthony's at Bremerton ★ SEAFOOD Overlooking the Bremerton Marina and the ferry dock, this waterfront restaurant is part of the Puget Sound's most reliable seafood-restaurant chains. The convenient location in the middle of all of Bremerton's naval attractions makes Anthony's your best bet for lunch or dinner on an exploration of this town. Northwest seafoods are a specialty here. The pan-fried Willapa Bay oysters and Dungeness crab cakes are both good bets and can be ordered either as appetizers or entrees. If you're not fond of fish, you'll find plenty of meaty options.

20 Washington Ave. ✆ **360/377-5004.** www.anthonys.com. Reservations recommended. Main courses $8–$28. AE, DISC, MC, V. Sun–Thurs 11am–9:30pm; Fri–Sat 11am–10:30pm.

SNOQUALMIE FALLS & THE SNOQUALMIE VALLEY

One of the reasons so many people put up with Seattle's drawbacks—urban sprawl, congested highways, and high housing prices—is that less than an hour east lie mountains so vast and rugged, you can hike for a week without crossing a road. Between the city and this wilderness lie the farmlands of the **Snoqualmie Valley,** the Seattle region's last bit of bucolic countryside. Here you'll find small towns, pastures full of spotted cows, "U-pick" farms, and a few unexpected attractions, including an impressive waterfall and a reproduction of a medieval village.

Snoqualmie Falls ★★, the valley's biggest attraction, plummet 270 feet into a pool of deep blue water. The falls are surrounded by a park owned by Puget Power, which operates a hydroelectric plant inside the rock wall behind the falls. The plant, built in 1898, was the world's first underground electricity-generating facility. Within the park, you'll find two overlooks near the lip of the falls and a .5-mile trail down to the base of the cascade. The river below the waterfall is popular for both fishing and white-water kayaking. To reach the falls, take I-90 east from Seattle for 35 to 45 minutes and get off at exit 27. If you're hungry for lunch, try the restaurant at **Salish Lodge,** the hotel at the top of the falls.

Snoqualmie Falls are located just outside the town of **Snoqualmie,** which is where you'll find the restored 1890 railroad depot that houses the **Northwest Railway Museum,** 38625 SE King St. (✆ **425/888-3030;** www.trainmuseum.org). The museum, an absolute must for anyone with a child who is a fan of Thomas the Tank Engine or *The Polar Express,* operates the **Snoqualmie Valley Railroad** on weekends from April through October. The 65- to 75-minute railway excursions run between here and the town of **North Bend.** Fares are $12 for adults, $10 for seniors, and $8 for children 2 to 12. Be sure to check the current schedule. The museum displays railroad memorabilia and has a large display of rolling stock. It's a big hit with kids!

Outside of North Bend rises **Mount Si,** one of the most hiked mountains in the state. Carved by glaciers long ago, this mountain presents a dramatic face to the valley, and if you're the least bit athletic, it is hard to resist the temptation to hike to the top. For more information, see p. 160.

Between North Bend and the town of **Carnation,** you'll pass several "U-pick" farms, where throughout the summer you can pick your own berries.

The Snoqualmie Valley is also the site of **Camlann Medieval Village,** 10320 Kelly Rd. NE (✆ **425/788-8624;** www.camlann.org), located north of

Snoqualmie Falls plummet nearly 300 feet in the Snoqualmie Valley.

Carnation off Wash. 203. On weekends, between late July and late August, this reproduction medieval village stages numerous medieval festivals and becomes home to knights and squires and assorted other costumed merrymakers. There are crafts stalls and food booths, and medieval clothing is available for rent if you forgot to pack yours. Throughout the year, the village stages a wide variety of banquets, seasonal festivals, and weekend living-history demonstrations. **Ye Bors Hede Inne** restaurant is open Tuesday through Sunday for traditional dinners ($19 per person). Fair admission is $10 for adults and $6 for seniors and children 6 to 12. Admission to both the fair and a banquet is $45.

On the way to or from Snoqualmie Falls, you may want to pull off I-90 in the town of **Issaquah** (15 miles east of Seattle) for a bit of shopping and candy sampling. Take exit 17 and, at the bottom of the exit ramp, turn right and then immediately left onto Northeast Gilman Boulevard. Just a short distance up the road, you'll come to **Boehms Candies,** 255 NE Gilman Blvd. (✆ **425/392-6652;** www.boehmscandies.com), which specializes in chocolate confections such as truffles, turtles, and pecan rolls. From Boehms, drive back the way you came (staying on Gilman Blvd. through the intersection that leads to the freeway), and you will come to **Gilman Village,** 317 NW Gilman Blvd. (✆ **425/392-6802;** www.gilmanvillage.com), an unusual collection of historic buildings that were moved to this site and turned into a shopping center full of interesting little shops.

Also here in Issaquah is the **Issaquah Salmon Hatchery,** 125 W. Sunset Way (✆ **425/391-9094** or 425/392-1118; www.issaquahfish.org), where throughout the year you can see the different stages of rearing salmon from egg to adult. In October adult salmon can be seen returning to the hatchery; every year on the first weekend in October, the city holds the Salmon Days Festival to celebrate the return of the natives. The hatchery is open daily from dawn to dusk; indoor exhibits are open daily from 8am to 4pm. Admission is free.

Where to Stay

Salish Lodge & Spa ★★★ Set at the top of 268-foot Snoqualmie Falls and only 30 minutes east of Seattle on I-90, the Salish Lodge & Spa is a popular weekend getaway spot for Seattle residents. With its country-lodge atmosphere, the Salish aims for casual comfort and hits the mark, though the emphasis is clearly on luxury. Guest rooms are designed for romantic weekend escapes, with wood-burning fireplaces, oversize whirlpool tubs, feather beds, and down comforters. A full-service spa makes this getaway even more attractive. The lodge's **country breakfast** is a legendary feast that will likely keep you full right through to dinner, and at night you can choose from one of the most extensive lists of Washington wines at any restaurant in the state. The lounge has a view of the falls.

6501 Railroad Ave. (P.O. Box 1109), Snoqualmie, WA 98065. www.salishlodge.com. ✆ 800/272-5474 or 425/888-2556. Fax 425/888-2420. 89 units. Summer: $189–$399 double; $579–$799 suite; Off-season: $189–$329 double; $509–$759 suite. All rates require a mandatory $15 resort fee. Children 17 and under stay free in parent's room. AE, DC, DISC, MC, V. Pets accepted ($50 fee). Amenities: 2 restaurants, lounge; bikes; exercise room and access to nearby health club; room service; sauna; full-service spa. *In room:* A/C, TV, fridge, hair dryer, MP3 docking station, free Wi-Fi.

THE WOODINVILLE WINE COUNTRY

Washington is home to one of the nation's most important and productive wine regions, and today produces more wine than any other state except California. Although the main wine country lies more than 200 miles to the east, in Central and Eastern Washington, there is a concentration of more than 50 wineries and tasting rooms a 30-minute drive north of Seattle, in and around the town of Woodinville. Most of these wineries and tasting rooms are open to the public, but the majority are only open on weekends (and sometimes just on Sat afternoon). The proximity of Woodinville to Seattle makes this an excellent day's outing, and with so many wineries in the area, you could easily spend 2 or 3 days wine tasting here. That Woodinville is also home to the Northwest's top restaurant (**The Herbfarm,** p. 292) and a gorgeous contemporary lodge (**Willows Lodge,** p. 292), makes this a great place for a romantic getaway.

Most of the wineries in the area charge a $5 to $8 tasting fee, but your fee is usually refunded if you buy any wine. For more information and a map to area wineries, contact **Woodinville Wine Country** (✆ **425/205-4394;** www.woodinvillewinecountry.com) or look for their wineries brochure at any area winery. If you'd prefer to let someone else do the driving, book a tour with **Bon Vivant Wine Tours** (✆ **206/524-8687;** www.bonvivanttours.com), which charges $85 per person for a day tour of the wineries.

To reach this miniature wine country from Seattle, head east on Wash. 520 or I-90 to I-405, drive north on I-405 and take the Northeast 124th Street exit, and drive east to 132nd Avenue Northeast. Turn left here and continue north to Northeast 143rd Place/Northeast 145th Street. Turn right and drive down the hill. At the bottom of the hill, you will find the area's two largest wineries.

The **Columbia Winery,** 14030 NE 145th St. (✆ **800/488-2347** or 425/482-7490; www.columbiawinery.com), has Washington's largest tasting bar

Chateau Ste. Michelle is in the heart of the Woodinville wine country.

and produces a wide range of good wines. It's open Sunday through Tuesday from 10am to 6pm, and Wednesday through Saturday from 11am to 7pm. This winery tends to be crowded on weekends, so try to arrive early.

Directly across Northeast 145th Street from the Columbia Winery, you'll find the largest and most famous of the wineries in the area, **Chateau Ste. Michelle ★**, 14111 NE 145th St. (✆ **800/267-6793** or 425/488-1133; www.ste-michelle.com). In a grand mansion on a historic 1912 estate, this is by far the most beautiful winery in the Northwest. It's also the largest winery in the state and is known for its consistent quality. Hours are daily from 10am to 5pm; if you take the free tour, you can sample several of the less expensive wines. A basic wine tasting is free, but you can also opt for $10 and $15 tastings that can include more expensive and older reserve wines. Because this winery is so big and produces so many different wines, you never know what you might find in the tasting room. An amphitheater on the grounds stages big-name music performances throughout the summer.

If you drive north from Chateau Ste. Michelle, Northeast 145th Street becomes Woodinville-Redmond Road (Wash. 202) and you soon come to the large and impressively modernistic **Januik Winery/Novelty Hill Winery,** 14710 Woodinville-Redmond Rd. NE (✆ **425/481-5502;** www.januikwinery.com or www.noveltyhillwines.com). Mike Januik is the winemaker for both of these wineries, and he crafts a wide range of reliable wines. The tasting room is open daily from 11am to 5pm. Along this stretch of road, you'll also find **Silver Lake Winery,** 15029 Woodinville-Redmond Rd. NE (✆ **425/485-2437;** www.silverlakewinery.com). This winery sometimes crafts good reds at good prices but can be hit-or-miss. The tasting room is open Monday through Saturday from 11am to 5pm and Sunday from noon to 5pm.

Continue a little farther to get to **DiStefano Winery,** 12280 Woodinville Dr. NE (✆ **425/487-1648;** www.distefanowinery.com), which is best known for its full-bodied red wines but also produces some memorable whites. The tasting room is open Tuesday to Thursday from 1 to 5pm, Friday from noon to 7pm, Saturday and Sunday from noon to 5pm.

If you want to visit some of the area's smaller wineries, head east a quarter-mile from Columbia Winery and Chateau Ste. Michelle on Woodinville-Redmond Road to the roundabout at 140th Place Northeast. Here you'll find the **Schoolhouse District,** named for the old Hollywood Schoolhouse, which dates from 1912. Here at this intersection, you'll find more than a dozen wineries, including the following, which are among my favorites.

In the lower level of the restored Hollywood Schoolhouse, you'll find **Alexandria Nicole Cellars,** 14810 NE 145th St. (✆ **425/487-9463;** www.alexandrianicolecellars.com), which in 2011 was named the winery of the year by *Wine Press Northwest,* a regional wine publication. The tasting room is open Thursday through Monday from noon to 5pm (Fri until 8pm).

In a separate building across the parking lot from the schoolhouse, you'll find four more tasting rooms. **Pepper Bridge Winery,** 14810 NE 145th St., Ste. A-3 (✆ **425/483-7026;** www.pepperbridge.com), which shares its tasting room with sister winery **Amavi Cellars,** is one of the most highly regarded wineries in the state and focuses on cabernet sauvignon, merlot, and Bordeaux blends. The tasting room is open Monday through Thursday from noon to 5pm, Friday and Saturday from noon to 7pm, and Sunday from noon to 6pm (shorter hours in winter). The adjacent **Ross Andrew Winery,** 14810 NE 145th St., Ste. A-2 (✆ **425/485-2720;** www.rossandrewwinery.com), which produces both cabernet sauvignon and syrah and an unusual cabernet-syrah blend, is also worth a visit. This tasting room is open Thursday, Friday, and Monday from noon to 5pm and Saturday from noon to 6pm. In this same building, you'll also find **Mark Ryan Winery** and the **J. Bookwalter Tasting Studio.**

Diagonally across the roundabout from the schoolhouse, you'll find several more good wineries. The **Carriage House Tasting Room,** 14421 Woodinville-Redmond Rd. NE (✆ **425/877-9472;** www.delillecellars.com), is the tasting room of **DeLille Cellars,** one of Washington's most prestigious wineries. Grapes used in the Bordeaux-style wines made here use grapes from the Klipsun and Ciel du Cheval vineyards, two of the state's top vineyards. Expect to pay $70 or more per bottle for wines here. The tasting room is open Sunday through Thursday from noon to 4:30pm, Friday from noon to 7pm, and Saturday from 11am to 4:30pm. Next door to the Carriage House, is the tasting room of **Brian Carter Cellars,** 14419 Woodinville-Redmond Rd. NE (✆ **425/806-9463;** www.briancartercellars.com), which is open daily from noon to 5pm. This winery makes wines in a wide range of styles, including Bordeaux-style blends, Rhone-style blends, Spanish-style red-wine blends, and even port-style dessert wines.

In the shopping center behind the Carriage House, you can visit **Sparkman Cellars,** 14473 Woodinville-Redmond Rd. (✆ **425/398-1045;** www.sparkmancellars.com), where big Bordeaux blends in the $40 to $50 range are produced. Grapes for many of the Sparkman wines are sourced from Washington's top vineyards. The tasting room is open Wednesday to Sunday from 1 to 6pm. In this same shopping center location, you'll also find **Dusted Valley Vintners** and **Gifford Hirlinger,** two of the better small wineries from Walla Walla, as well as the **Purple Café and Wine Bar** (p. 292).

From the Hollywood Schoolhouse neighborhood, drive north on 140th Place Northeast to downtown Woodinville, turn right on Northeast Woodinville-

Duvall Road, left on Northeast North Woodinville Road, and right on 144th Avenue Northeast. Here, in a warehouse industrial complex, you'll find more than 40 small wineries. Between April and September, many of these wineries are open from 4 to 8pm on the third Thursday of the month for the **Woodinville Warehouse Wineries Third Thursday Wine Walk** (www.woodwarewine.com). Admission to this monthly event costs $20 per person if you bring your own glass and $25 if you buy a glass. Your admission ticket gets you tastings at all the participating wineries. The following wineries are some of my favorites among these warehouse wineries.

For the most bang for your buck, head to 19495 144th Ave. NE, Ste. B240, a single tasting room that is home to **Smasne Cellars** (**© 425/485-9461;** www.smasnecellars.com), **AlmaTerra Wines** (**© 509/592-0756;** www.almaterrawines.com), and **Gård Vintners** (**© 509/346-1232;** www.gardvintners.com). What ties these three little wineries together is winemaker Robert Smasne, who has worked at numerous wineries across the state. The tasting room is open Friday from 2 to 7pm and Saturday and Sunday from noon to 6pm.

At **Anton Ville Winery,** 19501 144th Ave. NE, Ste. D300 (**© 206/683-3393;** www.antonvillewinery.com), you can sample a variety of good Bordeaux-style reds in the $30 price range. May through October, the tasting room here is open Friday through Sunday from 1 to 5pm; November through April, it's open Saturday from 1 to 5pm.

Cuillin Hills Winery, 19495 144th Ave. NE, Ste. A110 (**© 425/402-1907;** www.cuillinhills.com), produces primarily Rhone- and Bordeaux-style red wines, though with an emphasis on ripe fruit flavors. The tasting room is open Saturday from noon to 4pm.

If you're a jazz fan and your tastes run to sangiovese and zinfandel, be sure to stop by **Des Voigne Cellars,** 19501 144th Ave. NE, Ste. B500 (**© 425/415-8466;** www.desvoignecellars.com), which features jazz musicians on its labels. The winemaker here is the brother of the winemaker at Cuillin Hills Winery. While the emphasis here is on red wines, there is also a very good viognier-roussanne white blend. The tasting room is open Saturday from 1 to 5pm and most Sundays from 1 to 4pm.

Page Cellars, 19495 NE 144th Ave. NE, Ste. B205 (**© 253/232-9463;** www.pagecellars.com), focuses on cabernet sauvignon and sauvignon blanc but also does merlot, syrah, and a rosé. Keep an eye out for wines made with Klipsun Vineyard and Red Mountain grapes. The tasting room is open Saturday from noon to 4pm and Sunday from 1 to 5pm.

Red Sky Winery, 19495 144th Ave. NE, Ste. B210 (**© 425/481-9864;** www.redskywinery.com), does a variety of Bordeaux blends as well as semillon, syrah, and merlot. The tasting room is open Saturday from noon to 5pm, and, during the summer, is also open on Sunday from noon to 5pm.

Just because this is wine country doesn't mean you can't get a good pint of beer! The large **Redhook Ale Brewery,** 14300 NE 145th St. (**© 425/483-3232;** www.redhook.com), next door to Columbia Winery, is one of Washington's top breweries. Tours are available, and there's a pub here as well.

If you're up this way on a Saturday between early May and early October, be sure to stop by the **Woodinville Farmers Market,** at the Carol Edwards Center, Northeast 175th Street and 133rd Avenue Northeast (**© 206/528-2510;** www.woodinvillefarmersmarket.com), which is in downtown Woodinville adjacent to city hall. The market is open from 9am to 3pm.

Where to Stay

Willows Lodge ★★★ In the heart of the wine country, about 30 minutes north of Seattle, and adjacent to the much-celebrated Herbfarm (see below), this lodge is a beautiful blend of rustic and contemporary. From the moment you turn into the lodge's parking lot, you'll recognize it as someplace special. A huge fire-darkened tree stump is set like a sculpture outside the front door, and the landscaping has a distinctly Northwest feel. Inside the abundance of polished woods (some salvaged from a Portland, Oregon, port facility) gives the place something of a Japanese aesthetic. It's all very soothing and tranquil, an ideal retreat from which to visit the nearby wineries. In the guest rooms, you'll find beds with down duvets; slate tables made from salvaged pool tables; and all kinds of high-tech amenities.

14580 NE 145th St., Woodinville, WA 98072. www.willowslodge.com. ✆ **877/424-3930** or 425/424-3900. Fax 425/424-2585. 84 units. Summer: $249–$349 double; $599–$699 suite; off-season: $199–$259 double $379–$549 suite. Children 17 and under stay free in parent's room. AE, DC, DISC, MC, V. Valet parking $10. Pets accepted ($25 fee). **Amenities:** 2 restaurants, 2 lounges; bikes; concierge; exercise room; Jacuzzi; room service; full-service spa. *In room:* A/C, TV/DVD, CD player, hair dryer, minibar, MP3 docking station, free Wi-Fi.

Where to Eat

If you aren't out this way specifically to have dinner at The Herbfarm and just want a decent meal while you tour the area, try the **Forecaster's Public House** at the Redhook Ale Brewery, 14300 NE 145th St. (✆ **425/483-3232**). The Barking Frog restaurant at the **Willows Lodge** (see above) is another excellent choice in the area.

The Herbfarm ★★★ NORTHWEST The Herbfarm, the most highly acclaimed restaurant in the Northwest, is known for its lavish themed meals that change with the seasons. Wild-gathered vegetables, Northwest seafood and meats, organic produce, wild mushrooms, and, of course, fresh herbs from the Herbfarm gardens are the ingredients from which the restaurant creates its culinary extravaganzas. Dinners are paired with complementary Northwest wines.

The restaurant is in a reproduction country inn beside a contemporary Northwest-style lodge. Dinner highlights might include paddlefish caviar on crisp salmon skin; rosemary-mussel skewers with cucumber kimchi; oysters with sorrel sauce; Dungeness crab and wild mushroom "handkerchiefs"; salmon in a squash blossom with lemon thyme; perch on salsify puree with parsley-lovage sauce; lamb served three ways; truffled cheese; and, for dessert, muscat-poached peaches with anise hyssop ice. If you're a foodie, you need to have a dinner like this at least once in your life.

14590 NE 145th St. ✆ **425/485-5300.** www.theherbfarm.com. Reservations required. Fixed-price 9-course dinner $189–$195 per person w/6 or 7 matched wines. AE, DISC, MC, V. Seatings Thurs–Sat 7pm; Sun 4:30pm.

Purple Café and Wine Bar ★ NEW AMERICAN This stylish wine bar is convenient to all the wineries in the area and is my favorite lunch spot in Woodinville. It also makes a great place for an early dinner at the end of an afternoon of wine tasting. The menu is long and, as you would expect in a wine bar, features lots of great appetizers (including delicious grilled asparagus in the spring). Other dishes worth trying include the chopped salad and the penne pasta with Gorgonzola and pancetta. However, when I eat here, I usually opt for one of Purple's perfect pizzas.

14459 Woodinville-Redmond Rd. NE. ✆ **425/483-7129.** www.thepurplecafe.com. Reservations recommended. Main courses $11–$33. AE, DISC, MC, V. Tues–Thurs 11am–9pm; Fri–Sat 11am–10pm; Sun 11am–9pm.

NORTH OF SEATTLE: EVERETT'S AIR MUSEUMS

Before Bill Gates and Microsoft, Boeing, the aerospace giant, was the largest employer in the Seattle area. At that time, Seattle and Boeing were nearly synonymous, and while Boeing is no longer headquartered in Seattle, it still has large manufacturing facilities in the area. Consequently, there is a lot of aerospace history showcased around the Seattle area. If you have a fascination for airplanes both old and new, then you'll want to spend a half day or more visiting the air museums outside the town of Everett. To reach these Everett-area museums, drive 30 miles north from Seattle on I-5, take exit 189 to Wash. 526 west, and continue 4 miles to the intersection of Paine Field Blvd. and 84th St. SW.

Future of Flight Aviation Center & Boeing Tour ★★ While Microsoft and Amazon have plenty of clout around Seattle these days, Boeing is still a major presence in the city, and it has something that neither Microsoft nor Amazon can ever claim: the single largest building, by volume, in the world. The company's Everett assembly plant could easily hold 911 basketball courts, 74 football fields, 2,142 average-size homes, or all of Disneyland (with room left over for covered parking). This impressive building is open to the public by guided tour, and a visit to the plant is one of the most interesting tourist activities in Seattle. On the tour, you'll get to see how huge passenger jets are assembled. In the Future of Flight Aviation Center, from which the tours leave, you can stick your head inside a giant jet engine, climb into the cockpit of a Boeing 727, design your own jet on a computer, or go for a ride in a flight simulator.

The guided 90-minute **tours** are offered on the hour from 9am to 3pm, and tickets for same-day use are sold on a first-come, first-served basis; in summer, tickets for any given day's tours often sell out by noon. To check availability of same-day tickets, call the number below. It's also possible to make reservations 24 hours or more in advance by calling ✆ **800/464-1476** or 360/756-0086 daily between 9am and 5pm, or by booking online at the website below. If making reservations, you'll pay an extra $2.50 per ticket.

If you're in town without a car, you can book a tour to the plant through **Customized Tours** (✆ **888/554-8687** or 206/878-3965; www.ourtoursrock.com, which charges $59 and will pick you up at your Seattle hotel.

8415 Paine Field Blvd., Mukilteo. ✆ **888/467-4777** or 425/438-8100. www.futureofflight.org. Admission $16 adults, $14 seniors, $8 children 4 feet tall to age 15, no children under 4 feet tall on Boeing tour; exhibit hall only admission $10 adults and seniors, $5 children 6–15. Daily 8:30am–5:30pm. Closed Thanksgiving, Christmas, and New Year's Day.

Flying Heritage Collection Here at the Flying Heritage Collection, you can marvel at the 15 immaculately restored fighter planes that belong to Microsoft cofounder Paul Allen. Old fighter planes are another of Allen's interests, along with professional football (he owns the Seattle Seahawks), rock music, and science fiction (he owns EMP/SFM, the Experience Music Project/Science Fiction Museum). Many of the rare planes in this collection are in flyable condition, and two to three times a month during the summer, planes take to the air over Paine Field.

Paine Field, 3407 109th St. SW., Everett. ✆ **877/342-3404** or 206/342-4242. www.flyingheritage.com. Admission $12 adults, $10 seniors, $8 children 6–15, free for children 5 and under. Memorial Day to Labor Day daily 10am–5pm; other months closed Mon. Closed Thanksgiving and Christmas. From the Future of Flight Aviation Center, drive east on Wash. 526, turn right onto Airport Road, turn right again onto 12th Street SW, right again onto 30th Street West, and left onto 109th Street SW.

Museum of Flight Restoration Center The region's top aerospace museum is south Seattle's **Museum of Flight** (p. 141), and if you've already marveled at the immaculately restored planes at that museum, you may want to drop by this Paine Field facility. Here you'll see planes in various stages of restoration.
2909 100th St. SW, Everett. ✆ **425/745-5150.** www.museumofflight.org. June–August Tues–Sat 9am–5pm; September–May Tues–Thurs and Sat 9am–5pm. Admission $5 adults, $3 children 5–17. Call for directions.

LA CONNER: WASHINGTON'S TULIP CAPITAL

In a competition for quaintest town in Washington, La Conner would leave the other contenders wallowing in the winter mud. This town, a former fishing village, has a waterfront street lined with restored wooden commercial buildings, back streets of Victorian homes, and acres of tulip and daffodil fields stretching out from the town limits. Add to this three museums, numerous plant nurseries and gardening-related stores, art galleries, luxurious inns, and good restaurants, and you have a town almost too good to be true.

To reach La Conner, take I-5 north from Seattle and then take U.S. 20 west toward Anacortes. La Conner is south of U.S. 20 on La Conner–Whitney Road. Contact the **La Conner Chamber of Commerce,** 606 Morris St., La Conner (✆ **888/642-9284** or 360/466-4778; www.laconnerchamber.com), for more information on the area.

For a few short weeks each year, from late March to mid-April, the countryside around La Conner is awash with color as hundreds of acres of Skagit Valley tulip and daffodil fields burst into bloom in a floral display that rivals that of the Netherlands. These flowers are grown for their bulbs, which each fall are shipped to gardeners all over the world. The **Skagit Valley Tulip Festival** (✆ **360/428-5959;** www.tulipfestival.org), held each year during bloom time, is La Conner's biggest annual festival and includes dozens of events. Contact the festival office or stop by the La Conner Chamber of Commerce (see above), for a map of the flower fields.

Whether you're here in tulip time or not, you might want to stop by some of the area's farms, gardens, and nurseries. **RoozenGaarde Flowers & Bulbs,** 15867 Beaver Marsh Rd. (✆ **866/488-5477** or 360/424-8531; www.tulips.com), is the largest grower of tulips, daffodils, and irises in the country and has a gift shop. At **Christianson's Nursery & Greenhouse,** 15806 Best Rd., Mount Vernon (✆ **800/585-8200** or 360/466-3821; www.christiansonsnursery.com), you'll find hundreds of varieties of roses and lots of other plants as well. Nearby you can tour the beautiful English country gardens of **La Conner Flats,** 15980 Best Rd. (✆ **360/466-3190;** www.laconnerflats.com). Both of these nurseries are northeast of town off McLean Road (the main road to Mount Vernon).

The **Museum of Northwest Art ★★**, 121 S. First St. (✆ **360/466-4446;** www.museumofnwart.org), occupies a large contemporary building in downtown La Conner. The museum, which mounts a variety of exhibits throughout the year, features works by Northwest artists, including Morris Graves, Mark Tobey, and Guy Anderson, all of whom once worked in La Conner. This museum would be right at home in downtown Seattle, so it comes as a very pleasant surprise to find it in this tiny town. It's open Tuesday through Saturday from 10am to 5pm and Sunday and Monday from noon to 5pm; admission is $5 for adults, $4 for seniors, $2 for students and children ages 12 and over, and free for children 11 and under.

High atop a hill in the center of town, you can learn about the history of this area at the **Skagit County Historical Museum,** 501 S. Fourth St. (✆ **360/466-3365;** www.skagitcounty.net/museum). It's open Tuesday through Sunday from 11am to 5pm; admission is $4 for adults, $3 for seniors and children ages 6 to 12, and free for children 5 and under. A few blocks away, you'll find the **La Conner Quilt & Textile Museum,** 703 S. Second St. (✆ **360/466-4288;** www.laconnerquilts.com), which is housed in the historic Gaches Mansion. On the first floor of this museum, you'll find rooms furnished with antiques, while on the second floor there are quilt displays. The museum is open Wednesday through Sunday from 11am to 5pm (open daily during Apr); admission is $7 for adults, $5 for students, and free for children 11 and under.

Shopping is the most popular pastime in La Conner, and up and down First Street, you'll find lots of great galleries, boutiques, and gift shops filled with an eclectic assortment of must-have objects.

Where to Eat

On a dark, rainy night (or dreary afternoon), there's no better place in town to heft a pint of ale than at the **La Conner Brewing Company ★,** 117 S. First St. (✆ **360/466-1415;** www.laconnerbrew.com), right next door to the Museum of Northwest Art.

Seeds ★ AMERICAN Housed in what was for many years an old-fashioned seed company (thus the name), this casual restaurant on the edge of downtown La Conner has loads of historic character, which is what makes it one of my favorite places in town. With its battered wood floors and big windows, the renovated space still conjures up its seed-company heritage. The menu is simple, with an emphasis on sandwiches, salads, and a handful of more substantial entrees. I always go for the oysters. Be sure to notice the huge old beech tree growing through the deck near the front door.

623 Morris St. ✆ **360/466-3280.** www.seedsbistro.com. Main courses $10–$14 lunch, $10–$24 dinner. Reservations recommended. MC, V. Daily 11am–8:30 or 9pm.

TACOMA'S MUSEUMS & GARDENS

The cities of Seattle and Tacoma have long had an intense rivalry, and though Seattle long ago claimed the title of cultural capital of Washington, Tacoma has not given up the fight. Tacoma has two world-class art museums, and for anyone with an interest in art glass and famed Northwest glass artist Dale Chihuly, these two museums are a must. If it is Dale Chihuly's work in particular that brings you to Tacoma, be sure to stop in at **Union Station,** which is just up the street from the Tacoma Art Museum and contains a large Chihuly installation.

If you're in town on the third Thursday of the month, be sure to stick around for the evening **Artwalk** (✆ **253/272-4327;** www.artwalktacoma.com), which runs from 5 to 8pm. Participants include more than a dozen galleries and museums.

Hello, Dale, Is That You?

If you're in Tacoma on a Chihuly pilgrimage, be sure to bring your cellphone and dial the Ear for Art: Chihuly Glass Cell Phone Tour (✆ 888/411-4220). This self-guided walking tour of Chihuly artworks has five stops; at each one, just dial the toll-free number and punch in that stop number to learn more about the art you're seeing. You can also get a podcast of this tour by going to the Tacoma Art Museum website (www.tacomaartmuseum.org).

The Tacoma area is also home to some of the most outstanding public gardens in the state. Within a 20-mile radius, you can check out the orchids in a Victorian-era conservatory, tour an estate garden, and marvel at myriad species of rhododendrons.

To get to Tacoma from Seattle, take I-5 south for about 45 minutes. For more information on this area, contact the **Tacoma Regional Convention & Visitor Bureau,** 1516 Pacific Ave., Tacoma, WA 98402 (✆ **800/272-2662** or 253/627-2836; www.traveltacoma.com), which has its information center inside the Courtyard Tacoma Downtown hotel.

Museums

Museum of Glass ★★ Dale Chihuly's work inspired the construction of this museum, which showcases the very best art glass from around the world. A vast variety of glass artworks is featured in the galleries of this high-style building on the waterfront: Whether it's stained glass in the style of Tiffany, a traveling exhibit from a European museum, or the latest thought-provoking installation by a cutting-edge glass artist, you'll find it here. The highlight is the hot shop, a huge cone-shaped studio space where visitors can watch glass artists work at several kilns. Connecting the museum to the rest of the city is the 500-foot-long Chihuly Bridge of Glass, which spans the I-705 freeway. Adjacent to this museum, at 1821 E. Dock St., are the **Traver Gallery** (✆ **253/383-3685;** www.travergallery.com) and **Vetri** (✆ **253/383-3692;** www.vetriglass.com), which are outposts of **Seattle's Traver Gallery** (p. 195), the most highly respected art-glass gallery in the region.

1801 Dock St. ✆ **866/468-7386** or 253/284-4750. www.museumofglass.org. Admission $12 adults, $10 seniors, $5 children 6–12, free for children 5 and under. Free to all on 3rd Thurs of each month from 5–8pm; free for college students on Sun. Memorial Day to Labor Day Mon–Sat 10am–5pm (until 8pm on 3rd Thurs of each month), Sun noon–5pm; other months closed Mon–Tues. Closed New Year's Day, Thanksgiving, and Christmas.

Tacoma Art Museum ★★ Housed in a building designed by noted contemporary architect Antoine Predock, the Tacoma Art Museum may not have as big a reputation as the Seattle Art Museum, but it mounts some impressive shows. The building is filled with beautiful galleries in which to display both the museum's own collections and traveling exhibitions. The museum is best known for its large collection of art by native son Dale Chihuly, and fans of the glass artist can sign up for a walking tour of many of his works both here in the museum and around

Tacoma's Museum of Glass has some of the finest art glass around.

downtown. Tours are offered a couple of days a week, cost $15, and include museum admission. The museum also offers a cellphone tour of area Chihuly installations. You can find respectable collections of European Impressionism, Japanese woodblock prints, and American graphic art as well, and the museum regularly brings in large traveling shows.

1701 Pacific Ave. ✆ **253/272-4258.** www.tacomaartmuseum.org. Admission $9 adults, $8 seniors and students, free for children 5 and under. Free to all from 5–8pm on 3rd Thurs of each month. Wed–Sun 10am–5pm (until 8pm on 3rd Thurs of each month). Closed New Year's Day, Martin Luther King, Jr. Day, July 4th, Thanksgiving, and Christmas.

Washington State History Museum ★ ☺ A massive archive of Washington State history, this impressive museum is like no other history museum in the Northwest. A full barrage of high-tech displays makes history both fun and interesting. From a covered wagon to a sprawling model-railroad layout, a Coast Salish longhouse to a Hooverville shack, the state's history comes alive through the use of life-size mannequins, recorded narration, and "overheard" conversations. With loads of interactive exhibits and several films screened daily, it's obvious this museum is trying to appeal to the video-game generation, but older visitors will have fun, too. In 2011, there were plans to possibly close this museum for budgetary reasons; before planning a visit, make sure the museum is still open.

Wednesday Bargains

With the Museum of Glass, the Tacoma Art Museum, and the Washington State History Museum all within 3 blocks of one another, Tacoma is an even better museum town than Seattle. You can save on the cost of visiting these three museums by visiting on a Wednesday, when you can get into all three museums for $22 ($20 for seniors and $18 for students and children). For adults this is a savings of $7.

1911 Pacific Ave. ✆ **888/238-4373** or 253/272-3500. www.wshs.org/wshm. Admission $8 adults, $7 seniors, $6 students 6–17, free for children 5 and under. Free for all from 2–8pm on 3rd Thurs of each month. Wed–Sun 10am–5pm (until 8pm 3rd Thurs of each month). Closed Memorial Day, July 4, Labor Day, Thanksgiving, and Christmas.

Gardens

You'll find more public gardens at the sprawling **Point Defiance Park,** on the north side of town at the end of Pearl Street. This is one of the largest urban parks in the country, and in addition to a rose garden, a Japanese garden, a rhododendron garden, a dahlia test garden, and a native-plant garden, it's home to the Point Defiance Zoo & Aquarium, Fort Nisqually Historic Site, and the Camp 6 Logging Museum. Founded in 1888, this park preserved one of the region's most scenic points of land. Winding through the wooded park is **Five Mile Drive,** which connects all the park's main attractions (as well as picnic areas). There is also a network of hiking and biking trails. You can reach the park by following Ruston Way or Pearl Street north.

Lakewold Gardens ★ Formerly a private estate, this 10-acre garden, designed by noted landscape architect Thomas Church and located 10 miles south of Tacoma, includes extensive collections of Japanese maples and rhododendrons. There are also rose, fern, and alpine gardens that include numerous rare and unusual plants.

12317 Gravelly Lake Dr. SW, Lakewood. ✆ **888/858-4106** or 253/584-4106. www.lakewoldgardens.org. Admission $7 adults, $5 seniors and students, free for children 11 and under. Apr–Sept Wed–Sun 10am–4pm (until 8pm Wed July–Aug); Oct–Nov and Feb–Mar Fri–Sun 10am–3pm; Dec–Jan Fri 10am–3pm. Closed Thanksgiving weekend, Dec 24–Jan 1. Take exit 124 off I-5.

Rhododendron Species Foundation and Botanical Garden ★★ Covering 22 acres, this garden has one of the most extensive collections of species (unhybridized) rhododendrons and azaleas in the world. More than 10,000 plants put on an amazing floral display from March through May. Also included in these gardens are collections of ferns, maples, heathers, and bamboos. Inside the Rutherford Conservatory, you'll see numerous tropical species. For serious gardeners, this is one of the Northwest's must-see gardens. It's 8 miles north of Tacoma.

Weyerhaeuser corporate campus, 2525 S. 336th St. Federal Way. ✆ **253/838-4646** or 253/927-6960. www.rhodygarden.org. Admission $8 adults, $5 seniors and students, free for children 11 and under. Tues–Sun 10am–4pm. Closed New Year's day, Thanksgiving, Dec 24–25.Take exit 143 off I-5.

It's blooming pretty at the Rhododendron Species Foundation.

W. W. Seymour Botanical Conservatory ★ Constructed in 1908, this elegant Victorian conservatory is one of only three of this type on the West Coast and is listed on the National Register of Historic Places. More than 250 species of exotic plants (including more than 200 orchids) are housed in the huge greenhouse, which is built of more than 3,000 panes of glass. The conservatory stands in downtown Tacoma's Wright Park, which is a shady retreat from downtown's pavement.

Almond Roca® Rocks!

If you're as crazy about Almond Roca® candy as I am, you may be surprised to discover that it's made in Tacoma by the Brown & Haley company, in business since 1914. You can stock up on the addictive candies at the Brown & Haley Tacoma Outlet Store, 110 E. 26th St. (✆ 253/620-3067; www.brown-haley.com). This store, near the Tacoma Dome, is open 7 days a week. There's a second outlet in nearby Fife at 2105 Frank Albert Rd. (✆ 253/926-0240).

Wright Park, 316 S. G St. ✆ **253/591-5330.** www.metroparkstacoma.org. Admission by $5 suggested donation. Tues–Sun 10am–4:30pm. Closed New Year's Day, Thanksgiving to early Dec, and Christmas.

Where to Eat

If you're looking for someplace interesting to have a drink or an inexpensive meal, check out **The Swiss,** 1904 S. Jefferson Ave. (✆ **253/572-2821;** www.theswisspub.com), just uphill from the Washington State History Museum at the top of a long flight of stairs that links the museum with the University of Washington's Tacoma campus. The pub has not only a great beer selection and decent food, but also a collection of Dale Chihuly glass sculptures. ***Note:*** Because this is a pub, you must be 21 or older to eat here.

Harmon Brewery & Eatery AMERICAN In a renovated old commercial building across from the Washington State History Museum, this large pub is Tacoma's favorite downtown after-work hangout and casual lunch spot. The menu features primarily burgers and pizza, plus some interesting specials and, of course, plenty of good microbrews. The pub has an outdoor-sports theme.

1938 Pacific Ave. S. ✆ **253/383-2739.** www.harmonbrewingco.com. Reservations not accepted. Main courses $9–$18. AE, DC, DISC, MC, V. Mon–Thurs 11am–11pm; Fri 11am–midnight; Sat 10am–midnight; Sun 10am–9pm.

11

PLANNING YOUR TRIP TO SEATTLE

While knowing when it won't be raining may be the most important part of planning a trip to Seattle, you probably have plenty of other questions you'd like to have answered before you hit town. How do I get into town from the airport? What sort of public transit is there? Should I rent a car? In this chapter, you'll find answers to these and many other basic travel questions.

GETTING THERE

By Plane

The **Seattle–Tacoma International Airport** (✆ **800/544-1965** or 206/787-5388; www.portseattle.org/seatac/), most commonly referred to simply as Sea-Tac Airport, is served by about two dozen airlines. To find out which airlines travel to Seattle, please see "Airline Websites," p. 318.

GETTING INTO TOWN FROM THE AIRPORT

BY CAR To get downtown from the airport, take the Wash. 518 exit from the airport. Driving east on Wash. 518 will connect you to I-5, where you'll then follow the signs north to Seattle. Generally, allow 30 minutes for the drive between the airport and downtown—45 minutes to an hour during rush hour.

During rush hour, it can be quicker to take Wash. 518 west to Wash. 509 north to Wash. 99 (which becomes the Alaskan Way Viaduct along the Seattle waterfront).

BY TAXI, SHUTTLE, BUS, OR LIGHT RAIL A **taxi** into downtown Seattle will cost you around $35 ($32 for the return ride to the airport). There are usually plenty of taxis around, but if not, call **Yellow Cab** (✆ **206/622-6500;** www.yellowtaxi.net) or **Farwest Taxi** (✆ **206/622-1717;** www.farwesttaxi.net). The flag-drop charge is $2.50; after that, it's $2.50 per mile.

Downtown Airporter (✆ **855/566-3300;** www.downtownairporter.com) is your best bet for getting to downtown. These shuttle vans provide scheduled service between the airport and downtown Seattle daily, every 30 minutes from 5am to 9pm. Passengers are picked up at the Ground Transportation Center on the third floor of the parking garage. Shuttles stop at the following downtown hotels: Renaissance Seattle, Crowne Plaza, Fairmont Olympic, Seattle Hilton, Sheraton Seattle, Grand Hyatt, Westin, and Warwick. Fares are $15 one-way and $25 round-trip for adults, and $11 one-way and $18 round-trip for children 2 to 12. The biggest drawback of this shuttle service is that you may have to stop at several hotels before getting dropped off, so it could take you 45 minutes or more to get from the airport to your hotel. However, if you're traveling by yourself or with just one other person, this is your most economical choice other than a public bus.

OPPOSITE PAGE: **You can plan a flying trip to Seattle, or settle in for a longer stay.**

Shuttle Express (✆ **800/487-7433** or 425/981-7000; www.shuttle-express.com) provides 24-hour service between Sea-Tac and the Seattle, North Seattle, and Bellevue areas. Rates for shuttles to downtown Seattle hotels are $32 for one or two adults, $40 for three, and $52 for four; rates to University District hotels are $19 to $37 for one adult, $38 to $45 for two adults, $53 for three, and $69 for four. Children 12 and under ride free. You need to make a reservation to get to the airport, and reservations are recommended for going from the airport into town. To find the shuttle, simply head to the Ground Transportation Center on the third floor of the parking garage. If there are three or more of you traveling together, this will be your cheapest option for getting into town other than a public bus.

Sound Transit (✆ **800/201-4900** or 206/398-5000; www.soundtransit.org) operates the **Central Link** light-rail line between the airport and downtown Seattle. Monday to Friday trains operate every 7½ to 15 minutes between 5:05am and 12:10am, Saturday they run every 10 to 15 minutes between 5:04am and 12:10am, and Sunday they run every 10 to 15 minutes from 6:19am to 11:05pm. The light-rail station is outside the airport's parking garage (follow signs), and the fare is $2.50 for adults, 75¢ for seniors (with a "Regional Reduced Fare Permit"), and $2 for youths 6 to 18.

By Bus

Greyhound (✆ **800/231-2222;** www.greyhound.com) bus service provides connections to almost any city in the continental United States. Seattle's Greyhound bus station is located at 811 Stewart St. (✆ **206/628-5561**), a few blocks northeast of downtown. Several budget chain motels are located nearby, and you can grab a free ride into downtown on a Metro bus. If you will be traveling between several cities, look into the **Greyhound North American Discovery Pass.** The pass, which offers unlimited travel and stopovers in the U.S. and Canada, can be obtained from foreign travel agents or through **www.discoverypass.com.**

By Car

Seattle is 110 miles from Vancouver, British Columbia; 175 miles from Portland; 810 miles from San Francisco; 1,190 miles from Los Angeles; and 285 miles from Spokane.

I-5 is the main north-south artery through Seattle, running south to Portland and north to the Canadian border. I-405 is Seattle's eastside bypass and accesses the cities of Bellevue, Redmond, and Kirkland on the east side of Lake Washington. I-90, which ends at I-5, connects Seattle to Spokane in the eastern part of Washington. Wash. 520 connects I-405 with Seattle just north of downtown and also ends at I-5. Wash. 99, the Alaskan Way Viaduct, is another major north-south highway through downtown Seattle; it passes through the waterfront section of the city.

For information on car rentals and gasoline (petrol) in Seattle, see "Getting Around by Car," later in this chapter.

By Train

Amtrak (✆ **800/872-7245;** www.amtrak.com) service runs from Vancouver, British Columbia, to Seattle and from Portland and as far south as Eugene, Ore., on the *Cascades.* The train takes about 4 hours from Vancouver to Seattle and 3½ to 4 hours from Portland to Seattle. One-way fares from Vancouver to Seattle or from Portland to Seattle are usually between $30 and $50. Booking earlier will get you a less expensive ticket.

There is also Amtrak service to Seattle from San Diego, Los Angeles, San Francisco, and Portland on the *Coast Starlight,* and from Spokane and points east on the *Empire Builder.* Amtrak also operates a bus between Vancouver and Seattle, so be careful when making a reservation as you might be on a bus, rather than a train.

Like the airlines, Amtrak offers several discounted fares; although they're not all based on advance purchase, you'll have more discount options by reserving early. The discount fares can be used only on certain days and during certain hours; be sure to find out exactly what restrictions apply. Tickets for children 2 to 15 cost half the price of a regular coach fare when the children are accompanied by a fare-paying adult.

It is also possible to buy a **USA Rail Pass,** good for 15, 30, or 45 days of unlimited travel on **Amtrak.** The pass is available online or through many overseas travel agents. See Amtrak's website for the cost of travel within the western, eastern, or northwestern United States. Reservations are generally required and should be made as early as possible.

By Boat

Seattle is served by **Washington State Ferries** (✆ **800/843-3779,** 888/808-7977 within Washington, or 206/464-6400; www.wsdot.wa.gov/ferries), the most extensive ferry system in the United States. Car ferries connect Seattle's Pier 52 and Colman Dock with both Bainbridge Island and Bremerton (on the Kitsap Peninsula). Car ferries also connect Fauntleroy (in West Seattle) with both Vashon Island and the Kitsap Peninsula at Southworth; Tahlequah (at the south end of Vashon Island) with Point Defiance in Tacoma; Edmonds with Kingston (on the Kitsap Peninsula); Mukilteo with Whidbey Island; Whidbey Island at Coupeville with Port Townsend; and Anacortes with the San Juan Islands and Sidney, British Columbia (on Vancouver Island near Victoria). See "Getting Around," below, for fare information.

If you're traveling between Victoria, British Columbia, and Seattle, several options are available through **Victoria Clipper,** Pier 69, 2701 Alaskan Way (✆ **800/888-2535,** 206/448-5000, or 250/382-8100; www.clippervacations.com). Ferries make the 2- to 3-hour trip throughout the year, at prices ranging from $75 to $140 round-trip for adults (the lower fare is for off-season advance-purchase tickets). You can also expect to pay some sort of fuel surcharge. Some scheduled trips also stop in the San Juan Islands.

GETTING AROUND

Downtown Seattle is fairly compact and can be easily navigated on foot, but finding your way by car can be frustrating. Traffic, especially during rush hours, can be a nightmare. Drawbridges, one-way streets, I-5 cutting right through downtown, and steep hills all add up to challenging and confusing driving conditions. Here are some guidelines to help you find your way around.

MAIN ARTERIES & STREETS Three interstate highways serve Seattle. Seattle's main artery is I-5, which runs through the middle of the city. Take the James Street exit west if you're heading for the Pioneer Square area, take the

Seneca Street exit for Pike Place Market, or take the Olive Way exit for Capitol Hill. I-405 is the city's north-south bypass and travels up the east shore of Lake Washington through Bellevue and Kirkland (Seattle's high-tech corridor). I-90 comes in from the east, crossing one of the city's two floating bridges, and ends at the south end of downtown.

Remembering Seattle's Streets

Locals use an irreverent little mnemonic device for remembering the names of Seattle's downtown streets, and because most visitors spend much of their time downtown, this phrase could be useful to you as well. It goes like this: "Jesus Christ made Seattle under protest." This stands for all the downtown east-west streets between Yesler Way and Olive Way/Stewart Street—Jefferson, James, Cherry, Columbia, Marion, Madison, Spring, Seneca, University, Union, Pike, Pine.

Downtown is roughly defined as extending from the stadium district (just south of the Pioneer Square neighborhood) on the south to Denny Way on the north, and from Elliott Bay on the west to I-5 on the east. Within this area, most avenues are numbered, whereas streets have names. Exceptions to this rule are the first two roads parallel to the waterfront (Alaskan Way and Western Ave.) and avenues east of Ninth Avenue.

Many downtown streets and avenues are one-way. Spring, Pike, and Marion streets are all one-way eastbound, while Seneca, Pine, and Madison streets are all one-way westbound. Second and Fifth avenues are both one-way southbound, while Fourth and Sixth avenues are one-way northbound. First and Third avenues are both two-way streets.

To get from downtown to Capitol Hill, take Pike Street or Olive Way. Madison Street, Yesler Way, or South Jackson Street will get you over to Lake Washington on the east side of Seattle. If you're heading north across town, Westlake Avenue will take you to the Fremont neighborhood, while Eastlake Avenue will take you to the University District. These two roads diverge at the south end of Lake Union. To get to the arboretum from downtown, take Madison Street.

FINDING AN ADDRESS After you become familiar with the streets and neighborhoods of Seattle, there is really only one important thing to remember: Pay attention to the compass point of an address. Most downtown streets have no directional designation attached to them, but once you cross I-5 going east, most streets and avenues are designated "East." South of Yesler Way, which runs through Pioneer Square, streets are designated "South." West of Queen Anne Avenue, streets are designated "West." The University District is designated "NE" (Northeast), and the Ballard neighborhood "NW" (Northwest). So if you're looking for an address on First Avenue South, head south of Yesler Way.

Another helpful hint is that odd-numbered addresses are likely to be on the west and south sides of streets, whereas even-numbered addresses will be on the east and north. Also, in the downtown area, address numbers jump by 100 with each block as you move away from Yesler Way going north or south and as you go east from the waterfront.

STREET MAPS If the streets of Seattle seem totally unfathomable to you, rest assured that even longtime residents sometimes have a hard time finding their way around. Don't be afraid to ask directions. You can obtain a free map of the city from either of the two **visitor centers** operated by Seattle's Convention and Visitors Bureau **(www.visitseattle.org).** One of the visitor centers is in the Pike Street lobby of the Washington State Convention Center, and the other is in Pike Place Market at the corner of First Avenue and Pike Street.

You can buy a decent map of Seattle at most convenience stores and gas stations. For a greater selection, stop in at **Metsker Maps,** 1511 First Ave. (✆ **800/727-4430** or 206/623-8747; www.metskers.com).

If you're a member of AAA, you can get free maps of Seattle and Washington State either at your local AAA office or at the Seattle branch in the University District, 4554 Ninth Ave. NE (✆ **206/633-4222;** www.aaawa.com).

By Public Transportation

BY BUS The best thing about Seattle's **Metro** (✆ **206/553-3000;** http://metro.kingcounty.gov) bus system is that as long as you stay within the downtown area, you can ride for free between 6am and 7pm. The **Ride Free Area ★** is between Alaskan Way (the waterfront) to the west, Sixth Avenue and I-5 to the east, Battery Street to the north, and South Jackson Street to the south. Within this area are Pioneer Square, the waterfront attractions, Pike Place Market, the Seattle Art Museum, and almost all of the city's major hotels. Two blocks from South Jackson Street is Qwest Field (where the Seahawks play), 3 long blocks from South Jackson Street is Safeco Field (where the Mariners play), and 6 blocks from Battery Street is Seattle Center. Keeping this in mind, you can see a lot of Seattle without having to spend a dime on transportation.

The Ride Free Area also encompasses the **Downtown Seattle Transit Tunnel,** which allows buses and the Link light rail to travel underneath downtown Seattle, thus avoiding traffic congestion. The tunnel extends from the International District in the south to the convention center in the north, with three stops in between. Commissioned artworks decorate each of the stations, making a trip through the tunnel more than just a way of getting from point A to point B. The tunnel is open Monday through Saturday from 5am to 1am and Sunday from 6am to midnight. When the tunnel is closed, buses operate on surface streets. Because the tunnel is within the Ride Free Area, there is no charge for riding through it, unless you are traveling to or from outside of the Ride Free Area.

If you travel outside the Ride Free Area, fares range from $2.25 to $3, depending on distance and time of day. (The higher fares are incurred during commuter hours.) ***Note:*** When traveling out of the Ride Free Area between 6am and 7pm, you pay when you get off the bus; when traveling into the Ride Free Area, you pay when you get on the bus. Exact change is required; dollar bills are accepted.

BY MONORAIL If you are planning a visit to Seattle Center, there is no better way to get there from downtown than on the **Seattle Center Monorail** (✆ **206/905-2620;** www.seattlemonorail.com), which leaves from Westlake Center shopping mall (Fifth Ave. and Pine St.). The elevated train covers the 1 mile in 2 minutes and passes right through the middle of EMP/

SFM, the Frank Gehry–designed rock-music and science-fiction museum. The monorail operates daily from Sunday through Thursday from 8:30am to 8:30pm, Friday and Saturday from 8:30am to 11pm (in summer, Mon–Fri 7:30am–11pm, Sat–Sun 8:30am–11pm). Departures are every 10 minutes. The one-way fare is $2 for adults and $1 for seniors, and 75¢ for children 5 to 12.

BY STREETCAR Paul Allen's rapidly evolving South Lake Union development district, stretching from the north end of downtown Seattle to the south shore of Lake Union, is served by the **Seattle Streetcar** (**© 206/553-3000;** www.seattlestreetcar.org). There are 7 stops in each direction along the 2½-mile route, including Lake Union Park, which is home to several historic ships, and the adjacent Center for Wooden Boats. Downtown you can catch the streetcar at the corner of Westlake Avenue and Olive Way. Streetcars run every 15 minutes and operate Monday through Thursday from 6am to 9pm, Friday and Saturday from 6am to 11pm, and Sundays and holidays from 10am to 7pm. The fare is $2.50 for adults and 75¢ for seniors and students (children 5 and under are free). Metro passes and bus transfers are valid on the streetcar.

BY WATER TAXI A water taxi runs between the downtown Seattle waterfront (Pier 50) and Seacrest Park in West Seattle, providing access to West Seattle's popular Alki Beach and adjacent paved path. For a service schedule, check with the **King County Ferry District** (**© 206/684-1551;** www.kingcountyferries.org). The one-way fare is $3.50 for adults, $1.50 for seniors, and $3.50 for children 6 to 18 (free for children 5 and under).

BY FERRY **Washington State Ferries** (**© 800/843-3779,** 888/808-7977 in Washington, or 206/464-6400; www.wsdot.wa.gov/ferries) is the most extensive ferry system in the United States, and while these ferries won't help you get around Seattle itself, they do offer scenic options for getting out of town (and cheap "cruises," too).

From downtown Seattle, car ferries sail to Bremerton (1-hr. crossing) and Bainbridge Island (35-min. crossing). From West Seattle, car ferries go to Vashon Island (15-min. crossing) and Southworth (35-min. crossing), which is on the Kitsap Peninsula.

The Kitsap Peninsula can also be reached by ferry from the city of Edmonds, north of Seattle. One-way fares between Seattle and Bainbridge Island or Bremerton, or between Edmonds and Kingston via car ferry, are $12 ($15 from May 1 to the second Sat in Oct) for a car and driver, $7.10 for adult car passengers or walk-ons, $3.55 for seniors, and $5.70 for children 6 to 18. Car passengers and walk-ons pay fares only on westbound car ferries. One-way fares between Fauntleroy (West Seattle) and Vashon Island, or between Southworth and Vashon Island, are $16 ($19 from May 1 to the second Sat in Oct) for a car and driver, $4.55 for car passengers or walk-ons, $2.25 for seniors, and $3.65 for children 6 to 18.

By Car

Car rental rates vary as widely and as wildly as airfares, so it pays to comparison shop. Rates are highest in the summer and lowest in the winter, but you'll almost always get lower rates the farther ahead you reserve and if you prepay for your rental as you would for an airline ticket. However, the best way to save money, and I mean a *lot* of money, on a Seattle car rental is to **not** rent at the airport.

At Seattle-Tacoma International Airport, daily rates for a compact car currently range anywhere from $50 to $110 during the summer, with weekly rates ranging from $400 to more than $550. On top of this base rate, you'll pay additional taxes and surcharges of more than 40%! Your actual cost on a daily rental will be anywhere from $75 to $150, and on a weekly rental, you'll be paying between $600 and $800. Rent the same car in downtown Seattle or somewhere other than the airport and you might pay as little as $180 for a week's rental, with additional charges bringing the total to only $217. So, my advice is, if at all possible, try not to rent a car at the airport.

All the major car-rental agencies have offices in Seattle and at or near Seattle-Tacoma International Airport, including: Advantage (© **800/777-5500;** www.advantage.com); Alamo (© **877/222-9075;** www.alamo.com); Avis (© **800/331-1212;** www.avis.com); Budget (© **800/527-0700;** www.budget.com); Dollar (© **800/800-3665;** www.dollar.com); Enterprise (© **800/261-7331;** www.enterprise.com); Hertz (© **800/654-3131;** www.hertz.com); National (© **877/222-9058;** www.nationalcar.com); and Thrifty (© **800/847-4389;** www.thrifty.com).

If you are under 25, you usually have to pay a higher rate for a rental car, if the company will rent to you at all. International visitors should note that insurance and taxes are almost never included in quoted rental car rates in the U.S. Be sure to ask your rental agency about additional fees for these. They can add a significant cost to your car rental.

Before you drive into downtown Seattle, keep in mind that traffic congestion is bad, parking is limited (and expensive), and streets are almost all one-way. You'll avoid a lot of frustration by leaving your car in your hotel parking garage or by not bringing a car downtown.

Depending on what your plans are for your visit and where you're staying, you might not need a car at all. If you plan to spend your time in downtown Seattle, a car is a liability. The Link light-rail line connects Sea-Tac Airport with downtown, and the city center is well served by public transportation, with free buses in the downtown area and the monorail from downtown to Seattle Center. You can even take the ferries over to Bainbridge Island or Bremerton. Most Seattle neighborhoods that interest visitors are well served by public buses. But if your plans include any excursions out of the city, say, to Mount Rainier or the Olympic Peninsula, you'll definitely need a car.

If you're visiting from abroad and plan to rent a car in the United States, keep in mind that foreign driver's licenses are usually recognized in the U.S., but you may want to consider obtaining an international driver's license.

Gasoline is cheaper in the U.S. than in most other countries, but recent months have seen prices take a sharp climb upward. As of press time, gasoline averaged $3.88 a gallon in the Seattle area.

PARKING On-street parking in downtown Seattle is expensive, extremely limited, and, worst of all, rarely available near your destination. Most downtown parking lots (either aboveground or belowground) charge from $18 to $25 per day, though many lots offer early bird specials that allow you to park all day for around $10 or $12 if you arrive before a certain time in the morning (usually around 9am).

You can save money by leaving your car near the Space Needle, where parking lots often charge only $9 per day (but up to $15–$20 during special events). Some Pike Place Market merchants validate parking permits.

DRIVING RULES & TIPS A right turn at a red light is permitted after coming to a full stop. A left turn at a red light is permissible from a one-way street onto another one-way street after coming to a full stop.

If you park your car on a sloping street, be sure to turn your wheels to the curb. When parking on the street, check the time limit on your parking meter; some allow as little as 15 minutes of parking, while others are good for up to 4 hours. Also, during rush hour, be sure to check whether your parking space is restricted.

Stoplights in the Pioneer Square area are particularly hard to see, so be alert at all intersections.

By Taxi

If you decide not to use the public transit system, call **Yellow Cab** (✆ **206/622-6500;** http://yellowtaxi.net) or **Farwest Taxi** (✆ **206/622-1717;** www.farwesttaxi.net). Taxis can be difficult to hail on the street, so it's best to call or wait at the taxi stands at major hotels. The flag-drop charge is $2.50; after that, it's $2.50 per mile. A maximum of four passengers can share a cab; the third and fourth passengers will each incur a surcharge of 50¢. Taxis from downtown to Sea-Tac Airport charge a fixed rate of $32.

On Foot

Seattle is a surprisingly compact city. You can easily walk from Pioneer Square to Pike Place Market and take in most of downtown. However, the city is quite hilly and when you head in from the waterfront, you will be climbing a very steep hill. If you get tired while strolling downtown, remember that between 6am and 7pm, you can always catch a bus for free as long as you stay within the Ride Free Area. Cross the street only at corners and only with the lights in your favor. Jaywalking, especially in the downtown area, is a ticketable offense.

[FastFACTS] SEATTLE

Area Codes The area codes are **206** in Seattle, **425** for the Eastside (including Kirkland and Bellevue), and **253** for south King County (near the airport).

Business Hours The following are general guidelines; specific establishments' hours may vary. Banks are open Monday through Friday from 9am to 5pm (some also on Sat 9am–noon). Stores are open Monday through Saturday from 10am to 6pm and Sunday from noon to 5pm (malls usually stay open until 9pm Mon–Sat). Bars can stay open until 2am.

Car Rental See "Getting Around by Car," earlier in this chapter.

Cellphones See "Mobile Phones," later in this section.

Crime See "Safety," later in this section.

Customs Every visitor 21 years of age or older may bring in, free of duty, the following: (1) 1 liter of alcohol; (2) 200 cigarettes, 100 cigars (but not from Cuba); and (3) $100 worth of gifts. These exemptions are offered to travelers who spend at least 72 hours in the United States and who have not claimed them within the preceding 6 months. It is forbidden to bring into the country almost any meat products (including canned, fresh, and dried meat products, such as bouillon and soup mixes). Generally, condiments including vinegars, oils, pickled goods, spices, coffee, tea, and some cheeses and baked goods are permitted. Avoid rice products, as rice can often harbor insects. Bringing fruits and vegetables is prohibited since they may harbor pests or disease. International visitors may carry in or out up to $10,000 in U.S. or foreign currency with no formalities; larger sums must be declared to U.S. Customs on entering or leaving, which includes filing form FinCEN 105. For details regarding U.S. Customs and Border Protection, consult your nearest U.S. embassy or consulate, or **U.S. Customs (www.customs.gov).**

Disabled Travelers Most disabilities shouldn't stop anyone from traveling in Seattle. Thanks to provisions in the Americans with Disabilities Act, most public places are required to comply with disability-friendly regulations.

Almost all public establishments (including hotels, restaurants, museums, and such) and at least some modes of public transportation provide accessible entrances and other facilities for those with disabilities. For anyone using a wheelchair, the greatest difficulty of a visit to Seattle is dealing with the city's many steep hills, which rival those of San Francisco. One solution for dealing with downtown hills is to use the elevator at Pike Place Market to get between the waterfront and First Avenue. There's also a public elevator at the west end of Lenora Street (just north of Pike Place Market). This elevator connects the waterfront with the Belltown neighborhood. If you stay at the Edgewater hotel, right on the waterfront, you'll have easy access to all of the city's waterfront attractions, and you'll be able to use the elevators to get to Pike Place Market.

Most hotels now offer wheelchair-accessible accommodations, and some of the larger and more expensive properties also offer TDD telephones and other amenities for the hearing- and sight-impaired.

For information on public bus accessibility, contact **Metro** (✆ **206/263-3113;** http://metro.kingcounty.gov/tops/accessible/accessible.html). For Metro TTY service, call ✆ **711.**

The **America the Beautiful—National Park and Federal Recreational Lands Pass—Access Pass** gives people who are visually impaired or have permanent disabilities (regardless of age) free lifetime entrance to federal recreation sites administered by the National Park Service (NPS), including the Fish and Wildlife Service, the Forest Service, the Bureau of Land Management, and the Bureau of Reclamation. This may include national parks, monuments, historic sites, recreation areas, and national wildlife refuges. If you plan to visit Mount Rainier National Park or Olympic National Park, this pass is a must.

The America the Beautiful Access Pass can be obtained in person at any NPS facility that charges an entrance fee. You need to show proof of a medically determined disability. Besides free entry, the pass also offers a 50% discount on some federal-use fees charged for such facilities as camping, swimming, parking, boat launching, and tours. For more information, go to www.nps.gov/fees_passes.htm or call the **United States Geological Survey** (**USGS;** ✆ **888/275-8747**).

Doctors To find a doctor, check with the front desk or concierge at your hotel or look in the yellow pages of the local telephone book under "Physician." Also see "Hospitals," in this section.

Drinking Laws The legal age for purchase and consumption of alcoholic beverages is 21; proof of age is required and often requested at bars, nightclubs, and restaurants, so it's always a good idea to bring ID when you go out. Do not carry open containers of alcohol in your car or any public area that isn't zoned for alcohol consumption. The police can fine you on the spot. Don't even think about driving while intoxicated.

Driving Rules See "Getting Around," earlier in this chapter.

Electricity Like Canada, the United States uses 110 to 120 volts AC (60 cycles), compared to 220 to 240 volts AC (50 cycles) in most of Europe, Australia, and New Zealand. Downward converters that change 220 to 240 volts to 110 to 120 volts are difficult to find in the United States, so bring one with you.

Embassies & Consulates All embassies are in the nation's capital, Washington, D.C. Some consulates are in major U.S. cities, and most nations have a mission to the United Nations in New York City. If your country isn't listed below, call for directory information in Washington, D.C. (✆ **202/555-1212**) or check **www.embassy.org/embassies**.

The embassy of **Australia** is at 1601 Massachusetts Ave. NW, Washington, DC 20036 (✆ **202/797-3000;** www.usa.embassy.gov.au). Consulates are in New York, Honolulu, Houston, Los Angeles, and San Francisco.

The embassy of **Canada** is at 501 Pennsylvania Ave. NW, Washington, DC 20001 (✆ **202/682-1740;** www.canadainternational.gc.ca/washington). Other Canadian consulates are in Buffalo (New York), Detroit, Los Angeles, New York, and Seattle.

The embassy of **Ireland** is at 2234 Massachusetts Ave. NW, Washington, DC 20008 (✆ **202/462-3939;** www.embassyofireland.org). Irish consulates are in Boston, Chicago, New York, San Francisco, and other cities. See website for complete listing.

The embassy of **New Zealand** is at 37 Observatory Circle NW, Washington, DC 20008 (✆ **202/328-4800;** www.nzembassy.com). New Zealand consulates are in Los Angeles, Salt Lake City, San Francisco, and Seattle.

The embassy of the **United Kingdom** is at 3100 Massachusetts Ave. NW, Washington, DC 20008 (✆ **202/588-6500;** http://ukinusa.fco.gov.uk). Other British consulates are in Atlanta, Boston, Chicago, Cleveland, Houston, Los Angeles, New York, San Francisco, and Seattle.

Emergencies Call ✆ **911** to report a fire, call the police, or get an ambulance anywhere in the U.S. This is a toll-free call. (No coins are required at public telephones.)

Family Travel When I was a kid, I never wanted to do anything but go to the beach or the lake for family vacations, but if my parents had ever suggested that we take a city vacation, I would have wanted to go someplace like Seattle. This city is jam-packed with fun stuff for kids, whether toddlers or teens. Seattle Center, with the Space Needle, a children's museum and children's theater, a highly interactive science museum, and a combination science-fiction and rock-music museum, is the best place in the city to set the kids free. Then there's the waterfront, with its boat tours, aquarium, and tacky souvenir shops. Of course, you can keep your sports-fan kids happy by getting tickets to a baseball or football game. Kids can even watch salmon climbing a fish ladder and take a tour of the spooky Seattle underground.

To locate accommodations, restaurants, and attractions that are particularly kid-friendly, refer to the "Kids" icon throughout this guide.

Many hotels in Seattle allow kids to stay free in a parent's room; some even allow children to eat for free in the hotel's restaurant. Keep in mind that most downtown hotels cater almost exclusively to business travelers and don't offer the sort of amenities that appeal to families—like swimming pools, game rooms, or inexpensive restaurants. For specific hotel recommendations, see "Family-Friendly Hotels" (p. 63).

Many of Seattle's larger restaurants, especially along the waterfront, offer children's menus. You'll also find plenty of variety and low prices at the many food vendors' stalls at Pike Place Market. And there's a food court in Westlake Center shopping mall. For information on restaurants that cater to families, see "Family-Friendly Restaurants" (p. 79).

Note: If you plan to travel on to Canada during your Seattle vacation, be sure to bring your children's **passports** with you.

Gasoline Please see "Getting There By Car," earlier in this chapter.

Hospitals Hospitals convenient to downtown include **Swedish Medical Center,** 747 Broadway (✆ **206/386-6000;** www.swedish.org), and **Virginia Mason Medical Center,** 1100 Ninth Ave. (✆ **206/223-6600;** www.virginiamason.org).

Insurance For information on traveler's insurance, trip cancellation insurance, and medical insurance while traveling, please visit **www.frommers.com/planning**.

Internet & Wi-Fi As you might expect from a city that is home to both Microsoft and Amazon, Seattle is wired (and wireless) to the max. If you arrive by plane, you'll immediately find free Wi-Fi at Seattle Tacoma International Airport. Around the airport, you'll also find Internet-enabled phones that allow you to check email and access the Web. These phones charge 35¢ per minute with a $5 minimum. Almost all hotels in the city now offer Wi-Fi in guest rooms, although at the corporate business hotels, you will usually have to pay a daily fee for access. However, at some hotels that charge for access from the guest rooms, there is free Wi-Fi in the lobby. Likewise, espresso bars and cafes all over the city offer Wi-Fi. Among the cafes I frequent are Ancient Grounds, Bauhaus Books & Coffee, Cafe Allegro, Caffe Ladro, Caffé Vita, El Diablo Coffee Co., and Zeitgeist Art/Coffee. More information on all of these cafes can be found in chapter 5. There are also computers available at the **Seattle Central Library,** 1000 Fourth Ave. (✆ **206/386-4636;** www.spl.org). For a listing of free Wi-Fi locations, visit **www.wififreespot.com**.

Legal Aid While driving, if you are pulled over for a minor infraction (such as speeding), never attempt to pay the fine directly to a police officer; this could be construed as attempted bribery, a much more serious crime. Pay fines by mail, or directly into the hands of the clerk of the court. If accused of a more serious offense, say and do nothing before consulting a lawyer. In the U.S., the burden is on the state to prove a person's guilt beyond a reasonable doubt, and everyone has the right to remain silent, whether he or she is suspected of a crime or actually arrested. Once arrested, a person can make one telephone call to a party of his or her choice. The international visitor should call his or her embassy or consulate.

LGBT Travelers Seattle is one of the most gay-friendly cities in the country, with a large gay and lesbian community centered on Capitol Hill. Here in this neighborhood, you'll find numerous bars, nightclubs, stores, and bed-and-breakfasts catering to the gay community.

The first place to look for Seattle information is on the **Seattle Convention and Visitors Bureau**'s LGBT Web pages (www.visitseattle.org/visitors/discover/lgbt-travel.aspx). Once you're in Seattle, pick up a copy of the ***Seattle Gay News*** (✆ **206/324-4297;** www.sgn.org), available at area bookstores and gay bars and nightclubs.

The **Greater Seattle Business Association (GSBA),** 400 E. Pine St., Ste. 322 (✆ **206/363-9188;** www.thegsba.org), is Seattle's main LGBT business association and publishes a directory of gay-friendly Seattle businesses. This directory is a great resource and can be found wherever you find the *Seattle Gay News.*

The **Lesbian Resource Center,** 227 S. Orcas St. (✆ **206/322-3953;** www.lrc.net), provides community and business resource information as well as a calendar of upcoming events and activities.

The **Gaslight Inn** and **Bacon Mansion** are two gay-friendly bed-and-breakfasts in the Capitol Hill area; see p. 62 for full reviews on both B&Bs. For information on gay and lesbian bars and nightclubs, see p. 227.

Mail At press time, domestic postage rates were 28¢ for a postcard and 44¢ for a letter. For international mail, a first-class letter of up to 1 ounce costs 98¢ (75¢ to Canada and 79¢ to Mexico); a first-class postcard costs the same as a letter. For more information go to **www.usps.com**.

If you aren't sure what your address will be in the United States, mail can be sent to you, in your name, c/o **General Delivery** at the main post office of the city or region where you expect to be. (Call ✆ **800/275-8777** for information on the nearest post office.) The addressee must pick up mail in person and must produce proof of identity (driver's license, passport, etc.). Most post offices will hold mail for up to 1 month, and are open Monday to Friday from 8am to 6pm, and Saturday from 9am to 3pm.

Always include zip codes when mailing items in the U.S. If you don't know your zip code, visit **www.usps.com/zip4.**

Medical Requirements Unless you're arriving from an area known to be suffering from an epidemic (particularly cholera or yellow fever), inoculations or vaccinations are not required for entry into the United States.

Mobile Phones Just because your cellphone works at home doesn't mean it'll work everywhere in the U.S. (thanks to the fragmented cellphone system in the United States). If you live in the U.S., it's a good bet that your phone will work in America's major cities, but take a look at your wireless company's coverage map on its website before heading out; T-Mobile, Sprint, and Nextel are particularly weak in rural areas. (To see where GSM phones work in the U.S., check out **www.t-mobile.com/coverage**.) If you're visiting from another country, be sure to find out about international calling rates and roaming charges before using your phone in the United States. You could ring up a huge phone bill with just a few calls.

Options for staying connected in the U.S. include renting a mobile phone from a company such as **Roberts Rent-A-Phone** (✆ **800/964-2468;** www.roberts-rent-a-phone.com). However, you can also buy an inexpensive phone and prepaid minutes from such companies as **TracFone** (www.tracfone.com). These phones are readily available in such stores as Walmart and Target and usually cost less than $20. Prepaid minutes might cost $20 for 60 minutes, though double-minute plans can lower this cost. Another alternative if you are traveling with your laptop computer or have a smart phone is to install **Skype** (www.skype.com), a VoIP (voice over internet protocol) program/app that allows you to use your computer or smart phone as an internet-based telephone. Doing this allows you to call other Skype users at no charge.

Money & Costs Frommer's lists exact prices in the local currency. The currency conversions quoted below were correct at press time. However, rates fluctuate, so before departing consult a currency exchange website such as **www.oanda.com/currency/converter** to check up-to-the-minute rates.

THE VALUE OF THE U.S. DOLLAR VS. OTHER POPULAR CURRENCIES

$	Aus$	Can$	Euro (€)	NZ$	UK£
1	A$0.94	C$0.96	€0.69	NZ$1.27	£0.61

Credit cards are the most widely used form of payment in the U.S. It's highly recommended that you travel with at least one major credit card; options include **Visa** (Barclaycard in Britain), **MasterCard** (Eurocard in Europe), **American Express, Diners Club,** and **Discover.** MasterCard and Visa are the two most commonly accepted credit cards. You must have a credit card to rent a car, and hotels and airlines usually require a credit card imprint as a deposit against expenses.

You can withdraw cash advances from your credit cards at banks or ATMs, but high fees make credit card cash advances a pricey way to get cash. Keep in mind that you'll pay interest from the moment of your withdrawal, even if you pay your monthly bills on time. Also, note that many banks now assess a 1% to 3% "transaction fee" on **all** charges you incur abroad (whether you're using the local currency or your native currency).

The easiest and best way to get cash away from home is from an ATM (automated teller machine), sometimes referred to as a "cash machine" or "cashpoint." The **Cirrus** (✆ **800/424-7787;** www.mastercard.com) and **PLUS** (www.visa.com) networks span the country; you can find them even in remote regions. Go to your bank card's website to find ATM locations at your destination. Be sure you know your daily withdrawal limit before you depart. Four-digit PINs work fine in Washington.

In Washington, you'll find ATMs at banks in even the smallest towns. You can also usually find them at gas station minimarts, although these machines usually charge a slightly higher fee than banks. You can sometimes avoid a fee by searching out a small community bank, a savings and loan, or a credit union ATM. To avoid fees, you can also go into a grocery store, make a purchase, and ask for cash back on your debit card.

Beware of hidden credit-card fees while traveling. Check with your credit or debit card issuer to see what fees, if any, will be charged for overseas transactions. Recent reform legislation in the U.S., for example, has curbed some exploitative lending practices. But many banks have responded by increasing fees in other areas, including fees for customers who use credit and debit cards while out of the country—even if those charges were made in U.S. dollars. Fees can amount to 3% or more of the purchase price. Check with your bank before departing to avoid any surprise charges on your statement.

For help with currency conversions, tip calculations, and more, download Frommer's convenient **Travel Tools** app for your mobile device. Go to **www.frommers.com/go/mobile** and click on the Travel Tools icon.

What will a vacation in Seattle cost? Not as much as a vacation in London, New York, or San Francisco, but if you visit in summer, be prepared to spend $250 or more for an average hotel room. About the cheapest you can get a decent room in summer is around $150, but that won't be downtown. Visit during the rainy season and room rates will be half that. For meals, expect to pay $10 to $15 for breakfast, $15 to $25 for lunch, and $40 to $60 for dinner. Of course, you can eat for much less than this, but at these prices you'll be getting some of the city's more memorable dining experiences.

WHAT THINGS COST IN SEATTLE	$
Taxi from the airport to downtown Seattle	35.00
Double room, moderate	150.00–250.00
Double room, inexpensive	90.00–150.00
Three-course dinner for one without wine, moderate	30.00–40.00
Pint of beer	4.00–5.00
Cup of coffee	1.50–2.00
Latte	2.50–3.50
1 gallon/1 liter of premium gas	4.00/1.05
Admission to most museums	14.00–18.00

Newspapers & Magazines The *Seattle Times* is Seattle's daily newspaper. *Seattle Weekly* is the city's free arts-and-entertainment weekly.

Packing If you've already packed your umbrella in anticipation of your Seattle vacation, you might want to unpack it. No, it's not that I'm predicting sunny weather for your visit. It's just that Seattleites rarely use umbrellas. Sure it rains almost constantly for much of the year, but the rain often falls as little more than a light drizzle. Consequently, you're better off bringing a **rain jacket** rather than an umbrella. You'll stay dry most of the time, and you'll look more like a native. That jacket, or a sweater, will also come in handy almost any month of the year. Because of the cooling effect of Puget Sound, nights in Seattle can be cool even in the middle of summer. For more helpful information on packing for your trip, download our convenient Travel Tools app for your mobile device. Go to **www.frommers.com/go/mobile** and click on the Travel Tools icon.

Passports Virtually every air traveler entering the U.S. is required to show a passport. All persons, including U.S. citizens, traveling by air between the United States and Canada, Mexico, Central and South America, the Caribbean, and Bermuda are required to present a valid passport. ***Note:*** U.S. and Canadian citizens entering the U.S. at land and sea ports of entry from within the western hemisphere must now also present a passport or other documents compliant with the Western Hemisphere Travel Initiative (WHTI; see www.getyouhome.gov for details). Children 15 and under may continue entering with only a U.S. birth certificate, or other proof of U.S. citizenship.

Passport Offices

- **Australia Australian Passport Information Service** (✆ **131-232,** or visit www.passports.gov.au).
- **Canada Passport Office,** Department of Foreign Affairs and International Trade, Ottawa, ON K1A 0G3 (✆ **800/567-6868;** www.ppt.gc.ca).

- **Ireland Passport Office,** Setanta Centre, Molesworth Street, Dublin 2 (✆ **01/671-1633;** www.foreignaffairs.gov.ie).
- **New Zealand Passports Office,** Department of Internal Affairs, 47 Boulcott Street, Wellington, 6011 (✆ 0800/225-050 in New Zealand or 04/474-8100; www.passports.govt.nz).
- **United Kingdom** Visit your nearest passport office, major post office, or travel agency or contact the **Identity and Passport Service (IPS),** 89 Eccleston Square, London, SW1V 1PN (✆ **0300/222-0000;** www.ips.gov.uk).
- **United States** To find your regional passport office, check the U.S. State Department website (travel.state.gov/passport) or call the **National Passport Information Center** (✆ **877/487-2778**) for automated information.

Petrol Please see "Getting There by Car," earlier in this chapter.

Police To reach the police, dial ✆ **911.**

Safety Although Seattle is a relatively safe city, it has its share of crime. The most questionable neighborhood you're likely to visit is the Pioneer Square area, which is home to more than a dozen bars and nightclubs. By day this area is quite safe (though it has a large contingent of street people), but late at night, when the bars are closing, stay aware of your surroundings and keep an eye out for suspicious characters and activities. Also, take extra precautions with your wallet or purse when you're in the crush of people at Pike Place Market. Whenever possible, try to park your car in a garage at night; if you must park on the street, make sure there are no valuables in view—or anything that even looks as if it might contain something of worth. I once had my car broken into because I left a shopping bag full of trash on the back seat.

Senior Travel Don't be shy about asking for discounts, but always carry identification, such as a driver's license, that shows your date of birth—especially if you've kept your youthful glow. In Seattle, tour companies, the Washington State Ferries, and most museums and attractions offer senior discounts. These can add up to substantial savings, but you have to remember to ask.

The U.S. National Park Service offers an **America the Beautiful—National Park and Federal Recreational Lands Pass—Senior Pass,** which gives seniors 62 or older lifetime entrance to all properties administered by the National Park Service—national parks, monuments, historic sites, recreation areas, and national wildlife refuges—for a one-time processing fee of $10. Besides free entry, the America the Beautiful Senior Pass also offers a 50% discount on some federal-use fees charged for such facilities as camping, swimming, parking, boat launching, and tours. For more information, see "Disabled Travelers," earlier.

Smoking Smoking is banned in public indoor spaces throughout the state of Washington, so don't try lighting up—even in a bar.

Taxes The United States has no value-added tax (VAT) or other indirect tax at the national level. Every state, county, and city may levy its own local tax on all purchases, including hotel and restaurant checks and airline tickets. These taxes will not appear on price tags.

Seattle has a 9.5% **sales tax.** In restaurants there's an additional .5% **food-and-beverage tax.** The **hotel-room tax** in the Seattle metro area ranges from 10% to 16%. On **car rentals** at Seattle-Tacoma International Airport, you'll pay anywhere from around 50% to as much as 80% in additional taxes and fees (which is why, if you're renting a car, do it at a non-airport location)!

Telephones Many convenience groceries and packaging services sell **prepaid calling cards** in denominations up to $50. Many public pay phones at airports now accept American Express, MasterCard, and Visa. **Local calls** made from most pay phones cost either 25¢ or 35¢. Most long-distance and international calls can be dialed directly from any phone. **To make calls within the United States and to Canada,** dial 1 followed by the area code and the seven-digit number. **For other international calls,** dial 011 followed by the country code, city code, and the number you are calling.

Calls to area codes **800, 888, 877,** and **866** are toll-free. However, calls to area codes **700** and **900** (chat lines, bulletin boards, "dating" services, and so on) can be expensive—charges of 95¢ to $3 or more per minute. Some numbers have minimum charges that can run $15 or more.

For **reversed-charge or collect calls,** and for person-to-person calls, dial the number 0 then the area code and number; an operator will come on the line, and you should specify whether you are calling collect, person-to-person, or both. If your operator-assisted call is international, ask for the overseas operator.

For **directory assistance** ("Information"), dial 411 for local numbers and national numbers in the U.S. and Canada. For dedicated long-distance information, dial 1, then the appropriate area code plus 555-1212.

Time The continental United States is divided into **four time zones:** Eastern Standard Time (EST), Central Standard Time (CST), Mountain Standard Time (MST), and Pacific Standard Time (PST). Seattle is in PST. Alaska and Hawaii have their own zones. For example, when it's 9am in Seattle (PST), it's 7am in Honolulu (HST), 10am in Denver (MST), 11am in Chicago (CST), noon in New York City (EST), 5pm in London (GMT), and 2am the next day in Sydney.

Daylight saving time (summer time) is in effect from 1am on the second Sunday in March to 1am on the first Sunday in November, except in Arizona, Hawaii, the U.S. Virgin Islands, and Puerto Rico. Daylight saving time moves the clock 1 hour ahead of standard time.

For help with time translations, and more, download our convenient Travel Tools app for your mobile device. Go to **www.frommers.com/go/moblie** and click on the Travel Tools icon.

Tipping In hotels, tip **bellhops** at least $1 per bag ($2–$3 if you have a lot of luggage) and tip the **chamber staff** $1 to $2 per day (more if you've left a big mess for him or her to clean up). Tip the **doorman** or **concierge** only if he or she has provided you with some specific service (for example, calling a cab for you or obtaining difficult-to-get theater tickets). Tip the **valet-parking attendant** $1 every time you get your car.

In restaurants, bars, and nightclubs, tip **service staff** and **bartenders** 15% to 20% of the check, tip **checkroom attendants** $1 per garment, and tip **valet-parking attendants** $1 per vehicle.

As for other service personnel, tip **cab drivers** 15% of the fare; tip **skycaps** at airports at least $1 per bag ($2–$3 if you have a lot of luggage); and tip **hairdressers** and **barbers** 15% to 20%.

For help with tip calculations, currency conversions, and more, download our convenient Travel Tools app for your mobile device. Go to **www.frommers.com/go/mobile** and click on the Travel Tools icon.

Toilets You won't find public toilets or "restrooms" on the streets in most U.S. cities, but they can be found in hotel lobbies, bars, restaurants, museums, department stores, railway and bus stations, and service stations. Large hotels and fast-food restaurants are often the best bet for clean facilities. Restaurants and bars in resorts or heavily visited areas may reserve their restrooms for patrons.

VAT See "Taxes" earlier in this section.

Visas The U.S. Department of State has a **Visa Waiver Program (VWP)** allowing citizens of the following countries to enter the United States without a visa for stays of up to 90 days: Andorra, Australia, Austria, Belgium, Brunei, Czech Republic, Denmark, Estonia, Finland, France, Germany, Greece, Hungary, Iceland, Ireland, Italy, Japan, Latvia, Liechtenstein, Lithuania, Luxembourg, Malta, Monaco, the Netherlands, New Zealand, Norway, Portugal, San Marino, Singapore, Slovakia, Slovenia, South Korea, Spain, Sweden, Switzerland, and the United Kingdom. (***Note:*** This list was accurate at press time; for the most up-to-date list of countries in the VWP, consult http://travel.state.gov/visa.) Even though a visa isn't necessary, in an effort to help U.S. officials check travelers against terror watch lists before they arrive at U.S. borders, visitors from VWP countries must register online through the Electronic System for Travel Authorization (ESTA) before boarding a plane or a boat to the U.S. Travelers must complete an electronic application providing basic personal and travel eligibility information. The Department of Homeland Security recommends filling out the form at least 3 days before traveling. Authorizations will be valid for up to 2 years or until the traveler's passport expires, whichever comes first. Currently, there is a $14 fee for the online application. Existing ESTA registrations remain valid through their expiration dates. ***Note:*** Any passport issued on or after October 26, 2006, by a VWP country must be an **e-Passport** for VWP travelers to be eligible to enter the U.S. without a visa. Citizens of these nations also need to present a round-trip air or cruise ticket upon arrival. E-Passports contain computer chips capable of storing biometric information, such as the required digital photograph of the holder. If your passport doesn't have this feature, you can still travel without a visa if the valid passport was issued before October 26, 2005, and includes a machine-readable zone; or if the valid passport was issued between October 26, 2005, and October 25, 2006, and includes a digital photograph. For more information, go to **http://travel.state.gov/visa**. Canadian citizens may enter the United States without visas, but will need to show passports and proof of residence.

Citizens of all other countries must have (1) a valid passport that expires at least 6 months later than the scheduled end of their visit to the U.S.; and (2) a tourist visa. For information about U.S. Visas go to **http://travel.state.gov** and click on "Visas." Or go to one of the following websites:

Australian citizens can obtain up-to-date visa information from the **U.S. Embassy Canberra,** Moonah Place, Yarralumla, ACT 2600 (✆ **02/6214-5600**) or by checking the U.S. Diplomatic Mission's website at **http://canberra.usembassy.gov/visas.html**.

British subjects can obtain up-to-date visa information by calling the **U.S. Embassy Visa Information Line** (✆ **09042-450-100** from within the U.K. at £1.20 per minute; or ✆ **866-382-3589** from within the U.S. at a flat rate of $16 and is payable by credit card only) or by visiting the "Visas to the U.S." section of the American Embassy London's website at **http://london.usembassy.gov/visas.html**.

Irish citizens can obtain up-to-date visa information through the **U.S. Embassy Dublin,** 42 Elgin Rd., Ballsbridge, Dublin 4 (✆ **1580-47-VISA [8472]** from within the Republic of Ireland at €2.40 per minute; **http://dublin.usembassy.gov)**.

Citizens of **New Zealand** can obtain up-to-date visa information by contacting the **U.S. Embassy New Zealand,** 29 Fitzherbert Terrace, Thorndon, Wellington (✆ **644/462-6000;** http://newzealand.usembassy.gov).

Visitor Information For information on the Seattle area, contact **Seattle's Convention and Visitors Bureau,** 701 Pike St., Suite 800, Seattle, WA 98101 (✆ **866/732-2695** or 206/461-5840; www.visitseattle.org). If you're surfing the Web for information on the Seattle area, check out **www.seattle.gov/html/visitor**, the city of Seattle's visitor information site. For information on Washington, contact the **Washington State Tourism Office** (✆ **800/544-1800;** www.experiencewa.com).

One of my favorite Seattle **blogs** is *Seattle Times'* columnist Nancy Leson's "All You Can Eat" (http://seattletimes.nwsource.com/html/allyoucaneat/index.html), which is always full of good, up-to-the-minute restaurant information. Seattle-area restaurants are also the focus of *Seattle Metropolitan* magazine's **Nosh Pit** (www.seattlemet.com/blogs/nosh-pit). The friendly innkeepers of the Washington Bed & Breakfast Guild also have an informative blog: **http://blog.wbbg.com**.

If you want to load up your smart phone with Seattle-specific apps, there are some I recommend. For making restaurant reservations, the OpenTable app, available from the iTunes app store, is invaluable. For Seattle news and entertainment listings, get the *Seattle Times* mobile app, which will give you access to Nancy Leson's restaurant column while you're on the go. You can also find a list of Frommer's travel apps at **www.frommers.com/go/mobile**.

Wi-Fi See "Internet & Wi-Fi," earlier in this section.

AIRLINE WEBSITES

MAJOR AIRLINES

Aeroméxico
www.aeromexico.com

Air Canada
www.aircanada.ca

Air France
www.airfrance.com

AirTran Airways
www.airtranairways.com

Alaska Airlines
www.alaskaair.com

American Airlines
www.aa.com

British Airways
www.britishairways.com

Continental Airlines
www.continental.com

Delta Air Lines
www.delta.com

Frontier Airlines
www.frontierairlines.com

Hawaiian Airlines
www.hawaiianair.com

Icelandair
www.icelandair.com

JetBlue Airways
www.jetblue.com

Korean Air
www.koreanair.com

Lufthansa
www.lufthansa.com

Southwest Airlines
www.southwest.com

Sun Country Airlines
www.suncountry.com

United Airlines
www.united.com

US Airways
www.usairways.com

Virgin America
www.virginamerica.com

INDEX

Q

R

S

T

U

V

Accommodations

PHOTO CREDITS

p. i: © Howard Frisk; p. iii, iv, v: © Howard Frisk; p. viii: © Mike Coffey; p. 1: © Howard Frisk; p. 2: © Howard Frisk; p. 3: © Howard Frisk; p. 4: © Howard Frisk; p. 5: © Howard Frisk; p. 6: © Lindsay Kennedy; p. 8: © Lindsay Kennedy; p. 9: © Lindsay Kennedy; p. 10: © Marc Morrison / ZUMA Press / Newscom; p. 12: © Howard Frisk; p. 16: © North Wind Picture Archives / Alamy; p. 17: © Keystone-France / Gamma-Keystone via Getty Images; p. 19: © MGM / The Kobal Collection; p. 20: © Val Wilmer / Redferns / Getty Images; p. 21: © Howard Frisk; p. 27: © Howard Frisk; p. 29, left: © Lindsay Kennedy; p. 29, right: © Howard Frisk; p. 32: © Howard Frisk; p. 34: © Lindsay Kennedy; p. 35: © Lindsay Kennedy; p. 37: © Howard Frisk; p. 38: © Howard Frisk; p. 40: © Howard Frisk; p. 41: © Courtesy Fairmont Hotels & Resorts; p. 42: © Courtesy Arctic Club Seattle; p. 45: © Courtesy Kimpton Hotels, Photo by Jennifer Finch; p. 71: © Lindsay Kennedy; p. 72: © Lindsay Kennedy; p. 73: © Lindsay Kennedy; p. 82: © Lindsay Kennedy; p. 108: © Lindsay Kennedy; p. 109: © Lindsay Kennedy; p. 110: © Lindsay Kennedy; p. 111: © Lindsay Kennedy; p. 112: © Lindsay Kennedy; p. 113: © Lindsay Kennedy; p. 118: © Lindsay Kennedy; p. 119: © Howard Frisk; p. 122: © Howard Frisk; p. 123: © Lindsay Kennedy; p. 125, top: © Lindsay Kennedy; p. 125, box: © Howard Frisk; p. 126: © Howard Frisk; p. 127: © Lindsay Kennedy; p. 128, top: © Howard Frisk; p. 128, bottom: © Howard Frisk; p. 130: © Lindsay Kennedy; p. 131: © Howard Frisk; p. 132, top: © Lindsay Kennedy; p. 132, bottom: © Howard Frisk; p. 134: © Lindsay Kennedy; p. 135: © Howard Frisk; p. 136: © Howard Frisk; p. 137: © Howard Frisk; p. 138, left: © Howard Frisk; p. 138, right: © Howard Frisk; p. 139, top: © Howard Frisk; p. 139, bottom: © Lindsay Kennedy; p. 140: © Howard Frisk; p. 141: © Howard Frisk; p. 142: © Lindsay Kennedy; p. 143, left: © Lindsay Kennedy; p. 143, right: © Chuck Pefley / Alamy; p. 144: © Howard Frisk; p. 145: © Howard Frisk; p. 146: © Howard Frisk; p. 147: © Lindsay Kennedy; p. 148: © Howard Frisk; p. 149, top: © Howard Frisk; p. 149, bottom: © Howard Frisk; p. 151, left: © Lindsay Kennedy; p. 151, right: © Howard Frisk; p. 152: © Howard Frisk; p. 153: © Howard Frisk; p. 155: © Howard Frisk; p. 157: © Lindsay Kennedy; p. 158: © Howard Frisk; p. 159: © Howard Frisk; p. 161: © Lindsay Kennedy; p. 162: © Howard Frisk; p. 163: © Courtesy Summit at Snoqalmie; p. 165: © Otto Greule Jr / Getty Images; p. 166, top: © Andrew D. Bernstein / NBAE via Getty Images; p. 166, bottom: © Otto Greule Jr / Getty Images; p. 167: © Patrick Green / Icon SMI / Newscom; p. 168: © Paul Gordon / Alamy; p. 169: © Howard Frisk; p. 172, top: © Ron Yue / Alamy; p. 172, bottom: © Howard Frisk; p. 173, left: © Howard Frisk; p. 173, right: © Howard Frisk; p. 175: © Howard Frisk; p. 176: © Howard Frisk; p. 177: © Howard Frisk; p. 178: © Howard Frisk; p. 180, left: © Howard Frisk; p. 180, right: © Howard Frisk; p. 181: © Howard Frisk; p. 182: © Howard Frisk; p. 183: © Howard Frisk; p. 184: © Howard Frisk; p. 186, top: © Lindsay Kennedy; p. 186, bottom: © Howard Frisk; p. 187: © Howard Frisk; p. 188, left: © Lindsay Kennedy; p. 188, right: © Howard Frisk; p. 189: © Lindsay Kennedy; p. 190: © Howard Frisk; p. 191: © Lindsay Kennedy; p. 192, top: © Lindsay Kennedy; p. 192, bottom: © Howard Frisk; p. 198: © Lindsay Kennedy; p. 202: © Lindsay Kennedy; p. 203: © Lindsay Kennedy; p. 207: © Lindsay Kennedy; p. 208: © Lindsay Kennedy; p. 212: © Courtesy Seattle Repertory Theatre; p. 214: © Courtesy Seattle Public Theater at the Bathhouse, Photo by Paul Bestock; p. 215: © Howard Frisk; p. 216: © Lindsay Kennedy; p. 217: © Lindsay Kennedy; p. 218: © Lindsay Kennedy; p. 219: © Lindsay Kennedy; p. 220: © Lindsay Kennedy; p. 221, top: © Lindsay Kennedy; p. 221, bottom: © Lindsay Kennedy; p. 223: © Lindsay Kennedy; p. 225: © Lindsay Kennedy; p. 226: © Lindsay Kennedy; p. 227: © Lindsay Kennedy; p. 228: © Lindsay Kennedy; p. 230: © Howard Frisk; p. 235: © Courtesy The Whale Museum; p. 237: © Douglas Peebles / Danita Delimont Stock Photography; p. 239: © Charles Gurche / Danita Delimont Stock Photography; p. 246: © Rob Casey / Alamy; p. 247: © Roddy Scheer / Danita Delimont Stock Photography; p. 252: © David Svilar / Danita Delimont Stock Photography; p. 258: © Howard Frisk; p. 264: © Lindsay Kennedy; p. 265: © Howard Frisk; p. 268: © P Frischknecht / Blickwinkel / AGE Fotostock; p. 270: © Howard Frisk; p. 271: © Howard Frisk; p. 278: © Howard Frisk; p. 282: © Lindsay Kennedy; p. 285: © Lindsay Kennedy; p. 287: © Howard Frisk; p. 289: © Lindsay Kennedy; p. 297: © Howard Frisk; p. 298: © Howard Frisk; p. 300: © Lindsay Kennedy.

Restaurants